# Vilnius Between Nations
## 1795–2000

NIU PRESS / *DeKalb, IL*

# Vilnius Between Nations

## 1795–2000

Theodore R. Weeks

Northern Illinois University Press, DeKalb 60115
© 2015 by Northern Illinois University Press
All rights reserved

24 23 22 21 20 19 18 17 16 15      1 2 3 4 5

978-0-87580-730-0 (paper)
978-1-60909-191-0 (ebook)

Book and cover design by Shaun Allshouse

Library of Congress Cataloging-in-Publication Data
Weeks, Theodore R., author.
Vilnius between nations, 1795-2000 / Theodore R. Weeks.
    pages    cm
Includes bibliographical references and index.
ISBN 978-0-87580-730-0 (pbk.) — ISBN 978-1-60909-191-0 (ebook)
1. Vilnius (Lithuania)—History. I. Title.
DK505.935.W44 2015
947.93—dc23
2015035480

# Contents

ACKNOWLEDGMENTS   ix

LIST OF ABBREVIATIONS   xi

LIST OF ILLUSTRATIONS   xiii

Introduction: Nationality, Politics, Culture, Urban Space   1

1  Historical Background   11

2  A Center of Polish and Jewish Culture, 1795–1862   21

3  The Period of Russification, 1863–1914   59

4  World War I, 1914–1922   96

5  Vilnius as a Polish City, 1919–1939   124

6  The Destruction of Multinational Vilnius, 1939–1955   155

7  Socialist Normalcy in Vilnius, 1955–1985   189

8  Building a Lithuanian Capital City, 1985–2000   210

Conclusions   237

NOTES   243

SELECT BIBLIOGRAPHY   295

INDEX   303

To

J.W.B. (II)

M.J.C.W.

and

Z.D.W.

And their parents.

# Acknowledgments

The research and writing of this book could not have taken place without much support from a variety of sources, for which I would like to express my sincere gratitude. My thanks go out to the Memorial Foundation for Jewish Culture; the National Council for Eastern European and Eurasian Research; the Kennan Institute and East European Studies at the Woodrow Wilson International Center for Scholars in Washington, DC; the US Holocaust Museum and Memorial; Studium Wschodnie at the University of Warsaw; and the Fulbright-Hays program. Unfortunately, a number of these funds have been reduced or eliminated in the interim; I can only hope that American policymakers will reconsider the decision to gut research support in the humanities. The Slavic (now Slavic-Eurasian) Research Center of Hokkaido University in Sapporo, Japan, and the Imre Kertész Kolleg at the University of Jena, Germany, provided wonderful and stimulating places to write. None of these institutions, of course, is in any way responsible for the views expressed here. I would also like to express my gratitude to the Department of History at Southern Illinois University in Carbondale, which has been my academic home for two decades now.

A number of colleagues have kindly read and critiqued this manuscript at various stages along the way. In particular I would like to express my appreciation for the discussion of the book manuscript in Vilnius sponsored by the 12th International Conference "Recovering Forgotten History. The Image of East-Central Europe in English-Language Textbooks," organized by the Uczelnia Łazarskiego in Warsaw. In this context special thanks go out to Professors Felix Ackermann, Adam Kożuchowski, John Merriman, Vladas Sirutavičius, Bożena Szaynok, Jurgita Verbickienė, and Marcin Wodziński. Their critical comments are reflected on nearly every page of this book. The two readers from Northern Illinois University Press also helped me erase many embarrassing errors and trim down some of my habitual meandering verbiage. As usual, however, the final product with its various warts and infelicities can only be blamed on me.

Over the long decade I have been working on this book, the Lietuvos Istorijos Institutas in Vilnius provided a frequent scholarly home-away-from-home. My thanks to everyone there, from the kind staff at the library to the (usually) friendly *budėtojams*. Especial thanks to the institute's present director, Dr. Rimantas Miknys, who was even so kind and patient as to tolerate my broken Lithuanian without wincing. Drs. Darius Staliūnas and Vladas Sirutavičius provided intellectual companionship and stimulating criticism, not to mention *kepta duona su česnaku*. Many thanks to you all!

On a different level, my deep gratitude to several dear (if sometimes annoying) individuals is expressed in the dedication. Thanks, y'all.

# Abbreviations

Čaplinskas-2010 — Čaplinskas, Antanas R. *Vilniaus istorija. Legendos ir tikrovė.* Vilnius: Charibdė, 2010.

Feliksiak-1992 — Elżbieta Feliksiak, ed. *Wilno—Wileńszczyzna jako krajobraz i środowisko wielu kultur. Materiały międzynarodowej konferencji.* 4 vols. Białystok: Towarzystwo Literackie im. Adama Mickiewicza, 1992.

Feliksiak-1994 — Elżbieta Feliksiak and Marta Skorko-Barańska, ed. *Wilno jako ognisko oświaty w latach próby. Świadectwa o szkole (1939–1945).* Białystok: Towarzystwo Literackie im. Adama Mickiewicza, 1994.

Feliksiak-1996 — Elżbieta Feliksiak, ed. *Wilno i kresy północno-wschodnie. Materiały II międzynarodowej konferencji w Białymstoku.* 4 vols. Białystok: Towarzystwo Literackie im. Adama Mickiewicza, 1996.

Feliksiak-2000 — Elżbieta Feliksiak, ed. *Wilno i ziemia Mickiewiczowskiej pamięci.* 3 vols. Białystok: Towarzystwo Literackie im. Adama Mickiewicza, 2000.

Feliksiak-2002 — Elżbieta Feliksiak, ed. *Wilno i świat. Dzieje środowiska intelektualnego.* 2 vols. Białystok: Towarzystwo Literackie im. Adama Mickiewicza, 2002.

| | |
|---|---|
| USB | Uniwersytet Stefana Batorego (Polish university in Vilnius, 1919–1939). |
| VMI, vol. 1 | J. Jurginis, V. Merkys, A. Tautavičius. *Vilniaus miesto istorija nuo seniausių laikų iki Spalio revoliucijos.* Vilnius: "Mintis," 1968. |
| VMI, vol. 2 | H. Šadžius, R. Žepkaitė, J. Žiugžda. *Vilniaus miesto istorija nuo Spalio revoliucijos iki dabartinių dienų.* Vilnius: "Mintis," 1972. |
| VMID | Eugenijus Manelis and Romaldas Samavičius, eds. *Vilniaus miesto istorijos dokumentai. Vilniaus miesto istorijos skatinių chrestomatija.* Vilnius: Vilniaus knyga, 2003. |
| VMIS | Eugenijus Manelis and Romaldas Samavičius, eds. *Vilniaus miesto istorijos skaitinai.* Vilnius: Vilniaus knyga, 2001. |
| YdL | Leyzer Ran, compiler. *Yerushalayim de Lita / Jerusalem of Lithuania.* 3 vols. New York: Laureate Press, 1976. |

Illustrations

1   A photograph from the early 1960s juxtaposes the "Portrait Gallery" (as the deconsecrated Cathedral was known) with the Žirmūnai housing estate being built on the other side of the Neris River.   49

2   The Merchants' Club, built at the end of the Russian period on St. George's Avenue. Picture from the early twentieth century.   50

3   Statue of Collective Farmers on the Green Bridge spanning the Neris River.   50

4   Brick Gothic St. Anne's Church, Soviet-era monument to Mickiewicz, and Bernardine Church in background.   51

5   Post-Soviet monument of Vilnius' founder, Grand Duke Gediminas, unveiled 1996.   52

6   Monument to Frank Zappa erected by Vilnius Art School students in the early 1990s.   53

7   View of Castle Hill in Vilnius from the Neris River in 1917, showing how the upper castle looked before post-World War II Soviet reconstruction   54

8   St. Kazimierz's Church (1917), in Soviet times the Museum of Atheism.   55

9   The "Romanov" church, built in 1909 by the Russian authorities to emphasize the Russian Orthodox character of Vilnius. The church has survived into the twenty-first century.   56

10  The miracle-working icon of Ostra Brama (Aušros Vartai), photo from ca. 1917.   57

11  The Jewish district in Vilnius with one of its characteristic arches.   58

INTRODUCTION

# Nationality, Politics, Culture, Urban Space

IT IS A COMMONPLACE to point out that cities in East-Central Europe—indeed, cities more or less everywhere—bring together varied populations, speaking various languages, professing diverse faiths, self-identifying with different nations. At the same time, cities are the focal points of modern politics, especially where confessional and ethno-cultural identities are concerned. For all their emphasis on the peasantry, early nationalists were largely addressing their nationalist message to city dwellers. And the modern state, in its homogenizing and nationalizing efforts, uses the city—in particular the capital city—as the most intense workshop for representing the nation.[1] These themes—cultural diversity, nationalist rhetoric, state-sponsored efforts to nationalize urban space—form the center of this book's narrative. I hope that an examination of the unique historical experience of Vilnius over two centuries will contribute to our understanding of state-nation relations, the intersection between nationality and modern politics, and modes of interaction (both peaceful and violent) between diverse national-ethnic-religious groups in East-Central Europe and in urban spaces, here and elsewhere.

Why Vilnius? With no slight intended to other diverse, beautiful, and fascinating cities from Breslau/Wrocław to Baku (and beyond), I would argue that the importance of Vilnius to a variety of cultures (or nationalities, or ethnicities: these terms will be used more or less interchangeably according to specific contexts) is unparalleled. For Poles, Jews, and Lithuanians, Vilnius occupies a key position in national-cultural mythology. For Poles, the city of *Wilno* represented the locus of Polish Romanticism (Adam Mickiewicz and Juliusz Słowacki in particular) and the easternmost outpost of Polonism in the battle with Russian-Orthodox foes. For Jews, *Vilne* was a major center of religious study, home of the Vilne Gaon (Eliahu ben Shlomo Zalman, 1720–1797) and a center for rabbinical (and anti-Hasidic) thought. By the early twentieth century, the city was also known as an important city for modern Jewish political movements, in particular the socialist Jewish Bund and, to a lesser extent, early Zionism. For Lithuanians, Vilnius occupied a central place in national identity, as the capital of the early-modern Lithuanian Grand Duchy and the future capital of a Lithuanian nation-state. In the nineteenth century, Russians also "reclaimed" the city of *Vil'na*—if rather half-heartedly—after centuries of "perfidious" polonization. In the twentieth century Belarusians also laid claim to Vilnia as their future capital; plans were even mooted in the late 1930s to make the city the capital of the Belarusian SSR. In short, while East-Central Europe abounds with multiethnic, multireligious cities, none of these—not L'viv or Cluj, not Riga or Yerevan, not Łódź or Baku—figures so centrally in several different national mythologies as Vilnius.

One can observe through the history of this city how various regimes, from the Russian Empire to the present Lithuanian republic, have ruled over a city whose population exhibited extreme religious and cultural-linguistic diversity. Throughout the period of my study, from 1795 (the third partition of Poland) to the year 2000, Vilnius' population has never been overwhelmingly dominated by a single national-cultural group. In fact, until recently the only period during which a single ethnic group could claim a majority in Vilnius was during Polish rule in the 1920s and 30s.[2] Even ethnic Lithuanians did not make up 51 percent of the city's total population until 1989, according to official statistics.[3] Throughout the nineteenth century, Jews made up the largest single cultural-ethnic group, with Poles as the most prominent Christian nationality.[4] The Lithuanian claim on the city was always based on history (and a very specific understanding of history), not on demography: from the eighteenth century to 1939, this ethnicity never made up more than a small percentage of the city's population. Perhaps surprisingly, given present-day accusations of russifying policies during the Soviet years, the percentage of Lithuanians among Vilnius' inhabitants climbed steadily from 1949 onward.

Even more significant than demographic realities (which in any case are often disputed) is the rhetoric used by nations and states to claim the city. A case in point is the argument for Vilnius as a Lithuanian city. Although Lithuanians did not make up even one-tenth of Vilnius' population before World War II, this demographic fact in no way deterred Lithuanian patriots from claiming it. The ways in which they made their claim—essentially, by emphasizing a more-or-less mythologized national-Lithuanian history of the late medieval and early modern period (the Grand Duchy of Lithuania)—are typical of patriotic rhetoric that uses history and any other available tool to press forward national arguments. The Poles and Russians offered no less mythologized historical accounts, but the Polish case was strengthened by demographics since Poles had enjoyed a large physical presence in the city in recent centuries. Jews, for their part, made claims to the city based upon characterizations of Vilnius' history that largely ignored the presence of other national groups.

A recent article has captured the essence of this process in the phrase "symbolic appropriation."[5] As I will argue, in the nineteenth century—and even more intensively in the twentieth century—each national group expended significant energy in efforts to appropriate the city symbolically. The methods were diverse and included founding schools based on particular languages, erecting monuments, and writing travel guides. State power, at the same time, was far from neutral in this process. As we will see, the Russian, Polish, Soviet, and Lithuanian states all conceived and implemented a very specific type of national-symbolic politics. Such politics ranged from street naming and economic favoritism to the policies of bare genocide and ethnic cleansing employed by Nazis and early Soviet authorities in the 1940s. I do not, of course, equate genocide and cultural politics. I would, however, note that nationalist rhetoric can help pave the way for nastier policies. Apparently harmless movements advocating national revival, cultural development, or the goal of "reclaiming" a city can take on a life of their own and be used to justify brutal measures for the sake of achieving a culturally more homogenous city.

Rhetoric alone cannot, of course, "nationalize" a city: this process requires political power and both soft policies (propaganda, culture, education) and hard policies (repression, prohibitions of certain languages, restrictions on religion, and even the extremes of ethnic cleansing and genocide). Over the two centuries covered here, we will see ample examples of all of these state-political practices. They include the Russian Empire's restrictions on printing Lithuanian in Latin letters and using the Polish language in public; the Polish practice of favoritism toward fellow Poles in government hiring in the interwar period; and the evacuation of Poles from Vilnius during and immediately after World War II. This study will show, I believe, the modern state's relentless impulse toward achieving ethnic homogeneity or, at the very least, favoring one ethnic-cultural group while at the most tolerating the rest.

This study will not, however, treat Vilnius simply as an object of government policy or nationalist rhetoric. Part of the focus will be the city's everyday negotiations of nationality and the relations between ethnic groups, with particular attention to economic, social, and national categories. An important aspect of this topic is the range of reactions among Vilnius' population to state efforts at imposing a favored nationality on the cityscape: residents responded by resisting or ignoring those efforts, co-opting them, or exploiting them for their own personal advantage. It is also important to note that the interactions of the city's national and ethnic groups changed over time. Until the later nineteenth century, "parallel cultures" that intersected only in specific and limited contexts predominated.[6] In the twentieth century, and particularly after World War I, the incursion of the state into most parts of everyday life (from education to economic intervention to a growing state bureaucracy) brought different cultural-religious groups together more intensely, often engendering rivalry and frictions.

Nationality also played itself out in the city's urban spaces. The most obvious example is the Jewish quarter of town, but one can also point to streets and holy sites marked as Catholic by religious processions or to Soviet spaces used for rallies or marked with heroic monuments (such as the Lenin statue on Lukiškės Square). Here public perceptions and state policy sometimes dovetail and sometimes clash. As Yael Zerubavel has shown, state-sponsored patriotism can also be met by skepticism, rejection, and "refashioning" (e.g., of national heroes into silly or even obscene figures) by the public.[7] A more modest but also amusing example of a "shift of meaning" in Vilnius was found in the arch-Soviet statues on the Green Bridge. While some advocated their removal after 1990, most Vilnius residents clearly regarded the earnest statues of Soviet youth, farmers, soldiers, and industrial workers as an inevitable and rather amusing part of the landscape, in short, as "camp." Until 2015, the heroic statues remained in place. They were finally removed by a "liberal" mayor in a craven attempt to ingratiate himself to right-wing voters.

At this point a few words about key terms and concepts are in order. "Nation" and "state" are used here in a strict sense that is not always common in English. "Nation" refers to a group of people bound together by shared language, religion, perceived shared history, or common origins. I will use "nation," "nationality," and "ethnicity" more or less as synonyms. At times I will also use "culture" or "linguistic group" to describe the same people. The word "nation," on the other hand, will *never* be used here in the sense of a "country" or political unit—"state" will consistently refer to the political entity that exercises power, creates and enforces laws, levies taxes, wages war, and so on. In Western languages like English and French, "nation" and "state" are often conflated and confused, as in the phrase "our nation's capital." This is not the case—and is even linguistically impossible—in Central and Eastern Europe, where the words *Staat, państwo, gosudarstvo, valstybė* are difficult to confuse with *Nation/Volk, naród, narod/natsiia, tauta*.

A state, at least in the modern period, has fairly definite boundaries—which we all experience by showing our passports, applying for visas, changing money, going through customs, and so on—while the edges of the nation are much more porous and undefined. The modern state wants us to have a single nationality (and a single passport); human beings (as we will see) can vacillate between two or more nations, using different identities according to the situation (and adjusting for personal tastes and profitability). An individual named Schmidt who spoke no German could well have presented herself as a *Volksdeutsche* (ethnic German) during the Nazi occupation; a family of mixed Polish Jewish or Polish Lithuanian origins might have favored one identity over another in times of crisis. In Vilnius the primary markers of nationality were (and to some extent still are) religion and language. The few Muslim Tatars and the many (until World War II) Jews were in this context considered members of national, not just religious, communities. To be a Pole almost ipso facto meant to be Catholic, just as being Russian implied that one was Orthodox. This does not mean that there were no exceptions, but the very fact that people said (and still say), "he is Lutheran *but* a Pole" shows clearly where the "default" position lay for this nationality. As the example shows, particular religions and ethnicities were seen as going hand in hand.

Nationalists wish to ascribe a single nationality to individuals and, even worse, presume that they can work toward "uncovering" the "real" nationality of certain people.[8] I certainly do not wish to condone this approach. On the other hand, nationality is also not quite freely chosen. For most people, who speak one language (or are much more proficient in one language than in any other) and profess one faith, national identity is simple. But as in many of the most interesting cases in this study, the residents of Vilnius often confounded easy definitions and passed across "normal" national-cultural boundary lines. This boundary-crossing could mean the difference between poverty and state employment (as in the case of Poles or non-Poles married to Polish women during the period of russification in the Russian Empire) or even between life and death.

It is tempting to refer to Vilnius as a "multicultural" city: after all, in the adjective's most basic meaning—"having many cultures"—one can hardly deny that the term fits this city as well as many individuals who lived here. However, the term is laden with unfortunate present-day connotations and presupposes (at least in Europe and North America) a stable cultural arena in which one (or possibly two) languages dominate and where it is easy to tolerate—even embrace—"diversity" with a fairly minimal political, economic, or cultural cost. This was not the case in Vilnius, I will argue, until the later Soviet period. Up to the mid-twentieth century, accommodating cultural diversity demanded high costs that existing states either could not or would not bear. The Soviet period established a kind of bilingual cultural hegemony that after 1990 was translated into a (mostly) tolerant Lithuanian nation-state. Thus contemporary Vilnius is "multicultural" both in the ethnic makeup of its citizenry and its official embrace of cultural diversity. This is, however, an entirely different situation from Vilnius in 1800, 1860, 1914, or even 1939, where actual confessional-cultural diversity was strong enough to challenge (or at least appear to challenge) ethnic-political integration.

In a remarkable recent book on Sarajevo—another city exhibiting extreme religious-national diversity—Emily Greble warns against confusion of this traditional live-and-let-live system and present-day conceptions: "Multiculturalism in this context should not be confused with contemporary Western liberal ideas of diversity, integration, and secularism but should instead be understood as a model of tolerance and coexistence that reflected customary civic codes passed down from earlier generations."[9] In looking at Vilnius, I would further stress that "tolerance and coexistence" were based more on indifference and even contempt for other cultures than knowledge or respect. Originally I wanted to use the term "multiculturalism" to describe the cultural-religious situation in Vilnius but have since discarded it as imprecise and far too laden with present-day resonances to be helpful. Unfortunately, no good word exists to describe the cultural-confessional situation in the city so I will use, in different contexts, "multiethnic," "multilingual," "diversity of religion," and even "multicultural" to try to convey the reality of a city populated with people speaking different languages, professing different faiths, and at least to some extent (particularly before 1939) leading different everyday lives. The title I ultimately settled on emphasizes the distinct nature of these communities (whether based on linguistic or religious identity) and the struggle of different nations for this city.

Without falling into an ahistorical romanticization of the past as a golden age of mutual respect between diverse national-cultural and religious groups—I see little evidence of that—one can state that before 1939 diverse groups did live together mostly without violence though also with only limited mixing.[10] It is naive (and historically false) to blame interethnic violence in Vilnius (and elsewhere) exclusively on outside forces (the Russian Empire, the Poles from Warsaw, the USSR), but it was precisely during times of renegotiating the "terms of multicultural cohabitation" that violence erupted. However, the possibility exists of renegotiating these terms without violence, as the final decade of the twentieth century in Vilnius has shown.

At the same time, I do argue that the modern state is fundamentally a homogenizing instrument. Multiple languages and, to a lesser extent, religions tend to complicate the "efficient" running of a nation-state (the term itself indicates a tendency—or longing—toward a single ethnic-cultural unit) and as such were regarded with hostility by modernizing politicians. Even in the relatively rich and stable USA of the early twentieth century, Theodore Roosevelt spoke out against a "polyglot boarding-house" in advocating the total assimilation of immigrants. While the modernizing USSR advocated and even sponsored ethnic-linguistic diversity, even during its first twenty years, the function of Russian as a lingua franca (at least potentially) for all Soviet citizens was accepted as a given. The self-image and policies of interwar Poland and Lithuania were much more explicitly focused on a single ethnic-linguist group. One observes, in far milder form, this kind of ethnocentricity in the post-1990 period, albeit tempered by mitigating factors: globalization, the lack of any real threat from non-Lithuanian cultures, and the desire to gain access to the European Union (achieved in 2004).

The book's chapters reflect a periodization that may not be immediately familiar. The first chapter aims to give a very general historical background of the city's founding and growth in the early modern period. The "real" book starts, however, with the occupation of Vilnius by the Russian Empire in 1795. Some of the chapter's beginning and closing dates will be instantly recognizable: 1795 (the third partition of Poland), 1914 (outbreak of World War I), 1939 (Nazi Germany's invasion of Poland). Others will seem less familiar. For example, while the beginnings of both world wars in general historiography and in Vilnius coincided, the end dates did not: those wars did not really end for the city in 1918 or 1945. World War I continued in the form of a three-war conflict between Poland, Lithuania, and Soviet Russia until a tense de facto truce was reached in 1922. At the same time, efforts to incorporate Vilnius into the newly independent Polish Republic began already in 1919: for this reason, chapters 4 (World War I) and 5 (interwar) overlap chronologically by three years. World War II ended for Vilnius in a certain sense with the entry of the Red Army into the city in July 1944. I will argue, however, that radical measures to establish Soviet rule and culture in the city continued for some years afterward.

Similarly, while Lithuanians now celebrate March 11, 1990 as their (regaining of) independence day, at the time the possibility that the USSR would manage to claw back control over Lithuania could not be dismissed. Furthermore, although Soviet control over the city ended in the early 1990s, the process of recreating Vilnius as the capital of a Lithuanian nation-state was at that point only in its early stages. Thus I found it more appropriate to begin the final chapter, on the city's (re)-Lithuanization and de-Sovietization, with 1985, the year in which

Mikhail Sergeevich Gorbachev rose to power in the USSR. In her recent book on the Russian city of Nizhny Novgorod, Catherine Evtuhov has argued that local (or provincial) history requires its own periodization that is distinct from the time line of national or "universal" history.[11] I quite agree, and this book's organization reflects that.

Chapter 1 covers the history of Vilnius from the "earliest times," as background to show the competing visions of the city's past in Polish, Russian, Jewish, and Lithuanian historiography. In Lithuania, the period of the Grand Duchy (to the mid-sixteenth century) has been and continues to be a rich field of historical research. This chapter does not attempt to do justice to this historiography; the point here is very modest: to trace some of the main events in the city's history from its founding to the book's true beginning, the incorporation of Vilnius into the Russian Empire. I also wish to give the reader some idea of the classic historiography of the city while presenting certain commonly accepted key events. This book does not work to reformulate or strengthen national narratives, but these narratives undeniably predominate in most accounts of the city to this day. Still, realities apart from cultural and national boundaries have also formed the contours of the city's life: the physical growth of the city, its position in the larger European world, and economic conditions.

The next two chapters will cover the period of Russian rule over Vilnius, with the break between them coming after the disastrous Polish (or more properly Polish Lithuanian) January insurrection of 1863. I believe that this division is justified because, for all the measures taken against Polish culture in the pre-1863 period (most notably closing down the city's university after the 1831 November uprising), the hegemony of Polish and Jewish cultures in the city was not, to my mind, seriously challenged by the Russian authorities until after 1863. After 1863, russification took on more active forms, though, as I have argued before, in the end the entire policy of russification was not particularly effective and indeed was hampered by the contradiction between a would-be pro-Russian-nation policy and a nonnational, dynastic, and imperial state.[12] In the twentieth century, which properly only starts with World War I, the intensity and brutality of nationalizing measures increased considerably. For that reason the bulk of this book covers the period from 1914. Chapter 4 examines the period of war, revolution, and the three-sided conflict (Polish, Lithuanian, and Soviet) over Vilnius after 1914. This is followed by a chapter on the "Polish city" of Wilno under Polish rule, a period of less than two decades during which Lithuanian claims for the city were mainly articulated from across the border (though some schools educating in that language continued operation in Vilnius), Jewish culture flourished, and Poles made up a majority of the city's population for possibly the first and last time in history.

No one would deny the significance of World War II in redefining the boundaries, politics, ethnic makeup, and national memories in Eastern and East-Central Europe.[13] Vilnius exhibits an extreme example of the impact of this conflict: the city's population changed almost entirely in the decade after 1939. But the process of transforming a mainly Polish Jewish city into a Soviet Lithuanian capital did not end with the taking of the city by the Red Army in July 1944. I have somewhat arbitrarily selected the date of 1955 to end the World War II chapter because by that point radical changes in population, political legitimacy, and cultural policy had been put in place. The next few decades are characterized by a less turbulent situation that I will refer to as "socialist normalcy," which I argue characterized Vilnius as the capital of the Lithuanian Soviet Socialist Republic in the period 1955 to 1985.

The book's final chapter looks at another radical change in the city's "national face"—far less brutal than the changes of 1939–1955 but possibly more long-lasting. In the decade and a half after M. S. Gorbachev's rise to power, Vilnius was transformed from an ostensibly bilingual Soviet city to an undisputedly Lithuanian capital, albeit one that tolerated national minorities. The political policies adopted by the Lithuanian Republic since the reattainment of independence stress toleration and multiculturalism within the context of a Lithuanian nation-state.

Lithuanian and Polish colleagues reading this book in manuscript criticized my focus on only four national groups: Russians, Poles, Lithuanians, and Jews. Where, they asked, are the Tatars, Karaites, and Belarusians? Certainly the presence of these confessional-cultural groups in the city added to (and continues to enhance) its cultural richness. My response is mainly practical. Tatars and Karaites, while fascinating, never made up more than a tiny percentage of the city's total population. I do not see that either state policy or the city's main ethnic groups felt the need to take them into consideration when formulating rhetoric or policy to claim ("culturally appropriate") the city. The Belarusian example is more complex. Certainly this ethnic group was present in significant numbers in the city. In the twentieth century, Vilnius was even proposed as a possible capital of a Belarusian state (or Soviet Socialist Republic). In the city itself, however, the Belarusians never managed to organize in a way that threatened to dominate urban space (as, for example, Jews, Poles, and Lithuanians all did at different times). The Belarusian myth and reality of Vilnius constitute a topic that certainly deserves its own study but will not form a large part of this book.

The aim of this book is not to accuse or denounce, but simply (though in real life this is very far from simple) to understand. The history of Vilnius as a multicultural city and the negotiations (usually implicit) that allowed diverse national groups to inhabit a single urban space cannot provide "lessons" that can be easily applied to other diverse urban centers. The historical experience of Vilnius can, however, show how both nationalists and states worked to claim urban space as "properly" belonging to a specific national group. Perhaps the failures and, even more, the triumphs of these efforts will make us more sensitive to the need for extreme caution in formulating such exclusive cultural-nationalist claims.

• • •

A NOTE ON NAMES: as will be clear from this introduction, I reject the idea that "Vilnius" belonged "properly" to any one of the cultural-national-religious groups that lived in the city. However, in the interests of clarity, I will generally use the present-day (Lithuanian) name of the city: "Vilnius." In the notes, however, the city's name is left in the form used by the source; i.e., Russian *Vil'na*, Jewish *Vilne* (though the Hebrew form would resemble the Russian), Polish *Wilno*, and Lithuanian (and present-day) Vilnius. Along similar lines, to facilitate finding streets in the present-day city, I have generally (but not universally) used present-day (Lithuanian) spellings.

• • •

A NOTE ON CALENDARS: when Vilnius was a provincial city in the Russian Empire (1795–1915), its generally accepted calendar was that imposed by St. Petersburg—that is, the Julian calendar. This calendar ("old style," or "o.s.") was thirteen days behind the more precise Gregorian calendar ("new style," or "n.s.") used by the rest of Europe and North America. In general I have used the calendar used by a specific source (i.e., generally old style to 1915 and new style afterward). In cases that might be ambiguous, I have specified "o.s." or "n.s."

CHAPTER 1

# Historical Background

## Vilnius from "the Earliest Times"

THE HISTORY OF VILNIUS begins, as every guidebook will tell you, with Gediminas's dream of an iron wolf. The story goes that the wolf stood on a hill and howled with the power of a hundred wolves. Waking, Gediminas sought an explanation of the dream from a pagan priest. He was told that on this hill at the confluence of the Neris and Vilnia Rivers he should build his capital.[1] Following the priest's advice, so the story goes, Gediminas, the Grand Duke of Lithuania, transferred his capital there in the early fourteenth century.

Whether or not Gediminas actually dreamed about the iron wolf, he is generally credited with founding the city. And, it should be noted, Gediminas was not a legendary ruler but one of the major builders of the early Lithuanian state. As for the city itself, archaeologists have pointed out that a settlement existed there before the fourteenth century that had both economic and religious importance. But it was Gediminas who raised the city to the status of capital, supplanting the island fortress of Trakai. The first written documents from the city—letters from Gediminas to various European rulers, including the Holy Roman Emperor Louis IV—are dated 1323, so this year often appears as the beginning of Vilnius history.[2] Gediminas remained true to his pagan practices but established a tradition of religious toleration in the city that would continue for centuries.

In 1385 the Grand Duchy of Lithuania was linked to the Kingdom of Poland by the Union of Krewo. This union was cemented by the marriage a year later of Gediminas's grandson, Grand Duke Jogaila, to the Polish Princess Jadwiga. As part of this agreement, the Lithuanian state—and Grand Duke Jogaila/Jagiełło (the latter form is the Polish one) accepted Christianity in the Roman Catholic confession. In the ensuing centuries, Polish high culture came to dominate the nobility and church in the region, including in Vilnius.[3] Churches and followers of the Eastern Orthodox confession of Christianity continued to exist in Vilnius.

Events of the fourteenth century thus set the stage for the Lithuanian and Polish conflict over the city. No one denies that Gediminas was an ethnic Lithuanian, though historians point out that the Grand Duchy of Lithuania was certainly not a Lithuanian nation-state. Indeed, the language used by the bureaucracy of the Grand Duchy—"Chancery Ruthenian"—was a form of old Belarusian, a Slavic language much closer to Polish than to Lithuanian. Polish influences increased from the late fourteenth century. In any case, applying nationalist criteria to the late medieval and early modern periods is both fruitless and rather silly. Neither the Grand Duchy of Lithuania nor the Kingdom of Poland was organized, ruled, or conceived on national-ethnic lines. This did not, of course, prevent Poles, Lithuanians, and others from interpreting the region's history in national terms in the nineteenth and twentieth centuries.[4] The significance of Vilnius was from the beginning as a capital city but also as a commercial center on trade routes connecting Scandinavia with the Black Sea and Muscovy with central and western Europe. Already in 1387, just after the acceptance of Christianity, Vilnius' rulers granted the city's residents—that is, mainly artisans and merchants—far-reaching self-rule under the Magdeburg Law. Introduction of the Magdeburg Law allowed artisans and merchants to organize guilds and also to regulate business transactions as well as everyday behavior based on accepted legal norms.

Much of the city's economy was derived from its role as residential seat and capital for the Lithuanian Grand Dukes. Under the terms of the Krewo Union, Vilnius was also made a bishopric, with the first bishop arriving in 1388. By the early fifteenth century, Vilnius was already a thriving commercial and political center.[5] In subsequent centuries, magnate families such as the Radziwiłł and Sapieha clans built palaces in the city, giving employment to hundreds of servants, artisans, and other servitors.

Vilnius' growth in importance did not protect it from violent incursions in these unsettled times. The Teutonic Knights invaded and destroyed the city several times in the late fourteenth and early fifteenth century. A castle atop the elevation we now know as Gediminas Hill and a protective wall surrounding the city, completed with a number of gates, were built to protect the city from invaders but were only partially effective.[6] More important for the city's security would be the defeat of the Teutonic Knights at the battle of Grunwald (for Lithuanians, Žalgiris) in 1410.[7] Even so, a new defense wall would be built around the city in the early sixteenth century. For nearly two and a half centuries after Grunwald/ Žalgiris the city would be spared foreign invasion.

In the early 1400s the city was a bustling urban center. The Magdeburg Law was introduced in 1387, and some estimates of the city's population reach thirty thousand—though most scholars find this figure exaggerated and consider a population estimate of around twenty thousand much more realistic, even in the seventeenth and eighteenth centuries.[8] While we have no modern census figures, there seems no doubt that the city was populated by a number of different national groups, including Germans, "Ruthenians" (mainly, in this case, Belarusians but at any rate East Slavs), Lithuanians, Poles, Tatars, and others. Jews made their first appearance in the city in the fourteenth century and from around 1500 were a permanent presence in Vilnius. The fact that Grand Duke Sigismund I ("the Old") issued an edict in 1527 forbidding Jews from residing or trading in the city suggests that a Jewish community must have already been extant before that date. This prohibition, like many before and after in Jewish history, was soon overturned (and one wonders to what extent it was enforced).[9] The main synagogue that was to survive to the late 1940s dated from the first half of the seventeenth century, but many smaller prayer houses existed much earlier.[10]

The "Golden Age" of Vilnius dates, more or less, from the early sixteenth century and lasted for around a century and a half, until the Muscovite invasion in 1655 and subsequent six-year-long occupation of the city.[11] Before that cataclysm, political stability and a thriving economy allowed education, scholarship, and printing to develop. The first books printed in Vilnius in the 1520s were Eastern Orthodox religious texts that used the Cyrillic alphabet. In the second half of the sixteenth century each Christian confession (Orthodox, Calvinist, Lutheran, Catholic, Uniate) had its own printing presses in the city. Only much later, at the end of the eighteenth century, did Jews begin to print books in the city.[12]

The Reformation did not come immediately to Vilnius; the first indications of Protestant ideas (mainly reflected in Catholic prohibitions) only start to appear in the city from the late 1520s and later. By mid-century, however, important noble families with residences in and near the city went over to Protestantism, usually in its Calvinist guise. Among these families the most famous were the Radziwiłł, Sapieha, and Chodkiewicz clans. As throughout most of East-Central Europe, Lutheranism appealed primarily to townspeople of German ethnicity, but in Vilnius there was also a minority of Polish-speakers among Lutherans. By the 1560s, both confessions were established in the city.[13] Besides Christians and Jews, Muslim Tatars had formed a community in the city by this time.

With prominent noble families like the Radziwiłłs accepting (and strongly propagating) Calvinism and townspeople increasingly opting for Lutheranism (or remaining Eastern Orthodox), the Catholic Church in Vilnius saw its privileged position under threat. Crucially for future Polish and Lithuanian history, the Grand Duke/King never went over to the Protestants. Equally important, the Catholic Church's position in Vilnius and the region was strengthened by the establishment in 1579 of a Jesuit Academy there. It is difficult to overestimate the importance of this educational institution—a university starting in 1803—in the city's subsequent history.[14]

King Stefan Batory issued a "privilegia" on April 1, 1579 establishing the "academia et universitas" in Vilnius: for decades it would be the easternmost of all European universities (by comparison, the University of Moscow was founded nearly two centuries later). The institution would serve at least two purposes: it would be a center for the Jesuit Order and Catholic ("Counter") Reformation, and it would train teachers and clergymen for the region (and would be in this way also connected to efforts to recatholicize). From 1622 permission was obtained for the establishment of faculties of law and medicine, but it took some time for these faculties to open in Vilnius (law: 1641; medicine: 1781). Lectures were held, of course, in Latin, and many of the professors—even into the early nineteenth century—would come from central and western Europe. Initially under two hundred students attended the academy but by 1576 their numbers had grown to about five hundred.[15]

The academy quickly established its own publishing house, both for academic purposes and as a tool of the Counter Reformation. In Vilnius, unlike elsewhere, the Jesuits aimed not solely at converting Calvinists and Lutherans back into Catholicism but also at strengthening Catholicism against Orthodoxy. Vilnius' position on the western edge of Eastern Orthodoxy and the eastern edge of Catholic-Protestant struggles made it an obvious location for Jesuit activities. The university's first rector, Piotr Skarga, a brilliant preacher and thinker, is remembered by non-Catholics as a fanatical Jesuit who, while not directly advocating violence against heretics, expressed deep contempt for non-Catholics, whether Jews or Protestants.[16]

A decade before the university's establishment, the political relations between the Grand Duchy of Lithuania and the Kingdom of Poland had been significantly changed by the Union of Lublin (1569). The previous Union of Krewo linked the two states only through the person of their shared ruler. The Union of Lublin tightened the connection to a "real union" sharing monarch, currency, Sejm (parliament), and foreign policy. This real union increased the influence of Polish culture in Lithuania while, especially after the mid-seventeenth century, weakening the importance of Vilnius as one of the capitals of Poland-Lithuania. Thus ironically the seeds of decline were sown precisely in this period of cultural and economic blossoming.[17]

Relations between Roman Catholics and Eastern Orthodox believers had recently been complicated by the establishment at the Union of Brest (1595–1596) of the Uniate or (as it later came to be known) "Greek Catholic" Church. Uniates pledged loyalty to the Pope but retained their liturgy and practices, including married clergy and mass in Church Slavonic.[18] The Orthodox clergy regarded the Uniate Church with disdain, as a cynical instrument to convert to Catholicism and polonize local Orthodox people. In Vilnius the Uniate Church, including monasteries, would become an important site for the formation of Belarusian identity. Uniate churches and monasteries persisted in the city until the 1830s, when the Russian government gave them over to the Orthodox Church.[19]

As David Frick has shown, in the later sixteenth century and well into the seventeenth, Vilnius' Catholics, Uniates, Orthodox, Lutherans, and Calvinists not only lived side by side (to be sure, some streets were dominated more by a certain faith than others) but even had extensive economic and social intercourse.[20] Perhaps most surprising in Frick's detailed social history are the frequent instances of interconfessional marriages, business ties (including participation in the same guild, though not always), and much residential mixing. Still, he admits that members of the same religious group tended to cluster together: Muslim Tatars in the Łukiszki suburb; Jews in the city center; Lutherans on Castle and Glass Streets downtown and in the Antokol suburb; Calvinists near the Lutherans on Castle Street; and "Greeks" (the sources, Frick points out, seldom clearly differentiate between Uniates and Orthodox) on Subocz, Rudniki, Sawicz, Bakszta, and other downtown streets. Catholics resided throughout the city, but the nobles among them (by Frick's period, the seventeenth century, most Vilnius nobles were Catholic) in the very center of town along Dominican and Troki Streets.

Frick gives us a remarkably detailed picture of individual houses down to their rooms and rented "alcoves." His research confirms a general tendency toward spatial concentration of specific religious groups (no one in this period considered language or "nation" of particular importance) as well as much specific mixing—even in the same house and apartment. His documentation of the frequent residence of Jews in Christian houses is particularly surprising. It is well-known that no specific ghetto ever existed in Vilnius but that certain streets at certain times would be off-limits for Jewish residence. Jews were allowed to live in nobles' houses but were specifically forbidden from taking up residence in burgher houses. In fact, as Frick shows, in the seventeenth century the sources show Jews living both on "forbidden" streets and in Christian houses.[21]

Religious-ethnic differences were reflected not only in urban space but also in time. Different confessions and religious communities followed different calendars. The Orthodox and the Uniates, for example, celebrated different saints' days and calculated the date of Easter differently from their Roman Catholic (or protestant) neighbors. Jews, of course, used an entirely different calendar and observed their *shabbes* day of rest the day before the Christian Sunday. Further complicating calendric matters was the introduction of a correction to the Julian calendar dating to Ancient Rome. This Gregorian Calendar, named after the Pope who introduced it in 1582, was initially rejected by Protestants and not adopted by the Orthodox Church until the twentieth century (and even then not universally). Muslims and Karaites, furthermore, followed their own lunar calendars.[22] In practical terms, friction developed mainly when different confessions celebrated holidays or endured fasts at different moments. Thus a Lutheran, Uniate (who continued to follow the Julian calendar), or Jew might conduct business on a Catholic holy day when work was not allowed. Similarly, fasting was required of Roman Catholics and of Uniates (or Calvinists) on different days.[23] On the whole, despite the disparate calendric systems, it appears that the (mainly Catholic) authorities tolerated the chronological diversity even while disdaining non-Catholic practices.

Vilnius in the mid-seventeenth century was an impressive and wealthy city. While lands to the west suffered through the Thirty Years War (1618–1648), Poland-Lithuania—and also Vilnius, the dual state's "second" capital—prospered. Population estimates range wildly, with a Polish historian of the interwar period settling on the figure of 14,000 which seems very low. Whatever the true figure may be, the city could boast numerous publishing houses (the first book in Lithuanian published in Vilnius appeared in 1595), and a number of stone houses within the defensive walls. Noble palaces built by the Radziwiłł, Sapieha, Pac, and Chodkiewicz families were particularly noteworthy. The city was full of churches. Roman Catholics had some two dozen, Uniates seven, and Eastern Orthodox, Lutherans, and Calvinists each maintained both church and cemetery for their faithful. The large synagogue that would survive to World War II was the center of Jewish religious life, supplemented by numerous small prayer houses, primarily near the synagogue in the city center. On the edge of town (outside the walls) one could find the Tatar mosque.[24] While Poles and Catholicism predominated,

Vilnius' diverse religious and ethno-linguistic groups managed to live together in the fairly tight urban space without notable clashes.

The idyll was shattered in 1655. The Muscovite invasion and occupation of the city, while short-lived, can serve as a convenient caesura that indicates the end of the golden age. Invasion and occupation were accompanied by both a devastating fire that destroyed a great deal of the city and, for good measure, an epidemic. Figures for the number of deaths in the wake of the invasion range wildly and are all based more on conjecture than on solid documentation. It would appear, however, that the city lost the great majority of its population, though some of these residents had only fled the city and returned in the years after the Russians left the city. The city was rebuilt, the university continued its studies, and new churches appeared, but on a far less impressive scale than in the previous centuries.[25]

Russian invasions were followed by Swedish devastations in the Northern War of the early eighteenth century. The rise of Russian power coincided with neglect by the Polish rulers, still officially Grand Dukes of Lithuania but now resident in Cracow or Warsaw and only rarely visiting Vilnius. The wars and political instability destroyed the trade routes that had made Vilnius prosperous; fires and epidemics further reduced the city.[26]

Political and economic dislocation were paralleled by increasing religious intolerance. Lutheran and Calvinist communities dwindled, though they did not disappear entirely. Uniates and Orthodox believers remained, but Catholic supremacy had been established. At the same time, during the eighteenth century alleged (and probably, at least at times, real) persecution of Orthodox people by the Catholic authorities provided the Russian Empire with a convenient excuse for interference and even military invasion. Thus by the end of the eighteenth century, on the eve of the Russian Empire's incorporation of Vilnius, the city was a shadow of its former proud self.

## Historiography: Two Nineteenth-Century Views

Conceptions of Vilnius in the medieval and early modern period, particularly up to the early twentieth century, were heavily influenced by two monumental histories published in the first half of the nineteenth century. The first of these, Michał Baliński's *Historya miasta Wilna*, only managed to reach the year 1586 (the year of King Stefan Batory's death).[27] The second, by the indefatigable Polish writer Józef Ignacy Kraszewski, filled four sizable volumes and reached the mid-eighteenth century.[28] Both are traditional works of history, heavily emphasizing kings, battles, legal documents, and cultural history. Kraszewski, for example, begins with a long overview of semi-mythological Lithuanian princes going back to Roman times.[29] Both authors also contrast the "Lithuanian faith" (paganism) with Christianity, though mainly in a nostalgic folklorist vein. Both histories—though Kraszewski more than Baliński—often present the history of the city through the history of its rulers and cultural institutions.

In the introduction to a recent translation (into Lithuanian) of Baliński's history, Vytautas Berenis points out that of the two major nineteenth-century histories of Vilnius, Baliński's was more "local" and showed more openness to the idea of Lithuanian cultural differences, but it was stylistically inferior to Kraszewski's work.[30] This makes sense, as Baliński's entire life was linked with the city: he was born nearby, studied at Vilnius University, married the daughter of a famous professor of chemistry, and died in Vilnius in 1864.[31] Kraszewski, on the other hand, was born in Warsaw, died in Geneva, and in between wrote hundreds of books, becoming one of the most famous Polish writers of the nineteenth century. His history of Vilnius is thus more traditional, more "Polish," and less "local" than Baliński's work. Kraszewski also gives us access to sources that have subsequently been lost.

Baliński begins his history with an explanation of his motivations and goals in writing this history. In a sentence that stretches over two pages, he explains that he wanted not only to remind contemporaries of past events, setting down and retelling the circumstances of Vilnius' beginnings and the laws and privileges under which its inhabitants had lived. He has also set himself a second, equally important task of providing an explanatory background on some of the main events and rulers in Lithuanian history, "little known to ourselves [presumably, to Poles or to local people in Vilnius] and for Europe entirely foreign [obce]." Indeed, he continues, he hopes that this early story of their capital will serve as "a history of the Lithuanian nation." While Baliński does not define just what he means by "naród litewski" here, it is important to note that the Polish word *naród* never refers to the political unit (i.e., as a synonym for "the state") but always to the cultural-ethnic-demographic unit (i.e., as a synonym for "the people"). Baliński, it would seem, defined this "nation" in broad, inclusive terms rather than narrow linguistic ones. Thus he could include himself, as a man of Polish culture, within the Lithuanian nation.

The history itself follows a highly traditional pattern, with the succession of rulers providing the structure of the narrative. The city itself and its inhabitants do appear, but infrequently and almost as an afterthought. Baliński terms the period 1506-1586 (the reign of Zygmunt I to Stefan Batory's death—again, the rulers determine the periodization) the era of Vilnius' "Greatest Flourishing" [pomyślość][32] but devotes almost no attention to economics. Even more strangely, the creation of the university—for some, the proudest achievement of Batory's reign—is mentioned but hardly elaborated on. In the end, the history tells us much about Vilnius' rulers and political affairs but relatively little about the city itself.

Józef Ignacy Kraszewski's approach differs sharply from Baliński's. To start with, we should always remember that Kraszewski was a novelist, not a historian, and an astoundingly prolific writer. Where Baliński offers a few dozen pages of fairly dry political coverage, supplemented with documents, Kraszewski puts forth a hundred lush pages of political intrigue and conflict (certainly not lacking in these times). To be fair, however, Kraszewski also provides very serious material for the social historian, including information on artisans, trade, dress, and customs. In the end, Kraszewski may well be the better historian, at least for present-day tastes: political events and rulers certainly constitute the backbone of the narrative, but culture, economy, and physical aspects of the city also receive their due.

Both Baliński and Kraszewski wrote in the 1830s, before nationalism had reached its most fervent and chauvinistic stage. Both authors discuss the Lithuanians and their language, though perhaps more as a curiosity than as an examination of a living culture. Who could have known, after all, whether the almost exclusively peasant and oral language and culture of the 1830s would survive in the modern world? Neither author is hostile, to be sure, to things Lithuanian, and as we have seen, Baliński even speaks of the "Lithuanian nation (or 'people')," among whom he apparently included himself. On the whole, however, these works belong (mercifully) to a prenationalist historiography, taking for granted the influence and benevolence of Polish culture but not finding it necessary to oppose or denigrate other cultures or nations overtly.

Neither Kraszewski nor Baliński felt the need to "claim" Vilnius for the Polish nation. They were secure in the knowledge that for all the ethnic diversity the city exhibited, it was in the end both politically and culturally tied to the Polish nation. Even Baliński's praise for the "Lithuanian nation" does not contradict this position: at least as I would argue, he saw the Lithuanian and Polish "nations" as overlapping entities. As we will see, after these two classic works and even to the present day historiography turned much more nationalistic, sometimes in an aggressive vein but more often by focusing on one national-cultural group to the neglect or exclusion (often, to the unstated exclusion) of the others. The nationalist rhetoric of historians will figure in the present analysis as a factor equal in importance to the physical changes in the city and frictions between city dwellers, the state, and the nation to which they belonged (or to which they were ascribed).

• • •

This chapter has aimed to give a brief sketch of the first four and a half centuries of Vilnius' existence. From the start, the city's population showed a diversity of confessions, languages, and cultures. In this period—and long after—religion played a far more important role in an individual's identity and daily life than did language or ethnic origin. The state—whether the Grand Duchy of Lithuania in the earliest centuries or the Polish-Lithuanian Commonwealth later—tolerated religious diversity while paying little attention to what languages were spoken here. At the same time, by the sixteenth century Polish culture was increasingly crowding out the Ruthenian and Lithuanian languages, in particular among the nobility. In the eighteenth century the city experienced a significant decline against the background of war and natural disasters. At the same time the Polish-Lithuanian Commonwealth had entered a period of crisis that would culminate in the Partitions that would destroy that country entirely. One result of the Partitions would be the Russian occupation of Vilnius, which would last for over a century and to which we will turn in the next chapter.

CHAPTER 2

## A Center of Polish and Jewish Culture, 1795–1862

WITH THE THIRD PARTITION of Poland and the defeat of the Kościuszko Uprising, Vilnius came under Russian rule. For 120 years, St. Petersburg would be the ultimate authority over the city; in the twenty-first century one may still discern marks of that rule in its churches, architecture, and urban layout. For the first decades of Russian rule, however, it is difficult to speak of serious efforts to incorporate the city culturally into the larger empire (i.e., "russification").[1] True, the higher reaches of local administration were manned by Russians and considerable numbers of Russian troops were stationed there. But the university, city magistrate, printing, and in general Polish-dominated high culture continued to flourish until the early 1830s. Even after that point, Russian restrictions on Polish culture in the next three decades did not translate into any significant development of Russian culture there. Rather, Russians remained outsiders, a caste of officials and soldiers occupying foreign territory who only rarely remained in the city after their tour of duty.

Despite the hegemony of Polish culture in Vilnius, most likely not Poles but Jews formed the largest single ethnic group there. Visitors and locals alike remarked on the ubiquity of Jews, their prayer houses, shops, and "oriental customs." While Vilnius lacked a legally defined "Jewish ghetto," a fairly solid segment of the Old Town was dominated by Jewish residents. Jewish life in Vilnius remained traditional—the most famous rabbinical commentator of the city (and age), the Vilnius Gaon ("genius"), was still living in the city when it came under Russian rule (the Gaon died in 1797).[2] Certainly Jews and Christians came into contact on a regular, even daily basis, but it is difficult to speak of any "shared culture." Contacts remained on a practical, commercial level. As for Lithuanians, they have left little mark on the historical record of Vilnius for this period. Clearly many individuals of Lithuanian ethnicity must have lived in the city, and we have evidence of Lithuanian students at the university. Among these, the most famous was the 1819 graduate Simonas Daukantas, whose image adorns the present-day 100-litas bill. Still, like many other languages in East-Central Europe (Finnish,

Estonian, Czech, Ukrainian), Lithuanian would only be developed as a cultural and patriotic value in the second half of the nineteenth century.[3]

Periodization of Vilnius' history during the imperial era is a thorny issue, depending very much on whether one chooses to emphasize culture (and which one), politics, or economics. After some wavering I have selected somewhat arbitrarily to end this chapter in 1860, a year distinguished by no specific occurrence, but a convenient break before the tumultuous events of the 1863 anti-Russian uprising. Shortly thereafter, in 1862, Vilnius was connected to both Petersburg and Warsaw by rail; this connection had both political and cultural importance. A more traditional break might have been 1855 (the death of Tsar Nicholas I and ascension to the throne of Tsar Alexander II, the beginnings of the Great Reform period in the Russian Empire) or 1863 (the outbreak of the January Uprising). By selecting a year in between, I want to emphasize the break with past, more conservative forms of imperial rule (symbolized by the death of Nicholas I), and the advent of a more nationalist age, symbolized by the Polish Lithuanian Insurrection, its failure, and efforts by the Russian Empire to tie the city more tightly to the Russian center ("russification").

Between the incorporation of Vilnius into the Russian Empire and the insurrection of the early 1860s, Vilnius as a city and its population did not change radically. While these decades witnessed a continual tightening of imperial control over the city, the Russian rulers did not directly challenge (though they did bewail) the Polish Jewish character of the city. To be sure, after the November 1830 insurrection, the Russian authorities did close down the university—or rather, they moved it to Kiev, where it was resurrected as a Russian institution. This was certainly a great blow to Polish culture in Vilnius, but in a typical manner, the Russian Empire failed to follow up on this repressive measure with consistent policies that could better anchor the Russian nationality and Russian culture in this city. For such policies one needs to wait until after the subsequent 1863 insurrection.

This is not to say that the city did not change over these nearly seven decades—only that the change was gradual and not radical (in particular as compared to the ensuing half century). The city's population did increase, and work on what would become the fine St. George's Avenue (today's Gedimino) was begun. By 1862 one could travel from Petersburg through Vilnius to both Warsaw and East Prussia. The grand new avenue and railroad station accelerated communications and helped lay the foundations for a new, more "Russian" (or perhaps "imperial") Vilnius.

The structure of this chapter, like its end date, may well be somewhat unexpected. Basically, the chapter is divided into three unequal parts covering the city's growth and development (including population), major events of this period, and—by far the longest section—the city's cultures. The idea is first of all to construct, so to speak, a physical (statistical) and political substructure and then to build atop it a superstructure of cultural-national developments of over this half century. Obviously no exhaustive demographic, cultural, or even political history of the city can be attempted here. Rather, the point is to give an impression of how demography, politics, and (diverse) cultures worked together in this urban space during the early generations of imperial rule.

## City and Population

Statistics from the Russian Empire are notoriously faulty, so in the following one can at best gain only an approximate and relative picture of the city in the early nineteenth century. Soon after the Russian occupation of Vilnius in 1795, a kind of census—*reviziia*—was carried out. Each "long-term resident" (*obywatel starożytny*), usually a head of household, was asked, for example, to state name, the number of years of residency in Vilnius, the kind of real estate owned, and the names of all persons living on that property.[4] Unfortunately, as far as I can tell, neither city nor Russian authorities compiled this data, which could have given us an overall demographic picture of Vilnius in 1795.[5] According to an interwar Polish historian, Russian sources show a population of 25,430, of which 57.7 percent were Christian and 42.3 percent Jewish immediately after the incorporation of the city into the empire.[6]

One can certainly agree with the Soviet Lithuanian historians' assessment that "Statistical data on numbers of Vilnius' inhabitants in the first half of the nineteenth century are quite contradictory." These contradictions reflect the weakness of the sources—that is, the failure of Russian administrators to employ scientific statistical methods. In the first twenty-odd years of Russian rule, the population rose only slightly: by 1818, it had reached 33,568.[7] Whatever the exact figures really were, one thing is clear: Vilnius in the early nineteenth century was a small, provincial, and principally Polish Jewish city.

An invaluable source for information on Vilnius in the early nineteenth century is Michał Baliński's 1835 *Opisanie statystyczne miasta Wilna*. Baliński, whom we have already met as a historian of the city, was an indefatigable researcher and chronicler of Vilnius' history.⁸ Besides offering a wealth of statistics on the city's population, his book provides a description of the churches and other buildings in the town. About the city's physical aspect in general, Baliński makes the following remark: "A view of Wilno shows an exceedingly irregularly built city: there are nowhere straight or wide streets, nor well-formed squares [placów kształtnych]."⁹ Among the churches mentioned by Baliński, twenty-five (plus seven chapels) were Catholic and two (plus two chapels) were Orthodox. The city also had a Protestant ("ewangelicki") church and chapel as well as a wooden mosque and four main Jewish synagogues.¹⁰

The city's population by religion and confession must have roughly mirrored the same ratio, with the very significant exception of the Jews. Strangely, Baliński mentions no "Greek-Russian" (Orthodox) population (even stranger, the table on religions includes this category but without any figures). He lists only 273 Uniates, 162 Calvinists ("reformed"), and 482 Lutherans (Evangelical-Augsburg), whose numbers are overwhelmed by the 14,349 Catholics and 20,646 Jews (a total population of 35,922).¹¹ The actual numbers of Orthodox and Uniates must have been higher. Baliński admitted that his large figure for the Jews could not be considered precise but argued that a quick look at the "dirty and narrow lanes" of the Old Town where several (Jewish) families occupied a single small house might lead one to conclude that the real number of Jews in Vilnius was actually far higher. Indeed, the historian and statistician complained that Vilnius should be considered among the first cities of the empire, along with Riga, Petersburg, and Moscow, were it not for the "extraordinary abundance in Vilnius of Jews and on top of this their Asiatic garb and offensive slovenliness [obraźliwe nieochędóstwo]," which spoiled the view and reputation of the city.¹²

Christian clergy were present in the city in large numbers: 128 Catholic priests (kapłanów), 355 Catholic monks, and 177 nuns; a total of 34 Uniates, all but one monks and nuns; one Orthodox archimandrite, two priests, and five "Church servants" (possibly diaki / deacons); two Evangelical-Augsburg (Lutherans) priests; and two Reformed (Calvinist) priests.¹³ No Jewish or Muslim clerics are listed, though obviously there were numerous rabbis (strictly speaking, not "clerics") in the city.

A listing of houses in Vilnius carried out in 1800 cited a total of 1329 structures ranging from stone palaces to "huts" (chałupy), located mainly in what would now be considered the Old Town.¹⁴ Three decades later, Baliński noted 1552 houses making up the city, around one-third of which were wooden (i.e., the rest were stone or brick), so together with structures in "suburbs" (including such present-day downtown quarters as Lukiškės), the number of houses totaled around 1700. Baliński noted that in Riga, a city of similar size, there were more than twice as many houses—an indication of the extremely dense population in Vilnius. Among the largest private residences were those on Wielka, Trocka, and Wileńska Streets.[15]

Baliński only indirectly provides insight into the social make-up of Vilnius' population. By social estate the largest single group comprised nobles (6658), followed by townspeople (*mieszczanie*, 4930). "Active" and retired officials (*urzędnicy*) numbered 616 and 102, respectively, and 711 members of the clerical state and 319 serfs also resided in the city.[16] Baliński remarks that "Wilno cannot be counted among the industrial cities of the Empire." Artisans were still much more prevalent than industrial workers: Vilnius still counted thirty-one guilds, from bookbinders to milliners, in the early 1830s. Certain artisan trades, like those of tailors and furriers, were dominated entirely by Jews, but Christians were active or dominant in most others.[17] Small retail stores (*kramy*) were nearly all run by Jews, but larger stores (*sklepy* and *magaziny*) were owned by Jews and Christians alike.[18] Trade remained underdeveloped. In 1832 there were only two large merchants (of the first guild), both of whom were Christians. Jews dominated among petty merchants, with 33 Christians and 92 Jews belonging to the third guild.[19]

Baliński, probably reflecting his own sources and even more the mind-set of his age, gave no statistics on language or nationality. On the latter he remarked, "as for ethnicity [*ród*], the inhabitants of Wilno are Lithuanians, Russians, Germans, and Jews [Litwini, Rossyanie, Niemcy, i Żydzi]."[20] At first glance something seems to be missing: the Poles. Of course when Baliński wrote *Litwini* he did not have in mind ethnic Lithuanians but, rather, people of Polish culture, like himself, who resided in *Litwa*.[21] Similarly, "Russians" would include other eastern Slavs, such as Belarusians, who were particularly important in Vilnius. As we have seen, Baliński probably considered himself "ethnically" different from Poles of central Poland and saw himself chiefly as a *Litwin*, which is not the same as how we in the twenty-first century (with our emphasis on language and ethnicity) would define a "Lithuanian."

The Old Town core, in particular from Ostra Brama to the Castle Hill and the cathedral, would be readily recognizable to present-day visitors of Vilnius. Baliński mentions that the city was made up of 1552 buildings in total, but of these the most important ("in size or architecture") could be found on a handful of downtown streets.[22] Many main streets bore the same name (though of course not in Lithuanian) in the early nineteenth century as today, from "Castle" (Zamkowa/Pilies) to "Vilnius" and "German" (Niemiecka/Vokiečių) Streets.[23]

There were also numerous changes, however, in these decades. As Baliński mentions, the old bishop's residence across from the university was replaced by an "imperial palace" (*pałac cesarski*), the office of the governor general, in 1832.[24] Most striking for the city's image, the broad and straight avenue from the cathedral that today bears the name Gedimino was laid out in this period. In 1835 plans for the construction of a "new street from the Cathedral to Lukiszki Square" were mooted and the sum of 2066 rubles was allotted for this purpose.[25] Building this avenue was complicated not only by the general sluggishness of imperial Russian bureaucracy but, even more, by the competing interests of landowners and city government in buying up the necessary parcels of land needed to build the thoroughfare.[26] For all the delays, at length the grand new avenue—Georgievskii prospekt, named after St. George—took shape. A map of 1875 shows the straight line of this thoroughfare reaching all the way to the river—but even at that point there were few buildings lining the avenue beyond the square around a chapel to Alexander Nevsky (today Kudirka Square).[27] Thus the outline of the new, Russian Vilnius had been set out by the 1860s though that outline would be "filled in," so to speak, only in the century's final decades.

The building of the St. Petersburg to Warsaw rail line had a significant impact on the city. Construction on the rail line began in 1858, in 1860 Vilnius was connected to the north (to Daugavpils), and in 1861 the railroad station was completed. A year later trains were running between St. Petersburg and Warsaw through Vilnius.[28] Along with the railroad, the telegraph arrived in Vilnius: the first telegram was sent from the city in November 1859.[29] The railroad station, with its connections to other parts of the Russian Empire, "embraced" the Old Town to the south; to the west, St. George's Avenue formed the backbone of a new "Russian" (in spirit and architecture, though not so much in population) town.

By mid-century, Vilnius had grown appreciably since Baliński carried out his study. On the eve of the January Insurrection, the city's population was nearing 60,000.[30] As yet, the town retained its mainly Polish and Jewish character, overlaid by Russian officialdom and the Russian military presence.

## Three Events

Looking at the seventy years in Vilnius between two failed uprisings (the Kościuszko Insurrection and that of January 1863), three major political events stand out: the Russian occupation, the Napoleonic occupation of 1812, and the

November 1830 Insurrection. For most residents of Vilnius, in particular those who were neither Polish nor of the elite, the *longue durée* of 1795–1863 did not bring radical changes to life in the city. Certainly the city grew moderately, but the relative strength of Polish and Jewish culture there remained about the same. While Russian suspicion of the Polish elite became much stronger after the 1830–1831 insurrection (the "November Uprising" in Polish and Lithuanian historiography), Polish culture and wealth continued to dominate.

The occupation of Vilnius by Russian troops in 1794 put an end to a long period of turmoil and uncertainty about the future. The first governor general of the Lithuanian provinces, Prince Nikolai Vasil'evich Repnin, played a significant role in the city's life in the next three years. Repnin had decades earlier been Russian ambassador in Warsaw and was seen as friendly toward the Poles. At first, however, he set up his administration in Grodno rather than Vilnius as the latter city had been all too active in the Kościuszko Rebellion against the Russians.[31]

Both the city and the region were devastated from the insurrection, battles, and occupation. Repnin's first task was to assure future loyalty of the local population (particularly, of course, the nobles and clergy, as peasantry and townspeople enjoyed far less political importance) while attempting to get the region's economy back on track. While many Polish nobles initially demurred, first the clergy then the nobility declared their loyalty to the Russian tsarina within a year or two. Żytkowicz explains the lack of resistance to the general devastation and disorientation after the failed uprising.[32]

The Russian authorities confiscated numerous estates of Poles who had participated in the Kościuszko uprising. Setting a pattern that would be repeated time and again in the nineteenth century, these estates were given or sold at bargain prices to loyal, mainly Russian, officers and administrators. These efforts to increase Russian landholding in the region were ineffective, however, as most of the recipients either rented or sold the estates. In Vilnius, Repnin took over the Catholic bishop's palace for the Russian administration. The Russian authorities left religious communities more or less undisturbed, though they were from the start particularly hostile to the Uniates whom Tsar Paul I famously described as "neither fish nor fowl." While the Russians had no great love for the Roman Catholic Church, they regarded the Uniate establishment as simply a tool to convert Orthodox people to Catholicism.[33]

The single most important change to the cityscape in the early years of Russian rule was tearing down the old city walls. The walls, which had only been built in the early sixteenth century, had outlived their purpose in an age of muskets and cannons. Fighting in 1794 between the Polish insurgents and the Russian forces had caused widespread damage to the already crumbling walls. In September 1797 the governor general of Lithuania had recommended to the tsar that the walls be knocked down, but no action was taken. In August 1799 the civil governor of Lithuania petitioned the local military governor general to have the walls dismantled, pointing out that they served no purpose and exacerbated unsanitary conditions in the city.[34] The tsar agreed, and in the next few years (by 1805) the town walls had been nearly completely destroyed, leaving only a couple of distinctive gates, including Ostra Brama ("sharp" gate, today's Aušros Vartai), intact. Characteristically, the Russian administration undertook the action without any consultation with the still-existing town government (*magistrat*). Private individuals were allowed to cart away the stone from the old walls as long as they used it for constructing houses in Vilnius. Neither Russians nor Poles protested the destruction of the old walls.[35]

Looking at the larger European context, the first years of Russian rule in Vilnius roughly coincided with Napoleon Bonaparte's rise to supreme power in France. With the Treaty of Tilsit (1807) and the formation of the Duchy of Warsaw (later the "Grand Duchy"), the Napoleonic Wars inched very close indeed to Vilnius. The city was not included in the Duchy of Warsaw but the nearby presence of a kind of proto Polish state could not help but inspire hopes among Polish patriots for the resurrection of Poland. When the uneasy alliance between France and Russia was swept away by the extraordinary Corsican's invasion in early June 1812, Vilnius was almost immediately taken (without a battle) and would spend the rest of the year under French occupation.[36]

On June 12/24, 1812 Tsar Alexander I was attending a ball at the palace of governor general Benningsen just outside Vilnius at Zakret when news of the French invasion reached him. Frictions had been growing between Russia and France for some time, but the tsar hoped to buy time, fearing—like Stalin in 1941—that his army would not yet be equal to the task of taking on Napoleon's forces. The French troop build-up across the Neman River had not gone unnoticed by the Russians, but Alexander hoped that diplomacy could hold off an immediate clash. Napoleon chose instead to violate his pact with the Russian tsar in the hopes of bringing Alexander more in line with the French boycott of Britain known as the "Continental System."

Within days, the Russians pulled out of the city. Alexander himself left the town on June 14/26 for Sventsiany (today's Švenčionys), and Russian troops abandoned the city two days later, burning the Green Bridge behind them. That same day (June 16/28) French troops reached the city.³⁷ A Russian eyewitness wrote of a near-panic in the city, with residents rushing about in search of shelter, provisions, and reliable news on the intentions and position of the French. Rumors of French desecration of Orthodox churches and the looting of civilians abounded.³⁸ No effort was made by the Russian authorities to defend the city, and the *Grande Armée* was able to march into the city unopposed.

Despite all the misgivings, large crowds turned out in the city to welcome the French, in particular when Napoleon made his entry through the Ostra Brama gate at noon on June 16/28. Symbolically, the first troops to enter Vilnius were not French but Prince Dominik Radziwiłł's 8th Polish Ulans.³⁹ They were soon joined by thousands of other soldiers, many of whom had to camp in and around the city. Several noble residences, including the Nagurski, Sapieha, and Radziwiłł houses, were pressed into service to accommodate officers.⁴⁰ Napoleon himself lodged in the former bishop's palace (now the president's office) across from the university.

Napoleon was to reside in Vilnius for nearly three weeks, from June 28 to July 16 (n.s.). During that time he did his best to acquaint himself with the city, its inhabitants (to be sure, mainly of the "better sort"), and its environs. On the day after his arrival he took an equestrian tour of the city, guided by local magnates from the Pac, Sapieha, and other families. Like many other tourists in Vilnius, Napoleon was struck by the brick Gothic church of St. Anne. He even expressed his desire to transport the building to Paris.⁴¹ The French emperor similarly visited Castle Hill, the legendary site of the city's founding, climbing all the way to the top to examine the ruins of the upper castle, then descending and continuing along the Neris to the site of the now destroyed Green Bridge. As he passed through the crowded streets, Napoleon and his entourage were welcomed with shouts of "Vive Napoléon!"⁴² Many local Poles no doubt hoped that Napoleon would include the city in a newly resurrected Polish state ("Grand Duchy of Warsaw"). Napoleon himself, however, refrained from any specific promises for extending the Duchy of Warsaw geographically and politically. Instead, he spent his nineteen days in Vilnius getting acquainted with the city (mainly on horseback), meeting local dignitaries, and preparing his next military move against Russia—all the while hoping for concessions on the part of Alexander I.⁴³

During Napoleon's stay in the city, a major festival was organized there to celebrate the revolutionary holiday of July 14. In Vilnius the "French" holiday was given a Polish patriotic flavor by combining it with the solemn "act of confederation" signed by the Provisional Lithuanian Government.⁴⁴ While this act did not have great political significance—Napoleon had rather brusquely dismissed requests for the creation of a greater Poland, including the Lithuanian lands—symbolically it seemed to promise a future restored Polish state. At 11 a.m. a solemn mass was held in the cathedral, attended by local dignitaries, local guild representatives, numerous clergy, members of the Provisional Governmental Commission (Tymczasowa Komisja Rządowa), protected by battalions of the newly created National Guard (Gwardja Narodowa), and presided over by Bishop J. N. Kossakowski. After mass there were speeches by the president of the Provisional Government, Józef Sierakowski, and a reading of the act of confederation, ending with shouts of "Long live the union of Lithuania with the crown!" and "Long live Emperor Napoleon!" The city streets were decorated for the occasion, and the day ended with fireworks and a special gala performance of the patriotic Polish opera "Krakowiacy i Górali" at the National Theater.[45]

The departure of Napoleon in mid-July did not prevent a gala celebration of the emperor's name day (*imieniny*) a month later. A later account, based on contemporary stories in *Kurier Litewski* and *Tymczasowa Gazeta Mińska*, struck a patriotic, even fawning tone, claiming that "Lithuanians" (understood geographically, not ethnically) had long envied Poles their right to celebrate the great man's name day and thus the festivities were full of patriotism, joy, and "prayers and [best] regards ... which every Pole [now clearly including "Litwini" in this designation] offered up to Providence and to Napoleon."

The previous evening a cannonade had heralded the beginning of preparations. After a night of preparations for the festival, Napoleon's name day dawned with the gathering in Cathedral Square of military units serving under the emperor. The units were composed of "Poles, Bavarians, French, Imperial Guard." Generals and staff officers paid a visit to the Lithuanian governor general, count Dirk Hogendorp, and to the French foreign minister, the Duke of Bassano. A large altar with an (empty) throne was set up, surrounded by an honor guard made up of the recently formed (Lithuanian) National Guard. Accompanied by "sublime music," bishop Nikodem Puzyna held a solemn mass in honor of the day. A rousing sermon was heard, given by the prelate Michał Dłuski, who had recently caused a stir with his remarks in favor of emancipating the serfs. The church services concluded with a singing of hymns, including "Te Deum laudamus." The crowd surrounding the cathedral "filled the air with shouts of 'Long live Napoleon the Savior of the Poles!'"

From the cathedral the festivities then moved to the nearby square between the university and the bishop's residence. Here the mayor, Mykolas Römeris, pronounced a rousing speech, calling on all locals to do their patriotic duty to help the

A CENTER OF POLISH AND JEWISH CULTURE, 1795-1862    31

war effort and decreeing that henceforth the square would be known as "Napoleon Square" (which, incidentally, it still is, in the twenty-first century, though its name changed several times in the intervening two centuries). The evening was marked with a huge feast (*biesiada*) at which entire oxen, fowl, sheep, and rams were roasted. A patriotic play was performed "gratis" at the town theater, and afterward patriots made their way to a gala ball, which continued until six the next morning. Public buildings and main streets in the city were illuminated, and even "the Israelite school" and Jewish quarter were "richly lit." On Castle Hill a large sign (*transparent*) was erected declaring "Wilno—freed on June 28, 1812."[46] By celebrating Napoleon's name day, local Polish (or "Lithuanian") elites were able to express their own patriotic feelings and hope for the restoration of the Polish state in the not-too-distant future.[47]

Russians, despite their small numbers, are highly visible in the sources. We have the report of the monk M. Lavrinovich, whose supposedly eyewitness account of the 1812 events in Vilnius was published in 1897. In his almost breathless narrative, Lavrinovich speaks of fear as the Russian troops withdraw, jubilation (of some . . . ) upon Napoleon's entry, and such remarkable episodes as communicating with French soldiers in Latin.[48] Lavrinovich's account, with its theatrical speeches and moral sermonizing, may not be the most reliable source (though Russian historians have used it time and again), but it seems clear that some Orthodox people (the best definition for "Russian" in 1812) must have remained in the city, in particular in the poorer classes and as guardians of the various Orthodox churches there. Still, "silent evidence" that the Russian presence in Vilnius from July to December 1812 was minimal is the fact that subsequent Russian historians like Kudrinskii make no mention of the city's Russian population at all in their accounts.[49]

Everyone agrees that Jews were ubiquitous in Vilnius in 1812. They appear frequently in contemporary sources, though nearly always on the periphery, so to speak, of what is being discussed. The Jewish community shows up when special taxes are demanded, compensation for destroyed property is requested, and the like. Knowing well that in times of armed conflict they had much to lose and little to gain by supporting one side or the other, Jews mainly tried to avoid any entanglements in the French-Russian-Polish disputes. Jewish residents of the city suffered from having to feed and house French soldiers, and one later Polish commentator declares that "the attitude of the Jews toward Napoleon's army . . . was openly hostile, as is shown by all sources."[50] Later commentators often mentioned Jewish loyalty to the Russian side and to Alexander I personally.[51] While

Napoleon's name is generally connected today with the extension of civil rights to Jews in central Europe, in 1812 he would most likely have appeared to traditional Jews as a godless and secularizing Haman rather than as a liberator.[52]

The attitude toward the French on the part of Vilnius' Poles is not easy to gauge. To be sure, Polish society as a whole supported Napoleon as an ally against the partitioning powers. Many sources note that the general mood in the city was one of enthusiastic welcome for the French troops and their emperor.[53] It was only too clear that the Poles had little to offer Napoleon—aside from cannon fodder—and that Napoleon's policies in the Duchy of Warsaw and elsewhere had not shown a readiness to share power. One indication of a lukewarm attitude toward the French among the population of Lithuania, where the non-serf and non-Jewish population would have been mainly Polish, is the relatively small numbers of volunteers for Napoleon's army among this population.[54] Napoleon did form a "national guard" of Lithuanian (by geography, not necessarily ethnicity) volunteers, but on the whole recruitment from the "crown" (Duchy of Warsaw) was more successful.[55]

Polish society in Vilnius was in a difficult position. On the one hand, perhaps Napoleon could help resurrect the Polish state. On the other hand, the rule of Alexander I had not been onerous for local Polish-speakers ("*Litwini*"), who on the whole continued to use Polish in local institutions and, except at the highest levels, dominated the local bureaucracy. More than that, Alexander's educational policy carried out by Adam Czartoryski had been most favorable to Polish culture. Besides considerations of loyalty and gratitude toward Russia, there was also the simple fact that Napoleon could quite possibly lose the war. While the French military appeared very strong in summer 1812, Poles in Vilnius knew very well that supporting the French against Alexander would almost certainly bring negative repercussions in case of a French defeat.

After a promising summer for the French military, autumn events made the possibility of a change for the worse seem more and more likely. News of the clash at Borodino reached Vilnius on September 8 and was seen by local Polish society as a French victory. It appeared that with Moscow occupied by Napoleon's troops, Alexander would be forced to sue for peace—and, it was hoped, the peace terms would reward Poland for its support to the French war effort. Unfortunately for the Poles, they miscalculated.[56] As Napoleon sat and stewed in Moscow, tensions grew in Vilnius. Faced with empty coffers, the local military even taxed the clergy; shortages of salt and vodka were reported. On the other hand, a good harvest meant that the city had ample stores of grain as fall and winter arrived.[57]

In mid-October, after waiting for a month in a state of anxiety and poor health, Napoleon had had enough. He began the retreat of his now much reduced army from Moscow. The desperate situation for both Napoleon and his army (what remained of it) grew increasingly obvious. The Russians only narrowly missed entirely crushing the stragglers as they attempted to cross the Berezina River in late November. A week later Napoleon abandoned his army and rushed home to Paris. Unlike his leisurely stay in Vilnius in the summer, this time the emperor remained on the outskirts and did not even enter the city while en route. He even preferred rushing ahead to stopping and availing himself of the city's considerable food stores, which he might have used to provision his cold and starving army. The Russians entered Vilnius on November 28 (o.s., December 10, n.s.), ending the period of French occupation.[58]

A week or more before the actual French withdrawal, rumors had been circulating in Vilnius that the Russians would soon arrive in the city. Citizens barricaded themselves inside, hiding food and valuables, hoping that the storm would spare them. The French did mount a defense against the Russians, but outnumbered, in poor physical condition, and without strong leadership, they soon gave up and abandoned the city. They left behind thousands of sick and wounded soldiers in Vilnius, most of whom did not survive the ordeal. It is estimated that some 37,000 French soldiers are buried in and around the city.[59]

The year 1812 brought with it great hopes and terrible disappointments for Vilnius. The city and surrounding countryside were devastated more by the passage of troops and occupation than by any actual battles.[60] The disappointment felt by Poles at the failure to resurrect a Polish state was acute but mitigated by Tsar Alexander I's 1814 amnesty for those who had served the French during the Napoleonic occupation.[61] In Vilnius and Lithuania Polish cultural and economic domination remained strong; indeed, in the last decade of Alexander's reign the university and local schools became if anything more Polish than ever before (or after).

If 1812 in Vilnius formed part of a major world-historical context, the next major event of this period belongs squarely in the realm of Polish and Russian history. The November Insurrection of 1830 exploded after years of Polish dissatisfaction under Russian rule.[62] For the city of Vilnius specifically, however, the insurrection itself was far less important than its aftermath.

There was no love lost between Tsar Nicholas I (who reigned 1825–1855) and his Polish subjects. Some sort of clash between the autocrat and the Polish elite was probably inevitable, given the diametrically opposed views held by the tsar and the Polish nobility regarding the constitutional position of Poland within the

Russia Empire. For the Polish ruling class, the link with St. Petersburg was little more than a personal union, with the tsar of all the Russias ruling as the king of Poland, but within a constitutional framework.[63] For Nicholas, however, the Kingdom of Poland was just another territory of the Russian Empire, admittedly with its own history and separate privileges, but entirely subject to the monarch's will. Vilnius, of course, lay outside the Kingdom of Poland's borders, and while the local Polish-speaking nobility had many ties with Warsaw, legally they were subjects of the tsar not much different from the nobility in Tambov or Moscow provinces (though the Lithuanian statutes continued to form the basis of law here until 1840).

Tensions that had long been building were fomented by the events of 1830 in Paris and Belgium; the conspirators hoped that the new French government would support their own struggle to restore Polish independence. At the same time, few believed that an uprising could succeed without foreign help. The historian Joachim Lelewel—himself having been a major figure in the intellectual life of Vilnius in the decade before 1830—was asked by conspirators for advice in November 1830. A patriot but also a thinker, Lelewel tried to dissuade them from launching an uprising that would almost certainly be doomed to failure. Unfortunately, the conspirators found that they had little choice. The Russian authorities had caught wind of their plans, and orders were sent from St. Petersburg to find and arrest the ringleaders. Under these circumstances, the largely unplanned insurrection burst forth in Warsaw on November 29.[64]

News of the Warsaw events reached Vilnius in early December. The Russian authorities' concern that the "mutiny" (as they inevitably described the uprising) could spread to the east caused the Vilnius governor general Aleksander Rimskii-Korsakov to exile a number of students and the local notable (and mayor in 1812) Mykolas Römeris to the Russian interior on December 12/24.[65] A few days earlier the tsar had issued a manifesto admonishing the inhabitants of the Lithuanian provinces not to follow the example of Warsaw. In response to this manifesto, the district marshals of the nobility in Vilnius province published their own statement stressing their continued loyalty to the tsar.[66]

More worrisome than local landowners, at least at this point, were the students of Vilnius University, an institution that Russian administrators saw—correctly— as a center for Polish nationality, culture, and patriotism. University rector Wacław Pelikan did all he could to prevent students from joining the uprising, but with very mixed results. An appeal by the Russian field marshal Hans Diebitsch to the student body to remain loyal was reportedly greeted with whistles and stamping of feet, infuriating the military man (who would later help crush the uprising).[67] In the end Pelikan—who was very unpopular among the students already before 1830—could not prevent the participation of several hundred students (out of ca. 1500) in the uprising.[68]

Vilnius during the Polish-Russian war of 1831 was very much a case of the "dog that did not bark." The city remained in Russian hands throughout the year and no serious attempt by local citizens to rebel against the Russian authorities occurred. The closest that rebel forces came to Vilnius occurred in mid-April, but the Russian forces amassed in the city easily beat back the rebels.[69] After that point, despite widespread sympathy for the insurrection among Vilnius' inhabitants, the city remained on the whole passive. Gabriela Puzynina speaks of the hopes of spring and then the sense of disappointment and helplessness afterward.[70] The underground Komitet Centralny in the city did more, it would appear, to send volunteers out of the city to the rebels than it did to encourage rebellion at home.[71] In his later memoirs, one of the committee's members, Stanisław Szumski, gives the impression that they wished to support the insurrection more actively but that circumstances made this impossible. An indication of Szumski's double role is given by the fact that during this period the Russian authorities awarded him the Order of St. Anne, second class.[72]

Why did Vilnius fail to follow the example of Warsaw (or of western Lithuania) in supporting the rebels in 1831? Two answers may be given. One may blame the city's passivity on the failure of local notables, and especially the Komitet Centralny, to seize the initiative early in the year, before the Russians had amassed enough troops in the city to make this impossible.[73] Alternately, one may take the position that because of the troops stationed in the city and due to its location on the main road from the Russian interior to Warsaw, rebellion in Vilnius would have been hopeless.[74] In the end, the second argument carries more weight. Even in the Kingdom of Poland, which had its own army and political establishment, the rebellion had little chance of success. In army or political organization, the rebels in Vilnius could hardly prevail against the Russian army.

The crushing of the 1831 rebellion was followed by a series of repressive measures. The university of Vilnius was shut down by an imperial manifesto of May 1, 1832, leaving only the medical faculty intact for eight more years. Individuals who took up arms against the Russians stood to lose their property, their freedom, and even (if they were armed when apprehended) their lives.[75] On the other hand, the extreme policies advocated by Mogilev Governor M. N. Muraviev (who later achieved renown as the "hangman" of 1863) were not followed. Muraviev recommended a very strict policy against the Catholic and Uniate Churches; the abolition of the Lithuanian statute legal code, which was still in effect; and a government program to bring Russian settlers to the area.[76] Those recommendations hardly affected Vilnius and its immediate surroundings—this is particularly true of the conversion (or "voluntary return," from the Russian point of view) of Uniates in 1839. As before 1831, the bulk of government employees in Vilnius remained Poles. In short, despite the heavy blow to Polish high culture caused by the closing of the university, the Russian government made no serious attempt to challenge the cultural and linguistic dominance of Polish in the city.[77]

To be sure, repressions after 1831 were severe and affected many. In particular, those involved in the uprising, or even suspected of involvement, were likely to have their estates confiscated. These estates often ended up in the hands of Russian officials, usually through favorable auctions and similar measures. Many of the former insurgents, such as Czartoryski and Lelewel, left Poland for Western Europe, where they would live out their lives. The Lithuanian lands appear to have been harder hit by land confiscation and deportations than other regions. A historian of the uprising concludes, "It is quite clear that if anyone lost as a result of the war it was above all the gentry of the former eastern provinces."[78]

## Vilnius Cultures

Culturally and socially, Vilnius was at least three cities: one was Polish, one Jewish, and the other Russian.[79] They existed side-by-side with a minimum of mixing. Poles, of course, dealt with Jews on an everyday economic basis, in particular as most small shops were Jewish-run. Similarly, Poles could not avoid some contact with—or at least notice of—the Russians in the military and administrative spheres. There is evidence of Polish-Russian socializing at the higher reaches of society, and certainly Russian officials employed servants who would have mainly been recruited among local peasants, Polish, Lithuanian, or Belarusian by nationality. Still, Polish social life and culture for the most part went their own way, as did Jewish life, which was still dominated by religious culture. Russians played at most a minor role, mainly as temporary residents, in the social and cultural life of the city.

While probably outnumbered by Jews, Poles and their culture nonetheless dominated Vilnius in this period, at least in the sense of being most visible and predominant in the city. Jewish culture remained closed unto itself, intense but not dominant in the city space. Non-Jews neither understood nor were particularly interested in the beliefs and cultural practices of their Jewish neighbors except occasionally in an anecdotal sense, commenting on their "exotic" and "Asiatic" presence. Similarly, few Poles knew much about Russian culture, and the city's representatives of the Russian nation were not particularly inspiring—except, as we will see, as handsome young men in military uniforms. This latter group, however, hardly endeared themselves to their Polish counterparts.

## Polish Wilno

In the near-generation between Napoleon and the November Uprising of 1830, Polish civil society began to coalesce in Vilnius. "Civil society" has many elements, but here we will concentrate mainly on cultural aspects: the university, schools, and publishing. It was these institutions that bred other groupings such as the Szubrawcy, Filareci, and masons, which, in turn, further developed Polish civil society. The Insurrection of 1830/31 is probably best interpreted as an outcry of Polish society against Russian hegemony and restrictions. Publishing in Vilnius also contributed to the building of civil society, which requires, after all, some public forum to discuss and exchange ideas. While David Althoen has recently called into question just how widespread the Polish cultural renaissance of these years really was in Lithuania, at least for certain segments of Vilnius Polish society, these years were and remained a "golden age" of Polish culture.[80] The Jesuit Academy founded in 1579 had been officially transformed into a university—the largest in the Russian Empire at that time—by the ukaz of April 4, 1803 by Alexander 1.[81] The importance of the university in cultural life, publishing, and the development of civil society cannot be overestimated. Indeed, one of the best specialists on education in this period has called Vilnius the "Polish culture capital of the Russian partition" mainly because of the university.[82] The university managed to survive 1812 relatively unscathed, in good part because of the courageous actions of its rector, Jan Śniadecki. Even when the university was temporarily shut down so that its classrooms and clinics could be used to house sick and wounded soldiers, Śniadecki resolutely protected university property from the threat of pilfering, including from Russian soldiers. When a plan was mooted in late 1812 to disband the university, Śniadecki quickly prepared a memorandum for the tsar, including his diplomatic speech to Napoleon in which he had praised Alexander's support for the university.[83] In the end, the university was allowed to remain, and indeed the next two decades would be its most famous period, in particular connected with the name of the poet Adam Mickiewicz.[84] The importance of the university in the Russian Empire was also considerable: in this period its enrollment exceeded that of any other university in the empire, with 314 students in 1804 and over 1000 in 1829.[85]

Most students, however, did not study in the humanities. The largest number of students were enrolled in the Physics-Mathematical faculty (around one-third), with the Medical faculty close behind (ca. 25–30% of all students). Probably the most famous faculty was that of medicine, where the father-son team of Jan and Józef Frank, coming from Vienna in 1804, essentially created the medical school at Vilnius University.[86] In 1808 the younger Frank set up a vaccination clinic at the university, the first of its kind in Europe,[87] and the medical school would survive—though only for eight years—the closing of the university in 1832. At the time of Frank's retirement, his services to the university were deemed worthy of a generous pension.[88]

For the history of Polish society in Vilnius, the university was most significant for its student groupings, in particular the Filomaci ("Lovers of Knowledge") and Filareci ("Lovers of Morality").[89] These groups reflected the age of romanticism, and while there was probably no direct influence, they in many respects resembled the contemporary German Burschenschaften and Tugendbund.[90] These quite small student groups set up by Tomasz Zan, Adam Mickiewicz, and others around 1819 lasted less than five years. In Polish historiography, however, their importance as exemplars of noble, idealistic youth whose ideals and actions reflected a fusion of universal and patriotic values cannot be overestimated. In a sense, the Filomaci/Filareci (and related student groups) at Vilnius University play the same role as the contemporary (though somewhat older) Decembrists in progressive Russian historiography. In both cases, liberal and freedom-loving youth is contrasted with their reactionary, paranoid, and ultimately repressive elders in the Russian government. It must be admitted that this schema, though simplified, did reflect social and political realities of the time.[91]

One of the members of these groups, Ignacy Domeyko, recalled that the Filomaci arose when seven friends (later fourteen), all students at Vilnius University, following the leadership of Tomasz Zan decided to band together in a secret society that would organize lectures, share knowledge, and promote fellowship. In order to spread their goals of enlightenment more broadly, the Filomaci decided to found a different and broader association, the Filareci, which would be public and open to anyone who accepted its ideals and goals. Domeyko described the spirit in these groups as "purely national, patriotic, Polish—but free from plots and conspiracies, free of demagogic rants."⁹² While the Filareci were more political than the Filomaci (the latter charter specifically excluded politics, though it did mention "love for the fatherland"), in both cases it is difficult to see these groups as particularly dangerous to the political status quo. To be sure, they preached patriotism and a love for Polish culture but, unlike the contemporary Decembrists, did not formulate any more specific political plans.⁹³ Indeed, members of both groups generally expressed loyalty and appreciation to the tsar.

Unfortunately, the political atmosphere in Russia by the early 1820s was becoming increasingly paranoid and reactionary. But it was a specific, and rather trivial, incident that sparked the persecution of these student groups. In early 1821 the guards regiments led by Grand Duke Nicholas were transferred to Vilnius, as rumor had it, as punishment for some infraction.⁹⁴ From the start, neither the guards officers nor Nicholas were popular among the Vilnius students. Part of this animosity can be traced to feelings of national pride among the students, but more mundane matters—like the attraction of young men in uniforms for local belles— also played their part. Clashes between students and soldiers took place in theaters and on the street, considerably irritating both Polish society and the Russian authorities—Grand Duke Nicholas foremost among them.⁹⁵ Another incident in May 1823 involving schoolboys writing "Wiwat Konstytucja 3 Maja" (Long Live the [Polish] Constitution of May 3 [1791]) at a Vilnius secondary school further increased tensions (and led to the arrest and conviction of three youths).⁹⁶

A police investigation after one of these clashes uncovered "indecent verses" about Empress Catherine II (never popular among Poles) among the papers of one Jan Jankowski. When questioned by the police, Jankowski broke down and claimed that the Filareci had pursued patriotic, anti-government aims. Besides making the group out to be far more dangerous than it in fact was, Jankowski wrote down the names of numerous individuals connected with the Filareci.⁹⁷ Dozens of students were arrested, including Mickiewicz, Zan, Adam Suzin, and Jan Czeczot, and of these some twenty were exiled to the Russian interior and even (in the case of the ringleaders) Siberia.⁹⁸ With these arrests the atmosphere among Polish students and within all Polish society in Vilnius chilled considerably. While high society continued with its balls and festive occasions, as the memoirs of Gabriela Puzynina testify, the Vilnius Polish intelligentsia could no longer regard the Russian authorities or indeed Tsar Alexander I himself as benevolent.⁹⁹ Czartoryski's resignation in 1823 from his position heading the educational establishment in the region was just one indication of the growing breach between Polish society and Russian rule. Attitudes deteriorated further after the death of Alexander in 1825 and the succession at the end of that year by Nicholas, who had never made any attempt to hide his disdain—to put it mildly—for Poles and liberal ideas.

Masonic lodges also provided another venue for the development of civil society in Vilnius. As in other parts of the Russian Empire and throughout Europe, in Vilnius, too, masons pledged to work for enlightenment and brotherhood. All masonic lodges in the city closed down in 1812, but the lodge "Gorliwy Litwin" ("Zealous Lithuanian") took up its activities again at the end of that year. The lodge provided a site for discussion of current issues as well as a forum to organize benevolent work and charity. In 1817 the mason and marshal of the nobility from Upicki district, Szymon Zawisza, went so far as to propose that local landowners voluntarily renounce rights and privileges over their serfs, a suggestion that met with consternation not only from local officialdom but also from conservative landlords. Interestingly, however, the lodge was not closed down over this controversy but succumbed to the general reactionary trend in Russia when all masonic lodges were forbidden by the imperial ukaz of August 1, 1822.[100]

Another indication of a burgeoning civil society is the rise of the press and publishing. In the decade after 1812 there were two main scientific-literary journals in Vilnius, *Dziennik Wileński*, subsidized and published by the university, and *Tygodnik Wileński*, founded by the historian Joachim Lelewel in 1815 but closed down by the censors in 1822.[101] The liberal "Szubrawcy" society also published its own press organ, *Wiadomości Brukowe*, from 1816. Like *Tygodnik Wileński*, it was shut down (along with the society itself) in 1822.[102] The semi-official *Kurier Litewski* appeared daily throughout this period.[103]

The most famous printer in the nineteenth century was Józef Zawadzki, who arrived in the city in 1803.[104] By 1805 Zawadzki had entered into agreements with the university giving him the title "typographer of the Imperial University of Wilno."[105] Both books and periodicals were published for the university by Zawadzki, and this relationship continued, despite some frictions, for over twenty years. After the founder's death in 1838 the printing house was taken over by his son Adam and continued to be a major center for publishing in Vilnius until 1939.[106] Among the works published by Zawadzki were the first two volumes of Mickiewicz's poetry in 1822 and 1823.[107] Several other printers were active in the city, but Zawadzki's major competitors were Antoni Marcinowski and Teofil Glücksberg. In the period 1800–1832 several books appeared every year in Vilnius, ranging from a low of 27 new printings in 1802 to a high figure of 122 in 1823.[108]

The trajectory of Polish civil society's development reflected larger trends in the Russian Empire. Thus, in the period to ca. 1823, liberal views on serfdom, women's education, and the Jewish question (usually favoring incorporation of Jews into Polish society through education and assimilation) were expressed publicly.[109] After 1823, the public voice became considerably more circumscribed and liberal opinions could be expressed only very cautiously or in private. Particularly after the 1830/1831 insurrection, the Russian authorities came to regard Polish culture with grave suspicion, and the possibilities of open discussion and publication were severely curtailed.

For Polish culture in Vilnius, the single most painful punishment after 1831 was shutting down the university. The loss of the university left a gap at the center of Vilnius Polish society. A distinguished Polish literary scholar of romanticism described the situation this way: "the closing of the university created a new epoch in the biography of the city—from that point on, [the city] was deprived of cultural dynamism."[110] Certainly, Vilnius was never again so central for Polish high culture than in the decade and a half before 1830. Still, this narrow focus on high culture (i.e., Mickiewicz) distorts the view. While Warsaw was both culturally and economically more dynamic than Vilnius after 1831, the Lithuanian capital continued to be an important center of Polish culture even after the (far greater) post-1863 repressions.[111]

While Vilnius University was officially closed on May 1, 1832 and its library transferred to the St. Vladimir University in Kiev, one faculty did persist. The importance of the medical faculty for training specialists was simply too great to abolish it out of hand. Thus hundreds of students continued their medical studies until the final closure of the "Medical-Surgical Academy" in 1840. Enrollment at this academy amounted to nearly half—and even more—of the total enrollment of Vilnius University before 1831: 625 students in 1832 and 3865 students a year later.[112] Many faculty members also stayed on; courses were offered not only in science and medicine but also in languages and literature.

A graduate of the academy later wrote in his memoirs that initially its students were gathered from the less wealthy families of the region (richer parents could afford to send their sons to study in Dorpat or abroad). Though "children of Poland," these young men often had little understanding of the aims or inspirations of the 1830–1831 events. The general level of culture was low, with billiards and cards playing a more important part in student life than poetry or philosophy. However, the atmosphere—again following this memoir—began to change around 1835. At this time Franciszek Sawicz, from a poor family in the Pinsk area, enrolled at the academy and began to inspire his fellow students with patriotic ideas. Encountering Mickiewicz's *Books of the Polish Nation and the Polish Pilgrimage* (1832) in April 1836 was "like a comet" for these students. Inspired by these and other works by Mickiewicz, as well as Mochnacki's *History of Poland*, these young men banded together in 1838 to form the "Democratic Society," led by Sawicz and Szymon Konarski. The group was short-lived, however: the tsarist authorities caught wind of it and arrested the ringleaders and many others. Konarski received the ultimate punishment and was executed on February 15, 1839 (o.s.).[113]

Vilnius society was shocked by the severe treatment meted out to Konarski and his fellow conspirators. In her memoir Gabriela Puzynina speaks of the sadness and outrage felt among her aristocratic circle. Apparently fearful of public displays of support for the executed patriot, the Russian authorities posted a twenty-four-hour watch at his grave to prevent the laying of wreaths or any other such demonstrations.[114] Even the rather sober Stanisław Szumski, who was certainly not prone to patriotic ecstasies, describes Konarski in his memoirs with respect and admiration.[115]

Public organizations also suffered during this period. Indeed, the only civic organization that survived throughout this period was the Imperial Medical Society in Vilnius, which had been founded in 1805 by the indefatigable Józef Frank. Even in this case, however, the membership numbers stagnated, in particular after the closing of the Medical-Surgical Academy. Still, the Medical Society provided a public space for educated men to discuss—in Polish—professional matters and advances in the medical field. The society also published various works and collections of scientific essays, though irregularly.[116] Underground organizations certainly also existed, though their importance was almost certainly exaggerated by Marxist historiography.[117] Ethnic Lithuanians also began to make their mark—albeit modestly—in Vilnius organizations during this period; some were also active at the university.[118]

Upon Nicholas I's death in 1855, the new tsar appeared more open to public organizations in Vilnius, even those dominated by Poles. (At this point Polish dominance would have been inevitable.) One indication of this new more liberal policy was the foundation of the Vilnius Archaeological Commission by Count Eustachy Tyszkiewicz and others in 1856. This group aimed to collect historical and archaeological artifacts of the region, an activity that would inevitably be caught up with Polish (and other!) national memory. In the short period of its existence, the commission opened a museum and laid the foundations for a public library while also collecting material for publication.[119] Unfortunately, the outbreak of the 1863 insurrection and the repressions that followed resulted in the organization's forced "russification." However, even in that form the Commission carried out important scholarly work in the decades after 1864.[120]

Publishing in Vilnius also continued after 1831, though on a more modest scale. *Kurier Litewski* was transformed from a Polish periodical to a bilingual Polish-Russian mainly official organ, from 1834 bearing the title *Kurier Wileński*.[121] Zawadzki and other printers continued to publish books in Polish, with between 45 and 117 new titles appearing annually between 1832 and 1862.[122] In the 1840s the writer and publisher Adam Honory Kirkor took up residence in Vilnius, publishing several different journals in the next decades, including *Teka Wileńska*, *Pismo Zbiorowe Wileńskie*, and *Kurier Wileński*.[123] Along with his friend and colleague Władysław Syrokomla, Kirkor published accounts of travel in and around Vilnius.[124] Vilnius-related literature continued to appear in this period.[125]

Aside from the university, other schools in Vilnius also underwent significant changes in the period 1832–1862. In particular secondary education was the target of Russian attempts to "unify" the school system—or, from the Polish point of view, to russify it.[126] Still, throughout the period most subjects continued to be taught in Vilnius high schools (gymnasia) in Polish, and most teachers were local Poles. At the elementary level even less changed. Funding for schools did not rise, though the population did, so illiteracy was probably higher in 1860 than three decades earlier. The Russian authorities' general policy toward education was less one of active russification than restricting funding and closing down schools— but seldom opening new ones in their place.[127] Besides these official schools, however, there existed considerable numbers of "secret [i.e., illegal] schools" in which Polish literacy was taught. It is difficult to gauge the exact numbers of these schools but both official and memoir literature indicates that secret schools were ubiquitous.[128]

Still and all, Polish culture continued to dominate in Vilnius. Russian (and Belarusian) culture was limited to administrative activities and the Orthodox and Uniate Churches. (The latter was shut down in the late 1830s.) The first stirrings of the Lithuanian national movement could be discerned at Vilnius University even before 1832, but it is only in hindsight that we recognize this pioneering effort. In publishing, society, and religion, Polish culture remained predominant, restricted but not overtly attacked by the Russian authorities. This situation would change after 1863, though (as we will see) not quite as much as subsequent patriotic Polish historiography would have it.

## Yiddishe Vilne

While Polish high culture reigned supreme over much of the city's public space, Jewish culture rivaled it, though in a much less public way. While Polish culture predominated over the city as a whole, Jewish culture was less hegemonic. Living in an openly judeophobic Christian state, Jews cultivated their own religion and culture within the confines of the family and within their own educational and charitable institutions. Some Jews ventured out of their traditional world in this period, for example attending the university, but far more common was Jewish life within the boundaries, both geographic and moral, of tradition. In a city dominated by none-too-friendly Christian authorities, Jews tended to keep to themselves, even ignoring non-Jews in their descriptions of Vilnius.[129]

By all accounts, Jews were ubiquitous in Vilnius. The city had never had an official ghetto though there was certainly a Jewish quarter. The western part of the Old Town was heavily Jewish, with "German Street" (Niemiecka—also called Daytshe gos—today known as Vokiečių) as the central avenue of Jewish Vilnius. To the immediate east of the Jewish quarter, not more than a few minutes' walk, was the Christian axis of the city—that is, the thoroughfare running from Ostra Brama ("Sharp Gate," where the city's wonder-working icon was displayed, in present-day Vilnius, Aušros Vartai) to the Cathedral. In Polish times and into the early nineteenth century, Jews were prohibited from owning property or living on this street (present-day Didžiojo) or on Dominican Street. The ostensible reason for this prohibition was to avoid "offending Christian sympathies" along streets that would often be the sites of Catholic religious processions. In 1837 only thirty Jews were allowed to live along these "forbidden streets," but as a wonderfully detailed map indicates, several others owned property here, despite the prohibition. And to further complicate matters, other Jews petitioned the government to live and/or own property here, claiming to have enjoyed this privilege from Polish times. (A certain Gordon produced a document to this effect dated 1713.) Given the obvious mismatch between legal prohibition and the de facto toleration of Jewish ownership and residence, even along these "forbidden streets," the prohibition was officially ended in 1861.[130] After this date Jews could legally purchase real estate and reside anywhere in Vilnius. Nonetheless, the fundamental residential pattern continued with only minor alteration to the end of the nineteenth century.[131]

Vilnius was also a major center of Jewish learning and publication. Following the tradition of the Gaon, the city became both a real and symbolic center of traditional, Mitnagdic (anti-Hasidic) learning. To simplify matters somewhat, the serious and studious Mitnagdim rejected what they saw as a more enthusiastic and less intellectual brand of Judaism embraced and propagated by the Hasidim.[132] Besides the huge main synagogue, the Jewish quarter was honeycombed with small prayer and study houses. The introduction of compulsory military service for Jews in 1827 spurred a further expansion of yeshivoth (institutions of advanced Torah and Talmud study). According to a contemporary writing in the early twentieth century, young men hoped that if they showed themselves to be dedicated students of Torah, the Jewish community would spare them from the draft (handing over other young men instead).[133]

While traditional religious study remained dominant among Vilnius' Jews in the early nineteenth century, new intellectual movements could also be discerned. In particular the Jewish enlightenment, *Haskalah*, found a center in the city. Following the ideas of Moses Mendelsohn, the maskilim (followers of *Haskalah*) aimed at a modernization of Jewish life and religious practice in order to facilitate the integration of Jews into modern European society. To this end the maskilim denigrated Yiddish, advocating instead the cultivation of Hebrew and the learning of secular subjects, including the language of the surrounding (non-Jewish) population. The first maskilim in Vilnius came to the city in the 1780s but did not have a great impact on the community for some time. Conflict in the Jewish community continued to be mainly Mitnagdim versus Hasidic in this period, and when Prince Adam Czartoryski attempted to persuade Jews to attend Polish-language schools in the early nineteenth century, his efforts were thwarted by the traditional Jews still dominating the community.[134]

Vilnius was also a major center for Jewish publishing. In 1799 two Jewish printing houses were established in the city. When the Russian government decided in 1836 to restrict Jewish publishing to two cities (ostensibly to facilitate censorship), the brothers Romm took advantage of the government monopoly to expand their printing house, publishing, among many other things, an edition of the Talmud (despite many problems with government censors). Nearly all of these printed texts were, of course, in Hebrew during this period, but not exclusively: the first Yiddish-Polish dictionary was published here in 1827.[135]

Jews lived mainly from trade and artisan crafts, rarely earning more than just enough to survive. Certain trades such as tailoring and shoemaking were dominated by Jews. Small shops were almost by definition Jewish-run; this would begin to change (but slowly) only toward the end of the century. Jews also worked as pedlars throughout the region and could not be missed at fairs and markets in

Vilnius. Another overwhelmingly Jewish profession was that of *faktor*, a job title that is exceedingly hard to define precisely. Essentially a *faktor* was a "facilitator"—a gofer or runner who could help with the completion of almost any task. For a (probably Polish) nobleman, the *faktor* might help with the purchase of land, the furnishing of a residence, or the sale of produce. For this work the *faktor* earned a small fee. Besides the mass of artisans, petty traders, and *faktorzy*, there were also some (a very few) wealthy Jews. Jews made up a majority of merchants (i.e., wealthy businessmen registered in three guilds) in Vilnius during these years.[136]

Most Vilnius Jews spoke Yiddish (and Hebrew, at least among men, for prayers) and on the whole had little acquaintance with Polish or Russian culture. However, there were exceptions. As the interwar researcher Pinchas Kon has shown, at the beginning of the nineteenth century Jews were already enrolled (mainly in the medical faculty) in Vilnius University. Indeed, the university itself funded an elementary school for Jews in 1808, hoping thereby to reduce somewhat the barriers between Jewish and Christian culture.[137] There were also some discussions at the time about the importance of teaching Hebrew at the university itself.[138]

Much more important than this initiative of 1808—soon thwarted by Napoleon's invasion—was the founding in 1847 of the Rabbinical School and Teachers' Seminary in Vilnius. This institution, and others like it in Zhitomir and Warsaw, aimed to produce a new group of rabbis who would be conversant in both secular and religious topics and could also aid the Russian government in the registration of births, marriages, divorces, and the like. The seminar lasted not quite thirty years before the Russian government shut it down, noting the continued hostility toward it on the part of Jewish traditionalists and fearing that the graduates were more likely to embrace liberal or radical ideologies than to become loyal subjects of the tsar.[139] It is often noted that the seminar produced "not a single rabbi" because Jewish communities regarded its graduates as not entirely "kosher" and thus refused to hire them as local rabbis. As Verena Dohrn has argued, however, the Vilnius and other "Jewish seminars" actually did have a significant effect on creating a new, modern, and Russian-speaking Jewish elite.[140] Furthermore, the Vilnius "rabbi school" was not actually dissolved in 1873 but was transformed into a Jewish pedagogical institute that would survive to World War I. The Rabbi School was just one of the institutions through which the cultural and social distance between Jews and Christians was shrinking, as early as the 1840s. This process would continue and accelerate later in the century.[141]

A CENTER OF POLISH AND JEWISH CULTURE, 1795-1862    47

## Russian Vilna

Russian Vilnius consisted mainly of a rather small administrative elite and soldiers stationed in and near the city. The main barracks were in Šnipiškės, to the north of the Neris River, now part of downtown but at that time a rather disreputable suburb because of the large number of soldiers there and the establishments catering to them (e.g., taverns and houses of ill repute). There were few Russian landowners in the region before the 1860s and hence no Russian "society" (in the sense of relatively wealthy individuals who were both consumers and producers of culture, from masquerade balls to musical performances to journalism). To be sure, Russian officials and officers of higher rank sometimes mingled in Polish society.

When speaking of a Russian Vilnius in the early nineteenth century, one must start with churches. After all, even at the end of the Russian Empire the best generally accepted definition of "Russian" was religious: a believer in the Russian Orthodox tradition (*pravoslavie*). Before the 1830s, the distinction between Catholic and Orthodox was somewhat blurred by the continued existence of the Uniate Church, which combined allegiance to the Pope with rituals more in line with those of Orthodox believers. Among the major Uniate establishments in the city was the Basilian monastery. The annoyance felt by the Russian (Orthodox) rulers toward the Uniate Church—combined with the support of Uniate clergy for the November 1830 Uprising—led to the church's suppression in this region at the end of that decade.[142] Long before that, however, the equivalency between Russian and Orthodox had been firmly established. As David Frick has documented, already in the seventeenth century, Catholics, Uniates, and "Dis-unites" (a derogatory but common designation for the Orthodox) lived side by side.[143]

A Russian commentator (who certainly cannot be considered 100% objective) estimated that in the mid-sixteenth century Vilnius' population consisted of more or less equal numbers of Catholics and Orthodox, with a small but sizable population of Jews.[144] In any case, there can be no doubt that Orthodox believers—most of whom we would designate Belarusians by current national categories—did make up a significant part of the population. By the end of the eighteenth century Uniates and Catholics were numerically much stronger in the city than the Orthodox—but with the abolition of the Uniate Church in 1839 this situation changed. A map of 1859 shows a dozen Orthodox religious establishments, many of which had been Uniate before 1839, including St. Nicholas Cathedral, the Church and Monastery of the Holy Spirit, the Church of the Holy Trinity, as well as presumably smaller churches at the Lukiškės prison and another for soldiers ("Wojskowa") just across the Green Bridge from Šnipiškės.[145] Another indication of the continued permanent residency of Orthodox people in Vilnius is the cemetery there. Rather like Orthodox churches, the Orthodox cemetery had fallen into decline and disrepair in the eighteenth century and was renewed from the late 1830s.[146]

The Russians did, however, establish some educational institutions in the city. The Vilnius educational district was created in 1803 and from the 1830s became increasingly less Polish and more Russian.[147] A boys' high school (*gimnaziia*) that was set up in the city at the same time became a Russian-speaking institution after the closing of the university.[148] The presence of the provincial governor's office as well as that of the governor general of the Northwest Provinces also meant that numerous Russian officials were "stationed" in the city at any given time. But few of them stayed on after their terms of service, and few mixed with Polish society in the town.

Russians were an established presence in Vilnius by mid-century. The existence of Orthodox churches and an Orthodox cemetery in the city attests to the fact that not all Russians—or at least Orthodox believers—were transients. Still, most were. The city lacked a Russian theater and a Russian bookstore. Cultural life and society, even after 1831, was overwhelmingly dominated by Poles. Some Jews were learning Russian, and while their numbers were few, their influence in the generations after 1860 was considerable. In that year, however, Vilnius remained a mainly Polish Jewish city. The main object of tsarist political and cultural policy in the city during the ensuing half century would be to change that and to elevate the position of Russian culture in Vilnius.

A photograph from the early 1960s juxtaposes the "Portrait Gallery" (as the deconsecrated cathedral was known) with the Žirmūnai housing estate being built on the other side of the Neris River.

The Merchants' Club, built at the end of the Russian period on St. George's Avenue. Picture from the early twentieth century.

Statue of Collective Farmers on the Green Bridge spanning the Neris River.

Brick Gothic St. Anne's Church, Soviet-era monument to Mickiewicz, and Bernardine Church in background.

Post-Soviet monument of Vilnius' founder, Grand Duke Gediminas, unveiled 1996.

Monument to Frank Zappa erected by Vilnius Art School students in the early 1990s.

View of Castle Hill in Vilnius from the Neris River (1917), showing how the upper castle looked before post–World War II Soviet reconstruction.

St. Kazimierz's Church (1917), in Soviet times the Museum of Atheism.

The "Romanov" church, built in 1909 by the Russian authorities to emphasize the Russian Orthodox character of Vilnius. The church has survived into the twenty-first century.

The miracle-working icon of Ostra Brama (Aušros Vartai), photo from ca. 1917.

56. Gasse, Menschen und Torbogen

The Jewish district in Vilnius with one of its characteristic arches, ca. 1920s.

CHAPTER 3

# The Period of Russification, 1863–1914

THE HALF CENTURY THAT preceded the outbreak of World War I has often been characterized as the period of russification. According to this concept, during the decades after the January Uprising (1863), the Russian Empire became increasingly nationalistic, restricting the rights of the tsar's non-Russian subjects (around half of the total population), and attempting to assimilate non-Russians into the Russian nation. Except for the last claim, one can hardly dispute the overall characterization. One should not lose from view, however, the fundamental nature and mentality of the Russian Empire, which differed from those of a modern nation-state. Rather, the Russian Empire remained fundamentally a premodern, dynastic state, far more interested in specific personal loyalty of elites than in any putative ethnic connection between tsar and nation. Russian administrators in Vilnius and elsewhere did not particularly like or respect other cultures, but large-scale conversions (whether that meant cultural assimilation or religious changes) were rarely encouraged. While some ambitious (and nationalist) administrators proposed more ambitious programs to promote russification in culture (language) and religion (conversion to Orthodoxy), these policies were only seldom put into practice and, even then, carried out only for a short period.[1]

The event that triggered anti-Polish repressions and russification policies, to simplify somewhat, was the Uprising of 1863. This event is key to an understanding of Polish or Lithuanian history in the nineteenth century. In the years 1860–1862 there were a number of (Polish) patriotic meetings and conspiratorial circles in Vilnius. It appeared that Poles might gain broader freedoms for culture and education in their language, possibly even the reestablishment of the university.[2] Alas, these hopes were soon dashed. The uprising that broke out in Warsaw in January 1863 was doomed from the start—as the insurgents themselves recognized—though it did tie up tsarist troops for well over a year. The insurgents were not successful in taking Vilnius, whose position on the rail line from Petersburg to Warsaw made the city very important strategically. Thus for this city's history,

1863 is more important as a trigger for anti-Polish and anti-Lithuanian repressions than it is for developments in the city per se.[3]

The brutality of post-1863 Russian policy finds its embodiment within (Polish and Lithuanian) historical memory in the figure of Mikhail Nikolaevich Muraviev. The governor general of the Northwest Provinces (more or less present-day Belarus and Lithuania), Muraviev was appointed by Tsar Alexander II to put down the insurrection. Upon arriving in Vilnius on May 1, 1863, Muraviev energetically repressed the insurrection, not hesitating to hang Roman Catholic priests whom he considered implicated in the "mutiny" (as the Russians inevitably termed the uprising) against Russian power. Muraviev has gone down in Polish and Lithuanian history as the "hangman," but both at the time and (to a rather lesser extent) later, he was lionized by Russian society as a savior of the fatherland. He himself explained his policies as stern but necessary to prevent even worse disturbances and bloodshed. Thus for Russian patriots, Muraviev was not a brutal executioner but a stern paternal figure meting out severe but well-deserved and entirely necessary punishments.[4]

For Vilnius as a city, the post-1863 russification policies meant an intensification of already existing restrictions on other cultures. Now store signs were required to be at least bilingual with the non-Russian (in Vilnius, Polish or Yiddish) text below and not in larger letters than the Russian. All periodical publications in languages other than Russian were ended, and publishing slumped at least into the 1870s due to strict censorship.[5] The most absolute prohibition on publishing fell on the Lithuanian language: from the mid-1860s it was forbidden to publish anything in that language using Latin letters. The purpose of this restriction was to increase the distance between Polish and Lithuanian culture by forcing Lithuanians to use the Cyrillic alphabet. However, Lithuanian national elites—many of them Catholic clergymen—perceived the prohibition as an attempt at total linguistic and religious assimilation. Thus literate Lithuanians refused to accept the "Russian" alphabet, preferring instead to import (illegally) books printed in Lithuanian in East Prussia.[6]

While this period is often—including in this chapter's title—labeled as one of "russification," for Vilnius the measures restricting the public use of non-Russian languages were more a continuation of existing policies (though with increased severity and vigor) than a historical break. More important for this period was simply the process of modernization, which affected such mundane things as sewers, public transportation, and building new urban districts to accommodate in-migration. It should be noted, however, that this process of modernization was often seen as "Russian." Most likely this perception stemmed from the fact that the authorities pushing the changes were from Russia, along with much of the capital to finance the changes and the architecture employed to shape the city in the image of other "Russian" provincial cities. The distinction "Russian" versus "Polish/Jewish" often came down to "modern" (straight, broad streets at right angles to each other, the most prominent of which was St. George's Avenue) versus "old" (narrow and crooked streets, outdated sanitation, but also impressive Baroque and Classicist churches).

The city's population grew considerably in this half century. According to a census carried out in 1875, the city's total population (not counting soldiers) was 77,102.[7] There were considerably more women than men in the city (40,090 to 36,612), a statistic that is cited but not explained. Religiously the population broke down into 15.8 percent Orthodox Christians, 33.6 percent Catholics, and 45.9 percent Jews. Among Jews the youngest cohort (1–19 years of age) was a very large percentage: this fact indicates a high birth rate and/or low rates of infant mortality. The "estate" (*soslovie*) of the majority of Vilnius' inhabitants was that of "townspeople" (*meshchane*): they made up around 65 percent, reflecting the fact that Jews were routinely lumped into this estate unless they were wealthy merchants. Jews (62.8% of them) were far more likely to have been born in the city than Catholics or the Orthodox (respectively, 40.4% and 18.4%). Almost one-half of Vilnius' male population (42.7%) could read in Russian, with a quarter of women literate in that language (a figure that seems questionable given the fact that most inhabitants would have had rudimentary knowledge of the language at best). Nearly half of Vilnans earned their living by physical labor (23.2%) or in trade or handicrafts (24.5%). Industrial workers were still a rarity in the city.[8] This census did not include categories for "nationality" or "native tongue," but we can roughly surmise that most Catholics were Poles (though Lithuanians and some Belarusians would be among them) and nearly all Orthodox were Russians or Belarusians.

The first modern census in the Russian Empire was carried out in 1897. While nationality was still not used as a category, "native language" was. According to this census, the city boasted a population of 154,532 persons, 40 percent of whom were Jews (61,847 individuals), 31 percent Poles (47,795), 20 percent "Russians" (30,967; this figure would include Belarusians and, possibly, some Ukrainians), and 2.1 percent Lithuanians (3238).[9] These figures must be regarded with some suspicion: in particular the number of "Russians" is probably too high, and the figures for Poles and Jews are a bit low. The city grew rapidly between 1897 and the war; in 1910 Vilnius was the empire's fourteenth-largest city, with a population of 192,746.[10] On the eve of the first world war this figure had most likely exceeded 200,000 inhabitants.

## Building the City

As the population grew, so did the built-up area of the city. Looking at an 1881 map, one is struck by how little the city had expanded from the old Polish Jewish core. At the same time, the framework for later expansion had been laid. In particular, one notes that St. George's Avenue, the main avenue of the new, Russian city, had been completed, stretching from the Roman Catholic cathedral in the east to the Neris River in the west. But there it ended: the bridge over the river to Žvėrynas would not be built until 1906 (when it would be called "Nicholas Bridge," after the tsar). A large prison complex (marked "Turma" on the Polish map) was already present but few other buildings stood around it.

Lukiškės retained its character as a "suburb" rather than an integral part of the city. The Tatar mosque, small and made of wood, stood nearby along with the church of Sts. Phillip and Jacob and the Dominican monastery, which had been converted into the city's main hospital.[11] Aside from these few buildings, St. George's Avenue west of Vilenskaia Street (today's Vilniaus) was almost entirely unbuilt in 1881.

Closer to downtown, directly to the south of the Old Town, stood the railroad station, having been completed at the beginning of the 1860s. The station was located, so to speak, to the side of the city rather than in it. A straight avenue (marked only "Bulwar") ran from just west of the station toward the new avenue but dead-ended at the Lutheran Cemetery (this thoroughfare would later be extended, becoming today's Mindaugo/Tauro gatvės). As with Lukiškės, the broad boulevard led through a mainly empty landscape—its abrupt halt at the Lutheran cemetery indicated that the struggle between "old Vilnius" (to which the cemetery belonged) and new Vilnius (the "Bulwar") had not yet been decided. In the next few decades, new Vilnius would win out: in the 1890s the Lutheran cemetery was closed and the boulevard extended to connect up with St. George's.[12]

In 1881 the city was located almost entirely south of the Neris River. Only the Green Bridge (even then bearing that name) crossed the river and a version of today's Kalvarijų Street already existed, though that narrow road bore little resemblance to today's bustling thoroughfare. Only a few houses and, of course, the Russian military barracks were located nearby. The old Jewish cemetery still existed near the river across from Castle Hill but the map shows almost no houses anywhere in that area. Nor can one discern more than a sprinkling of buildings to the south of the rail line. Antakalnio Street, then as now, ran from Castle Hill along the river bank to the northeast, with its destination the suburb of Antakalnis. The arsenal and church of Peter and Paul were already present in 1881, but not much else. In other words, the town's layout in 1881—aside from the mainly empty St. George's Avenue and the railroad station—did not differ hugely from that visited by Napoleon in 1812.[13]

Thirty years later the city had expanded considerably. A new bridge linked the downtown to the "suburb" of Zwierzyniec (Žvėrynas)—originally the Grand Duke's hunting preserve (*zwierz* means "large animal, game" in Polish). On the 1881 map this neighborhood did not yet exist; by 1910 streets and buildings had been constructed, in particular small villas and wooden "summer houses" for the city's growing middle class.[14] To the north, numerous new buildings had been constructed on the right bank of the Neris and lining Kalvarijų Street. This district, Šnipiškės, retained its unfavorable reputation.[15] The road to Antokol (Antakalnis) was also lined with numerous new structures. Among these, the most famous was the sumptuous villa of the wealthy engineer and Lithuanian patriot Petras Vileišis. (The villa, built 1904–1906, now houses the Lithuanian Literature and Folklore Institute.)[16] Looking through an architectural description of new private residences constructed in these decades yields clear evidence of the "rise of the bourgeoisie." There are new palaces constructed by, for example, Ignacy Korwin-Milewski and Klementyna Tyszkiewicz, but dozens of villas, mansions, and residences were also erected by rich doctors, bankers, and engineers.[17]

By this time new streets and housing had also appeared north of the railroad line. Most remarkable of all, an entire "new town" (Nowo-Gród— today's Naujininkai) had appeared to the west/southwest of the old Polish Jewish core. Befitting its imperial character, the quarter's streets bore names harking to the Russian interior: Tver', Novgorod, Suzdal', Tambov, Arkhangelsk, Kiev, Smolensk.[18] Among the inhabitants of these new streets were Russian administrators, professionals, and acculturated Jews. Many of these individuals lived in rented apartments and housing suitable for the middle-class—but not wealthy—intelligentsia families that moved into the "new town" and along St. George's in these years.[19] The "modern" (though still Orthodox in religious practice) Choral Synagogue was constructed on the edge of the new town (and directly across from the old Jewish "ghetto") and opened in 1903. It is the only synagogue to survive to the present day.[20]

Members of the growing educated and professional class (the intelligentsia) in Vilnius could not afford their own villas but demanded a certain degree of comfort and style in their accommodations. For them, new styles of apartment buildings were constructed, as in other cities of the Russian Empire and throughout

Europe.²¹ Another solution to the housing demands of middle-class residents took the form of planned housing estates or "colonies," the most famous of which was constructed by the banker Józef Montwiłł next to Lukiškės Square. Following Western European models, Montwiłł planned and constructed a number of developments. While small by later twentieth-century standards, they were the first in Vilnius to project entire neighborhoods of two-to-three-story residences with courtyards and gardens. Montwiłł "colonies" were built to the south of the train station in Rasa, in the new town (Pohulanka), across the Neris River in Šnipiškės, and—most famously—squarely in the middle of the new downtown, next to Lukiškės Square. Here middle-class people could live in comfort in apartments that had water closets and baths, in a new community that was hygienic and modern.²²

As a middle-sized provincial capital, Vilnius could not boast the explosive growth and remarkable new architecture of St. Petersburg, Moscow, Odessa, or even Warsaw. Nearly all major administrative buildings were built in a style noticeably similar to contemporary architecture in Kiev, Helsinki, or even Tashkent.²³ In Vilnius this "imperial" style was associated with the Russian rulers and will be treated in the next section. But architects and architecture in the city can fairly be termed "European": the Jewish, Polish, Lithuanian, and Russian architects active here in the half century before 1914 did not create (or even wish to create) their own parochial style but instead drew on ideas and projects from other parts of Europe and modified these in accordance with local needs, as did Montwiłł with his housing estates.²⁴

## Making the City Russian

Russian administrators from Muraviev to the end of the empire never ceased insisting that Vilna was and would be a Russian city. Their constant remarks on this topic give the distinct impression that they did not actually believe their own rhetoric—if the city was so Russian, why all this harping? In fact the city was not, of course, very Russian at all. The Russians here were overwhelmingly administrators and soldiers who seldom stayed long or put down roots. For example, the city had a dozen governors general (the highest administrators) in the period 1863–1909, and only two remained in Vilnius as long as six years.²⁵

Still, the Russian authorities did their best to enhance the city's Russian exterior. After 1863, store signs had to be in Russian or at least bilingual, street names emphasized the city's imperial character, and many buildings in the new city or along St. George's Avenue could well have been in any provincial town of the Russian Empire. Any efforts to further "russify" the city were stymied by at least two factors: a lack of resources (and interest) on the part of state actors who were far more concerned with simply keeping order and, perhaps more profoundly, a lack of agreement on the very definition of "Russian" in this context. As a Russian official later recalled, despite ostensible hostility between Russians and Poles in the 1860s and 1870s, a good deal of mingling took place, in part due to the lack of fashionable "Russian society" in the city.[26]

The one aspect of Russianness that nearly all could agree on was religion: the Orthodox Church and Russian people were almost perceived as equivalent concepts.[27] Thus building and refurbishing Orthodox churches formed a major part of "russifying the land." As we have seen, with the abolition of the Uniate Church in this region, former Uniate churches and monasteries in Vilnius became (as the Russians portrayed it, "reverted to") Orthodox houses of worship. For example, the Basilian monastery close to Ostra Brama had become the "Holy Trinity" Orthodox monastery at that point, reverting to its pre-1596 status.[28] The nearby Orthodox cathedral of St. Nicholas the Miracle-Worker (Kafedral'nyi sobor vo imia sv. Nikolaia Chudotvortsa), which had been taken (back) from the Catholics in 1832, underwent in the 1860s a major rebuilding supported by 80,000 rubles of government funds.[29]

The Prechistenskii sobor, also very near the Old Town, had been Uniate from the late sixteenth to the late eighteenth century. In the early nineteenth century it had been further degraded, to a storehouse and then an anatomical theater (for the university's school of medicine). After 1863 it was essentially entirely rebuilt (though Russian commentators inevitably stress the continuity of the present structure with the original church dating from the fourteenth century), again with a good deal of state money (57,000 rubles), supplemented by donations from Moscow merchants (39,000 rubles).[30] Thus while the downtown core of Vilnius remained dominated by Catholic churches (the cathedral, Ostra Brama, St. Teresa, and many others), the Catholic religious hegemony was challenged by a number of impressive Orthodox houses of worship. By subsidizing the rebuilding, repair, and decoration of these churches, the Russian government asserted the importance of the Orthodox religion and the Russian nation in Vilnius.

Besides the new (that is, reconstructed or converted) Orthodox churches in the city center, two other new buildings would proclaim Vilnius' Russian character from two "strategic" points on the cityscape. Both structures date back to the turn of the century, a generation after the 1863 rebellion was crushed. The first was built in the new city in 1898: the impressive onion-domed Alexander Nevsky Church (also called the Romanov church). The site of this church is strategic from two points of view. First, it is located atop a hill that makes it easily visible from many other parts of the city, including from the Castle Hill in the Old Town core. Second, the church was located in the center of the new city, near the large railroad administrative building and apartment houses that echoed typical features of Russian imperial architecture. Thus Alexander Nevsky Church emphasized the Russian character of the new city quarter. In a similar way, a rather more modest but very noticeable church, in the unmistakable Byzantine style, was constructed in 1903 just across the Neris River from the end of St. George's Avenue. This Orthodox "Church of the Revelation of the Theotokos" (Tserkov' znameniia Bozhiei Materi) both served the practical religious needs of Russians who had built small houses in the new suburb of Žvėrynas and affixed on the city map a counterpoint to the Catholic cathedral that stood at the other end of the city's main new thoroughfare.[31] Thus by the early twentieth century, Catholic Vilnius was challenged from within, so to speak, by the newly magnificent Orthodox churches in the Old Town and at the same time "hemmed in" by the Alexander Nevsky and Znamenskaia churches in the new "Russian" districts.

Books and publishing were also used to mark the city as Russian. Vilnius' public library, offering mainly Russian-language books but also manuscripts and artifacts, was opened after 1863 and served as both a library and a museum. Among the artifacts presented in various showcases in the library were religious books in Russian and Ruthenian dating from the seventeenth centuries and earlier, images of Russian rulers (Peter, Anna, Peter III, Catherine, Alexander I) from the eighteenth and early nineteenth century, and a variety of books published in Church Slavonic in Vilnius from the early sixteenth century.[32] As a later Polish commentator remarked, the public library and museum were specifically organized after 1863 in a "Russian spirit," with the aim of demonstrating that Russian culture and the Orthodox religion were native to the region and were now "returning" to their proper historical place after centuries of polonization.[33] This is a quite fair summing up of the prevalent Russian attitude toward Vilnius and its region: the present-day ubiquity of Polish culture and the Catholic religion could not be denied, but these could be demoted to mere epiphenomena doomed to wither away as Russian culture returned to its proper historical place.

Another means of emphasizing the city's Russian character was through scholarship. In 1867 a branch of the Russian Geographical Society was created in the city and put forth an ambitious plan for archeological, geographical, and historical research in the region. Almost none of these proposed research projects was actually carried out; after a mere eight years of existence the Vilnius society closed, to be opened again only in 1910.[34] The ambitious plans and minimal follow-through of this organization is almost too perfect as a symbol of russifying efforts after 1863. For all the high-flown phrases about the region's eternal Russian character, even the most dedicated apostles of Muraviev's legacy (e.g., Ivan P. Kornilov, Pompei N. Batiushkov, Aleksandr I. Milovidov) had to be selective in their sources and arguments to argue for a historically Russian/Orthodox character of the city and region. And while they could (and did) point out that steps were taken toward "restoring" the proper Russian face of the city in the final decades of the nineteenth century, the fact remained that the city continued to show many more elements of Jewish and Polish culture than Russian.

Not by chance, many of the most prolific Russian authors on the (Russian) history of Vilnius and its surroundings were employees of the Ministry of People's Enlightenment (or, for a more prosaic translation, the ministry of education). These Russian patriotic historians tended to stress rulers, battles, and politics—but what to do when for several centuries (up to 1795) the Russian presence in Vilnius had been mainly that of an outside power that would sometimes destructively enter the city? In order to get around this problem, two tactics were adopted: first, rather than dwelling on the rulers, these historians emphasized the ruled and their Orthodox religion. Second, Russian patriotic writers emphasized the original *Russian* ruler before the Union of Krewo (1385), then spoke of the "Lithuanian-Russian state" (*Litovsko-Russkoe gosudarstvo*) thereafter, at least to 1569 (the Union of Lublin). By focusing on the large numbers of "Russians" (for us, Belarusians) and Orthodox believers living in the region and even in the city Vilnius, the writers (who left Lithuanians out of the equation entirely) were able to argue that while the upper classes may have embraced Catholicism and Polish culture, the masses remained true to their putative Russian roots.

For example, the pamphlet *Russkaia Vil'na*, published in 1865, consists entirely of a listing and description of Orthodox churches, monasteries, and other holy sites (or the ruins of former sites) in the city.[35] Many of these sites, to be sure, had in the succeeding centuries been taken over by the Uniates, but in the 1830s (when the Uniates of the region all converted to Orthodoxy, in part due to coercion) the holy places had been returned (in most cases) to the Orthodox Church or, failing that, were transformed from Catholic to Orthodox holy sites after 1863.

By including sites that were now mere ruins, the author could establish the ancient roots and legitimacy of Orthodoxy (i.e., Russianness) in Vilnius.

A short "history of Vilnius" published some years later also stressed the Orthodox connection but, following existing conventions, spent much more space on rulers and political history. Here the close contact with Russia (often in the form of armed conflict) is emphasized and one has the impression that only the general breakdown of Muscovite politics after the death of Ivan IV ("the Terrible") prevented the actual incorporation of Vilnius into Muscovy. Even so, the five-year period of Muscovite rule in Vilnius (1655–1661) receives nearly as much coverage as the subsequent period of more than century of Polish rule. The author leaves his Russian readers with the impression that, if not for the vagaries of history and the intervention of the perfidious Swede, Vilnius would once again have been "ours."[36]

A similar historical trajectory is traced by the longtime Russian educational official P. N. Batiushkov in his *Belorussiia i Litva*, published in 1890.[37] The subtitle of the volume is telling: "Historical fates of the Northwestern country," again hinting that while the Poles may have won out temporarily in the seventeenth and eighteenth centuries since 1795 the region had returned to its proper place under the Romanov scepter. Batiushkov argues that even in the seventeenth century there was a "revival of Russian national self-consciousness" and a "battle against Polish Catholics and Uniates" among local Russians. It should go without saying that local East Slavs were not Russian but Ruthenian/Belarusian and it is absurd to speak of "Russian national self-consciousness" at this point. Batiushkov takes the story all the way up to 1863, describing the desperate attempts by the Poles to retain power over "Russians" and continue to spread their influence, even after 1795, culminating in the Polish "mutiny" (*miatezh*) of 1863 and the realization— at last—that stern measures were necessary to tame the Poles and protect Russian influence here.[38]

A short historical work covering the post-1863 period and published just before the outbreak of the World War I provides a twist on this historical scenario. Writing in 1914, Muraviev's erstwhile lieutenant A. I. Milovidov looks back with satisfaction over a half century of "Russian Vilnius." Because his purpose is to show the change made in that period, Milovidov can openly state that almost nothing in the town was Russian in 1863—weights and measures, coinage, the language spoken in the streets, high culture (Russian books were only "by chance" to be found in the city), even the population (only 10% Orthodox, he claims). By 1914, however, a dramatic transformation from dark to light has occurred:

Russian historical studies of the town have been published, Russian books are for sale, those churches taken over by the Catholics have been restored to their rightful Russian Orthodox masters and new Orthodox churches built, Russian periodicals are published and read in the city. While Milovidov's pamphlet makes no claim of being a serious history of the town even in this relatively short period, it takes the narrative strategy of simply ignoring non-Russian elements to its logical conclusion. Here history's triumphant march toward a fully Russian Vilnius is documented.[39]

Perhaps the best-known means by which the Russian state attempted to leave its mark on the Vilnius cityscape was by constructing monuments. Three of these symbolized Russian domination in the city (and region). These were, in order of appearance, a statue of Governor General Muraviev on a pedestal in the courtyard of the governor general's palace (1898), a small bust to Pushkin placed at the foot of Castle Hill (1899), and a bombastic memorial to Catherine the Great (1904) near the entrance to the cathedral. The Pushkin monument, a simple bust on a pedestal, was placed in the park beneath Gediminas's Castle as part of the empire-wide Pushkin centenary celebration in 1899. On the pedestal one could read four lines of Pushkin in which the poet boasted of his spreading fame throughout "great Russia" in "all existing [in the Empire] languages." An illustration in Vinogradov's guidebook shows the strategic location of the Pushkin monument: just beyond it one sees in the background the remains of the original Lithuanian Grand Duke Gediminas's castle fortress.[40]

A short walk from the Pushkin monument passing the cathedral and turning onto "Palace Street" (*Dvortsovaia*—formerly Uniwersytecka) one found the monument to the Russian "hero" of 1863, M. N. Muraviev. This monument was constructed by public subscription (to be sure, many of the contributors were government employees—but from all over the empire) and was unveiled on November 8, 1898. The rhetoric and ceremony surrounding the construction and dedication of the monument combined a strong imperial patriotism with some conciliatory gestures to the Poles, who understandably viewed the monument with mistrust, if not loathing.

The beginning of actual construction—the laying of the monument's cornerstone on October 3, 1897—was surrounded by a ceremony at which a peasant, one Nikolai Morozik, read a speech of his own composition praising Muraviev's services to the Northwest territories.[41] The actual stone was laid by Ieronim, the local Orthodox archbishop, who also pronounced a speech for the occasion. Among the dignitaries present were the governor general, V. N. Trotskii, and the chief of the Vilnius educational district, Chepelevskii. The ceremony was also attended by the assembled schoolchildren of the provincial capital, and accompanied by festive singing by church choirs. After the festivities were over, the assembled civil and ecclesiastical dignitaries gathered together for a gala breakfast.[42]

The unveiling of the monument in early November 1898 was accompanied by ceremonies attended by local officials, both religious and administrative, as well as several important dignitaries from St. Petersburg. A flurry of telegrams from all corners of the empire greeted the opening of the monument. The telegrams and public statements consistently portrayed Muraviev as a stern but loving paternal figure—and vociferously denied that the monument was in any way aimed against the Poles. Tsar Nicholas II also welcomed the monument with a telegram: "Together with all true-Russian people I view with joy today's commemoration [literally: 'material immortalization'—*veshchestvennoe uvekovechenie*] of the memory of Count Mikhail Nikolaevich Muraviev in the very place of his great and fruitful activity."[43] A sympathetic commentator writing just after the ceremony summed up the meaning of the monument: "it will bear witness from generation to generation, century to century [of a man who gave this land] its true historical appearance and who, finally, with a firm hand, on an unshakable foundation, unfurled in Vilnius the banner: 'Here is Russia!'"[44] Despite efforts by the Russians to portray Muraviev in a positive light, for most residents of the city the monument symbolized the worst aspects of Russian rule.

If Muraviev was the man who saved Vilnius from the clutches of treasonous Poles, the person who had "returned" (following Russian patriotic rhetoric) the entire region to Russia had been Catherine II ("the Great" to Russians, but hardly to Poles). It was only natural that Catherine and her "historic deed" be commemorated in the city. The monument to Catherine had been anticipated for some years before its unveiling on September 10, 1904 (o.s.). The idea of a monument to Catherine in the most important city of the Belarusian Lithuanian provinces was not new and had received impetus from the construction of the Muraviev monument (opened in 1898). On February 9, 1899, on the personal recommendation of then governor general V. N. Trotskii, the tsar gave permission to construct a monument to the "main initiator of the return to Russia of the Belarusian lands torn away from her," as well as to collect donations throughout the empire for this purpose. In early 1902, A. Vinogradov published an article in *Vilenskii vestnik* which stated that the monument would be completed and probably opened (unveiled) in the present year. The renowned Vilnius-born sculptor Mark Antokol'skii was selected to create the statue and a granite pedestal for it. Antokol'skii died in July

1902 just as he was finishing this work in Paris, a circumstance that partially explains the delay in the monument's dedication.[45]

In essence, the controversy over the Catherine monument revolved around rival historical interpretations of Catherine the Great. For patriotic Russians, Catherine represented the continuation of Peter the Great's drive to strengthen, westernize, and expand Russia. From the Russian point of view, all of these were worthy goals pursued by an intelligent and energetic sovereign. The standard Polish interpretation, not surprisingly, was rather more negative. Catherine was a historical villain of the first order who not only interfered in Polish affairs, placing an ex-lover on Poland's throne, but, most damning of all, presided over the dismemberment of Poland. Conveniently for Polish nationalists, Catherine was both German and Russian, thereby bringing together the two most anti-Polish neighbors in one person. Perhaps Mickiewicz summed up the Polish attitude best in his *Books of the Polish Pilgrimage*: "The most debauched of women, a shameless Venus proclaiming herself a pure virgin."

The positive assessment of Catherine's impact on the Northwest Provinces (which included—using Russian spellings—Vil'na, Kovno, Mogilev, Minsk, and Grodno provinces) presumed that this territory was never truly Polish but at most had been "polonized" by an alien upper class. In P. N. Batiushkov's historical survey of the region, the author argued that this "truly Russian country" (*istinno-russkii krai*) had been subjected to religious and national persecution under Polish rule. Only after this region had been "regained" by Russia through the partitions, Batiushkov claimed, could Russian culture and Orthodox religion truly feel secure. Catherine was both the liberator of this oppressed land and a firm protector of things Russian and Orthodox, far more than her son Paul I or grandson Alexander I (who, after all, gave the Poles a constitution at the Congress of Vienna). Batiushkov only found fault with Catherine's overly magnanimous treatment of her new Polish subjects (the upper class, or *szlachta*), lenience that, he argued, allowed the process of polonization to continue even under Russian rule.[46]

Russian officials recognized that a monument to Catherine in Vilnius would not be popular among Poles. Governor general Petr Sviatopolk-Mirskii personally met with key members of the local Polish landowning nobility in an attempt to convince them that the monument was not meant as an anti-Polish gesture and that it would be in their interest to attend the ceremony. Sviatopolk-Mirskii was not successful in bringing all local Polish notables to the ceremony—in particular the absence of the Vilnius Catholic bishop, Edward Ropp, was noted.[47] Still, moderates and conservatives could hope that cooperation with the reform plans of Sviatopolk-Mirskii would bring about changes that would lessen or even eliminate existing legal restrictions on Poles. Probably with such considerations in mind, around fifty or sixty members (sources vary) of the local Polish landowning nobility attended the ceremony.[48]

According to the Polish and Russian press, Vilnius was decked out in flags and garlands on the day of the monument's dedication, with triumphal arches erected at the railroad station and Ostra Brama. The tsar's younger brother, Grand Duke Mikhail, attended the ceremony along with Governor General Sviatopolk-Mirskii, all six governors of the Northwest region, and other dignitaries. The monument itself, judging from the various images that have come down to us, shows Catherine looming over the crowd atop a base around three meters high. The empress is flanked by two eagles spreading (flapping?) their wings, and the inscription reads "Ottorzhennyia vozvratikh"—"that which was torn away, now returned."[49] Just as the Pushkin monument marked a Russian space in the shadow of the ancient Castle Hill and Muraviev stood guard next to the former bishops' palace gazing (glaring?) toward the former university, so Catherine stood mere meters from the Catholic cathedral, indeed in the shadow of its bell tower at the entrance to St. George's Avenue.

Vilnius was also becoming "russified," if that is the proper word, due to the increased cultural, educational, and commercial ties with central Russia. Most of the Lithuanian national elite of the first generation (e.g., the Vileišis brothers Jonas and Petras, Antanas Smetona, Augustinas Voldemaras, and Petras Klimas) attended Russian universities. This influence was also present in the artistic sphere. To take one example, the Vilnius-born Jewish sculptor of the Catherine monument, Mark Antokol'skii, went to Petersburg for artistic training and made his initial career there. Local artists could receive training at a local school for drawing founded in the 1860s; Russian artists also exhibited in the city.[50] Petersburg rivaled Warsaw in influence on budding artists in Vilnius.[51] Still, it is difficult to claim that these artistic exchanges left much of a permanent (Russian) mark on the city.

## Persistence and Change: Poles

While the Russians attempted to place a new stamp on the city, Poles and Jews in Vilnius tried to preserve their cultures while also changing with the times. And the changes that this half century brought for everyone were considerable.

Economic developments and Vilnius' position as an important stop on the St. Petersburg to Warsaw railroad brought new people and ideas to the city. New technologies like photography and, at century's end, the cinema made their appearance in the city. While Poles and Jews were subject to numerous legal and de facto restrictions, they also figured out ways to avoid and resist these disabilities, opening secret schools, forming underground political parties, and even at times opposing the Russian occupiers with violence. Obviously the political status and cultural development of Poles and Jews were quite different, but both were regarded with suspicion by the Russian authorities and both communities underwent wrenching internal changes over the two generations between 1863 and 1914.

After 1863 Polish culture in Vilnius was under attack. Post-1863 Russian laws and administrative practice were based on the fundamental assumption that in the "western provinces" (more or less today's Belarus, Lithuania, and right-bank Ukraine), Russian culture and landowning were to be encouraged in order to "turn back the clock" on the polonization that, following this conception, had befallen this territory since the early modern period. For several decades no Polish periodicals were permitted by the censor in Vilnius and in particular any kind of publications aimed at simple folk (alphabet books, popular scientific works, textbooks) were not allowed and even importing this kind of books was, at least initially, forbidden.[52] The fundamental attitude of the Russian authorities was that Poles in the Northwest territory, including Vilnius, were "newcomers" who could not be allowed to spread their culture (in particular the authorities worried about the polonization of Belarusian peasants). From a Polish point of view, though, it appeared that the Russian authorities were bent on pushing out all forms of Polish culture. To be sure, the Russians would have been quite pleased to do so had it been possible. In fact, however, Poles in Vilnius continued to speak their language, to teach it to their children (illegally), and to subscribe to Polish journals and newspapers published in Warsaw and Petersburg (legally). They also illegally brought in Polish publications from cities in the other partitions (e.g., Poznań or Cracow).

The strict censorship of Polish hit publishing in Vilnius hard. The Zawadzki firm, up to 1865 responsible for something like half of Polish-language publications in the city, essentially stopped publishing in Polish for forty years.[53] Figures from the Polish national bibliography show that numbers of Polish publications in Vilnius plummeted after 1865 and did not recover until after 1905.[54] And, as Andrzej Romanowski has shown, some few "periodicals" (mainly calendars and the like) were published in Polish in the region during this period.[55] The most repressive (or strict) years were the decade or so after the uprising; from the late 1870s in practice it became easier to get around the still-existing restrictions. One of Poland's best-loved and most popular writers, Eliza Orzeszkowa, concerned about the decline of Polish culture in the city, opened a bookstore in Vilnius in 1879.[56] According to a later account, Orzeszkowa's "mission" in Vilnius was to provide a place for the exchange of "free ideas" or, to put it another way, to establish an institution for liberal Poles and for the development of liberal Polish culture in the city.[57] Permission to open the bookstore and carry books in "all languages other than Yiddish" was given in July 1879, and the store opened for business in September. The authorities remained suspicious of the store and of Orzeszkowa as a liberal and an important Polish cultural figure. After the assassination of Alexander II on March 1, 1881 (o.s.), the further survival of the bookstore was doomed. Claiming that the establishment fomented anti-government and Polish patriotic sentiments, in April 1881 the governor general gave the order to close down "Orzeszkowa & Co." bookshop.[58] The short episode showed just how precarious Polish culture remained in Vilnius; the situation would improve markedly only with the 1905 Revolution.[59]

Education in the Polish language was also forbidden in Vilnius after 1863, though it continued nevertheless. From 1864 specific permission was required to open a school, thereby making illegal the many small schools—or simply private instruction—that existed in churches and homes. In reality, many of these schools continued operating illegally as there was no other way for Poles to teach their children literacy in their native language.[60] In his memoirs, Ludwik Czarkowski (born 1855) mentions that as a schoolboy in Vilnius he and his comrades collected money to buy Polish books and read them secretly.[61] Such references abound in Polish memoirs from this period. The Russian authorities were well aware of the existence of illegal schools and tried to fight them by arresting teachers (but rarely for long) and levying fines (which, officials complained, were often simply paid by the Polish landowners as a kind of patriotic duty).[62] Already in the 1870s and increasingly after that, it was rather apparent—even to Russian officials—that Polish culture in Vilnius had simply "gone underground" and was possibly even strengthened by Russian restrictions.[63]

A conservative nobleman, Stanisław Tarnowski, visiting from Cracow in the late 1870s described the terrible initial impression Vilnius had made.[64] The train station, the droshky (carriage) he took to his hotel, and even its driver appeared to him entirely Russian. Later, he admitted, the city's initial appearance was a bit like the driver's dirty Russian-style coat—just a shell, while the interior was different (just as, he implies, the Russian-looking driver was no doubt a Pole). But at first glance he found the scene before him "terrible": everywhere Russian signs, Orthodox churches, Russian soldiers, even tradesmen using Russian "out of fear." Ostra Brama was disappointing and to get there, one had to navigate dirty streets full of beggars and Jews. Prayers were held in Latin as the use of Polish, even in church, was forbidden.[65] The large numbers of Jews in the middle of the city rather horrified the nobleman, who remarked that it was as if Kazimierz (the Jewish quarter in his native town) were transferred to the center of town. "Inhabitants of Vilnius call it [the Jewish quarter] the black city, and rightly so," for no ray of sun reaches there. Jews spoke Yiddish among themselves, he noted, but used Russian when speaking to non-Jews, further adding to the Russian appearance of the city. In the end, however, despite his aversion to the classical cathedral, his remarks dismissing the town hall as commonplace—and his grumbling about dirt, poverty, Russians, and Jews—Tarnowski concluded that the main population in Vilnius "is just as Polish as in Warsaw or Cracow" and "The entire Russian appearance of Vilnius is simply an external dirty shell [skorupa]."[66]

## Tradition and Modernization: Jews

Unlike the Poles, Jews were not the primary objective of cultural and economic restrictions after 1863. The further narrowing of Jewish rights would come only a generation later, from the 1880s, and had only an indirect effect on Jewish life in Vilnius. Focusing on a broader level of change, however, Jewish culture was certainly subject to the same modernizing trends that confronted traditional Polish culture. For Jews modernization was a particularly painful process as the very concept of a "modern Jew" had to be created. To be sure, Poles were also handicapped in this process by their lack of a state, but Jews were doubly disadvantaged: they neither possessed a state nor, at least in the 1860s, a "nation." That is, while the Polish elite (at least) thought in terms of a Polish nation including magnates, petty nobles (*szlachta*), townspeople, and peasants—all bound together by culture and a sense of shared history—Jews in the 1860s remained a religious community, albeit one with many characteristics of a nation (languages, tradition, self-consciousness, history). This would change over the next two generations. Some Jews would embrace liberalism, others socialism (in different guises), and still others, nationalism (again in various forms). But the concept of Jews as *only* a religious community would hardly survive to 1914.

Vilnius without Jews was simply inconceivable, even for judeophobes. Jews lived in large concentrations in the very center of the Old Town and "German

Street"—Daytshe gos—was the main thoroughfare of Jewish Vilnius.[67] While Polish and Russian businesses, signs, and conversation might dominate on St. George's or on Castle Street (now Pilies), in the small streets nearby, Jews and Yiddish set the tone. Aside from their numbers, Jews were also more likely to be natives of the town: in 1875 almost two-thirds of the city's Jewish population had been born in Vilnius while only two-fifths of Catholics and not even one-fifth of Orthodox believers could make that claim.[68]

Economically, Jews in Vilnius made up the bulk of the city's "middle class," between Polish landowners and Russian officials on the one side and mainly Catholic (and also probably Polish or Lithuanian) servants and laborers on the other side. Jews were largely excluded from government jobs, though a small number worked as teachers in the city's Jewish teachers' institute (up to 1873 the government-sponsored "Rabbinical School"). Most Jews earned their living as artisans, merchants, shopkeepers, and "agents" of various types. Several thousand Jews (in 1875) worked as laborers, but this kind of physical work was much more typical for Catholic Vilnans.[69] It was as traders, artisans, and shopkeepers that Jews dominated in the city's occupational structure. Half of all construction workers, two-thirds of leather workers, and nearly all tobacco workers were Jews.[70] The Jewish tailor and shopkeeper are almost legendary—but in this case, the legend is based on solid statistical evidence. Less commonly spoken of are Jewish prostitutes. A one-day census in 1875 found 120 women active in this trade—likely a gross underestimate—of whom half were Jewish.[71] A generation later, in 1903, a police file on prostitution in Vilnius mentions numerous Jewish names among madams running houses of ill fame.[72]

In 1881 Jewish education continued to be carried out mainly in Jewish schools using Yiddish and Hebrew as the languages of instruction, most commonly the *heder* and for more advanced students the *yeshiva*. Shemarya Gorelik recalled that Vilnius in the 1890s was full of Jews studying at various formal and informal institutions.[73] The state-run Rabbinical School was shut down in 1873 but reopened shortly thereafter as a Teachers' Institute for Jews and in that form existed until 1915.[74] Hirsz Abramowicz later recalled his own experiences in this and other government schools for Jews where all subjects—even religion and prayers— were taught in Russian. As Abramowicz remembered, speaking Yiddish in public was forbidden these students, even outside of the school itself.[75] Among these *maskilim*, the preferred spoken language was Russian—never Yiddish—but this group was quite small in 1881. Still, in 1875 a Russian statistician found that over a quarter of Vilnius' Jews were literate or "semi-literate" in Russian: this figure gives some idea of the spread of the language within the Jewish community.[76]

Far more typical was the *heder* where boys learned rudimentary Hebrew skills and usually little else. Despite constant attempts by both Russian authorities and *maskilim* to reform these small, usually cramped and unhygienic schools, here most Jewish lads received their only formal education.[77] It has been estimated that in the late nineteenth century there existed one heder for approximately every twenty-eight school-age youngsters.[78] The heder teachers, as is often recounted in memoirs, were usually far more interested in their own studies than in teaching a crowd of small boys. The 1875 census found 202 melamdim (heder teachers) in Vilnius, only 36 percent of whom were literate in Russian.[79] Most likely the number of actual melamdim was higher. Learning Hebrew letters was often accompanied by harsh words and physical blows for the lazy or dull. At the same time, it is almost certain—though hard to prove—that Jews were the most literate people in Vilnius. Even among Orthodox people in Vilnius, around one-third were illiterate or "half-literate" in 1875. Very few adult Jewish men could not at least make out Hebrew letters and, as we have seen, over one-fifth of them were also literate in Russian.

The Russian authorities' distaste for Jews is well-known. However, in Vilnius it may be argued that the Russians mistrusted and despised Poles even more than they did Jews. This was certainly the case with the most infamous governor-general of Vilnius, M. N. Muraviev, who considered Poles (particularly the Catholic clergy) especially dangerous.[80] On the whole the Russian officials evinced little sympathy for the Jews but tended to see the Poles—in particular the Catholic clergy—as far more dangerous. Younger Jews, however, were often singled out as seditious trouble-makers, as in 1881, when the governor of Vilnius province wrote in an annual report that the younger generation of Jews was being influenced by "enemies of public order." He concluded, however, that this phenomenon was of "insignificant dimensions."[81] It is also worth remembering that in summer 1881, when pogroms broke out in the southwestern provinces (today's Ukraine) and even in Warsaw in late December, Vilnius was spared.[82] One reason that pogroms did not spread into this region could be the decisive action of the governor-general of Vilnius, Count Eduard Ivanovich Totleben. Immediately upon receiving word of the Elizavetgrad pogrom in mid-April, Totleben sent out orders to military and civilian authorities warning them to take all possible measures to prevent any clashes between Christians and Jews. A circular of May 6, 1881 to the governors of Vilnius, Kovno, and Grodno provinces clearly stated measures to be taken. First, all false rumors and agitation among the people were to be "vigilantly pursued"; authorities were to pay "painstaking attention" to "unknown individuals." If a disturbance broke out, local authorities were ordered to suppress it immediately and inform local military units. If need be, these military units were to aid civilian authorities in reestablishing order.[83] The correspondence between Totleben, local authorities, and the Ministry of the Interior in Petersburg shows that all were concerned with maintaining public order. In the end, despite alarming rumors and fears, Vilnius' Jewish community was spared.[84]

A unique witness to the situation of Jewish Vilnius was Dr. Isaac Rülf, a rabbi from Memel (now Klaipėda) who visited the city in late summer 1881, wishing to observe the conditions of "Russian Jewry" firsthand. Rabbi Rülf's short sojourn in Russia—a bit over a week in total—was spent in Vilnius and Minsk. As an acculturated but religiously Orthodox German Jew, Rülf felt both alienated from and attracted to Vilnius' Jewish population. He noted that the court of the main synagogue (*Schulhof*) took up a large area "cut through with different irregular streets running hither and thither, badly paved and not entirely clean."[85] Houses crowded the street, some containing apartments and others housing different charities and associations (*khevros*). Each association had its own prayer house (*beyt midrash/ kloyz*). The decorations in the Great Synagogue he describes as "massive, very old [*uralt*] and gnawed on by the tooth of time."[86]

Rülf noted that the Jewish community in Vilnius was not unified. Dozens of prayer houses and small synagogues existed, practically one for each Jewish association (*khevrah*), with only the Great Synagogue and the cemetery uniting all. Vilnius lacked a chief rabbi though it did have a crown rabbi, Dr. A. Gordon. Most Jews did not consider crown rabbis, trained at state institutions, their true spiritual leaders, but they depended on them to carry out many functions such as performing marriage ceremonies. Several different rabbinical courts existed in the city, each with its own "clientele."[87]

Another visitor to the city in the 1880s, and one far more familiar with the realities of Jewish life in the Russian Empire, was the economist and journalist Andrei Pavlovich Subbotin. Whereas Rabbi Rülf was more concerned with the religious life of Vilnius' Jews, Subbotin primarily reported on economic conditions. He noted that Jews dominated in trade (2752 out of 3194 individuals were engaged in trade) and made up just over half of the artisans in the city (5962 of 10,534). Factories in the city tended to be small, barely more than large artisanal shops, engaged in brewing, cigar-making, leather goods, and glass manufacture. Vilnius was remarkable for its huge number of tiny shops (*lavki*)—one for every twenty inhabitants—which were overwhelmingly run by (impoverished) Jews.[88] Just over 40 percent of all houses in the city were owned by Jews but because of the high cost of living in Vilnius, many Jews lived in wretched quarters or even simply slept in prayer houses or in charitable institutions.[89]

Like Rülf, Subbotin noted the large number of educational establishments here, providing the surprising statistic that among 139 schools, 112 were Jewish—but only 3223 of 7563 pupils studied there.[90] This would correspond with much anecdotal evidence about Jewish *hedarim* at which only a handful of boys were instructed. Like the German rabbi, the Russian economist remarked that nearly all Jews tried to speak Russian, contrasting their attitude unfavorably with that of local Poles.[91]

Rülf stressed the persistence of traditional life among Jews in Vilnius, but Subbotin emphasized the harbingers of change that were also visible. Most of the youth, both agreed, could at least understand Russian, and graduates of the state Rabbinical School and other state Jewish schools formed a small but growing Russian-speaking Jewish elite. The grinding poverty in which most Vilnius Jews lived was reflected in both men's descriptions. This poverty—along with legal restrictions that grew in strength after 1881—would fuel Jewish radicalism. In particular from the 1890s, the figure of the "Jewish nihilist" would become widespread, troubling both traditional Jews and Russian authorities alike.

In 1897 the Jewish "Bund," the first Jewish socialist party, was founded in the city, and by 1905 it is estimated that one-quarter of the city's Jewish workers were members of that party.[92] Long before this, the Russian authorities had uncovered "illegal circles" of "socialist-revolutionary" Jewish youth, for example in 1875 at the Jewish teachers' institute.[93] But those were schoolboy affairs compared to the Bund, which quickly spread "revolutionary propaganda" among the town's workers—local authorities had confiscated almost a dozen brochures by 1898.[94] Four years later, a Bund sympathizer, Hirsh Lekert, fired two shots at the detested Vilnius governor Victor von Wahl. Despite the governor's minor wounds, Lekert was tried and executed a mere three weeks later.[95] Not without reason did the governor of Vilnius province in his 1903 report call the Bund "the most serious and most zealous Jewish movement."[96]

Political Zionism was also gaining strength in Vilnius. Theodor Herzl visited in 1903 and was greeted as "king of the Jews."[97] At the same time St. Petersburg sent out a circular warning local authorities to keep a close watch on Zionist activities, which it considered "in contradiction with principle of the Russian state idea."[98] From 1905 to 1911 Vilnius served as the location for the central organization and publishing activities of the socialist movement Poalei Tsiyon (Workers of Zion).

Still, most Vilnius Jews—as even Governor General Pahlen recognized—were indifferent or even hostile to Zionism.[99]

It is easy in retrospect to exaggerate the importance of radical politics in Vilnius' Jewish life. At the time, however, other things were more visible. For example, there was the grand new synagogue in the Moorish style, built in 1903 on the edge of the Jewish quarter.[100] Here more "respectable" Jews could worship in sumptuous surroundings, avoiding the grime and ruckus of the Old Synagogue. However, even here Orthodoxy was maintained; religious reform had few adherents among Vilnius' Jews. In the absence of a dynamic form of modern religious Judaism, Vilnius' youth was faced with a stark choice: remain within the constraints of conservative Orthodoxy or abandon the Jewish religion entirely. The number of "non-Jewish (by religion) Jews" in Vilnius, while remaining a small percentage of the total, was a visible and—for some—threatening group by the early twentieth century.[101]

## Tourism and the City

The railroad brought Vilnius closer to the rest of the Russian Empire and, indeed, to the rest of Europe. While few foreign visitors made their way to the city before World War I (Rabbi Rülf was an exception), afterward it was easy enough to board the train from Petersburg or Warsaw and visit the city. As Laimonas Briedis has shown, a number of prominent Russian writers, including the playwright Aleksandr Ostrovsky and novelist Fyodor Dostoevsky, visited the city after the railroad link to Petersburg was completed.[102] Thousands of other less famous Russians made their way through the city, as tourists or on business. Several guidebooks in Russian and Polish portrayed Vilnius for these visitors, each revealing their own specific interests and interpretation of the city's past and present.

Russian guidebooks to Vilnius reflect the kind of patriotic history described earlier in this chapter. Inevitably they begin with a short "capsule history" of the town. Take, for example, Dobrianskii's *Staraia i novaia Vil'na*, which was in its third edition by 1904. Dobrianskii, who published several historical works aside from this popular guidebook, notes at the outset that "From ancient times the Lithuanian tribe has been in close contact with the neighboring Russian tribe and for this reason Vilnius from the first days of its historical existence was half-Russian in population. The very name of the city is obviously [*povidimomu*] of Russian origin."[103] Emphasizing the use of Russian (for present-day scholars, Chancery

Ruthenian) as the official language of the Grand Duchy of Lithuania, he notes that the first book printed in Vilnius was in Russian. As in the histories cited above, Dobrianskii remarks on the persecution of the "Orthodox Russian nation" under Polish rule and makes the charge that, by encouraging the Jesuits in the religious sphere and the Jews in the economic one, the Poles held tight to their control over Vilnius, but to the detriment of the local inhabitants.[104] The city that passed into Russian rule in 1795 was, in his view, a mere shadow of its former self, and Russian policy during the nineteenth century attempted to restore its greatness.

Dobrianskii's guidebook also emphasizes the Russian nature of Vilnius in its discussion of the city's "sights." More than twice as many pages are devoted to Orthodox churches, monasteries, and chapels (including ones that no longer existed) as to Catholic sites. Of the four monuments discussed, three were recent and Russian—statues of Muraviev, Catherine, and Pushkin. Most of the secular sites were either built under Russian rule (St. George's Avenue), re-rebuilt (the Green Bridge), or extensively remodeled and connected with recent Russian history (the Governor General's Palace, where Napoleon had stayed in 1812). Public organizations (*obshchestva*) listed here were mainly Russian, as were the educational institutions. In short, the guidebook did not ignore non-Russian Vilnius—it dutifully described Jewish sights and Catholic churches—but treated these elements as "nonessential": real Vilnius was Russian.[105]

Polish guidebooks also exhibited a one-sided view of the city, no doubt reflecting what the author thought the reader's interests would (or should) be. An author we have met before, Adam-Honory Kirkor, composed several descriptions of Vilnius and its surroundings for visitors.[106] An edition issued in 1880, long after Kirkor had left the city for Cracow, begins with the obligatory historical background (over fifty pages). Here Russians make an appearance only as invaders, merchants, and eventually rulers from the later eighteenth century; the real heroes are Lithuanians (*Litwini*) and Poles (though the latter culture is implied, not explicitly stated, possibly due to censorship constraints). Jews also figure in this story, in particular as merchants, allowed in 1633—according to Kirkor— to live in the city only on the streets between St. Nicholas Church and German Street (which remained the main Jewish quarter into the twentieth century).[107] The story is taken into the mid-nineteenth century and features the university (and the archaeological museum that occupied its place from the mid-1850s), Napoleon, visiting emperors, and a few bouts with cholera. The historical section ends with the opening of the railroad to Warsaw in 1862, thereby avoiding the difficult period of the next few years.[108]

Not quite one-third of the guidebook is dedicated to tourist sights, and while these include Orthodox and Protestant churches, the mosque and synagogues and also descriptions of Catholic churches make up the bulk of these pages. Partly this reflects, of course, the simple fact that there were more Catholic churches than those of other confessions, but the inclusion of a dozen "no-longer existing" Catholic churches in the guidebook suggests that something else is at work. These churches reflected the historical past of Vilnius and in a sense its most profound nature. With few exceptions, the Orthodox churches were of fairly recent date (or at least extensively rebuilt in recent decades); Catholic churches had dominated the city for centuries.[109] As Kirkor explained in the preface to the guidebook, much had changed in Vilnius since he left the city in 1868. Most of his contemporaries had passed away or, like him, no longer resided there. The "historical guidebook" thus becomes a way of preserving both the city as he had known it and—implicitly—its Polish culture.

A guidebook published three decades later, in 1910, is much closer in format and coverage to present-day tourist guides. The book starts with historical comments but these are kept to a minimum, and the city—including its new, Russian-built neighborhoods—is presented in a series of walks (*wędrówki*). The author, "W. Gizbert" (Wacław Gizbert Studnicki), was a well-known member and archivist of the Vilnius Calvinist community. His guidebook begins with the remark that after several decades of lethargy at present cultural life, press, theater, and art were flourishing. "Vilnius is awakening and while looking back over its once-holy past, with greater satisfaction it gazes into the unknown future."[110] Any contemporary Pole would understand what Gizbert does not state directly: since the 1905 Revolution, Polish culture had recovered much lost ground.

To underscore this point, Gizbert divided the city's past into three epochs: (1) the pre-Christian, (2) "Vilnius modeling itself on Cracow", and (3) "Vilnius in decline" from 1794 to the Russo-Japanese War. With that war (and the unmentioned 1905 Revolution), a more favorable period for Poles and their culture in Vilnius had dawned. Gizbert mentions Russians (the "Orthodox population") and Jews, even noting that the latter made up around one-half of the city's population, but the city's culture, history, and future are portrayed as really belonging to the Poles.[111] As we have seen, Russian rule ushered in a period of decline, and "Jewish commerce" is similarly linked to decline (*upadek*) in an earlier period.[112] The positive achievements and "sights" of the city are products of Polish culture.

## 1905 in Vilnius

For Gizbert and many others, a new era in Vilnius' history began with the loosening of restrictions on Polish culture during the Russo-Japanese War and the ensuing 1905 Revolution. These events shook Vilnius, from its ruling elite to the most modest denizens. Even more important than the violent events of that year were the political reforms that followed. These reforms allowed the rapid development of a contentious public sphere in the next few years. Before 1905, Vilnius lacked both an unofficial periodical press and citizens' organizations. From 1905 onward, both press and public organizational life would rapidly develop for Jews, Lithuanians, Poles, and even Belarusians. In 1904, Vilnius was a city ruled by the Russian authorities.[113] Afterward, Russian administrators had to contend with an increasingly organized and vocal civil society.

In Vilnius, as in other cities of the empire, it was news of "Bloody Sunday" in St. Petersburg that set off the revolution. Word arrived in Vilnius by telegraph on the evening of January 23 (n.s.) that unarmed demonstrators had been brutally shot down in the Russian capital. Almost immediately after the event thousands of leaflets were distributed among workers of Vilnius and caused—in the words of the provincial governor Count Pahlen—"very strong excitement" (*vozbuzhdenie*).[114] The next day strikes began. While most enterprises opened for work that morning (January 24), many workers failed to show up, in particular shoemakers. In the course of the morning other workers followed their example, walking off the job. Around lunchtime a group of "unknown individuals" showed up at the Rivkind factory on Lukiškės Square, urging the workers there to walk off the job, which many of them promptly did.[115] In the next few days, dozens of factories and thousands of workers went on strike, and protest marches were held in the city. Police arrested dozens of marchers and strikers. Count Pahlen warned workers that not showing up for work could lead to arrest.[116] On the whole, however, government reactions were restrained and violence was avoided.

The efforts of the Russian authorities to reestablish order had some effect. On the January 26 the printers at the Syrkin shop (where the official *Severo-Zapadnoe slovo* was published) came back to work and the following day other printing shops were working again. Thus by January 28 on the whole order had been restored in the city. On that day *Vilniaus Žinios* (*Vilnius News*), which had hardly mentioned any strike activity on January 12, printed a short notice: "In Vilnius factories and print shops, printers laid down their work these past days, and for this reason our newspaper has not appeared for two days."[117]

The first labor disturbances of 1905 in Vilnius thus lasted a mere three days and were not characterized by violence or significant property damage. It is difficult—even impossible—to identify specific strikers or workers, but one matter is clear: Jewish workers played a very significant part. Jewish workers predominated in the small artisan shops, tobacco and leather factories, and needle trades—all branches of industry that were hardest hit by the strikes. Practically the only group of mainly non-Jewish workers mentioned specifically by the governor in his report seems to have been the printers, though there could certainly have been Jews among these, too. Not only the workers but also the factory owners (Zalkind, Segal) appear to have been mainly Jewish. To be sure, this is hardly a scientific sample, and more detailed research would be needed to confirm this general impression, but it seems impossible to avoid the conclusion that the January 1905 strikes disproportionately involved Vilnius' Jewish population.

Lithuanian and Russian Social Democrats (SD) were also active in the city. Amid the strike the Lithuanian SD party issued a manifesto demanding among other things an end to the war, a constitution, amnesty for all political prisoners, and civil liberties (e.g., freedom of speech, religion, and assembly). The Lithuanian SD also specifically demanded that Lithuania be given autonomy with its own parliament (*seimas*) in Vilnius.[118] The Russian SD and Polish PPS were also active in the city and cooperated with the Jewish Bund in organization and propaganda.[119] On the street, however, it appears that the Bund was by far the most noticeable socialist force.

For the next several months the situation in Vilnius remained tense. News of continuing defeats on the battlefield in Manchuria and rumors of strikes in other parts of the empire fueled hopes that the tsarist regime's days might be numbered. In particular, despite censorship, news of dramatic and violent events in neighboring Russian Poland reached Vilnius' workers.[120] Revolutionary propaganda spread widely among the workers and strikes broke out frequently.[121] The social democrats tried to convince workers that strikes over low pay and poor working conditions were shortsighted. Instead, workers should look beyond mere economic gains and work to overthrow the existing order. Only a general strike, it was claimed, would bring both economic and political progress. One example of these, an appeal by the Vilnius group of the Russian Social Democratic Party of February 19, 1905, combined economic demands (an eight-hour workday, workers' insurance, higher wages) with political demands (freedom of speech and the press, the right to assemble and strike, the calling of a constituent assembly, amnesty for arrested workers).[122]

In late March governor Pahlen complained that agitators had organized a series of strikes in Vilnius. Government agents among the workers kept the authorities well informed concerning agitation, propaganda, and planned strikes. The continuing agitation and unrest, Pahlen wrote to the governor general, demanded the introduction of a state of "heightened security" (*usilennaia okhrana*) in the city, which governor general Freze recommended from April 1.[123] In February and March strikes occurred at forty-six factories in Vilnius province, most of which were in the city of Vilnius.[124] Throughout spring and summer strikes continued unabated; May 1 was celebrated with demonstrations and widespread strikes.[125]

Sporadic strikes continued through the summer, but only in autumn did real revolution come to Vilnius. The events of October 1905 nearly brought about the collapse of the Russian Empire. Beginning in Moscow in late September, strikes in the center of Russia mushroomed into a massive general strike that paralyzed the country, including Vilnius.[126] For a moment, it appeared that the entire edifice of tsarism might crumble. The desperate situation compelled Tsar Nicholas II—much against his will—to issue a short manifesto promising basic civil rights, a loosening of legal restrictions based on nationality, and the convening of an elected legislature, the Duma. This document, issued reluctantly by the tsar (he never forgave his advisor Sergei Witte, who urged him to do so) has gone down in history as the October Manifesto.[127]

In Vilnius, too, October was marked by strikes, demonstrations, and police violence.[128] A strike of railroad workers expanded into a general strike, demonstrations were fired upon by the police, and the ensuing funerals were then transformed into even greater anti-government protests. Workers' strikes were augmented by strikes in Vilnius' schools and in the post and telegraph offices. In short, during October no inhabitant in the city could feel sheltered from the revolutionary events.[129] The strike in Vilnius was led in particular by the railroad workers who, as we have seen, had begun striking already in late September in Moscow. The decision by railroad workers to lead a general strike throughout the empire was reached on October 10 and the actual strike began two days later. One worker, Mariia Vasilevskaia-Zhebrovskaia, recalled that when she received a telegram from Moscow saying "October 10 Nina departs," this meant that the strike would start on that day.[130]

On the 14th (o.s.) a front page article in *Vilniaus Žinios* described the effects of the strike on Vilnius, noting that newspapers from Moscow were not reaching the city and that local railroad workers were also staying away from their jobs. The issue for October 14, 1905 (no. 249) was to be the last one for ten days. On the front page of the October 25 issue (no. 250) the editor explained that the reason for the nonappearance of the newspaper during the intervening days was the general strike in Vilnius. The announcement noted that the general strike had not yet entirely died down, but that the workers in "our print shop" had begun to return to work.[131] In the interim Vilnius had witnessed the largest public demonstrations of the year as well as the greatest violence.

The Lithuanian socialist Kipras Bielinis also recalled that it was the railroad workers in Vilnius who started the general strike on October 14. Many other workers, including postal and telegraph employees, soon joined the strike.[132] On October 16 the railroad workers even met with Governor General Pahlen, asking him to remove troops from nearby Kherson Street (now Jakšto). The governor general agreed to this but troops remained on the main downtown thoroughfare, St. George's Avenue.[133] As large numbers of workers attempted to push onto this street, the military shot into the crowd, killing five and injuring thirty.[134]

The violence of October 16 galvanized outrage in Vilnius against the government. On October 17 the funerals of the demonstrators who had been killed became mass anti-government rallies. In the words of the Vilnius chief of security (*okhrana*), these rallies featured "deputations of anti-government organizations with signs bearing extremely criminal slogans."[135] Workers and professionals came together three days later at a meeting that condemned the government for its role in the events of October 16. The gathering resulted in the following demands of the government: the total withdrawal of Cossacks and the military from the town; the establishment of an independent commission to investigate the events; and an official denial of rumors that martial law was to be introduced in Vilnius.[136] Unfortunately (though unsurprisingly), the government ignored these demands, and the day after this resolution another bloody clash took place between demonstrators and the military, this time leaving seven dead and twenty wounded. The erstwhile government paper *Severo-Zapadnoe slovo*, now exhibiting considerable independence, published a list of twenty-three individuals who had been wounded in the two clashes, the great majority of them apparently (judging from names) Jews.[137]

Not only workers but even schoolboys joined the anti-government demonstrations. On October 22 the upper classes of the Vilnius *real'noe uchilishche* (practical high school) issued a resolution calling for reforms in schools. For example, they demanded the following: an end to obligatory church attendance; the right to pray in one's native language; an end to "spying and searches"; the acceptance of practical high school graduates into universities; and an end to the *numerus clausus* that restricted access to higher education for Jews.[138] Even before this resolution many pupils had gone on strike to demand civil and national rights in the secondary schools of Vilnius. The revolutionary parties actively spread propaganda among these secondary school students, calling on them to expand their demands beyond school reform to general political revolution.[139] These strikes began to end only in November and December, after St. Petersburg had conceded the right of pupils to be taught in Polish and Lithuanian.[140]

The famous "October Manifesto" of October 17, 1905 (o.s.) did not significantly calm the situation in Vilnius. Bielinis speaks of the "days of freedom" from the day the manifesto was issued until approximately December 7/20. During these six weeks socialist parties organized freely in Vilnius, publishing newspapers without censorship, and openly called—as in a Lithuanian SD proclamation of November 6, 1905—for an armed insurrection against the tsarist government.[141] A conservative Polish commentator noted that "Vilnius stormily celebrated the announcement of the constitution." The next ten days, he continued, were marked by repeated clashes between the public (in particular he mentions "Jewish self-defense forces") and government troops. Meanwhile, the only Polish newspaper in the city, *Kurier Litewski*, began republishing (after a week of strikes) on October 23 without censorship, declaring "Niech żyje wolne słowo polskie na Litwie." (Long live Polish freedom of speech ["the free Polish word"] in Lithuania!)[142] The freedoms promised in the October Manifesto also allowed the first mass meeting of Lithuanian patriots, which took place in the city during November (of which more below). The government appeared to have lost control in the city.

However, appearances were deceptive. To start with, middle- and upper-class inhabitants were becoming weary of revolutionary proclamations, disruptions, and bloodshed.[143] Already in July the liberal-conservative *Kraj* (published in St. Petersburg in Polish) had complained of the "bloody slogans" (and deeds) of the revolutionaries in Łódź, and it seems likely that such sentiments were widespread among its educated and privileged readership.[144] The promise of an elected legislature, even though details were yet to be worked out, seemed to many a reasonable step toward a more liberal order in Russia. And the anti-religious and anti-bourgeois rhetoric of the revolutionary parties made it appear that a reformed Russia might very likely be more consonant with their interests than a revolutionary one.

In the end, however, the event that effectively ended the "days of freedom," like the railway workers' strike that forced the government to issue the October Manifesto, began not in Vilnius but in Moscow. On December 7 workers there began a general strike that soon turned into an armed uprising. The workers had overestimated their strength; government forces bloodily crushed the uprising first in Moscow, then throughout the empire. By the end of December 1905, while acts of violence continued, the government had regained the upper hand.[145] Events followed a similar pattern in Vilnius. Major strikes began on December 11. Two days later there were large demonstrations, and a crowd of some three thousand was dispersed on Pylimo Street by armed government troops. A general strike continued to December 17, once again preventing the publication of *Vilniaus Žinios* (which failed to appeared from December 12 to 17). On December 20 the newspaper could report that the general strike was over, without bloodshed ("Kraujo praliejimo nebuvo").[146]

While Vilnius certainly never experienced bloodshed on the scale reached in Moscow, on December 13 troops did open fire on protesting crowds and disperse them.[147] During these days the rather frenzied dissemination of propaganda flyers by the socialists (Bund, PPS, and Russian SD) suggests that these groups foresaw their own failure.[148] By the end of the month life appeared to be returning to normal in Vilnius. The main articles on the front page of *Vilniaus Žinios* for the last two days of 1905 bore the headlines "The Suppression/Calming of Revolts" and "How Calm Was Restored in Lithuania." Calm may have been restored, but despite subsequent repressions, life did not return to pre-1905 normalcy.

## Claiming the City: The Lithuanians

Up to now, a certain cultural-ethnic group has been largely missing from our story: the Lithuanians. The reason is simple: during this period (not just the nineteenth century but reaching back to the Reformation or so), few ethnic Lithuanians were living in Vilnius and their language was seldom heard in the city. While Lithuanians lived nearby in the countryside, their language was mainly considered a peasant tongue by Vilnius residents, and indeed, the Russian government itself considered the written language so weakly established that they attempted to force a new alphabet onto the Lithuanians. By the late nineteenth century, however, Lithuanian efforts to reestablish their culture in written form and to organize as an ethnic-cultural group were successful enough to draw the (mainly negative) attention of the Poles. From 1905 onward, the Lithuanian presence in Vilnius, while still numerically weak, grew in strength and self-confidence.

The Lithuanian national movement came to maturity in the generations after 1863. Among the milestones of that movement were the periodicals *Auszra*

THE PERIOD OF RUSSIFICATION, 1863-1914   89

(Dawn) and *Varpas* (The Bell), which began to be published in the 1880s. At the same time, more and more books were printed in Lithuanian—in East Prussia, outside the Russian Empire—and smuggled across the border. This period in the Lithuanian national movement became known as the "book carriers' time" and by the early 1900s, even Russian officials recognized the failure of the prohibition on books published in the Lithuanian language using Latin letters. Thus by the eve of 1905, a fully fledged Lithuanian national movement was in place, to the considerable consternation of most local Poles.[149]

The modern Lithuanian revival was in part (but only in part) a reaction to Russian efforts to force Lithuanians to accept the Cyrillic alphabet for their language. Probably, however, the generous treatment of ethnic Lithuanians in the serf emancipation of the post-1863 period was even more important. The emancipation, aimed at punishing Polish nobles, had the unintended effect of creating a new class of relatively well-off peasants whose sons, often as Catholic priests, would become both producers and consumers of the new Lithuanian-language written culture. Churches were often the flashpoints of the new Lithuanian self-assurance. When older priests (often themselves of ethnic Lithuanian stock) used Polish, they would be challenged by a younger generation that wanted hymns, prayers, and homilies in Lithuanian (the actual mass was, of course, in Latin).[150] Perhaps ironically, despite the failure of Russian policy to divide Lithuanians from Poles through imposing the Cyrillic alphabet, the Lithuanian national movement tended to be anti-Polish.[151] Poles, for their part, generally viewed Lithuanian culture and national pretensions with scorn and accused Lithuanian nationalists of collaborating with the Russian authorities to gain their ends (an accusation not entirely untrue). Polish-Lithuanian frictions were heightened by the struggle—before World War I in verbal form—over the city. By the early twentieth century, the Lithuanian national movement was poised to express its claims on the city it viewed as the eternal capital of the Lithuanian nation: Vilnius.[152]

As we have seen, the actual numbers of Lithuanians in Vilnius were rather small, a bit over three thousand, or 2.1 percent of the total population in 1897. To be sure, the definition of "Lithuanian" was not always clear at this point, and some ethnic Lithuanians in Vilnius may well have preferred to identify with the Polish educated/upper class.[153] Even while agreeing that this statistic seriously understates the real numbers of Lithuanians, no one can (or did) claim that Vilnius at the turn of the century was demographically a Lithuanian city. Rather, the city's history and centrality for Lithuanian culture were emphasized. It was a matter of great pride for the Lithuanians that the first non-Russian newspaper published in the city after the 1860s (in late December 1904) was *Vilniaus Žinios*, though Polish and Yiddish periodicals rapidly followed it.[154]

Without a doubt, the most important event in 1905 for the Lithuanian national movement was the "Great Seimas" held in Vilnius late in that year.[155] The gathering had been inspired and organized in great part by the energetic and cantankerous Dr. Jonas Basanavičius, one of the fathers of Lithuanian nationalism. Basanavičius, a writer and ethnographer, returned in summer 1905 to Vilnius after nearly a quarter century abroad.[156] On November 11, 1905 *Vilnius Žinios* published Basanavičius's call for a gathering in Vilnius to discuss national demands of the Lithuanian people.[157]

This assembly convened on December 4, 1905 at the Vilnius town hall (*miesto salė*), a grand and recently completed (1902) building that now houses the philharmony. As was expected, the Lithuanian social democrats refused to take part in this bourgeois affair of middle-class notables and priests, though in the end some socialists did, in fact, take part in the discussions.[158] In the end the assembly reached important decisions on Lithuanian autonomy, schools, and the church. These decisions were published in *Vilniaus Žinios* on 7 December.[159]

Despite some revolutionary rhetoric ("a happier life can be had only by winning the struggle against the old order"), the actual demands were rather more cautious. All Lithuanians should work together, regardless of class or party affiliation, to achieve autonomy within a new, reformed federal Russia. In order to bring this autonomy about, Lithuanians in Kaunas, Vilnius, and Gardinas (Grodno) provinces should refuse to serve in the army, keep their children from attending school, and withhold all taxes from the government. "Purely national" schools should replace the present ones, and all inhabitants should be taught in their "native tongue" (understood in the context to be Lithuanian but never stated). Even more controversially, "since in Lithuanian churches of the Vilnius bishopric the Polish language is used in prayers for political purposes" the assembly wished all "fighting Lithuanians" success against the polonizing priests and called for the use of Lithuanian in these churches.[160] Economics or relations with the Jews were not mentioned. Despite limiting their demands to autonomy within Russia, the Lithuanian patriots hereby set themselves up against both the Russian government (as it was presently constituted) and the existing Polish-dominated hierarchy of the Catholic Church in the region.

While the Great Seimas was in itself of crucial importance for the Lithuanian national movement, perhaps even more important was the publication of its resolutions in *Vilniaus Žinios*. Here we see the interplay between political action and the press. In a sense the newspaper itself was part of the "action"—Vileišis was certainly no passive observer of the Seimas. By spreading the word of the Seimas's meeting, deliberations, and resolutions, *Vilniaus Žinios* was not only providing information: it was also demonstrating to Lithuanian speakers that their language and culture deserved the same rights and respects as all others.

After the revolutionary year Lithuanian culture, despite government repressions, continued to develop in Vilnius. Many reforms of 1905—including a less strict censorship law—were not rescinded. The press continued to expand, despite government fines and arrests. In her important bibliographical work on Vilnius Lithuanian periodicals, Jadvyga Kazlauskaitė counts nearly fifty journals and newspapers published in the city in the decade from 1905 to the first year of World War I.[161] To be sure, many of these had very small circulations and were of short duration. The periodicals even included legal socialist organs in Lithuanian, such as *Naujoji gaudynė*, *Skardas*, and *Žarija*, though these were rapidly all shut down by 1908.[162] In 1914 a dozen Lithuanian periodicals appeared in the city, ranging from literary monthlies to two daily papers, *Viltis* and *Lietuvos Žinios*.[163]

Periodical publishing—especially for dailies—had changed radically compared to the pre-1905 situation. Now newspapers could publish without preliminary censorship, but they could then be taken to court by the government for any article deemed inappropriate. Not infrequently the government would place an "arrest" on an issue of a journal or newspaper, confiscating all copies still to be found and pressing charges against the editor.[164] While sometimes newspapers were shut down out of hand—such had been the case with the socialist titles mentioned above—in general the government took a different tack, relying more on the fear of the financial consequences of confiscations. Not government interference but market forces and bad administration presented the main threat to Lithuanian periodicals (and those in other languages) in Vilnius.[165]

Even Petras Vileišis's *Vilniaus Žinios* was unable to make ends meet. In 1909, faced with mounting debts, Vileišis was forced to shut down the daily.[166] Only months later, however, his brother Jonas opened another newspaper in Vilnius, *Lietuvos Žinios*, its title not only harking back to the first Lithuanian-language daily in the empire but also openly declaring that this was a newspaper for all of Lithuania. A year later another Lithuanian-language daily, *Viltis* (Hope), opened in Vilnius. Both periodicals would continue publication until the autumn of 1915, when the German army occupied Vilnius.

Lithuanian civil society expanded significantly in the decade between 1905 and the German occupation. Despite sparse funding and a not entirely benevolent government, dozens of periodicals, clubs, and Lithuanian organizations were set up. Schools were organized, along with lectures and courses to teach basic literacy. Parallel with the development of periodicals, Lithuanian literature grew. Poems, songs (*dainos*), stories, and even novels and plays appeared.[167] The establishment of a Lithuanian bookstore by Marija and Jurgis Šlapelis, like the staging of Lithuanian plays and exhibitions of Lithuanian art, served to "legitimize" Lithuanian culture in the city's urban space.[168]

By the eve of the First World War, Lithuanian civil society was growing in Vilnius—and elsewhere—despite all obstacles. While many Lithuanians, no doubt, continued to identify themselves more with village and religion than with nationality, this was changing—in significant part because of the activities of Vilnius-based Lithuanian organizations, publishing, and cultural activities.

## Vilnius on the Eve

The years between the suppression of the 1905 Revolution and the outbreak of World War I witnessed a remarkable flourishing of the city. As we have seen, Lithuanian culture in the city expanded rapidly after 1905 and the more established Jewish and Polish cultures similarly launched new newspapers, periodicals, and voluntary associations. The growing visibility and (at least potential) strength of Lithuanian culture exacerbated relations between Poles and Lithuanians, but for the moment these tensions remained confined mainly to print polemics. At the same time, all inhabitants of the city—regardless of nationality or native tongue—were affected by the development of the city's infrastructure and campaigns for elections to the Duma. Vilnius was becoming a modern city, with a growing educated class, modernizing infrastructure, and increasing political awareness. Election campaigns and growing political sophistication tended to increase national consciousness, but at the same time local efforts also helped create a local (rather than national-cultural) identity bridging the city's cultural gaps. The most important of these efforts is associated with the *krajowcy* (from Polish *kraj*: "land," "country"). In short, in summer 1914 one could be optimistic about the future of a modern and multicultural Vilnius/Wilno/Vilna.

Vilnius, like most cities in the Russian Empire after the Great Reforms, had a city government elected on a narrow franchise. After 1905 the city Duma showed a new activism in tackling issues of city planning, economy, and infrastructure. After the revolution had been suppressed, the Duma generally met every two weeks and concerned itself with matters of hygiene, road building, transportation, sanitation, and trade (within the city).[169] As the city grew, the need for efficient public transport became more apparent. Thus in early June 1907 the city government discussed bringing an electric tramway to Vilnius; in the end, however, the horse-drawn tram remained, barely challenged by a dozen or so automobiles (sixteen registered in 1913) and around one thousand bicycles.[170] For water, most residents still relied on public wells, though from the 1890s modernization of water supply and sewers had been taking place. Still, only a few downtown streets were served by water pipes (and sewers) and even there, most house owners preferred to avoid the expense of a water-sewer connection.[171] As an energetic city official could point out in 1913, very much remained to be done to assure modern conveniences in the city.[172]

As in city infrastructure, in politics much of the old remained. The main novelty of the post-1905 period were elections to the State Duma. The details of these elections are less interesting than the fact that political mobilization tended to solidify and enhance national-cultural identity. To put it another way, politics made ethnicity matter more. On the other hand, the restricted suffrage from 1907 and obvious weakness of the Duma itself limited interest in legal politics. Still, a number of parties and groupings existed, each of which mainly appealed to (certain elements within) a certain national-culture group.

In Vilnius, political organizations existed primarily among Poles and Jews, mainly because of their numerical predominance in the city. Certainly Lithuanians claimed the city, but they tended to see politics in an "all-Lithuanian" manner and considered their main representatives to be four ethnic Lithuanians, none of whom was elected from Vilnius province.[173] To simplify hugely, among Jews the two strongest trends were Zionist and Bundist, with the more traditional—as well as the more acculturated—elements of Vilnius Jewry disdaining both. Acculturated Russian-speaking Jews, in Vilnius as elsewhere, tended to support the liberal Kadet party. In the disappointments and repressions of post-1905, many Jews simply turned their backs on the political institutions of the time.[174]

Among Poles various political parties and groupings developed in the Duma period. Traditional conservatives—a group that Darius Szpoper has dubbed "the successors of the Grand Duchy [of Lithuania]"—were prominent.[175] The Catholic bishop of Wilno, Edward Ropp, was elected to the First Duma in 1905 and hoped that his "Constitutional Catholic Party" and political work among Vilnius workers would prevent the spread of radicalism. Unfortunately for Ropp, the Russian authorities regarded him—quite unfairly—as an arch-Polish nationalist and had him exiled from Vilnius in 1907; with him the prospect of a modern political Catholicism in the region also disappeared.[176] Given the narrow franchise and limited power of elected organs, whether local or imperial, it is not remarkable that Polish politics here remained on the whole embryonic or traditional-conservative.[177]

In the almost-decade from 1905, Polish culture once again flourished. Numerous newspapers and journals vied for the Polish public's attention; among the dailies were *Przegląd Wileński, Gazeta Wileńska*, and *Kurier Litewski*.[178] A prominent journalist and political figure of the time, Czesław Jankowski, served as editor of the latter in 1906–1907 and vividly described the financial, political, and personal frictions of those years in his polemical memoir.[179] Cultural organizations such as the "Lovers of Antiquity" and the "Museum of Science and Art" also appealed mainly to middle- and upper-class Poles in Vilnius.[180] Polish theater—moribund since 1864—also developed rapidly.[181] Efforts were made to set up a proper monument to the local boy and national poet Adam Mickiewicz, though these (even in the interwar, as we will see) did not come to fruition.[182] And in these years cinema, already present in the city before 1905, grew in popularity. Not only could residents choose from a half-dozen movie houses by 1914, but several films—entertainment as well as documentaries—were produced in the city, apparently mainly by Poles, before the war.[183]

With lighter censorship and a larger literate public sphere in various languages, the cultural variety of Vilnius was far more evident than before 1905. Newspapers and journals appeared not only in Polish but also in Yiddish, Russian, Belarusian, and Lithuanian.[184] In part, no doubt, the growing visibility and assertiveness of non-Polish cultures contributed to increased Polish chauvinism, in particular toward Jews, during these years.[185] But in Vilnius relations between Poles and Jews did not change significantly during these years; the main potential threat to Polish culture here was seen in Lithuanian claims to the city and the region. Catholic churches in mixed Polish Lithuanian parishes witnessed fistfights and conflicts over the language of hymns, prayers, and homilies. In Vilnius itself the Polish domination of the Catholic Church was nearly total; only one church (St. Nicholas) in the city used Lithuanian exclusively.[186] Despite the advances of Lithuanian culture in the city and in general, the "threat" to Polish cultural hegemony in Vilnius was of a long-term nature, not an immediate one. Still, polemics between Poles and Lithuanians became increasingly bitter and the dogged Lithuanian position that Vilnius was and must be their capital city augured ill for the future.[187]

After 1905, Poles in Vilnius recognized the growing strength of other cultural-national movements, in particular those of Lithuanians and Jews. Chauvinism and antisemitism was one response to this development, but another more humane approach was that espoused by the so-called *krajowcy*. This movement, espousing a regional rather than ethnic-cultural identity, arose in Vilnius in the post-1905 years. Among its most important thinkers were Tadeusz Wróblewski, Mykolas Römeris, Roman Skirmunt, and his cousin Konstancja Skirmuntt. The krajowcy had a vision of a multicultural, peaceful Litwa (Lithuania, but defined by geography and history) in which all cultural-national groups—Belarusians, Poles, Lithuanians, Jews, Tatars, Karaites—would live together in harmony and mutual respect. The attractiveness of this vision is obvious, but the practical difficulty of transforming the ideal into reality should not be underestimated.[188]

The fate of the krajowcy is reflected in the biography of Mykolas Römeris, born into Polish culture but after World War I, despite desperate attempts to reconcile Poles and Lithuanians, forced by circumstances to choose between the two cultures. Römer, unlike most Polish-speaking intellectuals, chose Lithuanian. The krajowcy deserve more attention from historians because their ideal of a multilingual, multicultural Vilnius and Lithuania provides a refreshing alternative to the chauvinistic and murderous "solutions" of the twentieth century. Even at the time, however, the krajowcy were of marginal political importance and their proposals, if noticed at all, were generally dismissed or scorned. Perhaps if not for the First World War and the intense heightening of nationalism that it brought, the krajowcy's ideal could have been realized. Events of the twentieth century cast doubt, however, on that possibility.[189]

CHAPTER 4

# World War I, 1914–1922

THE WAR DECLARATIONS OF late July to early August 1914 put an abrupt and unexpected end to an era. For an entire century, since the end of the Napoleonic Wars, European power and wealth had increased exponentially. Wars on the European continent during those four generations were relatively short in duration and peripheral in significance. The few exceptions to the latter generalization (e.g., the Crimean War and the Franco-Prussian War) are remembered more for their indirect consequences (the Great Reforms in Russia and the unification of Germany) than for their military significance. Now Europe was faced with a conflict that, like the Napoleonic Wars more than a century earlier, would change the political landscape of Europe and, indirectly, the world.

The war that began in late July 1914 was utterly different from the conflicts of the past century. In this war the technological, financial, logistical, and cultural achievements of the long nineteenth century were employed to mobilize, energize, and slaughter unprecedented numbers of human beings. Very rapidly military and political developments revealed the inability of the Russian Empire to deal with the kind of mass mobilization of resources demanded by merciless modern war. After an initial foray into East Prussia, Russian forces were beaten back and from August 1914 onward the Russian army would never again threaten German territory.[1]

Had it not been for the overwhelming demands the Western Front placed on the German army, it seems likely that the Russian Empire would have collapsed far earlier than in March 1917.[2] As it was, the Russian forces could not withstand the organizational and technological superiority of the German troops. A new offensive in summer 1915 forced the Russians to relinquish Warsaw in July and Kaunas at the end of August. Vilnius was next in line and was taken on the eve of Yom Kippur, or September 18, 1915.[3]

The German occupation lasted over three years. While the German authorities were, of course, far less predatory than their successors in the Second World War, policy was nonetheless geared mainly toward exploiting the local area in order to provision the troops. This unwise (and inefficient) policy alienated all inhabitants of Vilnius, regardless of nationality. At the same time, both Poles and Lithuanians were working behind the scenes to assure a favorable postwar situation that included rule over the city.

Traditionally the end of the war is clearly marked: the eleventh hour of the eleventh day of the eleventh month in 1918. For Vilnius this demarcation makes no sense. November 1918 changed little for the city except to usher in a period of even greater chaos and suffering. Over the next two years the city would change hands a half-dozen times between Red Army and the Polish and Lithuanian forces. Finally the Polish general Lucjan Żeligowski took the city in October 1920 and put an end to this chaotic period, but the Polish occupation faced strong protests from the Lithuanians. After a (flawed) plebiscite showing overwhelming support for Polish sovereignty over Vilnius, the city was officially incorporated into Poland in March 1922. The failure of the Polish and Lithuanian governments to find a compromise over Vilnius led to a complete breakdown of diplomatic relations, a rift that would last until 1938. In Vilnius, as elsewhere, the outcomes of World War I in many ways set the stage for the tragedies of World War II.

## The War's First Year: August 1914 to September 1915

Perhaps the most remarkable characteristic about the historiography of World War I in this region is the general lack of interest that historians have shown in the conflict as it played out "in the East." For the national states that emerged after 1918, the war is relegated to a kind of antechamber to independence. In the USSR, World War I was treated primarily as one main cause for the revolution of October 1917; even in the post-1992 years the conflict has not become central in Russian historical research.[4] Specifically for Vilnius, there is a striking dearth of information, whether in primary sources or in the historiography, about the first year of the war. Several books analyze German policy in the city and its region but even general accounts leap from August 1914 (the war's outbreak) to 1915 (the taking of Kaunas).[5] Published memoirs, such as that of the future Lithuanian foreign minister Petras Klimas, also tend to start in late 1914 or even in summer 1915.[6] The somewhat scanty coverage of the period 1914–1915 here reflects the relative lack of sources.

The "war enthusiasm" shown elsewhere in Europe (though the extent of this phenomenon has been challenged in recent years) also appeared in Russia, though much less so in Vilnius.[7] Poles and Jews had little reason to be enthusiastic for an empire that treated them, at best, as second-class citizens, and the Russian population of Vilnius was overwhelmingly made up of officials and soldiers. Patriotic Poles hoped that the war would weaken the empire and thereby make a rebirth of an independent Poland possible. The few politically thinking Lithuanians in Vilnius also harbored hopes for more cultural autonomy at war's end, and Jews for the most part simply tried to keep their heads down and earn a living (although this became increasingly difficult once the war interfered with commercial ties).

At the beginning of the war, both Poles and Lithuanians hastened to declare their loyalty to the tsar and their support in the conflict, but it was clear that if the war should go badly, their support might easily switch to the other side.[8] Like Poles in Warsaw and other cities, Vilnius Poles had to consider which side had more to offer them. In his diary Stanisław Cywiński noted that in November and December 1914 "russophilism" (*rusofilstwo*) was still quite prominent among Poles in the city.[9] Writing after the war, Polish activist and writer Wanda Dobaczewska agreed that Poles had expressed support for the Russian war effort early in the war, but she added that in Vilnius pro-Russian enthusiasm never reached the heights seen in Warsaw: "In Wilno no one ever threw flowers at Cossacks."[10]

The largest ethnic group in Vilnius (at war's outset), the Jews, saw little possibility of any good coming from the war, and Jewish anti-Russian feeling was considerably stimulated by the brutal treatment of Jewish civilians by the Russian military authorities.[11] A sympathetic (though not particularly judeophilic) Polish observer wrote in August 1915 that "the nonpoliticized Jewish masses instinctively favored the Germans and in their souls warmly desired Russian defeats. This was more than Germanophilism: this was an idealization of the Germans."[12] The brutal deportations of Jews carried out by the Russian military could only strengthen Jewish loathing for the tsarist regime.[13]

Polish journalist Czesław Jankowski's diary remarks on early Polish support for the Russian war effort. Noting the battles over Warsaw in November 1914 and the city's fall to the Germans in early August 1915, Jankowski speaks of orders to carry out obligatory (though paid) labor to strengthen Vilnius' defenses in July 1915. He also recalls requisitioned livestock being driven through town.[14] After the German army entered Kaunas—barely one hundred kilometers from Vilnius—on August 18, 1915 it was clear that Vilnius was next in line. Evacuations of banks, government offices, and even the monuments to Empress Catherine the Great and Governor-General Count M. N. Muraviev were set in motion.[15]

By August 1915 it was clear that the Russians' days in Vilnius were numbered. On August 15 an 11 p.m. curfew was announced that was to begin on August 18. After this curfew all streetlights would be turned out, all windows had to be covered with black paper (to block out interior light), and no one was permitted on the street. All able-bodied men from eighteen to fifty years of age still resident in the city were required to report to local police stations to be organized into work battalions to dig defense trenches around the city.[16] Perhaps in an unconscious admission that they could not themselves keep order, in that month the Russians allowed a volunteer city police force, or militia, to be organized.

One Jewish militia member, the teacher and writer Hirsz Abramowicz, recalled that, by joining the militia, men hoped to protect themselves and their families from deportations into Russia. As Abramowicz recalled, most members of the militia were Polish, but a few were Jews. Their duties were to regulate traffic and in general to maintain public order.[17] By early September, the city was full of rumors of impending deportation, aerial bombing, and worse. Many fled the city as the Russian troops withdrew and the Germans approached, fearing reprisals and brutality from the Russians now that their military defeat seemed assured. German bombs were dropped on the city, newspapers ceased to appear, and daily life was heavily disrupted. On September 15 one eyewitness wrote, "Vilnius is already becoming cut off from the world." On September 18 the retreating Russians attempted to blow up the bridges over the Neris River, but in their haste they only succeeded in damaging them. The same day the Germans entered the city.[18]

## The First Months of German Occupation

When the Russians left Vilnius, very few residents regretted their departure. Under the Germans, it was felt, life would at least be more orderly and predictable. Patriotic Poles and Lithuanians also hoped that the German occupation would be a first step toward independence or at least autonomy. In any case, the arrival of German troops was seen—at first—as a liberation.[19] Jews, meanwhile, tended to see Germans as more civilized than Russians and hoped for better treatment than under the tsarist regime.

On Saturday, September 18, German troops began to stream into the city across the damaged but still intact Green Bridge. Czesław Jankowski noted in his diary, "After a month's siege, the Germans forced the Russians to withdraw to the east and took Vilnius—without a shot." Jankowski also remarked on the apparent lack of major damage to any structures in the city and noted that despite the numerous explosions heard in the night, both the railroad station and the gasworks remained intact. By noon a declaration in five languages (Polish, Belarusian, German, Lithuanian, Yiddish) announcing the German occupation of Vilnius was being plastered along the city's streets.[20]

The proclamation, signed by Graf Pfeil, began by announcing that "German forces have expelled the Russian army from the Polish city Wilno," noting that the city was "always a pearl in the glorious Kingdom of Poland." No other national group aside from Poles was mentioned here; the proclamation left the impression that the city and its surroundings were populated exclusively by Poles. As one might expect, Graf Pfeil also warned against any attacks on German soldiers but did this, so to speak, apologetically, adding, "I do not wish to carry out any punitive measures [*Strafgewalt*] in Wilno. God bless Poland!"[21] Abramowicz notes tartly that, despite the generous words (for Poles, anyway) in Pfeil's proclamation, "This Prussian 'freedom' endured for barely an hour," after which this proclamation was taken down and replaced by far stricter ones.[22]

Abramowicz's "hour" may be a figure of speech, but the tenor of German proclamations did change quickly, and for the worse. On September 21 residents of Vilnius were informed that any messenger pigeons (*Brieftauben*) had to be killed within two days; residents were also admonished that "it is forbidden for women to sell themselves to German soldiers." In response local wags wondered aloud whether this was a suggestion that female Vilnans should offer themselves for free.[23] Further restrictions followed, from obligatory muzzles on dogs (loose animals would be "caught and killed") and a hefty thirty-mark fee (in cities) for obligatory registration, to a prohibition of street trade in food and drink, to restrictions on public gatherings.[24] In short, it was clear that life under German occupation was to be more orderly, but possibly no less trying, than the previous year under Russian rule.

As Graf Pfeil's initial pro-Polish proclamation had shown, the Germans were vitally interested in using nationalist feelings among the local population to their own advantage. General Erich von Ludendorff's assessment of the nationality situation in the region reflects German priorities: "The Lithuanians believed the hour of deliverance was at hand, and when the good times they anticipated did not materialize, owing to the cruel exigencies of war, they became suspicious once more, and turned against us. The Poles were hostile, as they feared, quite justifiably, a pro-Lithuanian policy on our part. The White Ruthenians [i.e., Belarusians] were of no account, as the Poles had robbed them of their nationality and given nothing in return. . . . The Jew did not know what attitude to adopt, but he gave us no trouble, and we were at least able to converse with him, which was hardly ever possible with the Poles, Lithuanians, and Letts."[25]

The Polish attitude toward the Germans was not, at least initially, so negative as Ludendorff indicated in his memoirs.[26] Fundamentally, however, Polish and German interests did not coincide. The Poles mainly wished to incorporate the Vilnius region into an independent Poland while the German occupying authorities concentrated on more immediate considerations: waging a war, feeding and supplying soldiers, and maintaining public order. A report by a certain von Beckerath to Hindenburg of May 1916 indicated that while some Poles were dissatisfied with German policies, on the whole the German occupying authorities had to take the Poles into consideration as they made up the "relative majority" in Vilnius and its region.[27] Von Beckerath may have been trying to put a good face on the situation. Writing at the end of September 1915, Czesław Jankowski noted down in his diary some of the main reasons for increasingly strained relations between Poles and the German occupiers: the quartering of officers and soldiers in Polish homes, the indiscriminate and outrageous thievery of German soldiers (sometimes under the guise of requisitions "compensated" by worthless scraps of paper), and the ignoring of the "citizens' committee" set up by (mainly) Poles to help administer the city.[28] Complaints of this sort would only increase in the subsequent years of German occupation.

Even Jankowski, who as a sympathizer with the National Democrats could hardly be suspected of pro-Jewish sentiments, noted that "At the present time [September 29, 1915] the most irritated and embittered are the Jews. For example, when Jews petitioned to the city commander von Treskow against an order that they keep stores open on the sabbath, the commander rejected their petition, remarking that he had not had a Sunday off for a year: "This is war, gentlemen!"[29] The German authorities were not so much antisemitic as simply inflexible and intolerant of Jewish religious requirements. For example, the Germans required that all corpses be buried enclosed in a coffin (which of course violates Jewish religious law). The Germans restricted trade, which had been nearly a Jewish monopoly in the region, requiring that grain, fruit, nuts, and even fish be sold (for very low prices) to the occupying authorities. In such a situation, with hunger and even starvation a real and growing possibility, the inevitable consequence was a thriving black market in which Jews as experienced merchants and traders played an important role. Despite increasingly draconian threats and punishments, the Germans were unable to control the market (or to feed both the army and the local population) and succeeded mainly in antagonizing the local Jews. But, as Hirsz Abramowicz noted in his memoirs of that period, "The German occupation during World War I oppressed everyone more or less equally." Jews were not singled out for special restrictions and in some cases survived better under German occupation than did Polish townspeople, in particular because of the similarity between Yiddish and German.[30]

Nor were Lithuanians particularly happy about the German occupation. To begin with, there was Graf Pfeil's provocative description of Vilnius as a Polish city. Then, as we have seen in the von Backerath memorandum, the Germans did not appear to take the Lithuanian national movement very seriously, quite aside from the Vilnius question. A protest signed by leaders of the Lithuanian national movement on the occasion of a German census of Vilnius argued that since their arrival in the city the Germans had "further encouraged aggressive Polish policies."[31] A year later, in summer 1917, the prominent Lithuanian leader Dr. Jonas Basanavičius penned a pamphlet in which he documented the sufferings of Lithuanians under German occupation, from peasants having their land and produce confiscated to the spread of disease occasioned by chronic hunger and germs introduced by German soldiers to attempts to "germanize" Vilnius by putting up German language signs in the city.[32] In short, at least as early as 1916 the Lithuanians were just as unhappy with the German occupation as their Polish and Jewish neighbors were.

In great part the dissatisfaction stemmed from the terrible economic situation. The disruptions of trade caused by war, combined with the German army's enormous requirements for foodstuffs, meant that hunger threatened the general population as early as 1916 (and only got worse after that point). Already in July 1915, two months before Vilnius had been occupied, the Germans ordered all grain crops confiscated and established strict price controls. This order was extended to the Lithuanian territories and Vilnius with the advance of the German armies.[33] It was decreed that local merchants were obliged to accept both German and Russian currencies (at the exchange rate—favorable to the Germans—of first 1.5 marks to a ruble and later 2.0 marks to the ruble).[34] A new "Ostrubel" was also introduced in an effort to prop up the money supply, but locals with anything to sell (usually illegally, as the Germans had forbidden or strictly regulated nearly all trade) were increasingly unwilling to accept the German script. Requisitions of grain, fruit, meat, horses (for haulage), potatoes, and essentially any other food items were frequent, onerous, and never coordinated, leading to extreme frustration bordering on despair on the part of landowners and peasants.[35] These highly restrictive policies had economic as well as political outcomes, both very negative. Economically the German attempt to seize total control over the economy meant that peasants and landowners had little initiative to produce foodstuffs; this in turn led to dire shortages in late 1916 and 1917. Politically the German restrictions alienated every national group so that by 1917 the initial (at least potentially) favorable attitudes toward the Germans—on the part of Lithuanians and Jews, and to a lesser extent Poles—had been almost totally extinguished.

In cultural policy, the Germans early on adopted a seemingly liberal line. A decree of December 1915 stated explicitly that "The language of instruction should be the mother tongue [of the pupils]." The same decree forbade the use of Russian as a language of instruction (though the language could be taught as a subject in secondary schools), and it was specifically noted that "Weißrussisch" (Belarusian) was *not* Russian and thus not subject to any restrictions. It further stated the expectation that "as soon as possible all educators [*Lehrpersonen*] will acquire a knowledge of the German language."[36] Pukszto points out that by the end of 1915 there were four Polish high schools (gymnasia), eight "partial" gymnasia (with only a four-year course), and thirty elementary schools operating in Vilnius. These Polish schools together enrolled over five thousand pupils.[37] On a practical level Jewish schools continued to operate with the main change that Russian-language schools now switched over to Yiddish or Hebrew. The Germans frowned on the use of Yiddish in schools and attempted to introduce "pure" German, but with indifferent results.[38] There was no restriction on Lithuanian-language schools in Vilnius, and a "People's University" with lectures in Lithuanian was set up in the city.[39] But any gratitude the Lithuanians might have had toward the Germans was later undercut when the latter forbade the "People's University." Their unsubtle efforts to force schools to serve the German cause by propagandizing and germanizing the population further antagonized members of all nationalities.[40] Liulevicius concludes, "Ultimately, schools policies were another failure, for natives fell back on a tradition of clandestine schooling, and education became a focal point for sullen resistance."[41]

Another German policy that angered and alienated the local population was their demand for labor. As a recent study has shown, thousands of Poles, Lithuanians, and Jews were obliged to work for the Germans building roads, cutting trees, and performing other types of physical labor. While this work was in principle paid, like the compensation given for confiscated goods and crops, the pay was rarely adequate and the forced labor often required individuals to spend weeks or longer away from their homes. And, like most compulsory labor forces, these work battalions were on the whole of questionable utility to the German work effort.[42]

## War Fatigue and German Kulturarbeit, 1916–1917

By the end of 1915 few inhabitants of Vilnius could have entertained any illusions about the nature of the German occupation. The exigencies of the war blotted out any other considerations in the eyes of the German military occupiers, who were on the whole uninterested in restricting language use (except for teaching in Russian) and unwilling to expend resources for this purpose. The German occupiers expected local residents to behave like good Prussians: to pay taxes, surrender a good deal of their produce to feed German soldiers, and remain quiet. Given the hard conditions of life in Germany itself, one could hardly expect provisions and everyday life to be easier in occupied territories. Still, the Germans did sponsor a surprising number of cultural events, publications, concerts, and the like. We will consider these under the rubric of *Kulturarbeit*. At the same time, one should not lose sight of the fact that for most local residents cultural activities remained a luxury rather far removed from their everyday life of inadequate nourishment and uncertainty as to what the future would bring.

In 1916 the population of Vilnius was exhausted and hungry, unhappy with the German occupation and longing for peace. Conditions would only deteriorate the following year. The 1917 revolutions in Petrograd only complicated the situation. The first (in March, n.s.) appeared initially to invigorate the Russian war effort (and allowed Woodrow Wilson to bring the United States in on the Allied side), but by year's end the conflict at home knocked Russia out of the war. On the level of everyday life, however, the "sullen resistance" mentioned by Liulevicius continued with little change. In 1916 inhabitants of the German-occupied *Ober Ost* had endured compulsory labor duties; confiscation of crops and horses; new taxes on everything from dogs to matches; and prohibitions on fishing, trading in foodstuffs of any kind, and owning bicycles (which were confiscated by the Germans). In 1917 belts were further tightened with the introduction of new taxes on salt, new confiscations of horses and crops, and the German authorities' decision as of July 24, 1917 not to accept Russian rubles any longer. An indication of the widespread misery in Vilnius was the steep drop in the city's population, from over 200,000 at the beginning of the war to around 139,000 by September 1917.

Of these, 110,000 were being fed (sparsely) in the 130 public soup kitchens set up by citizens' committees in the city.[43] Help from international charities and assistance from relatives in North America were further restricted after the American entry into the war in April 1917.

Both anecdotal and statistical evidence shows that 1917 was the single worst year of the war for all Vilnius residents, regardless of nationality. Among Jews, for example, mortality in 1917 was over three times higher than in the prewar period while births plummeted to less than one-third of the 1911–1913 figures.[44] Among Polish residents mortality in the first three months of 1917 was over double the figure for 1915. A Polish report on the state of the city in spring 1917 argued that the combined effect of requisitions, forced labor, and increased taxes was "simply the annihilation of the country [zagłada kraju]."[45] The Lithuanian writer Liudas Gira's diary for February and March 1917 is full of complaints about the cold (the schools were so inadequately heated that many children did not attend) and steadily increasing prices for every kind of food.[46] The Jewish librarian and writer Khaykel Lunski probably put it best when he wrote just after the war that, while the year 1914 had been filled with the wails and moans of families as their young men were taken from them for the war effort, by 1917 no one even had the energy to whimper anymore.[47]

And yet cultural and political life, of a sort, continued during these dismal years. In 1916 the Germans published several guides to the city and sponsored exhibitions on local culture and art. Liudas Gira continued, despite badly heated classrooms, to teach classes of Lithuanian children. Several newspapers in German (*Wilnaer Zeitung* and *Zeitung der X. Armee*), Lithuanian (*Dabartis* and from autumn 1917 *Darbo Balsas*), Polish (*Dziennik Wileński*), Belarusian (*Homan*), and Yiddish (*Letste nayes*) continued to appear and even increased circulation numbers.[48]

Vilnius exerted its fascination not just on its longtime residents, Jewish poets, and Lithuanian or Polish patriots; the German occupiers too were captivated by the city. In a fascinating chapter of his book on *Ober Ost*, Vejas Liulevicius attempts to trace what he calls the "Mindscape of the East" that the Germans created during this period. The Germans produced a remarkably large body of published texts on the eastern territories they occupied, even before 1918. Liulevicius sees several factors predominating in their discourse of the "new eastern lands," including vastness/emptiness, filth, menace, *Unordnung*, and interesting but primitive peoples. According to his interpretation of these texts, the Germans saw their role in "straightening out" (both metaphorically and literally) these lands, cleaning them up, and bringing them *Kultur*.[49]

Looking more narrowly at German writings of this period that focus on Vilnius, we find precisely the same tropes and "cultural tasks." Take, for example, an impressionistic guidebook published first in serial form (in *Wilnaer Zeitung*) and then as a booklet (and already in its second edition by 1916), written by the soldier Paul Monty. The very first words of the guidebook emphasize the exotic, crooked, and disorderly nature of the city: "Crooked and confusing the streets and alleys wind 'round, one's eye seeks in vain straight lines that would somehow reveal the logic and meaning of the whole urban organism."[50] The alien use of space is emphasized when the author comments on the strange location of the railway station, essentially cut off from the city (the Old Town, that is), without even a proper street connecting the two. As for the city's squares and places, these are also peculiar: "Cathedral Square" is not a "square" at all, but a park, and "Lukischplatz" is rather sniffingly dismissed as "really just the raw material for a square, with a truly Russian waste of space without any kind of design, without reference to the surrounding buildings, more an empty spot than a living piece of the city."[51] Once again clearly reflected is the author's sense of unease with disorderly space lacking proper limits, connections, and form.

Monty took particular interest in describing the Jewish population of Vilnius. Starting with the main thoroughfare of the Jewish part of town, "German" Street, the guidebook describes the many signs "in the most impossible German offering the broadest possible array of items for sale." The "impossible German" almost certainly reflected attempts by the local Jews (who would in any case have made up the majority of retail traders in Vilnius) to fashion their native Yiddish into "proper" German. Similarly, in front of the railway station travelers are accosted by individuals with Yiddish accents ("schennes Zimmer?") offering meals and lodging.[52]

The Jewish part of town (Monty uses the term "Ghetto") is described in some detail. "As on an island in the sea the people of Israel live on their own streets, just like long ago, in the middle of the large city Vilna." Tradition and piety predominate in this "city within a city." A description of the crowded, narrow, and not particularly hygienic conditions in this quarter merits quotation: "A dark cloud appears to hover over these roofs, no matter what the weather. Walking in these gloomy streets arouses claustrophobia in a western person [i.e., a German]. All senses rebel against the stroller's impressions. The eye sees misery, the ear hears dissonant sounds, and the nose—oh the nose!—the nose has very good reason to feel personally insulted." Endless numbers of tiny stores line the streets, offering everything possible for sale. Everywhere one looks there are hawkers and children under foot. Only on *shabbes* do the stores close and the hubbub on the street dies down. But finding the Great Synagogue is no easy matter as "it hides itself" amid a warren of little streets and tiny courtyards, each harboring another small prayer house. Here, within a few steps all the necessities of Jewish life are available: places to buy and sell, places to pray, a bathhouse, and a large library (the famous Straszun library).[53] Despite the jocular style, we again see the menace of disorder, filth "insulting the nose," the confusion of countless twisting alleys, the impossibility of gaining a clear image of the whole. The Jewish part of Vilnius is only the most disorderly, exotic, and alien quarter; the entire city's charm for the German soldier-tourist lies in its exoticism and vaguely menacing confusion.

The boundary line between order and chaos is set down clearly in the guidebook: an imaginary line dividing the railroad station from the Old Town. Order reigns in the station: "The railroad station does not belong to the city: it serves the great ruler [*er dient dem grossen Herrscher*]."[54] But as soon as one ventures out from the station, the foreign world of Jewish hucksters, crooked streets, mud, and disorder begins. A remarkable feature of Monty's guidebook is its almost total lack of human figures, aside from a few Jewish merchants. The Catholic churches of the city are described but without any reference to their (mainly) Polish congregations or to the Lithuanian peasants who came to the city to work as servants and laborers. To be sure, the guidebook genre encourages the privileging of permanent objects (churches, statues, squares, monuments) over humanity, but reading Monty's guidebook one would literally not know what languages the inhabitants of this city spoke. Perhaps acknowledging the culture of Vilnius' inhabitants would run counter to the "exotic" tone of the guidebook.[55]

Other German publications, perhaps aimed at a broader audience of Germans who would never see the city itself, did devote more time to local languages and culture. In his travelogue entitled *Neu-Ost*, Paul Listowsky gave a quick description of Polish cities and culture from Częstochowa to Grodno, and while he referred to Vilnius as "Lithuania's capital," he failed to make clear whether he understood "Lithuania" in an ethnic or geographic sense (in any case he did not go into specific ethnic Lithuanian claims on the city).[56] A more scholarly work on the geography of Poland and Lithuania published in the war's final year argued that, since the German occupation in 1915, "City and countryside alike have very successfully been cared for by the German administration . . . . The city has thus entered the newest phase of its cultural development, which has swept away the earlier periods of Lithuanian, then Polish, and finally Russian influence."[57] One could hardly state more explicitly the German self-image as *Kulturträger* to a benighted land.

At the same time, certain publications indicate a fondness and respect for the local culture that the Germans found in Vilnius and its region. It is rather remarkable that at a time of war and faced with all sorts of material shortages the Germans could publish, for example, a guidebook to an exhibition on "Antiquities and Art" in the region of Vilnius-Minsk.[58] Even more impressive is a well-produced volume of artistic photographs of the city, ranging from a general view of the city shrouded in snow to images of the Jewish part of town to photographs of Orthodox and Catholic churches. Even here, however, the editor could not restrain himself from remarking on the "filth" and "nasty smells" that might otherwise go unnoticed by the viewers of the photographs.[59] In the most sophisticated and longest of the Vilnius guides of this genre, *Wilna. Eine vergessene Kunststätte*, the author, Professor Paul Weber, complains that the Russians treated the city "like a stepchild"; he also notes that "The German eye will miss cleanliness and order," but he nevertheless extols the city's cultural and architectural beauty.[60] In short, not only did the German occupation have a significant impact on Vilnius but Vilnius and its region also exerted its influence on the Germans who came in contact with it.

## Antechamber to Independence, 1917–1918

On November 5, 1916 the Central Powers announced the formation of an independent Polish state without, however, allowing Poles to actually take control of administration in any region. A few months later, the startling events in Petrograd encouraged both Polish and Lithuanian movements to press for more concessions. As Tomas Balkelis has recently argued, it was only during the actual war years that Lithuanian patriots began to demand independence (as opposed to some form of autonomy).[61] While the demand for independence had a longer history among Poles, it could only be expressed openly after the war was well under way.[62]

One of the most important questions to be considered involved the borders of future states. In late May 1917 a group representing "all Polish political orientations in Lithuania" addressed the German chancellor with a memorandum on the future status of that land. Here the Poles argued that Poles represented the only "native cultural element" and insisted that ethnographic Lithuanian territory was more or less limited to the former Kaunas/Kowno province. Given the dominance of Polish culture among both the educated and the more wealthy population here, Lithuania could only exist in a close alliance with Poland. This so-called memorandum of the 44 (signatories) infuriated Lithuanians partly because of the arguments it made for Polish dominance but probably even more because of its blithe refusal to even recognize the legitimacy of Lithuanian political and cultural claims.[63]

Lithuanian activists soon made public their rebuttal to the Polish pretensions to the region. Their memorandum (also sent to the German chancellor) insisted that unlike "aggressive polonism," Lithuanians did not lay claim to the entire territory of the erstwhile Grand Duchy of Lithuania, but only to the ethnically Lithuanian and mixed areas (in the latter case the argument becomes somewhat murky, of necessity). As for Vilnius itself (not even mentioned in the Poles' declaration), its population had long been mixed, and just because some elements of the "simple people" used the Polish language, this could hardly mean that they belonged to the Polish nationality. And even the "Lithuanian nobility" who at present mainly supported the Poles did so out of willful ignorance of their own past and Lithuanian roots. Vilnius was located in a mainly Lithuanian ethnographic region and was populated by Lithuanians and polonized Lithuanians—"Polish immigrants" should not be allowed to usurp the proper place of Lithuanians in their own capital city. In this argument Jews disappear entirely: the dispute is reduced to a binary contest between Polish and Lithuanian state ideas.[64]

The future Lithuanian foreign minister, Petras Klimas, describes the growing organization and resoluteness of Lithuanian proto-statehood in Vilnius during 1917. To be sure, the Poles had a head start and enjoyed more support among the local elite and nobility, but the Lithuanian movement was gaining strength from summer of that year, and in particular after the September conference of that year, attended by 264 Lithuanian activists.[65] The most important outcome of this conference was the formation of a council of twenty representatives, the Lithuanian *Taryba*, a kind of proto-government.[66] From this point onward, with the American entry into the war and at year's end the collapse of imperial Russia, events moved quickly: there was even a call (to be sure, from abroad) in November 1917 for Lithuanian independence.[67]

The increasing visibility of the Lithuanian movement was so disturbing to local Poles that they addressed various petitions to German authorities and politicians defending their position in Vilnius and insisting on the city's Polish history and identity.[68] A memorandum drawn up by Władysław Zawadzki of the Vilnius

Polish committee (Komitet Polski w Wilnie) in early November 1917 saw three possibilities for the future of Lithuania: (1) a connection between Lithuania and Poland; (2) Independence for occupied Lithuania; (3) A looser confederation with Poland. Zawadzki differentiated between "Litwini" (the normal Polish word for "Lithuanians," but also a term used by local Polish cultural figures like Mickiewicz) and a rather grotesque neologism coined by himself, "Lietuwi," by which he meant ethnic Lithuanians of an ardently anti-Polish bent.[69] He expressed his concern that the "Lietuwi," "the most chauvinistic and anti-Polish group," could gain the upper hand in part through their single-mindedness, not to say fanaticism. By creating a new and entirely negative word, the Polish activist aimed to separate out "good" Lithuanians (who would not be hostile to some form of Polish cultural or political hegemony) from "chauvinist" "Lietuwi" who demanded their own state. Obviously these categories had more to do with Zawadzki's anti-Lithuanian polemics than with any actual ethnographic or political facts. He concluded by insisting that if an independent Lithuania were to arise, the (future) Polish state would have to "categorically demand that any so-formed Lithuania limit itself to lands settled in the majority by Lithuanians." In particular "Vilnius and its region" (Wilno i okręg wileński) would then form part of Poland.[70] Unfortunately for future Polish-Lithuanian relations, this demand clashed directly with the Lithuanian insistence that Vilnius become the capital of a future Lithuanian state.[71]

With the Bolshevik revolution in Petrograd (November 1917, n.s.) and Russia's exit from the war, it appeared that the Germans had free rein in the east, including Vilnius. Poles in the city were well aware of Lithuanian claims and feared that the Lithuanians could even succeed in gaining control over Vilnius with German connivance. On January 13, 1918 Stanisław Cywiński wrote in his diary, "The fate of Wilno lies in the balance.... It would be truly a scandal and stupidity if Wilno were to become the capital of Lithuania!—all because the Lithuanians do not want to come to an agreement with the Poles!"[72]

Vilnius as the capital of Lithuania seemed an absurdity to Cywiński, but for the Taryba there was no real alternative (nor any desire to seek one out). On February 16, 1918 Lithuanian leaders announced—characteristically, in Vilnius—the reestablishment of the Lithuanian state.[73] To be sure, declarations are easy to make, but actual states are rather more difficult to create. As Alfred Erich Senn has pointed out, the unilateral declaration of independence annoyed the Germans, but in spring 1918 they recognized Lithuanian independence. The actual statement issued by the Taryba, headed by Basanavičius, declared the "restoration" of an "independent Lithuanian state, resting on democratic foundations, with its capital in Vilnius."⁷⁴ Despite the Lithuanian proclamation, however, the actual borders of a future Lithuania remained unclear. Behind the scenes Lithuanians were negotiating with the German authorities about the creation of their future state, on July 11 selecting Duke Wilhelm von Urach of Württemburg as the future Lithuanian monarch.⁷⁵ The collapse of imperial Germany in November 1918 prevented him from accepting the Lithuanian crown as King Mindaugas II.⁷⁶

## The War Ends, the War Continues: 1918–1920

The year 1918 began with German victory on the Eastern Front and ended with the crushing defeat of Germany by the Western powers. While traditionally World War I ends with this year, in Vilnius and elsewhere east of the Odra River, war conditions continued for at least two more years, making 1918 not the war's final year but a period of transition from a relatively stable situation to one of near chaos. The German signing of an armistice officially ending the war on November 11, 1918 was thus something of a nonevent in Vilnius and neighboring regions.

The city's economic misery continued unabated as the political situation seemed to spiral out of control. With the Kaiser's abdication and the signing of the armistice agreement in November 1918, the German troops in Vilnius found themselves in an impossible situation: in principle stationed in a foreign land serving a government that no longer existed, surrounded by incomprehensible nationalist struggles, and threatened by foreign intervention from east (the Red Army) and west (Poland). The Germans remained in Vilnius for some weeks longer, evacuating in mid-December, though the soldiers of the tenth army elected their own council (Soviet/*Rat*) in November 1918.⁷⁷

The Red Army marched into Vilnius to fill the power vacuum left by the retreating Germans. Already on December 8, 1918 the central committee of the Communist Party of Lithuania and Belorussia had announced the formation of a "Provisional Revolutionary Workers' Government in Lithuania." Tellingly, the declaration was made in Vilnius.⁷⁸ Also in December elections for the Vilnius Soviet of Workers' Deputies took place. It is noteworthy that the Soviet members were divided almost equally between communists and "sympathizers" (that is, those who wanted a closer alignment with Soviet Russia) and more independent socialists. Ninety-six members of this first Vilnius soviet belonged in the pro-Bolshevik group while the more independent-minded (though also socialist) Jewish

Bund elected sixty deputies. The Menshevik Internationalists elected twenty-two, and the Lithuanian Social Democrats fifteen. The socialists went on to form the "Provisional Revolutionary Workers' and Poor Peasants' Government of Lithuania" on December 8, 1918 in Vilnius. Among the government's eight "ministers" were four Lithuanians, two Poles, and two Jews, including Semen Dimanshtein, who later gained fame as a nationality specialist in the USSR and, later still, was purged by Stalin.[79]

While communist agitation was noticeable in the city throughout the chaotic month of December, at the same time the Lithuanians were rushing to establish their own state institutions in the city.[80] Local Poles hastened to set up "self-defense" units to protect Polish Vilnius from the Red Army and possible Lithuanian threats.[81] A document issued in 1919 by members of the German soldiers' council, which asserts that the German command favored Polish conservatives, is probably accurate. It is doubtful, however, that at this point the German military cared very greatly about anything other than extricating itself from the region.[82] In the first days of 1919 Lithuanians and Poles alike (political leaders, that is), recognizing their inability to resist the approaching Red Army, evacuated Vilnius. Residents of the city—still mainly Polish and Jewish with very few industrial workers—were nonetheless shocked when the Red Army entered the city unopposed on the night of January 5, 1919. Abramowicz described life under the Bolsheviks in 1919 as "unbearably hard," with almost nothing to eat, and with anyone capable of doing so abandoning the city for friends and relatives in the countryside. Still, after a few weeks the Bolsheviks allowed merchants to open their shops again; the Russian soldiers even set up musical entertainments and—of course—propaganda meetings for the locals.[83]

Bolshevik rule in Vilnius lasted barely three months; the city was taken by Polish armies led by the marshal (and political leader) Józef Piłsudski on April 19, 1919.[84] Though Polish control of the city did not continue unbroken after this date, the April 1919 "liberation" would be celebrated by Vilnius Poles throughout the interwar period.[85] A celebration of the fifteenth anniversary of the date in 1934, for example, produced a booklet with poems, photos of military heroes, and memoirs. The exalted tone of the memoirs can likely be linked to the fact that the city was taken from the Bolsheviks on the day before Easter. Special masses were held to celebrate the defeat of the Red Army and the return of Vilnius to a strong, independent Poland. Of particular importance was the leading role of Piłsudski, the local-born national hero, in a military operation that helped to determine the fate of the city.[86] Taking Vilnius was not only important for local Poles, it was possibly even more significant for the entire Second Polish Republic as an event that shaped its future eastern frontiers.[87]

For non-Poles living in Vilnius, the memory of April 1919 was considerably more bitter. The Polish entry into the city was accompanied by attacks on Jews that left dozens dead (Jewish sources speak of at least sixty victims) and resulted in significant property damage.[88] Besides the violence—the longtime community leader Jakub Wygodzki wrote of three "horrible days" of attacks from April 20 to 22—many Jews were arrested, and (to the great detriment of future Polish-Jewish relations) the Jewish community as a whole was treated as complicit with the Soviet occupiers.[89] The bitter memory of the April 1919 pogrom by Polish soldiers made Vilnius Jews fear for their future under a Polish government; this fear made them more sympathetic to the Lithuanians.[90] The Polish authorities, for their part, denied any specific violence targeting Jews but argued that Jews had collaborated with the Soviet occupiers. This pogrom, along with those in Lwów, Białystok, and many smaller places, had a disastrous effect on relations between Poles and Jews. To simplify a painful and complex situation, one may say that the Jews feared that the Polish state had no interest in protecting their rights or even their personal safety. Poles, on the other hand, were angered by what they regarded as exaggerations and anti-Polish biases in the portrayal of this violence.[91] Neither argument can be dismissed, though (as is nearly always true in such matters) both are one-sided.[92]

Even while the Poles celebrated their military victory, however, the Lithuanians were planning their own return to the city. As Česlovas Laurinavičius has shown, the Lithuanians actually preferred the Poles to the Red Army—at least in April—and may have been willing to compromise with Piłsudski in 1919, but the opportunity was lost.[93] The Poles set up a "Civilian Administration of the Eastern Lands" in February 1919 that was to exist until September 1920 and under whose auspices Vilnius fell.[94]

Almost immediately, Polish culture made a comeback in the city, with Polish theaters, periodicals, and schools opening.[95] Most importantly, the university, closed for over eighty years, was resurrected as a Polish institution. Officially the university was opened—now bearing the name of its original founder from the sixteenth century, Stefan Batory—by a decree signed by Józef Piłsudski on August 28, 1919 declaring that "By means of my decree the University of Wilno, closed by forces hostile to us [Poles] eighty-seven years ago, is once again called back to life [został powołany do życia]."[96] Between this August declaration and the official opening of the university some six weeks later, there was a frantic rush to get the buildings in shape to receive students, organize the university library, and prepare for the festive opening. This inaugural ceremony began on October 10 with special afternoon masses at the chapel in Ostra Brama, with its miracle-working image of the Virgin, an obvious Polish symbol, thereby connecting up the modern university with its religious origins. This was followed by a festive mass the following day at the cathedral; the inauguration ceremony in the university's Columned Hall (*Sala Kolumnowa*), which involved the head of state ("Naczelny Wódz," as Piłsudski was called) handing over to the university rector the university insignia; and finally an evening ball hosted by Piłsudski. The leader pronounced a long speech for the occasion and signed the act officially opening the university under its new title, "Uniwersytet Stefana Batorego" (USB). As the first rector later recalled, even the Jewish population of the city regarded the opening of the university with interest and sympathy.[97] Lithuanians, too, established schools and periodicals in the city despite Polish censorship and general malevolence, but they were unsuccessful in their desire to create the first Lithuanian university in the city.[98]

When the Red Army marched on Warsaw in summer 1920, the Lithuanian government saw its chance to take advantage of Polish weakness and restore Lithuanian power over their declared national capital.[99] The Red Army entered the city on July 14, 1920 and handed it over to Lithuanian control on August 26, immediately after the Polish defeat of Soviet armies at the so-called Miracle on the Vistula.[100] With the Soviet defeat, Lithuania probably had no chance to retain its grasp over the predominantly Polish city, but it took the "revolt" of a friend and fellow officer of Piłsudski's, Lucjan Żeligowski, to bring Vilnius back under Polish control, where it would stay until autumn 1939. The extent to which Piłsudski knew of (or even ordered) Żeligowski's attack on the city seems disputed, but once the latter's troops had taken the city from the Lithuanians on October 9, 1920, Piłsudski did not disavow or criticize his friend's actions.[101] Resistance was minimal and the city fell into Polish hands without serious fighting.[102]

Since ostensibly Żeligowski's actions constituted a "revolt," it would have been unseemly to attempt an immediate incorporation of the territory into Poland. Instead, the peculiar entity of "Middle Lithuania" was created while a plebiscite of the population was prepared (about which more below).[103] There was little doubt that the end result of the plebiscite would be favorable to the Poles—which is the main reason the Lithuanians vociferously opposed it. And, as foreseen by all, in early 1922 Middle Lithuania ceased to exist except as an eastern region of the Polish Republic. The "liberation" of October 1920 (from a Polish point of view) or "illegal occupation" (from a Lithuanian) would quickly petrify into two opposing myths. For patriotic Poles, Żeligowski was a hero; a downtown thoroughfare in Vilnius bore his name during the interwar years. For Lithuanians, on the other hand, the October attack was an illegal and cynical power grab on the part of the Poles and the beginning of a two decades' long occupation of the true capital of Lithuania.[104]

## Diplomatic Battles over Wilno/Vilnius

Even as the city was being contested by Polish, Lithuanian, and Red Army troops, the Poles and Lithuanians were launching another offensive, on the diplomatic front. The outlines of the future Polish and Lithuanian states only began to take real shape in the chaotic period 1919–1920 and, unfortunately, the basic concepts held by political-diplomatic actors on either side were difficult to reconcile, to put it mildly. Few Poles could imagine an independent Poland without eastern cities such as Vilnius (Wilno) and L'viv (Lwów), and the Lithuanian political elite had dedicated itself to the idea of Vilnius as their eternal capital (there was, in any case, no city with an ethnic-Lithuanian majority; the population of Kaunas/Kowno was similarly dominated by Poles and Jews, though the city was at least located in the middle of a solidly Lithuanian region). Even before the war ended, as we have seen, both sides were advancing their claims vis-à-vis the warring powers. From the end of 1918, when fledgling governments and diplomatic corps were hastily set up, Polish and Lithuanian diplomats went on an offensive to claim "their" city.

The diplomatic notes and exchanges between the Polish and Lithuanian delegations at the League of Nations reflect their different strategies. While the Polish documents tend to emphasize recent history, high culture, the specific Polish language and culture, and the present population of the city, Lithuanians stressed geography, history before the nineteenth century, and the idea that "Lithuania" (and "Lithuanian") needed to be understood as more than simply the region where in the present day the Lithuanian language was dominant. They also argued that population statistics were biased against the Lithuanians as a mainly rural, nonnoble, and less affluent nation. These rhetorical strategies crop up, obviously in somewhat different form, again and again in this extended "dialogue" that took place throughout the 1920s and even beyond. While specific authors do vary their arguments to some extent, the general rhetorical strategies of Lithuanian versus

Polish are remarkably similar. For this reason I will discuss only two diplomatic documents of this early period.[105]

The first of these documents, an "exposé" (as it was called in French) issued by the Lithuanian Delegation at the Paris peace conference and dated September 29, 1919, was signed by "Prof. A. Voldemar," the later right-wing nationalist Augustinas Voldemaras. The document begins with a statement that recently Polish "political spheres" had been engaged in intense propaganda demanding the detachment of Vilnius from Lithuania and its attachment to Poland, while also calling for a plebiscite of the local population. Following this statement are the Lithuanian arguments for keeping Vilnius and for not allowing a plebiscite.[106]

The first arguments are historical: "Vilna is the historical capital of the Lithuanian state and is located in a region which from times immemorial has made up an integral part of an ethnographically purely Lithuanian domain."[107] Tellingly, Voldemaras does not actually claim that the city itself is mainly Lithuanian, and his rather high-flown language skirts the issue of whether in the present day the region is mainly—much less "purely"—ethnically Lithuanian. Similarly, the statement "The history of the city of Vilna is the history of Lithuania and vice versa"[108] is a rhetorical flourish devoid of any actual reference to recent times but typical of Lithuanian "claiming rhetoric."

The document's second point touches upon practical considerations: "The city of Vilna constitutes, at the present moment, the economic, political, and intellectual center of the country and is also the principal transportation hub. The vital forces of the Lithuanian people nourish it."[109] The first sentence here presents a fairly unassailable statement of fact, but it begs an important question: what exactly is meant by "the country" in this case? Poles, too, would have agreed that Vilnius as a city was of major importance for the region—the question of course was whether this "country" formed a part of Poland. The second sentence here is again more of a rhetorical flourish than a statement of fact: "vital forces" of nations can hardly be measured by any traditional means, and while Lithuanian patriots may have urgently desired Vilnius, the case for Jewish and Polish "vital forces" in the nineteenth century seems more convincing. Still, there was a degree of truth to the statement that because of Lithuanian publishing houses, artistic associations, and scholarly societies in Vilnius, "to separate Vilna from Lithuania would be exceedingly prejudicial to the country and would damage the city itself."[110]

Point three of the document has it that in order to attach the city to Poland, it would be necessary for Poland to annex the entire *gouvernement* (obviously thinking in terms of Russian imperial administrative boundaries) as well as part of Grodno and Minsk provinces. Turning here to statistics of 1897, Voldemaras noted that in that census Poles made up a mere 10 percent and 8.17 percent (respectively) of the population in these provinces, and furthermore, their numbers were much smaller in reality. Furthermore, according to the fourth point, "From the ethnographical point of view, Poles [of this region] have nothing in common with Vilna and its surroundings. The element which has taken on the name 'Pole' is composed principally of those Lithuanian landed proprietors who are accustomed to spending the winter in the Lithuanian capital and whose origins, in general, are not Slav but entirely Lithuanian." To sum up, Voldemaras argues that the number of Poles was small, and even these figures were exaggerated because the citizens in question were not Poles at all, but Lithuanians.

After these key points, the rest of the memorandum is devoted to broader issues. The entire mass of "common people" in the region was purely Lithuanian, but in the repressive anti-Catholic atmosphere of the Russian Empire this backward and "très peu cultivé" group tended to confuse faith with nationality, as did the Russian authorities. For this reason, and in a situation where "the national language [Lithuanian] was banned," Polish-speaking clergy and elites did their best to polonize hapless Lithuanians.[111] In such a situation, recently much exacerbated by war, pogroms, and Polish occupation, Voldemaras concludes, a plebiscite would not show the true will of the people. As a kind of codicil, Voldemaras notes that he was attaching a report by M. Rozenbaum, Undersecretary of State for Foreign Affairs, which "clearly shows the immense danger a plebiscite in Vilna would present for Jews of Poland, Galicia, and countries occupied by the Poles."[112] The idea that a plebiscite in Vilnius could not be carried out fairly under present conditions of Polish occupation and the threat of violence appears again and again in Lithuanian accounts. And, in fact, one cannot deny that local Jews—at the very least—were unwilling to participate in the plebiscite that did occur, though the Jewish community refused to take a clear stand in favor of a boycott.[113]

If Lithuanian diplomatic arguments claiming Vilnius were one-sided and full of half-truths about recent history, demography, and urban economy, Polish diplomats advanced similarly self-serving theses to make their case that Vilnius was an entirely Polish city. One example of these arguments can be found in a memorandum presented to the Bruxelles Conference on Vilnius in May 1921. This conference had been called by the Belgian foreign minister, Paul Hymans, in an effort to find a solution to the Vilnius question through a confederation agreement between Poland and Lithuania.[114]

This particular document, another memorandum, began with bravado: "Polish rights to the territory and to the city of Wilno are clear and irrefutable," and for this reason Poland "has consented to confer the decision as to the destiny of this land to the will of its inhabitants."[115] Knowing that most non-Poles would very likely boycott the plebiscite, the Poles could be confident in trusting in a favorable outcome for a plebiscite. As for the historical arguments of the Lithuanians, the Polish memorandum archly pointed out that the term "Lithuania" has two meanings: a historical region of Poland and an ethnographic area. In fact, as this document charged, the Lithuanians purposely confused the two concepts in order to advance their claims on Vilnius, when in truth (as the Poles insisted) even the earliest documents of the Grand Duchy of Lithuania were published in Slavic, not Lithuanian, and since at least the Union of Lublin (1569), the Grand Duchy of Lithuania and "the crown" have simply been two parts of one unified Polish Republic. Nor did the Polish population in the Grand Duchy differ in any significant way from that in the Crown, and while the word "Lithuanian" was often used by individuals in the Grand Duchy to refer to themselves, this usage was devoid of ethnographic significance.

From the late eighteenth century (the Kościuszko rebellion) and to the present day, the memorandum continued, Vilnius and its region shared the sentiment, enthusiasms, and fate of other Polish lands. "During the last two Polish insurrections, in 1830 and 1863, the inhabitants of Wilno mixed their blood with that of their brethren in the rest of Poland."[116] While Russian administrative boundaries attempted to cut Vilnius off from Poland, the Germans in 1915, following ethnographic evidence, separated Kaunas and ethnic Lithuania from "the Polish territories of Wilno."[117] According to the memorandum, only later, following their general anti-Polish policy, did the Germans establish the capital in Vilnius, setting in place the Lithuanian Taryba. With this rather questionable statement (in terms of both historical fact and interpretation), the Poles aimed to dismiss the Lithuanians as mere agents of the Germans.

Polish claims on Vilnius went beyond the historical, patriotic, and ethnographic. Culture was a vital reason that Vilnius was Polish: "That progress which has been achieved by the Wilno region, all of its creative and vital civilization, are par excellence of Polish genius."[118] Indeed, Vilnius was the cultural and scholarly center of "historical Lithuania, but in no way of the Lithuanian people." The university, literature, press, church life, and scholarly societies were and had been in recent generations dominated by Poles. True, Lithuanians had a historical claim on the city, but if one were to accept the Lithuanian argument that this claim from centuries earlier gave them the right to possess Vilnius in the twentieth century, "a similar criterion could lead us to conclude with far more reason that Granada belongs to the Moroccans, Cracow to the Germans and Petrograd to the Italians."[119] Having rather sniffingly dismissed Lithuanian pretensions to the city with this comparison, the Poles went on to cite statistics proving their ethnographic dominance (as usual, generally leaving out Belarusians and Jews).

Polish patriots were completely unable to appreciate the Lithuanian claims to Vilnius, and Lithuanian patriots were similarly blind to Polish arguments. With both sides arguing largely if not primarily from mythic rather than practical or objective considerations, the possibility of mutual understanding and compromise remained minimal.

## Wilno in "Middle Lithuania," 1920–1922

After Żeligowski's liberation or illegal seizure of the city in October 1920, there was little chance that the Lithuanians would succeed in gaining control over Vilnius without foreign intervention. While the Soviet authorities were very willing to endorse the Lithuanian claim over the city, no doubt more as an anti-Polish measure than as a reflection of pro-Lithuanian sentiments, the Entente was decidedly chilly about the prospect of sending troops to the region.[120] In any case, the Lithuanian claims did not seem more convincing to the French or British than the Polish arguments.

Given the obviously provisional character of Middle Lithuania and its non-democratic, military origins, elections needed to be called quickly and would be of major importance for the territory's future. On October 12, 1920, Żeligowski declared himself the territory's "commander in chief" (*Naczelny Dowódca*) but promised that any decrees issued by him would have to be ratified post facto by the Middle Lithuania's legislature (*Sejm Ustawodawczy*) upon its convocation. At length the date for elections was set for January 8, 1922. From late 1920 and throughout 1921 Żeligowski and the Polish administration of Middle Lithuania did all they could to persuade all inhabitants of the territory to participate in the elections. From the start, Lithuanians seemed unlikely to participate—both the Kaunas government and local Lithuanian intellectuals like Mykolas Biržiška called for a boycott of what they regarded as an illegal election. There was hope, however, that the Jews could be persuaded to vote, and the authorities of Middle Lithuania went out of their way to woo potential Jewish voters during this period.

Żeligowski enjoyed a positive reputation among Jews and was not connected with the anti-Jewish violence that unfortunately had not been a rare occurrence among Polish troops over the past two years. The general's "Order No. 1" did not specifically favor any one nationality and stated simply that the "savage Bolshevik hordes" had been expelled from the city and that an elected legislature would decide the territory's fate.[121] While Żeligowski's most obvious constituency was the Poles, he also hoped to gain Jewish support for the incorporation of the city into Poland. For this reason, it was vital that Middle Lithuania avoid any appearance of antisemitism. Jewish commentators agree that policy toward the Jews during 1920–1922 was "soft" and that Żeligowski and other officials of Middle Lithuania tried to woo Jews over to their side.[122]

At the same time, the Lithuanian state had shown a very favorable attitude toward its Jewish citizens from the start, going further than any other European country in granting Jews not just equal rights but also cultural autonomy and even a minister of Jewish affairs.[123] In the years leading up to World War I, Polish-Jewish relations had become very strained; Lithuanians, on the other hand, had remained fairly neutral on the Jewish question (their main national rival being, of course, the Poles). The Polish record was further spoiled, from the Jewish point of view, by the apparent reluctance of the newly formed Polish state (and the Polish public) even to agree to the minority rights treaty demanded by the Allies at the Paris peace talks in 1919. The memory of pogroms in Lwów (November 1918), Vilnius (April 1919), and elsewhere further tarnished the image of Poles among Jews.[124] While many Jews recognized that only a minority of Poles had participated in or approved of such atrocities, the fear that the Polish state would be unwilling or incapable of protecting its non-Polish citizens was widespread. On the other hand, this fear also made Jews hesitate before taking any actions that might provoke their Polish neighbors—like openly supporting Lithuanian claims to Vilnius.

While there is considerable evidence that many Vilnius Jews would have preferred that the city pass to Lithuanian hands, few declared this position openly, probably for fear of antagonizing the Poles. For example, Jacob Wygodzki noted in his memoirs that the previously neutral policy adopted by Jews toward the occupying powers (from the Germans onward) needed to be changed to one of active support for the Lithuanians once they had taken Vilnius and spoke of the situation of Jews in "Kovno-Lita" ("Kaunas-Lithuania") as "paradise" (*gan eden*). However, once the city was back in Polish hands a much more cautious approach was again the order of the day.[125]

By December 1920, according to a Middle Lithuanian internal report, Jewish political life was returning to normal. At a meeting of the Jewish community, its president, Dr. Wygodzki, spoke of the "inordinately positive impression" that General Żeligowski had made on him, but he also stressed that both Poles and Jews must work together in preventing any further excesses and toward improving mutual relations. The Poles must respect the terms of the Versailles Treaty (here Wygodzki was referring most likely to the rights for national minorities guaranteed there). Wygodzki also explained to those assembled "about the formation of Middle Lithuania" and spoke about federation (though from the vague mention in this report it is not clear just what he meant: a federation with Lithuania?). Like Wygodzki, Vilnius chief Rabbi Isaac (Yitshak) Rubinsztejn mentioned recent violence against Jews in and around the city, stressing that this violence had been caused by agitation on the part of "some secret organization" (that is, not by direct orders of the Polish authorities). All speakers stressed the need to work with the authorities in schools and in the press to combat antisemitism.[126]

It is difficult, perhaps impossible, to gauge exactly the attitude of the Vilnius Jewish community toward the prospect of the city's incorporation into Poland.[127] One report from early 1921 claims that Jews suffered terribly under the Polish occupation and did not openly oppose incorporation simply because of their fear of Żeligowski's troops. However, this account, found in the files of the Lithuanian Foreign Ministry, is simply too patently anti-Polish and pro-Lithuanian to be taken seriously, as the following quotation (English in the original) shows: "The Poles declare that they intend to exterminate the Jews, should Vilna not be ceded to Poland. . . . Under the [sic] Lithuanian rule . . . the Jews of Vilna enjoyed all the privileges of equal citizenship. . . . It is therefore only natural that the Jews . . . should wish to vote that Vilna should remain Lithuanian."[128] True, many Jews probably would have ideally supported incorporation in Lithuania, but the authorities of Middle Lithuania were careful to cater to Jewish sensibilities. The president of the Temporary Ruling Commission (the highest civilian authority in Middle Lithuania), Aleksander Meysztowicz, even insisted on speaking Yiddish with a Jewish delegation.[129] In the end, however, Jews had nothing to gain and much to lose from taking a clear stand either for or against participation in the elections (which, given the Polish majority in Middle Lithuania, was equivalent to supporting incorporation into Poland). Thus in late 1921 the Jewish leadership (of various parties) came out with a neutral declaration, endorsing neither participation nor a boycott. This declaration was probably little more than a diplomatic tactic, an attempt to avoid overtly offending the Poles while recognizing that whether or not Jews openly opposed participation in the plebiscite, the Poles would win the majority of the vote.[130]

An internal Polish report on attitudes of non-Poles toward the plebiscite, as it had come to be known, portrays relations between Poles and Jews with rather shocking frankness: "Support for the Polish orientation in the Vilnius question does not lie in the interest of the Jews as all Jews perfectly sense [*wyczuwają*] the antisemitism of all classes [*warstwa*] of Polish society." Jews would of course prefer to live in a state where they are not the only minority (strangely in these discussions the large Belarusian, Ukrainian, and German minorities in Poland disappear), such as with the incorporation with Lithuania or "on the other hand [through] a direct union with the Jews of Soviet Russia or with Germany." No Jew, the report continues, forgets that Jews are "at the helm of power" (*u steru rządów*) in Soviet Russia though some prefer a connection with the economically more advanced Germany.[131] For all its antisemitic tone and prejudices, the report was probably correct at least in its assessment of Jewish misgivings about becoming Polish citizens. The Polish state clearly tended toward a self-definition as a would-be nation-state of Poles, which could only mean that non-Poles would end up in the category of second-class citizens. But most Vilnius Jews no doubt saw the incorporation of their city into Poland as inevitable and, like so many times before in Jewish history, tried to keep their heads down and to avoid exacerbating anti-Jewish feelings among either Lithuanians or Poles.

The elections to the Vilnius Sejm took place, as planned, on January 8, 1922. As expected, most Poles voted and most non-Poles did not. Lithuanians were least likely to go to the polls: official figures showed that 8.2 percent of rural Lithuanians voted and a mere 1.2 percent of Lithuanians living in cities did. As for Jews, 15.3 percent of those in rural areas and 6.3 percent of urban dwellers voted. Finally, among Poles 83 percent of urban dwellers and 80.3 percent of rural residents voted.[132] In other words, among more nationally conscious individuals (peasants at this point would almost certainly be less nationally oriented than townspeople), Jews and Lithuanians refrained from voting, while Poles participated. In Vilnius itself 83.6 percent of Christian Poles voted (but only 75.6% of all Christians; in other words, Lithuanians and Belarusians generally boycotted the elections). A total of 68 Muslims voted (60.2%), while a grand total of 303 Jews in the city (1.4%) cast their ballots.[133] The official view that the Bundists supported participation in the elections while the Zionists opposed it seems false, given this almost complete rate of nonparticipation.[134]

As everyone had expected, the Vilnius Sejm met for just a month, convening on February 1, 1922 and voting to dissolve itself on February 28. On February 20 the Sejm passed its most important—indeed, only important—law: a request that Middle Lithuania be incorporated into the Republic of Poland.[135] On March 2 a delegation from the Vilnius Sejm arrived in Warsaw with a request to the Sejm Ustawodawczy of the Republic of Poland that was accepted on April 6. On April 18, 1922, the eve of the three-year anniversary of the liberation of Vilnius from Soviet rule (but for Jews the occasion of a murderous pogrom), "Middle Lithuania" was officially incorporated into the Republic of Poland with ceremonies in the city attended by Piłsudski, Żeligowski, Aleksander Meysztowicz, three bishops, and other dignitaries.[136]

• • •

In Vilnius as elsewhere in Europe, World War I sharpened national aspirations and conflicts. The war also had catastrophic effects on the city's economy and population. The optimistic growing city of early 1914 had declined into a considerably smaller, hungrier, and more isolated city by 1922. The Poles "won" the contest for the city but their victory was a hollow one indeed, bringing in its wake a total breakdown in relations with Lithuania. The city also became much more homogenous in the period 1914–1922 with the departure of almost all Russians and a significant reduction of the Jewish population. Still, as we will see in the next chapter, the multicultural nature of the city continued on even in interwar "Polish" Vilnius.

CHAPTER 5

# Vilnius as a Polish City, 1919–1939

VILNIUS WAS UNDER POLISH control, informally and formally, for just under twenty years, but this short period managed to produce an incredible number of memoirs, conferences, scholarly monographs, and histories. Not surprisingly, most of these works are in Polish and deal with Poles and their culture in the city they call Wilno. To be sure, the majority of city's population was—for the first time in the modern period—Polish by culture and language, as were the university and most other cultural institutions and publications. Because of this wealth of Polish cultural history of interwar Vilnius, in this chapter I will concentrate on the actual process of "making the city Polish," while a good portion of the city's population was not of this cultural-ethnic group. For example, Jewish culture continued to be strong and ubiquitous, though the hold of traditional religious beliefs and even of Yiddish was noticeably weakening by the later 1930s. As for Lithuanians, they were present in some numbers in the city but their Vilnius was constructed mainly in publications and declarations from the other side of the Polish Lithuanian frontier (less than fifty kilometers to the west). Belarusians, Tatars, and Karaites also continued to make their home in the city, even producing significant scholarly work in these years.[1]

Compared with the decades before 1914, the city developed and changed rather little in the interwar years. With the nearby Polish-Lithuanian border sealed (though one could illegally sneak across) and the Soviet border (which was also less than one hundred kilometers away) closed for trade and commerce, Vilnius found itself stranded and mainly neglected by the government in Warsaw, which, after all, had many other pressing matters to contend with in this turbulent period. The city's population did rise, though the dearth of reliable statistics, in particular after 1931, when the last prewar census was taken, makes it difficult to know the exact size and makeup of the city at the end of this period. According to official (Polish) statistics, the city's population in 1923—the first full year of "official" Polish rule—was 167,454, a figure that grew to 208,478 by 1937. Considering that the city's population in 1910 had been 186,461 and had probably been close to 200,000 by 1914, the growth rate was rather anemic.[2]

Very soon after Vilnius was incorporated into the Polish republic, Władysław Studnicki published a pamphlet outlining the economic situation and future prospects of Vilnius and its region. As the pamphlet's first lines indicate, Studnicki was writing before the official incorporation of Vilnius into the Polish state; he pointed out that "Middle Lithuania" was a "temporary formation" with "accidental borders." The region had suffered greatly during the war years (into the early 1920s), Studnicki wrote, with great losses among horses and cattle, and the lowest agricultural yields in the Polish Republic. The devastation of local agriculture meant that nobles of the Vilnius region had a difficult time carrying out their role supporting (Polish) cultural and educational efforts. Commerce was mainly in the hands of Jews, who owned some 70 percent of retail shops in "Middle Lithuania." Studnicki insisted that without the lands east of the so-called Curzon line (almost half of the territory of the interwar Polish Republic), "any significant development of the Polish nation and [Polish] independence are impossible." As for the city itself, Studnicki opined, "[it is] a hearth of civilization which influences [literally, 'irradiates'] our entire northeast," just as Lwów [L'viv] did for the southeast. Studnicki, like most local Poles, was convinced that Vilnius must remain a Polish city not only for itself, but to anchor and strengthen Polish civilization in the republic's eastern territories.[3]

The importance of Vilnius for the Polish state—strategically, culturally, even spiritually—could not be denied. At the same time, faced with numerous more urgent tasks in building a unified state, Warsaw failed to subsidize the city or finance new infrastructure or government buildings. A brochure from 1930 remarked that, for most of the 1920s, Warsaw had considered the Vilnius region "a ball and chain" (*kula u nogi*).[4] The interwar period failed to see any significant new construction, whether of public buildings, housing, or new urban districts, partly because of the modest growth of the city as a whole and its generally depressed economic condition.

Nonetheless, the city did change and modernize during these years. Several new large buildings put up in this period remain modest landmarks in Vilnius to this day. On Mickiewicza, as the main downtown avenue was renamed, two rather stark modernist structures went up side-by-side in the late 1930s, both housing banks. Both buildings consist of a main square corpus with minimal decoration, reflecting contemporary modernist and functionalist architectural styles.[5] A few steps down the same thoroughfare the Jabłkowski brothers had their elegant department store. The building, begun just before the war, was completed only in 1923. Another few minutes' stroll further on, another square modernist office building was constructed in 1937–1939 for the public insurance company Ubezpeczalnia społeczna. Off Mickiewicza but less than a quarter hour away on foot, a large university dormitory was completed just before the Red Army invaded in fall 1939.[6]

Remarkable about all of these buildings is their Spartan modernist architecture and, perhaps, the fact that several generations and changes of regime later, nearly all continue to be used for the same purpose for which they were originally built (the only, partial, exception is the insurance building, now occupied by the Ministry of Health at Gedimino 27). Another building that deserves mention is the YIVO (Yiddish/Jewish Scientific Institution) center on Wiwulski Street (Vivulskio) in the New Town. Built, like the buildings mentioned above, in the modernist style, this office and classroom building was completed in 1933.[7]

Already at this point some voices protested what they saw as the threat of "modern urban planning," in particular with reference to the city's many impressive buildings (mostly, of course, churches) from the sixteenth to eighteenth century. The priest Marian Morelowski, for example, complained that modernist city planning—in particular efforts by the city government to recast the square around the cathedral—threatened to destroy Vilnius' centuries-old beauty and harmony.[8] On a rather more sober note, Stanisław Lorentz, who was responsible for the conservation of historical monuments in the region in the early 1930s, recalled in his memoirs the intense interest local artists and intellectuals had in maintaining the historic beauty of Vilnius.[9] Even the small wooden mosque near Lukiškės Square was maintained and restored during the 1930s only, unfortunately, to be destroyed after the Second World War.[10]

The city did not, however, entirely stand still. True, most residents of the city depended on wells for water and could only dream of electric light at home. The unsanitary conditions and ripe odor in warm weather of the densely populated Old Town (and not just its Jewish quarter) reflected the lack of sewer lines and modern hygienic facilities in most residences. Electricity use in the city remained low, not just compared with the West but also when compared with Polish cities such as Warsaw, Cracow, or even Lwów. Still, in the 1930s the use of electricity shot up significantly, though from a very low level. Similarly, the sewer system and delivery of running water to homes expanded at this time. A hydroelectric plant and the tapping of new sources of clean water for the city were also in the works in the late 1930s, despite chronic city budget deficits.[11] As in other cities of interwar

Poland, the desire to create a more modern and healthy city were often checked by empty government coffers as well as by the public's general reluctance to bear the cost of such improvements, whether in direct charges or in taxes.[12]

Interwar Vilnius remained a fairly compact city, so transportation was less of an issue than it would become in the second half of the twentieth century. Still, residents could choose from motorized taxi and bus services within the city, while at the same time the old horse-drawn droshky and trams remained. The first motorized autobuses were purchased in 1926 from the Swiss firm "Arbon"; hence locals spoke not of traveling by "bus" but of taking the "arbon." By 1930 rather small buses carrying fourteen to fifteen passengers ran along three lines going from the center to the city's outskirts. At 20 grosz bus tickets were not cheap: the price corresponded to that of a kilo of sugar. People of more modest circumstances saved bus fare by walking. Nonetheless, in 1932 the few dozen buses running transported more than 5 million passengers.[13] Automobiles remained rare in Vilnius; only the wealthiest could afford the still unreliable, expensive, and inconvenient machines. The army, high state officials, and from 1926 firemen were transported in automobiles; one could by 1938 also travel by one of the 170 city taxis (mostly Fiats).[14] Even in 1939, however, most Vilnans had never ridden in a private car or taxi.

Movie theaters had made their appearance in Vilnius before the war, indeed, before the turn of the century. In the twenties, however, the number of movie houses expanded significantly. By the end of that decade one could choose from around a dozen movie theaters in the city, the most opulent and well-known among them bearing the international names Lux, Helios, Casino, and Pan (not, presumably, in the Polish meaning of the word—"Lord" or "Mister").[15] According to Čaplinskas, in autumn 1939 there were a dozen large movie theaters in Vilnius that could seat 400 or more viewers, with the largest being Pan (1000 seats), Mars (1200), and Helios (1000). Czesław Miłosz recalls the Helios cinema from his childhood, across the street from the Jabłkowski department store on Wileńska Street.[16] Looking more or less at random through posters advertising various forms of entertainment in Vilnius in 1927 and 1936, from boxing matches to public lectures but also including cinema, one notes posters from the Lux, Helios, Polonja, Światowid, Pan, and Casino movie houses with offerings from a number of countries including the USA, Germany, France, Hungary, the USSR, and Austria. Among the stars that figure in these posters are Claudette Colbert, Eddie Cantor, Errol Flynn, Borys [sic] Karloff, and Shirley Temple. One could choose film versions of famous literary or operatic works (e.g., *David Copperfield* and *Madame Butterfly*), popular comic, amorous, or adventure movies, or even one Hungarian film (1927) intriguingly entitled *Sodom and Gomorrah*.[17] In the cinema, at least, a resident of Vilnius could be a citizen of the world.

Perhaps the single most important technological innovation in communications of this period was radio. The new technology was slow to spread in Poland due to the poverty both of the central government and of the average Pole. Still, by the mid-1920s radio stations were being set up in most Polish cities.[18] Polskie Radio organized the first broadcast from Vilnius in autumn 1927. The official founding of Polskie Radio Wilno took place in January 1928; in 1935 it moved into a larger studio on Mickiewicz Avenue. Offerings varied from light music to classical concerts and also included plays, lectures, and news. There were also limited broadcasts in Lithuanian and Belarusian.[19] In 1936–1937 Czesław Miłosz worked at the Polskie Radio Wilno studio. Even in 1939, however, radio receivers remained large and expensive, beyond the reach of an average Vilnius family.[20]

Town planners in Vilnius recognized that much remained to be done to modernize the city. A fictional "conversation" between a "layman" (*laik*) and "city planner" (*urbanista*) penned by two Vilnius planners and published in 1939 reflects the tension between needs and accomplishments. The planner points out that Vilnius is in fact two distinct cities—a beautiful old one and a new, mostly ugly one. Explaining the beauty of the Old Town as not only the buildings themselves but also their harmonious placement relative to each other, the planner also recognized that, as the city's population grows, the needs of industry, hygiene, and communications had to be taken into account. Nevertheless, modernization should not come at the expense of harmony. The planner appears to dismiss the entire nineteenth century as esthetically barren, but he does not advocate any radical measures against the modern parts of town (the largest part of the city, after all). In the end, the city planner's suggestions are general and hardly controversial: they amount to the "regulation" and "ordering" of more recent city quarters while "preserving" the historic beauty of the city.[21]

Politics in interwar Vilnius tended to be dominated by conservatives and nationalists, but left-wing opinions and agitation were also present, if not always openly displayed. And it seems certain that Soviet historiography overemphasized and exaggerated the importance of these trends, though it is equally clear that they did not simply invent them. Wiktor Sukiennicki, who was later to write a number of important works about Vilnius, remembered helping found the "Union of Progressive Youth" (Związek Młodzieży Postępowej) at the university in the early 1920s. In 1934 Sukiennicki was able to visit the USSR as a worker at the

Research Center on Eastern Europe in Vilnius, returning with "half a railroad car of material." Sukiennicki insisted that this research institute (which sadly remains almost entirely unresearched by later historians) was neither pro-Soviet nor, as the writer and later communist functionary Jerzy Putrament would claim, a center for anti-Soviet espionage.[22] Certainly there was a communist "underground" in the city, and its members were often connected with pro-Lithuanian and pro-Belarusian liberation movements, but this was not always the case.[23]

More typical than pro-Soviet or even mildly socialist sentiments was the political outlook of Stanisław Cat-Mackiewicz. To be sure, it is risky to characterize this figure and his views as in any way "typical." However, Mackiewicz ("Cat" was his pen name) and the conservatives of the daily *Słowo*, which he edited in the 1920s, certainly were closer to the political mainstream in Vilnius than were leftists.[24] Mackiewicz attacked nearly the entire political spectrum from socialists to the National Democrats. He dismissed liberal-bourgeois democracy as unsuitable for Poland; a monarchy or, failing that, a very strong executive who could override a fractious parliament would be the ideal government form. In this way he could, at least partly, support Piłsudski after the latter's coup of May 1926. Mackiewicz saw Polish culture in the region as vastly superior to any other and seldom missed a chance to mock the nationalist pretensions (from his point of view) of Lithuanians, Belarusians, or Ukrainians. Like many conservatives of the old school, Mackiewicz did not harbor favorable attitudes toward Jews but, unlike the National Democrats, antisemitism was not a central issue for his political philosophy. In short, Janusz Osica's description of Mackiewicz and his circle as "politicians of anachronism" fits rather well. His ideal of a paternalistic, hierarchical state led by a monarch and nobles (whether they attain their rank by birth or ability) hardly had a chance in the political context of interwar Poland. In the end, Mackiewicz's press polemics were read, one may argue, more for their stylistic fire than for any actual program they might have contained.[25]

## Making Wilno Polish

Long before Vilnius had officially become part of the Polish state, Polish residents had begun the process of "repolonizing" the city. A key component of Vilnius' Polish cultural scene in the past—as we have seen—was the city's university. Even before the withdrawal of German troops from the city in 1918, plans were afoot to reopen the university. The university was of key importance not just as a center of learning and practical training but also as an indication of the strength and continuity of Polish culture in the city. No literate Pole had to be reminded that Adam Mickiewicz had studied in Vilnius and produced his earliest poetic works there. The closing of the university after the November 1830 Insurrection was seen as part of the greater tragedy of the Polish nation. Thus resurrecting an institution of higher learning (and memoirs of the time often use this biblical word) was crucial for reestablishing Polish Vilnius.[26]

After the decision taken on December 13, 1918 to reestablish the university, an enormous amount of practical work had to be carried out under very difficult circumstances. A budget of just over six million Polish marks was set for the period July 1 to December 31, 1919 to get the university buildings in shape to receive students, to recruit professors, and the like. The humanities held a privileged position in the university, probably partly due to the tradition of Mickiewicz but equally due to financial and practical considerations. According to the first "proto-rector," A. Wrzosek, efforts were made to recruit at least one Lithuanian professor for a chair of Lithuanian philology, "naturally, [one] not hostile to *polskość*." Among those considered for the post, if we can believe Wrzosek, were Mykolas Biržiška (despite the fact that he was "exceedingly unpopular among the Polish society of Vilnius") and Augustinas Voldemaras (though he was seen as "a person hostile toward Poland").[27] In the end no chair for Lithuanian language and literature was created (whether because of direct anti-Lithuanian hostility or simply because no suitable candidate could be found, it is difficult to say). Similarly, despite appeals from the Jewish community, no chair for the study of Hebrew—much less Yiddish—would be created at the university.

The university officially opened under the name of its original founder from the sixteenth century, Stefan Batory, by a decree (*dekret*) signed by Józef Piłsudski on August 28, 1919: "By means of my decree the University of Wilno, closed by forces hostile to us [Poles] eighty-seven years ago, is once again called back to life."[28] Between this August declaration and the official opening of the university some six weeks later there was a frantic rush to get the buildings in shape to receive students, organize the university library, and prepare for the festive opening. This inaugural ceremony began on October 10 with special afternoon masses at Ostra Brama Madonna, an obvious Polish symbol, thereby connecting up the modern university with its religious origins. This was followed by a solemn mass the following day at the cathedral and the inauguration ceremony at the university. During these solemnities, Józef Piłsudski himself handed over the university insignia to the institution's rector. Later that evening the head of state hosted a gala ball. The leader pronounced a long speech for the occasion, and at the signing of the act officially opening the university, the title "Uniwersytet Stefana Batorego" (USB) was used for the first time. As the first rector later recalled, even the Jewish population of the city regarded the opening of the university with interest and sympathy.[29]

Writing in the late 1920s, the first rector of the newly resurrected USB, professor M. Siedlecki, stressed the university's efforts and successes in maintaining good relations with Vilnius society, including its non-Polish elements. For example, Vilnius Jews, he maintained, had "a rather strange idea of Polish scholarship [*nauka*]" due to their experiences under Russian rule and at first were rather reserved toward the university. Soon, however, "they recognize that the existence of an institution of higher learning in Vilnius could bring them significant benefits [*znaczna korzyść*]," and even the important Zionist leader Rabbi Isaac Rubinsztejn sent his daughter to study at the university. Siedlecki even wanted—or so he later wrote—to set up a lectureship for Hebrew "but . . . was unable to find an appropriate candidate [to fill the post]." A lectureship was created for Belarusian, and according to the rector's later recollection, attempts were made to reach out to local Lithuanians. But when two Poles, Witold Abramowicz and one Mr. Krzyżanowski, approached Siedlecki in spring 1920 with the request that a chair (*katedra*) of Yiddish (*język żydowski*) and another for Lithuanian language be created so that there could be at least one professor of "the Jewish nationality" and one Lithuanian on the faculty, the rector rejected the appeal out of hand, noting that only scholarly qualifications would be the basis of hiring decisions, not "politics." Clearly, for Siedlecki, and probably for most Vilnius Poles, it was taken for granted that the university should and would be a bastion of Polish culture.[30]

Toward the end of the first full academic year at USB, the approach of the Red Army forced the evacuation of university personnel and students. Many students joined the volunteers to fight the Bolsheviks with the rector's explicit blessing. In early July 1920 it became clear that Polish troops would not be able to defend the city, and the rector prepared to evacuate faculty and the most valuable moveable property of the university. With five train cars provided on July 10, Siedlecki left the city, ending up in the western Polish city of Poznań, where he received a telegram from General Żeligowski with the welcome news that Vilnius was back in Polish hands. Within days he was back in the city and was relieved to find that for the most part, the university had not been damaged under Bolshevik or Lithuanian rule. During the period of "Middle Lithuania," the rector complained, the representatives of the League of Nations in Vilnius completely failed to understand "the mood [*nastrój*] of the people of Wilno" and made no effort to comprehend the city (and region's) *polskość*. Perhaps in part due to this frustration, in late 1921 Siedlecki left the city and returned to Cracow.

After the incorporation of Vilnius into the Polish Republic, the university was able to operate on a more regular, not to say routine, basis. There were six faculties: "1) the Arts, 2) Theology, 3) Law and Social Sciences, 4) Mathematics and Natural Sciences, 5) Medicine and 6) the Fine Arts."[31] Among the most pressing issues of the university's first decade of existence were continual financial problems, finding decent housing for faculty and students, improving the university library, and setting up appropriate clinics and laboratories.[32] Enrollments went up from 547 students (251 of whom were women) in 1919/1920 to 3177 (1086 women) in 1928/1929, a figure roughly equal to that of 1938/1939 (3110).[33] Jews always made up a large percentage of students in this period, 19 percent in 1928/1929 but falling thereafter to around 13 percent ten years later.[34] Fewer Belarusians studied at USB (never more than 3% of the total student body), while Lithuanians were even less numerous, rarely more than 1 percent of the total enrollment. There were, however, both Belarusian and Lithuanian student organizations at the university.[35]

Reading memoirs of USB students—nearly all written after a more-or-less reluctant emigration from the city, one is struck by the elegiac quality of the memories.[36] To be sure, remembering one's youth later in life is perhaps always an exercise in reliving past joys of a vanished time, and this is all the more true when the place of those youthful joys has changed so radically and in a certain sense has disappeared altogether.[37] The presence of non-Poles is often remembered, but rarely in hostile or antagonistic terms. Irena Sławińska (clearly exaggerating a bit) suggests that between one-quarter and one-half of students were Jews, but she does not note any tensions between these Jewish students and Christian Poles.[38] Just before her departure after the war, Maria Znamierowska wrote in the context of her ethnographic studies that in her dreams she "heard music and song in Polish, Belarusian, Lithuanian, Yiddish" and remarked that USB had been not just a place of study and research but also one of "rest and contemplation on the fleeting forms of life."[39] Thus both in contemporary accounts and postwar memoirs, USB was a place where diverse national cultures and ethnic groups came together and interacted in a cultured and conflict-free manner. But it must be noted that the fundamental assumption and precondition of this conflict-free interchange was the acceptance of the hegemony of Polish culture at the institution. By taking for granted this Polish hegemony, both contemporaries and memoirists could "allow" other cultures to share the institution—but never to claim it as their own.[40]

The restored Polish university in Vilnius functioned as a spiritual and intellectual center for the strengthening and propagating of Polish culture. But students never numbered much over 3000 and never as much as 2 percent of the city's total population. The physical presence of the university at the "heart" of the city functioned, to be sure, as a reminder of the hegemonic culture in Vilnius. For most residents, however, university studies and scholarship in general must have been rather far removed from their everyday lives. What measures did the city authorities take to make the city's face, so to speak, more Polish? For one thing, streets were renamed in appropriate Polish fashion. "Suvorovskaia" became "Św. Anny," "Gubernatorskaia" was renamed "Żeligowskiego," and "St. George's" became "Mickiewicza." Streets named after distant points in the Russian Empire generally received new names referring to local or at least Polish places: Kavkazskaia, Vladimirskaia, and Orenburgskaia Streets were renamed Góra Bouffałowa (after the hill it passes), Dynaburska, and Śmigłego-Rydza, respectively. Some street names associated with Russian Orthodoxy (Blagoveshchenskaia) received more Catholic names (Dominikańska). But some changes are rather more difficult to explain: why rename "Avtomobilnaia" as "Szara" ("Gray")? And most street names did not change, except for the accent: Niemiecka, Żydowska, Mińska, Fabryczna, Dobra, and Karaimska remained unchanged, though of course now signs would be in Latin letters instead of Cyrillic. In any case, it seems likely that inhabitants continued to use the old names for streets (as in Ilf and Petrov's *Twelve Chairs* for post-revolutionary street names in Russia) for some time. Jews for the most part would have used the Yiddish names, in any case—e.g., Daytshe gos (ul. Niemecka)—and one imagines that they continued to speak of Glezer and Yatkever (Jatkowa) even when the "official" names of these streets in the Jewish quarter had been changed to Gaona and Juljana Klaczki.[41]

Numerous Polish publications, both scholarly and popular, aimed to emphasize the Polish nature of Vilnius and to glorify its "liberation" from Lithuanians, Soviets, or both. An early brochure posed the rhetorical question, "What does every Pole need to know about Wilno?" A series of questions and answers are presented, the questions naïve and ignorant, the answers clear and confident, exhibiting a thoroughly Polish point of view. Most importantly, these publications argued, Poles (and others) should not confuse the present "little country" of Lithuania with the large, mainly Slavic territory of "Litwa," dominated by Polish culture, that had existed in the early modern period. As for Vilnius itself, though founded by the Lithuanian prince Giedymin (Gediminas), the city had very little to do with ethnic Lithuanians. Their language in the fourteenth century had no literature and was incapable of supporting an advanced culture. Gediminas himself had invited Polish artisans, artists, and merchants to the city. To the question, "So, was Wilno ever Lithuanian?" the answer is clear and stark: "Never." In order to defend (Polish) Vilnius, local inhabitants are called upon to "ceaselessly appeal and aspire to Poland and only to Poland" (*Bez przerwy wołać i dążyć do Polski i tylko do Polski*). For all its lack of sophistication, this pamphlet exhibits in concentrated form, so to speak, broadly held conceptions about Polish Vilnius.[42]

In a rather more sophisticated form one finds the same arguments in a pamphlet published in French in the late 1920s. Russian imperial policy, the author argues, encouraged anti-Polish sentiment among Lithuanians (and, it is implied, helped engender the entire Lithuanian national movement). Vilnius was not in an ethnic Lithuanian region, nor had it ever been peopled by Lithuanians; the Lithuanians had violated neutrality by siding with Soviet Russia against Poland in 1920; the plebiscite of early 1922 proved the desire of the local population to live under Polish sovereignty. Like the popular pamphlet, this booklet mentions the domination of Polish culture (and its long-standing importance and influence in the region), but the effort to tar Lithuanians with the Russian and Soviet brush is a clever maneuver to influence foreign opinion, which on the whole—and in particular in France and Belgium—was heavily anti-Soviet.[43] In both of these pamphlets, for domestic and international consumption, the fundamental argument is clear: Vilnius was and is a Polish city; it would be a crime and an absurdity to hand it over to the Lithuanians, whose culture was less advanced and whose historical claims to the city were without foundation. Neither of these pamphlets—in typical fashion—devotes much space to the Jews of Vilnius, who continued to make up a considerable part of the city's population.

A number of interwar publications aimed to remind Poles of Vilnius' (Polish) culture and history, including its glorious recent past (i.e., the early 1920s). A short book published in the mid-1930s provided guidance for local schoolteachers on incorporating the historical monuments of Vilnius in their instruction. Here it is interesting that national minorities (i.e., non-Poles) in the city past and present are mentioned, and while the tone is patriotic, it is not chauvinistic. Third-graders, for example, would visit sights such as the tomb of Piłsudski's mother (where the marshal's heart would soon be buried) and be asked questions about the man and his importance for Vilnius. Similarly, visits to graves of those fallen in 1919–1920 and in the 1863 Insurrection would be connected to different generations of Poles fighting and dying for their homeland. Visits to the town hall, royal graves (in the cathedral), the university, and the cathedral itself would be accompanied by lessons on how earlier the city and country were administered and ruled. Another topic of instruction was the role that faith and education played in the lives of earlier Poles in Vilnius.[44] Innumerable books considered every aspect of the military campaigns of 1919–1921 that saved Vilnius from Lithuanian occupation.[45] History—in particular recent history—was actively coopted into the discourse of Polish Vilnius.

In the religious sphere, local Catholic churches and clergy tended to identify themselves strongly with Polish patriotism. Bishop Jerzy Matulewicz attempted to adopt a neutral position between the competing claims of Lithuanians and Poles, but this only earned him the enmity of both sides and a premature retirement.[46] Much anecdotal evidence supports the contention that the Catholic Church in the region was conservative and strongly supported Polish patriotic ideals, but the specific case of Catholic clergy in the Vilnius region during the interwar needs more study. Neal Pease has shown convincingly that the Catholic Church in interwar Poland was not as predictably conservative as traditionally thought, and no doubt Catholic clergy in this region, too, were ideologically more diverse than is often supposed.[47] Still, the general position of the Catholic Church in Vilnius against political liberalism—and its suspicion of the "neo-pagan" Lithuanian state—seems rather well documented.[48]

Despite the weak economy and the city's position far from the political and cultural centers of Warsaw and Cracow, the literary scene in Vilnius was very active. Indeed, this aspect of interwar Vilnius is vastly better researched than any other. In part this is due to the fact that one young poet of the interwar, Czesław Miłosz, later achieved world fame and was awarded the Nobel Prize (1980), while another, Miłosz's close friend Teodor Bujnicki, had a son who devoted a good deal of his scholarly life to culture in Vilnius.[49] As the literary scene in interwar Vilnius is far better known than other aspects of life, a few words and references to more serious studies will have to suffice here. Interwar Vilnius was home to a wide variety of writers, from journalists like the older Stanisław Mackiewicz (Cat) to the more radical, experimental, and generally more left-wing "Żagary" group (to which both Miłosz and Bujnicki belonged).[50] For a relatively small, out-of-the-way, and poor provincial city, Vilnius could boast an astonishing literary scene and has left an important mark on the history of Polish literature. Jagoda Hernik Spalińska's book on the 371 "literary Wednesdays" that took place in Vilnius between 1927 and 1939 shows vividly the breadth and vitality of the literary scene.[51] Some of the poetry and shorter works produced were published in the numerous periodicals—both specifically literary and more general—published in interwar Vilnius.[52] Besides publishing, Vilnius also boasted an active theatrical life.[53] In literary culture, then, interwar Vilnius was indisputably an important Polish city.

When thinking of literature and Vilnius, most Poles would immediately invoke the national poet, Mickiewicz, whose poetic beginnings in the 1820s are associated with the city. And yet Vilnius lacked a proper monument commemorating the poet. Public art, in particular monuments, is an obvious way to mark and memorialize a city's (national) past. Only a few such works of public memorial art were constructed in Vilnius in the interwar period. One of these was a small memorial to the Polish writer Eliza Orzeszkowa (who spent most of her life in nearby Grodno, though she had many close ties to Vilnius), set up on the square now dominated by a monument to Vincas Kudirka (who wrote the words to the Lithuanian national anthem). Aside from this, surprisingly little was done to adorn the cityscape with new monuments or public art, most likely because of the lack of finances. Plans to construct an enormous (over twenty meters high) monument to the city's most famous son, Adam Mickiewicz, caused a great deal of public debate resulting in two large models—but no final monument. In and of themselves, however, the controversies over the Mickiewicz monument are indicative of the difficulties of "properly" monumentalizing national heroes.

There is some irony in the fact that, when Mickiewicz monuments were erected in Cracow (1898), Warsaw (1898), and Lwów (1904), none was constructed in the city most linked with the artist's life and work.[54] Of course the reason for this is not hard to understand: Mickiewicz symbolized Polish culture, and while such a monument could be allowed even in Russian-occupied Warsaw (though grudgingly), it would send an unacceptable message in Vilnius—that is, it would mark the city as culturally Polish. Nonetheless, there had been repeated efforts before the outbreak of World War I—associated in particular with the journalist Czesław Jankowski—to erect a monument, and several thousand rubles had been collected for this purpose.[55]

Once the city was firmly (though not yet officially) in Polish hands after October 1920, efforts were renewed to properly remember Mickiewicz in the town of his youth. The "Committee for the Construction of a Monument to Adam Mickiewicz" was set up in 1921, and a model for the future monument by the sculptor Zbigniew Pronaszka was completed the following year.[56] Unfortunately, the cubist style of the proposed monument (and model) was not to the liking of most Vilnius Poles. As a well-known art historian at USB and Vilnius enthusiast, Juljusz Kłos, noted in a contemporary guidebook, "twelve meters high . . . in cubist forms [the model] called forth an instinctive protest in most viewers."[57]

VILNIUS AS A POLISH CITY, 1919-1939    137

While Pronaszka's model continued to stand, as far as I can tell, throughout the 1930s, its modernist form made it unacceptable to the monument's potential sponsors. Already in 1925 a new competition for the Mickiewicz monument had been announced.[58] The competition was limited to Polish artists, regardless of their place of residence. The jury judging the entries (there were sixty-eight in all) was headed by General Żeligowski and included a number of dignitaries, from a banker to professors of art and architecture to a Poznań literary figure. The majority of the jury members were not from Vilnius but represented all parts of Poland, emphasizing the national importance of the future monument. After a great deal of discussion and negotiation lasting for years, the project of Henryk Kuna was accepted, by an overwhelming number of votes, in 1932. The monument was to be placed in the center of the city, at the intersection of Wileńska and Mickiewicza in the middle of the latter avenue and was, like Pronaszka's model, to tower above the city, the five-meter tall statue of the Bard placed atop a base (decorated with bas relief motifs from Mickiewicz's works) over twice as high.[59]

Unfortunately, Kuna's monument was to prove just as unacceptable to large segments of Vilnius Polish society as Pronaszka's had been. The style, structure, and location of the monument were all criticized, in particular in press polemics encouraged by the conservative Vilnius daily, *Słowo*. Here a new factor came into play: Kuna's Jewish origins. While Kuna had been born into an Orthodox Jewish family, he had converted to Catholicism and was a well-known Polish artist. The polemics over whether a Polish patriot of Jewish origins should be allowed to memorialize the Polish national poet—himself of mixed and "questionable" origins—indicated that a form of racial antisemitism had entered Polish public discourse by the 1930s. On the other hand, we should also not discount petty factors such as personal rivalries, the cynical use of antisemitism to sell newspapers, and sincere misgivings over the monument's intrinsic merits. In any case, in the face of press polemics the Vilnius town council proved reluctant to support the project and the monument remained only a wooden model when World War II broke out.[60] The difficulties of remembering and memorializing Mickiewicz in Vilnius give us some insight into the complications of public and national commemoration in interwar Poland.

Interwar Polish Vilnius was also an artistic center. True, Vilnius artists rarely counted among the avant-garde and, unlike the city's writers, tended to be rather conservative in themes and technique. Patrons of the arts in the city were mainly noble landowners who wanted art that emphasized the city's great past and links with Polish culture. Ferdynand Ruszczyc embodied this tendency, with his indefatigable work for the university and its school of fine arts.⁶¹ At the same time, modernist tendencies in art could be found in the city, in particular reflected in the work of the artist Ludomir Slendziński and the "Wilno school."⁶² While the artistic scene was dominated by Poles, a number of Jews and even a few Lithuanians left their mark.⁶³ The most important institutions for interwar Vilnius artistic life were the university's faculty of fine arts and the Vilnius Society of Visual Artists (Wileńskie Towarzystwo Artystów Plastyków).⁶⁴

Interwar Vilnius lives on in an amazing variety of publications about the period in Polish. Even into the twenty-first century new memoirs from the period continue to be published. These reminiscences differ from other memoirs of youth in that they attempt to re-create a city that, in a cultural and national sense, no longer exists. As befits members of the intelligentsia (nearly all memoir authors come from this educated and cultured class), these memoirs stress cooperation and national-culture toleration, acknowledging the Jewish and Lithuanian presence in the city, while also depicting Vilnius as a Polish milieu.

Helena Obiezierska's memoirs are in many respects typical. The recollections of a woman who studied at USB and ended up as a teacher, they were written at the end of her life and published only after her death. Obiezierska specifically refers to her own life in the context of the history of the Polish people in the twentieth century, no doubt referring to the shared experiences of regained statehood, Nazi and Soviet occupations, but also to trends in Polish culture. Born in 1899, Obiezierska comments that she grew up during the period of "Młoda Polska," when old forms of artistic representation were being challenged. She was precisely old enough to have firsthand experience of Russian schools (in Minsk) as well as the dislocations of the war years. After various peregrinations from Minsk (when the Bolsheviks took the city) to Warsaw, she finally ended up in Vilnius, where she enrolled at USB.⁶⁵

Among Obiezierska's first impressions of Vilnius, the Jewish community loomed large. While, as she insisted, [she was] "not an antisemite," she found the Vilnius Jews slovenly in their dress and rude. The older generation, she recalled, acted loyal toward Poland but spoke among themselves "exclusively in Russian." The "two enthusiasms" among Jews—finding ways of enriching themselves and their admiration for Russian culture—"created in the generation of the first half of the twentieth century enormous contempt and dislike for Poles and their strivings for independence." At the same time, she recalled in a more positive vein the Jews (mainly female) enrolled with her in Polish philology courses.⁶⁶ The city impressed her, mainly negatively, as dirty and run-down. Still, she came to like the city and her work teaching at various high schools. By the time anti-Jewish disturbances became endemic at the university (from ca. 1931), she was mainly concerned with her own teaching. She mentions in passing the periodical demands by nationalist students that Jewish medical students supply "their own corpses" (i.e., that they not be allowed to work on "Christian" cadavers). She remembers with disapproval the "pseudo-national propaganda" for restricting Jewish access to university (and even secondary) education but admits to not buying at Jewish stores in order to support "the still weak Polish commerce in Wilno."[67]

Obiezierska's memoirs are notable for their frank dislike of Jews, despite her formulaic statement that "I am not an antisemite, but. . . ." Clearly for her, as for most Poles of the time (and even later), "Jew" and "Pole" were more or less exclusive terms, and the Jews in Vilnius were not only alien but basically hostile to Polish national aims. It should be noted, however, that Jews appear perhaps on a few dozen pages—if that—of her memoir of over 500 pages. Far more important were her efforts in education and internal Polish politics.

A very different memoir, that of the librarian Janusz Dunin-Horkawicz, which was published just before his death, also remembered Jews as alien, though not necessarily as hostile. At the same time, Belarusians too, inasmuch as they retained their national identity once educated, were also considered traitors to the Polish cause, and Dunin-Horkawicz states intriguingly that Jews were not afforded an "entry into Polish society"—except among communists. The latter statement suggests one reason for the over-representation of Jews in leftist circles. Russians were few in interwar Vilnius, but on the whole they enjoyed friendly relations with Poles. As for Lithuanians, he could recall only a servant girl.[68] For Dunin-Horkawicz, Vilnius was mainly memorable for its position between East and West, its old-fashioned, slow-paced life (the prevalence of horse-drawn drozhki, even in the late 1930s), the peculiarities of Polish spoken there, and religious traditions and festivals. Probably because of his youth during the 1930s (he was born in 1931), Dunin did not comment on politics or cultural events but, rather, on the kind of thing that a boy would remember: festivals, funerals, food, and play.

An unusual pair of memoirs is that of a father and son: Stanisław Mianowski (born 1889) and his son Krzysztof (born 1923). The father attended the "II gymnazjum" located on the premises of the old university and remembered the festive unveiling in 1898 of the nearby Muraviev monument, "the height of ugliness." In his final years at high school (after 1905), he recalled, Lithuanian priests whipped up "chauvinism" and hatred toward Poles. After graduation Stanisław Mianowski, like many other sons of local nobles, studied in Dorpat (Iur'ev, today's Tartu), where he joined the fraternity "Polonia." Rather more unusually—though he mentions the presence of numerous other Poles—he continued his education (in law) at Kazan University on the Volga before returning to the Vilnius region only a few weeks before the outbreak of World War I.[69]

Taken prisoner by the Germans, Mianowski-père mentions the presence of numerous Jews whom he divides into "Russian-speaking" and "Polish-speaking" groups, reserving harsh words for the former but only singling out two individual polonized Jews for positive recollections.[70] Returning to Vilnius on leave in October 1919, he was able to attend the festive opening of the university before his military duties took him away again, after which he came back to stay right before the plebiscite of early 1922. In this context he noted the bitter opposition expressed by Lithuanian propaganda (he does not mention Jews here). Mianowski's relations with Jewish lawyers (who, it should be recalled, were not few in interwar Poland and Vilnius) seem to have been somewhat conflicted. On the one hand, he specifically remarked that he "respected" the Jewish attorneys Izrael Kapłan and Miron Wygodzki. But on the other hand, he mentioned one Henoch Korngold, who had earlier spoken scornfully of "these Litwaks" (Korngold was from Warsaw) but in November 1939 "showed his true face" by remarking, "finally your [*wasze*] Polish rule has come to an end." Jewish lawyers in Vilnius behaved loyally toward the Polish state, on the whole, but spoke among themselves in Russian.[71] Stanisław Mianowski went on to be a judge, a position he held when the Red Army invaded in September 1939.

The memoirs of the younger Krzysztof Mianowski, born 1923, are rather different in tone—not those of a grown man but recollections of boyhood and youth. He was born in a house on the banks of the Neris (Wilia) River, across the river from the wooden monument to Mickiewicz by sculptor Pronaszka, which he remembered people mocking for its modernist style. As a boy he remembered the death of Piłsudski and the ceremonial burying of the leader's heart in Rossa Cemetery in Vilnius (1937). Jews appear in these memories as neighbors and more-or-less kindly adults, though he does recall pouring sand on the heads of Jewish neighborhood children (apparently playmates, at least known by name) and being scolded by "an old Jewess."[72] Among his fellow pupils at school were Poles, Jews, Tatars, Russians, and Karaites, as well as French and German children. The only Lithuanian he recalls was, typically, one of the family's cooks. Mianowski's recollections lack any hint of hostility or friction between nations though he seems to have socialized mostly with Poles (as one would expect).

Krzysztof Mianowski recalls many details that would have been of interest to a boy and teenager. His family lacked a radio, but their neighbors had one that cost 300 złoty—a month's salary for a mid-grade civil servant. Like many other youngsters, he spent many afternoons on Mickiewicza Street, which the elderly still called "Jerek" (after the Russian designation, St. George). Sweetshops and bakeries, movie theaters, restaurants, a flower shop, the Jabłkowski Brothers' department ("universal") store, officers' club, and the two most elegant hotels in Vilnius ("George" and "Bristol") were among the delights of Mickiewicz Street.[73]

One of the pioneers of Polish radio, Tadeusz Łopalewski recalls another part of Vilnius life in the 1920s and 1930s, in particular literary and artist circles. Like many immigrants to Vilnius in these years, Łopalewski had grown up in the Russian interior (St. Petersburg) and tried his luck (with no success) in the Polish capital before landing in Vilnius in the early 1920s. About the locals, Łopalewski noted that they liked to eat "well and a lot" and that restaurants served tasty and inexpensive dishes. A tradition of "graphomania" existed in the city, combined with sharp practices "from the time of Mickiewicz" among publishers (the memoirist was a young writer).[74] Very soon upon arriving in the city, Łopalewski was in the thick of the theater and literary world there and recalled the controversies about the Mickiewicz monument contest(s), including one entry (not to the taste of most locals) of the poet naked with an eagle drinking his blood à la Prometheus. Like many, Łopalewski recalled the flood of spring 1931 and the sensational uncovering in a crypt under the cathedral of the remains of King Alexander Jagiellończyk and Barbara Radziwiłłówna, both untouched for several centuries.[75] At literary gatherings from that time Łopalewski became acquainted with Witold Hulewicz, a writer and the later program director (from 1927) of Polskie Radio in Vilnius.[76] From the start Łopalewski was involved with the Vilnius radio station and recalled that no one had any idea how to program radio and that in any case the audience remained small in the 1930s because of the expense of radio sets. Lectures, concerts (including folk music with village musicians), radio plays, recitations, and topical broadcasts or news made up programming in the early years. For the burial of Piłsudski's heart in Vilnius, "an especially important, many-hour program" was planned, but the announcer Limanowski, who was expected to provide a running commentary on the processions, organizations, dignitaries present, and the like, instead rambled on about the day's weather, clouds, Mickiewicz, and other topics.[77] In autumn 1939, when the Red Army invaded and the city was given over to the Lithuanians, Łopalewski remained at Polskie Radio (until dismissed, along with other Poles, by the Lithuanian authorities). Remarkable about

Łopalewski's memoirs is the almost total absence in them of non-Poles, though this may be explained by censorship considerations (the book was published in the mid-1960s) and by his close involvement with Polish-language culture.

## Wilno as a Tourist Destination

In the interwar period, Vilnius was touted as a tourist destination even though relatively few Poles could afford to travel for pleasure and when they could, they only infrequently visited cities in the country's eastern borderlands. After all, even in Western Europe, travel as a leisure activity had only become a mass phenomenon in the mid-nineteenth century (e.g., Thomas Cook's famous outings, including his visit to the Crystal Palace Exhibition in London).[78] Still, the idea of tourism did exist, and efforts were made to put Vilnius on the Polish tourist's mental map. A proper tourist needed, of course, a guide—or at least a guidebook (the Polish *przewodnik* can serve for either meaning). As we have seen, there had been Polish guidebooks to Vilnius (or guidebooks to Polish Wilno?) before 1914, and some of these were expanded, and many more new guidebooks appeared in the interwar years.[79] These books adopted various strategies to present Polish Vilnius, in part simply by their focus on Catholic and Polish sights but also by portraying non-Polish elements in the cityscape as somehow foreign, exotic, or even unnatural (the last mainly in the case of Orthodox and Russian elements introduced in the later nineteenth century). In many cases the guidebooks presented much more than a mere listing of "sights" or practical information; they included a significant amount of historical, artistic, and even geographical information about Vilnius and its surroundings. Guidebooks helped polonize Vilnius in at least three ways: first, by presenting the city as naturally forming part of Poland and Polish history; second, by noting and emphasizing the predominant position of Polish culture and the Roman Catholic faith in the city; and finally, by encouraging Poles from outside Vilnius to get to know (and love) the city as part of their shared cultural and national heritage, whether they hailed from Mazovia, Great Poland, or Galicia.

Probably the most popular of these guidebooks was that penned by Władysław Zahorski, first appearing in 1910 and going through a number of editions after the author's death in 1927, well into the 1930s. Zahorski also published a number of pamphlets on specific sights such as the churches of St. Anne and St. Nicholas. Born in 1858 near Vilnius, Zahorski spent his youth in the Russian interior, where his father was exiled after 1863. He attended Moscow University and graduated in 1883 with a medical degree, returning to Vilnius only in 1893.[80]

Zahorski was not a professional historian but an enthusiast of the city, which may explain the popularity of his guidebook. In various editions, it began with a short outline of the city's history then plunged into the city's streets, beginning with Ostrobramska and Zamkowa Streets—that is, starting at the site of the miracle-working image of the Virgin and then walking down to the foot of Castle Hill. Specific houses along this route were identified and described, usually in connection with their Polish past. Because of the guidebook's organization by streets, then by churches and cemeteries, it had the effect of removing non-Poles and non-Catholics from sight. This is not to say that Zahorski left out, for example, Jewish Vilnius: he mentions that with Szklana (Glass) Street the so-called Black City (Czarne Miasto), or Jewish quarter, began.[81] The 1935 edition even includes a short entry titled "Jewish district" describing this quarter as including Szklana, Klaczki, Żydowska, Gaona, and Szwarcowego Streets and mentioning the Great Synagogue.[82] On the other hand, Zahorski's account of Niemiecka (German) Street, described by Czesław Miłosz as "exclusively Jewish" at this time, does not mention Jews at all.[83] For Zahorski, it would seem, the Jewish residents of Vilnius were a passing and not particularly interesting part of the eternal and Polish city.

Another guidebook, or more properly a kind of mixture of city history and guidebook, by Jerzy Remer, took a different approach. Rather than inviting the reader to wander through the city's streets, identifying specific houses and other sights with the Polish past, Remer divided his book into topics related to the city and its region. Indeed, the city as such only begins to dominate after some thirty-odd pages on its natural surroundings and the peasant population (where it seems likely that the *chłop litewski* ["Lithuanian peasant"] pictured on page 11 is meant as a local variety of Pole). Proceeding chronologically, Remer dedicates an entire chapter to the sacred image at Ostra Brama, speaking lyrically of the generations who have prayed before her and concluding, "But the most expressive documents of the miraculous power of the Mother of Mercy of Ostra Brama are the testimony plaques [*wota*], innumerable links of the enormous chain of human joy and pain."[84] While Poles are not mentioned specifically, Remer's readers would have certainly connected—at least in part—this "joy and suffering" with the past of a Polish-Catholic city under foreign and Orthodox domination.

In a chapter entitled "Along Streets and Alleys" (*Ulicami, zaułkami*), Remer advises the visitor to stroll aimlessly and without plan through Vilnius. In particular he emphasizes the city's "Latin quarter" (his phrase) around the university and points out the various places connected with Mickiewicz's life and works. Passing from the university district toward the Rossa Cemetery, Remer does not fail to note the Jewish quarter. But, as for Zahorski, for Remer, this district was only a secondary sight along one's way to the more important cemetery where the remains of various famous Poles were interred. Among those buried in Rossa, Remer duly remarks, are the Lithuanian painter "Czurlanis" (Mikalojus Konstantinas Čiurlionis) and the thinker "Basanowicz" (Jonas Basanavičius)—but the casual reader would hardly notice these individuals' nationality.[85] In particular Remer's chapters on the nineteenth-century city ("The Polish Athens," "A Symbol of Brotherhood and Heroism") portray the city in exclusively Polish terms, as part of the Polish nation and suffering for the Polish cause. In a similar way, the subsequent two chapters ("Liberation," "The Republic's Fortress") tell of the Bolshevik hordes threatening the city and of its eventual redemption by Piłsudski and Żeligowski, but it fails to mention discordant elements such as the pogrom of April 1919. The city's past and present fate, Remer's narrative stresses, are connected inextricably with the larger fate of Poland. Whether or not the population of the city is of mixed nationality thus loses all significance: the city itself certainly belongs to the Polish past and future.

Another popular guidebook that was published in three editions in the 1930s was that of Professor Juljusz Kłos of USB. Kłos was an architect and art critic, a major figure in interwar Vilnius. The author's friend, the well-known photographer Jan Bułhak, called Kłos's work a "guidebook to human souls" (*przewodnik po duszach ludzkich*). Kłos died suddenly in 1933 in his early fifties, and the final edition of the guidebook (1937) was published after his death. Possibly due to his training as an architect, Kłos dedicated considerable space to the topography and architectural past of the city. But perhaps the most remarkable feature of his guidebook was its enthusiasm, an enthusiasm the author attributed to the city itself, as exemplified by Mickiewicz's "Oda do Młodości" (Ode to Youth). Kłos explicitly stated that this enthusiasm would certainly penetrate the soul of any sensitive visitor, "not only every Pole, but even foreigners coming from distant lands."[86] Like Remer, Kłos described Vilnius' past and present as part of a larger Polish narrative involving oppression, resistance, and eventually triumph to freedom. Speaking of the city's history from the time of the hated "hangman" M. N. Muraviev to the city's redemption in the early 1920s, Kłos gave the impression that the city was populated exclusively by Poles; he mentioned no other nationality except obliquely (i.e., if 65% of the population voted on January 8, 1922 for Poland, who were the others?).[87]

VILNIUS AS A POLISH CITY, 1919-1939    145

Kłos's guidebook did dedicate a bit more space to the Jewish quarter, here defining it as the triangular area between three streets: Wielka, Niemiecka, and Dominikańska. Unlike the other two authors discussed here, Kłos also described the main synagogue (which is illustrated here as well) with real interest. As for the Jewish inhabitants themselves, Kłos mentioned a single one: the critic and art historian Juljan Klaczko, "a friend of Słowacki's" who was born here (but later converted to Christianity and was a convinced Polish patriot). As for the rest, Kłos remarked on the exotic and "original" aspects of the Jewish quarter but continued, "This [positive] impression is unfortunately weakened by the typically Eastern slovenliness [*niechlujstwo*] of the inhabitants of this unhygienic [*antyhigjeniczna*] quarter and its unbearable stench [*zaduch*] make it impossible for a cultured European, in particular on hot summer days, to visit these alleyways."[88] Some individuals of Jewish birth, like Klaczko, could leave behind the "Eastern" ways of their people and become "cultured Europeans." But in general Jews were an exotic and backward element, included among but not properly constituting the true (Polish) Vilnius.

## Jewish Vilna

World War I and the insecurity of the early 1920s had taken a heavy toll on Jews in Vilnius. Many had died and even more had emigrated both abroad and to other parts of the Russian Empire (initially) and Poland. Jews would never recover their numerical predominance in the city. Still, the Jewish presence was large, even ubiquitous. The census of 1931 (the only one carried out in the city in the interwar period) showed nearly 55,000 Jews residing in Vilnius, or almost 28 percent of the total population.[89] And Vilnius remained an important center for Jewish culture and learning, both of the traditional and of the "modern" varieties. When in the final years of the interwar republic Shaul and Yitzhak Goskind made six short films of principal Jewish towns in Poland, Vilnius was among them.[90]

Relations between Jews and Poles in these decades were uneasy but not uniformly hostile. The back-and-forth of the city between the Red Army, Poles, and Lithuanians in the 1918-1920 period had placed Vilnius Jews, to use a German researcher's apt phrase, "between all fronts."[91] The interwar Polish Republic saw itself, first and foremost, as the homeland of ethnic Poles. While ethnic minorities (who made up one-third of the total population) enjoyed legal equality and in principle had rights to state support for education in their native tongue, in reality the Polish state fairly consistently privileged the Polish language, Polish schools, and ethnic Poles.[92] This is hardly remarkable and in no way unusual for East-Central Europe in the interwar period: every would-be "nation-state" in the region favored the main national group for government employment, financial assistance, and the like.

In the previous chapter we have considered the elections in 1921 to the "Wilno Sejm" that would decide the fate of the city and its environments ("Middle Lithuania"). Jews (and Lithuanians), as we have seen, chose to boycott the election rather than insert themselves between Poles and Lithuanians in this very sensitive matter. Unfortunately, the local authorities interpreted the nonparticipation of Jews in the plebiscite as an indication of anti-Polish feeling. A Polish official remarked in an internal memo from late 1921 that Jews recognized widespread antisemitism among Poles and for this and other reasons would prefer to live under Lithuanian rule.[93] The generalized distrust expressed toward Jews in this memo was far from unusual among Poles. Even Polish-speaking Jews (of whom there were increasing numbers) were rarely considered (even by themselves) as "Poles."

At the same time, it would be wrong to dwell on the negative. As Czesław Miłosz and many others have recalled in their memoirs, Poles and Jews interacted in many ways on an everyday basis and on the whole these interactions were businesslike or even friendly. As Jarosław Wołkonowski has shown, Jews served on the Vilnius city council throughout this period, even after 1935, when relations took a decided turn for the worse.[94] During the interwar period the forces of secularization and acculturation were also at work in Vilnius; by the late 1930s many young Jews spoke Polish as a native language and no longer frequented the prayer houses that had made the city so renowned. While Yiddish continued to dominate as the native language of Vilnius Jews, Jews in 1939 were at least culturally and linguistically much more integrated into local Polish society than had been the case at the beginning of the century.

A Jewish community (that is, as an official bureaucratic body) continued to exist in the interwar period. As Samuel Kassow points out, the *kehile* elected in late 1918 was democratic and secular, elected by all Jewish residents twenty years of age or above. Already during the war, Vilnius Jews had banded together to protect their interests in the face of harsh war conditions and the hostility of the Polish National-Democratic Party supporters. After the April 1919 pogrom, the *kehile* called on the Polish authorities to respect Jewish rights and assure the safety of all residents, including Jews. Already at this early stage, the *kehile* was strongly but not exclusively influenced by the left (especially the Bund) but represented the diverse political stances and interests of the entire Jewish community.⁹⁵ As a center for community action, Jewish charity, and education, the *kehile* was active throughout the period.⁹⁶

Most commentators at the time emphasized the economic decline of Vilnius' Jewish community in the interwar period. In a famous essay, Arcadius Kahan described the Jewish quarter in terms of three "concentric circles": the densely populated, mainly poor, and traditional core in the middle of the Old Town; a second circle on the edge of the Jewish Old Town, featuring businesses and extending to the more spacious (and expensive) residences of wealthier and often less traditional Jews; and finally an outer circle, only loosely connected with the core, of Jewish housing (usually poor) on the edges of town. Kahan estimates that some 35 percent of Vilnius' Jewish population worked in trade, 30 percent as artisans, 25 percent as wage earners (i.e., in factories or workshops), and around 10 percent in services or unemployed (his estimates, admittedly rough, add up to 110%). More than 2000 Jews were enrolled in eleven guilds, a similar number belonged to an artisans' union, and more than a thousand individuals belonged to merchants' and retailers' associations. Vilnius Jews also had their own physicians', dentists', engineers', nurses', and teachers' organizations as well as a wide variety of charitable groups. Despite differences in education, piety, and wealth, Kahan claimed, social differentiation among Vilnius Jews lacked rigidity: "I would maintain that, in comparison with the communities of Warsaw and Cracow, Lemberg and Lublin, Białystok and Odessa, Vilnius had the shortest social distance."⁹⁷

It is possible, of course, that Kahan's portrayal of the city of his youth is somewhat rose-tinted (which is entirely understandable, of course, given his life experiences). While he does not deny the existence of poverty in the city, contemporary reports are more bitter in their evaluation of economic and demographic trends. In an overview looking at the period 1911-1928, the physician and well-known Vilnius figure Cemach Szabad noted the very unfavorable position for social scientists looking at the city, the lack of scientific statistics, and the dearth of demographic works on Jews in the region. Using the statistics available to him (death certificates), Szabad calculated that Jewish mortality had increased significantly during the war, peaking in 1917-1918 and only returning to normal around 1921. More important than higher mortality rates for the reduction of Jewish population, however, was the flight of thousands of Jews across the border to Lithuania and elsewhere out of fear of pogroms. As for the birth rate among Jews in Vilnius, it had declined continually in the 1920s, by more than one-third between 1923 and 1928. While a declining birth rate among urban populations was typical of the period, the low number of births also contributed to the stagnant size of Vilna's Jewish community.[98]

The economist and sociologist Jacob Lestschinski (Leshchinskii) portrayed the development of Jewish Vilna since the war in darker hues, entitling his essay on the subject "the decline of a Jewish city." More than any other city, Lestschinski claimed, Vilna suffered from the war: not from violence and pogroms specifically, but in the sense of losing its economic base. Walking around Vilna, he went on, one sees elderly men and women selling a motley variety of rags, cakes, old trousers, herring, rolls, and apples out in the open. Speaking with some of the traders, Lestschinski learns that their children are earning good money as emigrants in New York and Argentina. Young Jews in the city were eagerly studying practical subjects in the hope of earning a better living than their parents. But the cards were stacked against them: the Polish government encouraged migration of peasants to the city to establish new stores and artisan shops in direct competition with Jewish businesses. For this reason, Lestschinski asserted, Jewish commerce in Vilna had shrunk by at least one-third and the future did not look promising.

As an example of the difficulties faced by Jewish artisans and commerce, Lestschinski used the tailoring business. Before the war, Jewish tailors dominated in the city though already at that point Polish competition was increasing. In the 1920s, however, Polish officers and civil servants avoided Jewish tailors and dry goods stores, preferring Polish establishments even when their prices were higher. As for the Polish businesses, these enjoyed cheap credit terms not available to their Jewish competitors. Furthermore, Poles were using these favorable terms to build modern workshops and factories with which the typical, small Jewish tailoring shops simply could not compete. In other branches of the clothing, glove, shoe, and haberdashery business, Jews had lost access to the Russian market upon which they had depended before the war, and Polish tariff politics had lately shut out access to the German market. In short, Lestschinski was unable to provide any optimism about economic developments in Jewish Vilnius since 1918.[99]

If the interwar period was not particularly prosperous in the economic sense for Vilnius' Jews, their cultural scene was abundantly rich. As Cecile Kuznitz has pointed out, interwar Jewish poets and intellectuals saw their city as a melding of ancient tradition, folk culture, and modernity. Despite the cost of doing so, most merchants preferred to use both Yiddish—and, as required, Polish—in their shop signs to underline the Jewish character of their business and their city. At the same time, Jews in Vilnius—reacting in part to complaints about unhygienic conditions—organized to pave the court of the old synagogue (the so-called *shulhoyf*) and in other ways repaired and beautified the Jewish quarter and the nearby new town (Pohulanka), where institutions such as the Jewish People's Bank, Hebrew Immigrant Aid Society, and—most famous of all—YIVO were located.[100]

YIVO, the Yiddish acronym for Jewish/Yiddish Scientific Center, may fairly be called the most striking and influential cultural experiment launched by interwar Vilnius Jews.[101] The idea behind the institution, set up in 1925, was simple: to create a modern research university, with the goal of training future scholars and carrying out research, all using the Yiddish language. It is no coincidence that in the same year the Hebrew University of Jerusalem was founded. The creators of YIVO, in particular Zalman Rejzen, Nochem Shtif, Elias Chernikover, and Max Weinreich, organized the institute into four sections: philological (including folklore and linguistics), economic-statistical (which, among other things, published work by J. Lestschinski), historical, and pedagogical-psychological. The institute also functioned as a bibliographic center for Yiddish publications and published a bibliographical yearbook. The YIVO's library and archive aimed to collect and preserve important works and artifacts having to do with various aspects of the Jewish past and present.[102]

YIVO depended on private donations for its operations. Many of the scholars involved with the institute supported it by long hours of free or poorly paid work. Unlike the Hebrew University, YIVO did not aim to educate undergraduates. Rather, it offered courses to advanced students, akin to a doctoral program (though it did not have the right to issue degrees). The institute avoided politics but was obviously close to other Yiddish-language educational and social organizations. Its historical section saw as its role both the collecting of historical documents and the furthering of a sophisticated analysis of Jewish history using the medium of the Yiddish language. In this effort the great Russian-Jewish historian Simon Dubnov supported and worked with the institution.[103]

The amazingly rich outburst of Yiddish poetry in the interwar period paralleled the bourgeoning of Polish literature at the same time. This aspect of Jewish culture is better researched than any other; suffice it to say that the members of "young Vilne" in their own way created a modern artistic city that was not limited to the written/spoken word alone.[104] Vilnius also enjoyed an active and dynamic theater life in Yiddish.[105] Similarly, readers could choose from a variety of periodicals and other publications in that language; a researcher on the topic of the Yiddish press has called 1928 "in a statistical sense... the peak year of the Yiddish press," with a dozen periodicals appearing in Vilnius (though of course many others published in Warsaw and other cities would have been available).[106] A survey of cultural, scholarly, and artistic life in Vilnius published in 1935 filled nearly five hundred densely printed pages.[107] In short, Jewish culture—whether in Polish, Hebrew, or Yiddish (though most obviously in the latter language)—continued to prosper in this period.

Jews also participated in "Polish" cultural life in the city. Indeed, the process of linguistic acculturation among Vilnius Jews helped weaken the cultural divide that had been so strong just a generation earlier. Throughout the interwar period, Jews made up a significant percentage of students at Stefan Batory University. According to Arcadius Kahan, the highest enrollment of Jews occurred in the very middle of this period, in the academic year 1929–1930, when around one-quarter of students at the university declared Yiddish or Hebrew as their native tongue.[108] At the university there was a student mutual aid society; the Esperanto club at the university was also popular among Jewish students.[109] Jews also participated in sports in the city, having a number of clubs for football (soccer), swimming, and other sports.[110] Football club "Makabi" had its own field where regular matches with other teams (not only Jewish) were held.[111]

Vilnius' reputation as a center for traditional religious life also endured in the interwar years. It seems, though, that this reputation was nurtured as a "lost paradise" of simple, true Jewishness. This image comes through clearly in several publications of these years, including two that used the still relatively new technology of photography to portray the traditional Jewish city. In both of these books, both the one published locally with Yiddish text and the other published abroad with (minimal) text in German, showed traditional scenes of Jewish life, religion, trade, and everyday interaction, including poverty. Looking at these remarkable photographs, one feels that even at this point (the books were published in 1925 and 1931), the authors sensed that the traditional Jewish life in Vilnius was on the wane.[112]

At the same time that these romanticized images were published, strains in Polish-Jewish relations in Vilnius were apparent. Often the university was the flashpoint for these conflicts. Nationalist Polish students took to blocking access to the university for Jewish students, leading in November 1931 to a clash in which a Polish student was struck by a rock and killed.[113] While calm was eventually restored without further bloodshed, Polish-Jewish relations at the university remained tense throughout the 1930s.[114] These tensions reflected an increased level of antisemitism throughout Poland, including efforts to segregate Jews at universities to specific seats ("ghetto benches"). Several professors at USB (Antoni Zygmund, Juliusz Rudnicki, Manfred Kridl, Wiktor Sukiennicki) refused to comply with this law and are remembered with honor by Kahan in his article/ memoir about the interwar university.[115]

## Imagining a Lithuanian Capital

The Lithuanians had lost the initial battle for Vilnius, but they had not given up the struggle for what they considered their rightful capital. Throughout the interwar period the Lithuanian government steadfastly—not to say inflexibly— maintained that their capital was Vilnius and that the city was under illegal Polish occupation. At the same time, Lithuanian culture and learning did not disappear entirely from the city in this period. While the Poles were less than cordial toward Lithuanian publishing and schools, they did not ban them either (though specific publications and schools were at various times shut down). On the whole it would seem that the Polish authorities were far more concerned with—and ruthless in punishing—signs of Belarusian and Ukrainian patriotism than Lithuanian, possibly because of the much larger numbers of Belarusians and Ukrainians within the Polish state.[116]

Among the most remarkable and indefatigable of Vilnius Lithuanian patriots were the Biržiška brothers, Mykolas (1882–1962), Vaclovas (1884–1956), and Viktoras (1886–1964). Strangely, their family was not from Vilnius or even from the region—their hometown of Viekšniai is nearly as far as one can get from Vilnius and remain in Lithuanian territory. Be that as it may, all three enthusiastically propagated the Lithuanian claim to the city both as active participants in the city's Lithuanian community (especially in the immediate post–World War I period and after Lithuania regained Vilnius in October 1939 and into the Nazi period) and even more as zealous and energetic writers and cultural workers for the Lithuanian Vilnius cause. Mykolas, trained in law at Moscow University but active later primarily as a historian, dedicated his professional life most completely to the Vilnius cause, against the Poles in the interwar period and against Soviet rule after 1944. All three brothers emigrated, via Germany, to the United States after World War II.

Mykolas and his brothers eloquently put forth the case for Lithuanian Vilnius from 1918 but also after 1920, when Polish rule appeared inevitable, at least in the short run. During the confused period 1918–1920, Mykolas published a number of periodicals, in both Polish and Lithuanian, arguing that Vilnius should become a part of the Lithuanian state. The numerous articles he published in Polish are particularly interesting. Here he argued that present-day Polish-speakers from Vilnius and its region had only recently—that is, only in the late eighteenth century or later—come to think of themselves as "Poles." They were descendants of Lithuanians who had only in the last few generations come to be polonized. In any case, in a Vilnius ruled by the Lithuanians, such (Polish-speaking) individuals had nothing to fear, either for their culture or for their individual rights: the Lithuanian state would treat all languages and national groups equally.[117] This was the consistent, and probably sincere, line that Mykolas, his brothers, and official representatives of the Lithuanian republic followed.

Mykolas Biržiška also argued that the Polish government had shown itself to be chauvinistic and unfair toward non-Poles. In particular, the October 1919 pogrom in Vilnius was blamed on local administrators. While anger at the excesses of the Bolshevik occupation was understandable, Mykolas argued, he did not understand how the local leadership (*sfery kierownicze*) could "tolerate the most horrible outbreaks of the mob or of specific depraved individuals."[118] Here and later the conclusion was clear: the Polish government could not be trusted to protect the personal safety—much less the basic individual rights—of non-Polish citizens. The Lithuanian republic, Mykolas pointed out repeatedly, was doing far more for its Jewish and even Polish citizens.

After the official incorporation of Vilnius into the Polish state, Mykolas Biržiška was arrested by the Polish authorities but later released and deported (with some thirty other Lithuanian activists). From Kaunas, Biržiška continued his agitation for Lithuanian Vilnius. His book *The Golgotha of Vilnius* presents a chronicle of the repressions and even atrocities (including the October 1919 pogrom) carried out by Poles and/or the Polish government in the 1920s.[119] He does, however, note small concessions by the Polish government such as permission to celebrate the seventy-fifth birthday of Jonas Basanavičius, the grand old man of the Lithuanian national movement, in Vilnius in November 1926 and his burial in the Rossa (Rasų) Cemetery in February 1927.[120] In general, however, Biržiška's writings on interwar Vilnius (which concentrate mainly on the 1920s, and in particular the early 1920s) present a clear picture of a beleaguered Lithuanian community and repressive Polish state power.[121] Ironically for Mykolas Biržiška, who always despised and opposed the communists, coverage of the culture in the interwar period in the one large-scale history of Vilnius published in the Soviet period follows a very similar line.[122]

Despite the small numbers of ethnic Lithuanians in the city, parents could send their children to (private) Lithuanian schools and from March 1927 there was even a Lithuanian student association at USB.¹²³ There was also a small Lithuanian press as well as a Lithuanian bookstore throughout the period, and even Lithuanian theater in Vilnius did not die out in the interwar years.¹²⁴ Lithuanian culture remained alive in the city, albeit on a small scale, though Lithuanians at the time and subsequent historiographers have probably exaggerated the importance of Lithuanian culture for the Polish authorities.¹²⁵

Mykolas Biržiška was exceptional in his energy and dedication, but his rhetoric and arguments fit in closely with a dominant Lithuanian discourse about Vilnius. Dozens of works from the time (and even after 1939) vociferously argue that Polish rule over the city was historically unjustified and characterized by repression toward non-Poles. The Lithuanian government, to be sure, encouraged and propagated this line, but there seems little doubt that Lithuanian intellectuals on the whole agreed.¹²⁶ In Kaunas (Lithuania's "temporary capital") in 1925 the "Association for the Liberation of Vilnius" was set up. This association set up dozens of local chapters in the next dozen years. Among other things, the association produced "Vilnius passports" that allowed bearers to show their support for the Lithuanian city. Hundreds of thousands purchased these passports, helping support the propaganda efforts of the association and keeping the idea of Lithuanian Vilnius alive. At the same time, the association's efforts were confined mainly to areas under Lithuanian control and had little effect on Lithuanian cultural life in Vilnius itself.¹²⁷

One should not underestimate the effect of the pro-Vilnius propaganda in Lithuania. It seems likely that in 1919 few Lithuanians (except among the educated—a relatively small group) had a powerful interest in Vilnius. Twenty years later, the pro-Vilnius feeling expressed when the city was incorporated into Lithuania (through Stalin's help) was overwhelming. In great part this widespread enthusiasm can be attributed to educational efforts on behalf of Vilnius by the Lithuanian state and private organizations like the Association to Liberate Vilnius. These organizations published numerous guides to the region, discussing its geography, climate, and nationalities (which included Lithuanians, of course, but also Jews, Tatars, Karaites, and Roma).¹²⁸ Indeed, an entire (short) guidebook to the city, complete with the Lithuanian versions of its street names, was published shortly before Vilnius returned to Lithuania.¹²⁹ While the Lithuanian authorities did not accept all of Narbutas/Biržiška's street names, in the majority of cases they adopted them. Thus the "imagined Vilnius" was translated, at least in part, from the page of this guidebook to the actual cityscape after October 1939.

## Vilnius on the Eve

While the Lithuanians never relinquished their claim on Vilnius, the Poles managed to bully them into opening diplomatic relations in 1938. Typically, both sides displayed crassly undiplomatic attitudes and behavior, with the consequence that even though from spring 1938 onward one could in principle travel from Vilnius to Kaunas, in reality relations remained icy to actively hostile, just at the time when both Poland and Lithuania were under serious threat from Nazi Germany to the west.[130]

Even after diplomatic relations had been established, the Vilnius question remained open. The final Lithuanian constitution of the interwar period, promulgated in May 1938, referred to Kaunas (as had all previous constitutions) as merely the "temporary capital." Summer 1939 was tense. Nazi aggression against Czechoslovakia had made clear that the next victim would be Poland. The annexation of Memel/Klaipėda in March 1939 added to the anxiety that worse was to come.[131] A cartoon published in *Kurier Wileński* earlier that month entitled "Fashions for 1939" depicted a couple dressed in elegant evening apparel—and wearing gas masks.[132] The grim political atmosphere did not improve in ensuing months. Lucy Dawidowicz recalled that in June 1939, "The threat of war darkened our days. We lived in the shadow of the storm that had been gathering all year. Every day we awoke to premonitions of disaster."[133]

By summer 1939 it appeared that the only effective curb on Nazi aggression against Poland would be the Soviet Union. Since the 1920s the USSR had consistently supported the Lithuanian claims to Vilnius, more out of cold realpolitik than from any political or diplomatic principle. The USSR had its own territorial claims on Poland (western Ukraine and Belarus) which bordered the Vilnius area to the immediate east and south. Soviet-Polish relations had never been good, and even in the face of a mutual foe—Hitler's Germany—these relations did not warm up much. But the ideological and political antagonism between Moscow and Berlin appeared to afford Poland at least some possibility of playing the one against the other. News that the German minister of foreign affairs, Joachim Ribbentrop, was meeting with his Soviet counterpart, V. Molotov, sent shock waves through Polish society.[134] The Molotov-Ribbentrop Pact of August 23, 1939 opened the way for the German invasion of Poland, as was widely understood.[135] From this point onward everyone realized that war was mere days away.

CHAPTER 6

# The Destruction of Multinational Vilnius, 1939–1955

THE SECOND WORLD WAR brought overwhelming devastation down upon Vilnius. The Soviet and Nazi occupations of the city caused major upheavals, violence, and the death of many residents. For Poles, the period was characterized by a reduction of their status and rights and, after the war, exile from the city. Obviously Jews were vastly more threatened by the Nazis than by the Soviet occupation, but one should keep in mind that many Jews were arrested by the NKVD, and middle-class Jews had their property confiscated by the Soviet authorities. Vilnius' Jews were nearly all killed by the Nazis, while Poles suffered from Nazi policies but were not immediately targeted for genocide. Lithuanians, on the other hand, were favored by the Nazis, though the Nazi occupation also targeted them to enlist their labor for the war effort (both as soldiers and as workers). At best, German policy toward the Lithuanians may be characterized as condescending; at worst, Lithuanians were arrested, pressed into forced labor, and—in particular if they had attempted to aid Jews—executed.

One consistent factor throughout this period was the increase of Lithuanians living in the city, whether under the auspices of the "bourgeois" republic (1939–1940), the Lithuanian Soviet Socialist Republic (1940–1941, 1944 onward), or the Nazi occupation (1941–1944). In the post-1944 years the Lithuanian Soviet authorities succeeded in having nearly all Poles "repatriated" (expelled) from the city. By the late 1940s the city's population was almost entirely different from that of 1939. During the decade after 1944 major building campaigns attempted to transform Vilnius into a proper Soviet capital. By the mid-1950s most direct damage from the war had been repaired or at least cleared away and a new, socialist, bilingual (Russian Lithuanian) city had been created.

With the destruction of Vilnius' centuries-old Jewish community and the "repatriation" of the Poles, the city's character changed irretrievably. While Jews (mainly from the Russian interior) and Poles (mainly from nearby rural districts) would settle anew in the city, they could not and did not challenge the Soviet Lithuanian cultural hegemony over the city. To be sure, this "cultural hegemony" was more an ideal than a reality in the early 1950s. One was more likely to hear Russian (or some form of East Slavic) than Lithuanian spoken here for some time. The ideal, however, was important: the university and other cultural agencies were decidedly and consistently Lithuanian in language, and following stated ideals (and realities) of Soviet nationality policy, a "socialist in content, national in form" bilingual Russian Lithuanian culture took shape in the city.

I will argue that these years saw the destruction of old, traditional, multinational Vilnius and the first steps toward the creation of a new city: a bilingual Soviet capital. Up to 1939, a number of ethnic-cultural groups—the largest among them Poles, Jews, possibly Belarusians, and Lithuanians—not only resided in the city but could trace their culture's (and often their own family's) history back several generations—or more. That changed after the cataclysm of World War II. With slight exaggeration, one may say that the capital of Soviet Lithuania in the latter 1940s represented a demographic tabula rasa that would be specifically cultivated as Lithuanian and Soviet/Russian. I end this chapter in 1955 not due to any specific event but because by this point, I will argue, the initial, radical phase of this process had been completed. After 1955 to the end of Soviet rule in Lithuania, the program of demographic and cultural Lithuanization with a distinct Soviet accent would continue, but in a less radical, more self-assured, and more gradual way.

## Red Army in Vilnius: September–October 1939

On September 1, 1939 Germany invaded Poland. Vilnius, far to the east, received word of the fighting with dread and worry. The Luftwaffe bombed the city's radio station and the neighborhood of Antokol (Antakalnis), but little serious damage was done.[1] Vilnius still felt far from the military action; it was hoped that with the entry of France and England into the war against Hitler, Poland could be saved.[2] Thus the invasion by the Red Army on September 17 came as a complete surprise to the Poles. Vilnius was less than a hundred miles from the border and by this point the Polish army was nearing collapse.[3] The units remaining around the city crossed the border into Lithuania rather than destroy themselves in senseless battles with an overwhelming foe.[4] At dawn on September 19 Soviet tanks were attempting to cross the Neris near the Green Bridge and within days had established control over the city, promptly setting up an NKVD office in the court building on Mickiewicz Street where the Soviet secret police was to remain in residence—aside from the short period of Lithuanian and German occupation—until January 1991.⁵

The Polish population was in a state of shock at the rapid collapse of their army and the destruction of the Polish Republic. In particular middle-class inhabitants viewed with great trepidation the entry of the Red Army into Vilnius. Bolshevik propaganda since 1917 had consistently portrayed Poles as reactionaries and tools of the Western (capitalist) powers, and the general Polish conception of the communists was hardly more positive.⁶ Added to this were long-standing antagonisms deriving from Russian rule over Poles that had ended only a generation earlier. Any Polish inhabitant of the city aged forty or older would have had personal memories of Russian soldiers and administrators, the monuments to anti-Polish figures like Tsarina Catherine II and Count M. N. Muraviev, restrictions on Polish culture, and other humiliations. Now Poles were entirely at the mercy of what they certainly perceived as Russian imperialism in its newest form, Soviet imperialism. To be sure, some left-wing Poles welcomed the introduction of a workers' regime in the city, but these were certainly minority voices.⁷ Much more typical were the numerous young Poles who quickly organized clandestine groups to resist Soviet (and later, Lithuanian) rule.⁸

Jews saw the Soviet occupation of the city in contradictory ways. On the one hand, there was no denying that the Red Army was to be preferred over Hitler's troops. Indeed, thousands of refugees from western Poland (not entirely, but mostly Jewish) streamed into the city, severely straining the ability of charitable organizations to deal with them. Among the refugees was Herman Kruk, who arrived in Vilnius on October 10, 1939 after over a month on the road from his Warsaw home. He remembered that already at this early date Jewish charities like the "Joint" (American Jewish Joint Distribution Committee, JDC) and the OZE/TOZ (Society for Preserving the Health of Jews) had set up soup kitchens and dormitories to aid the refugees, though their resources were overwhelmed by the enormous numbers of hungry, dirty, and exhausted displaced Jews.⁹

Many Poles later recalled young Jews welcoming the Soviet troops with red flags; while the frequency of such incidents may be questioned, it seems impossible to dismiss them.¹⁰ Certainly, many acculturated (at least linguistically) Polish Jews felt alienated in the 1930s by the continuing and even strengthening antisemitism and not infrequently—as in Isaac Bashevich Singer's novel *Shosha*—sought an answer in a naïve confidence in the USSR. Writer Aleksander Wat's communism in the 1930s similarly reflects this milieu (also typical was Wat's mistreatment by the Soviets and subsequent disillusionment with the communist ideal).¹¹ Most Vilnius Jews, however, viewed the outbreak of war as a catastrophe and the arrival of Red Army soldiers as a direct threat to their property, livelihoods, and religious practices.[12]

For Lithuanians in Vilnius, the defeat of the Poles who had "occupied" (as the Lithuanians had it) the city for two decades seemed a kind of historical justice.[13] But they too remained cautious. The Kaunas government maintained strict neutrality in the war (toward both the USSR and Germany) but also allowed many Polish soldiers to flee across the border to avoid destruction.[14] The Lithuanian foreign minister discussed the present political situation with advisors at a meeting on September 18. The meeting's attendees noted the "difficulty" of present relations and expressed the opinion that the Soviet-Lithuanian pact of 1920 could—and should—be interpreted to mean that Vilnius would be turned over to Lithuania. However, cautious approaches from the Lithuanians had been met by silence from Moscow. One advisor asserted that the entire country was in serious danger as it would be very easy for a small group to "request" Soviet intervention (a very prescient opinion, as it turned out); everything had to be done to avoid provoking such a step. For the present, then, the Lithuanian foreign ministry could do nothing but wait and hope for the best.[15]

Meanwhile in Vilnius, the Soviet authorities quickly established an 8 p.m. curfew and began seeking "enemies," whom it started detaining within days of the army's arrival. Hundreds were arrested and deported into the USSR. Certain groups were particularly targeted: anyone active in politics (from city self-government to members of political parties), intelligentsia (lawyers, doctors), and businessmen. Looking over the lists of the arrested, one notes that nearly all the names are Polish, though a significant number of Jews, Russians, and Belarusians (especially intelligentsia) also appeared. Some Lithuanians also figured among those arrested.[16] On September 20 residents were given twenty-four hours to turn in all weapons and explosive materials to the Soviet authorities. Many residents preferred to take the risk of hiding weapons, and indeed underground resistance units were already being formed (almost exclusively by Poles) at this time.[17]

At the same time a systematic looting of citizens' property, from furniture to entire factories, began.[18] Bronisław Krzyżanowski recalled that the Soviet authorities packed up the "ELEKTRIK" radio factory and shipped it off to the Russian interior.[19] Vilnius' main department store, the Jabłkowski Brothers', was systematically emptied of its goods. Other factories and even the railroad yards provided machinery and equipment that was transported east. X-ray machines, medicines, and electrical goods disappeared with the Red Army, who also took with them the library of the Institute for the Research of Eastern Europe and local archives.[20]

One possible reason for the quick action on the part of Soviet officials in Vilnius was their knowledge that the city would not remain for long in their hands. On September 29 the USSR signed a supplementary protocol to the Molotov-Ribbentrop Pact (essentially transferring Lithuania from the German to the Soviet sphere of interest). Immediately the USSR began negotiations with the Lithuanians to hand Vilnius over to them, and a pact to this effect was signed on October 10.[21] The agreement was not, however, without its dangers for Lithuania. In accepting the "gift" of Vilnius from the USSR, Lithuania also pledged its friendship to the USSR, accepting the stationing of Soviet troops on its territory. The following summer, these troops would be used as a Trojan horse to end Lithuanian independence entirely.

For the moment, however, news of the "return" was met with public jubilation throughout Lithuania.[22] Within Vilnius itself, nearly the entire population heard the news with relief, believing that a Lithuanian occupation would in any case be preferable to the Soviet one.[23] The date of the actual handover was set for October 28.

## Vilnius in the Lithuanian Republic, October 28, 1939–June 1940

For Lithuanians, the "return" of Vilnius on October 28, 1939 was an occasion of momentous national joy.[24] For Poles the entry of Lithuanian troops into "their" Vilnius called forth anger and incomprehension. As for Jews, they hoped that Lithuanian rule would be able to preserve them from the Nazis. With very rare exceptions, everyone was happy to see the last of the Red Army.

On October 28, 1939 Lithuanian soldiers marched triumphantly into the city, greeted enthusiastically by the city's Lithuanian residents and with reserve by Poles and Jews.[25] Throughout Lithuania, the occasion was celebrated as a major triumph for the government and the Lithuanian people.[26] Flyers were distributed assuring Polish residents that the Lithuanian government did not aim to restrict their language or discriminate against them and calling on them (in Polish) to work together for the freedom and prosperity of "our mutual fatherland—Lithuania!"[27] A number of one-day newspapers were published in Polish welcoming Lithuanian rule, though a later researcher has argued persuasively that in fact the Lithuanian authorities were behind them.[28]

For Lithuanians, the march of their army into the city was the undoing of a historic wrong, not an act of aggression.[29] Even the sober law professor and Lithuanian-by-choice Mykolas Römeris argued that, according to international law, the city belonged to Lithuania.[30] The city's population—comprising very few who could even understand Lithuanian—was assured that all languages and ethnicities would be treated equally. Like other self-declared nation-states, however, Lithuania soon adopted policies favoring its own nation, language, and culture.[31]

Almost immediately the Lithuanian authorities set about changing street names, starting with the main downtown thoroughfare, known under the Poles after the national poet Mickiewicz and now renamed Gedimino, after the medieval Lithuanian Grand Duke. The street name changes were facilitated by the fact that this topic had already been extensively discussed in the Lithuanian press, and as we have seen, a recent Lithuanian guidebook to the city provided new Lithuanian names for all major streets.[32] Some of the changes were mere translations (or transcriptions) of the Polish names, but others were more substantial. For example, Żeligowskiego (after the general who had taken the city for the Poles in 1920) became Klaipėdos (after the Baltic port lost to the Germans in March 1939), Piłsudskiego became Algirdo, the 3rd of May (the Polish constitution day of 1791) became the 16th of February (Lithuanian independence day). Deceased Lithuanian national figures such as Basanavičius and Maironis also got their own streets. By May 1940, a full 490 streets had received new names, though the changing of street signs lagged behind.[33] At least on maps printed in early 1940—though probably not consistently on the ground—Vilnius' streets had received proper Lithuanian names.[34]

Poles were quickly antagonized by what they saw as flagrant attempts to Lithuanize the city. Many civil servants, policemen, and teachers (overwhelmingly Polish as of September 1, 1939) lost their jobs and were replaced by Lithuanians. The Lithuanian authorities of course sought to extend the use of their language over Polish, whether in businesses, on the streets, or in schools. From the Lithuanian point of view this was a natural thing to do in their own capital city.[35] To Poles these actions seemed an outrageous attempt by Lithuanian chauvinists to destroy Polish culture (and Polish outrage was certainly exacerbated by the widespread Polish superiority complex vis-à-vis Lithuanian culture).[36] In churches, too, pressure was put on the mainly Polish hierarchy to allow more sermons, prayers, and hymns in Lithuanian.[37] The Lithuanian security forces denied the veracity of rumors about Poles organizing resistance underground, but they admitted that relations of the Polish population to the new authorities left much to be desired and noted that Jews were on the whole more friendly toward the Lithuanian government.[38] As Poles readily admit, the underground organizations formed from September 1939 to oppose Soviet rule continued to exist and plan for resistance to Lithuanian infringements on Polish rights.[39]

The terrible events of September 1939 heightened Polish national sensitivities and made cooperation with the Lithuanian authorities seem very close to treason.[40] Already in December 1939 strikes broke out over plans to introduce Lithuanian into schools in the city.[41] Writing (in Polish) in his diary, Mykolas Römeris—who better than anyone symbolized the possibility of cooperation between Poles and Lithuanians—was pessimistic. In early 1940 he complained that the atmosphere in Vilnius was "nasty" (*paskudna*), partly because of the attitude of the Poles ("Going from a psychology of being the masters to that of tolerated renters is not easy") and partly because of the Lithuanians' "linguistic-lithuanizing radicalism." The only way forward, he wrote, would be with significant changes in both Polish and Lithuanian attitudes—the former giving up their arrogant assumption of cultural superiority and the latter allowing the Poles as large a measure of cultural and national autonomy as possible. At least in the short run, neither change seemed likely.[42]

Economically the city was in very bad shape in late October, with even basic foodstuffs in short supply. The new regime, even the Poles admitted, quickly improved the city's supply of food and other necessities.[43] Prices were high, however, and many shopkeepers (often Jewish) began refusing to accept Polish currency for fear that it would soon be worthless.[44] One can hardly blame merchants for not wishing to accept a currency from a now nonexistent state, even though permitted to do so by the Lithuanians. But the continued circulation of the Polish złoty was absurd and could not last, for both political and economic reasons. The Lithuanian government decided to allow residents to exchange their Polish money for Lithuanian at the rate of two złoty for one litas.[45] While this was a lower rate than had prevailed before the war, under the circumstances the currency reform could not fairly be called exploitative or anti-Polish. The currency exchange took place between November 2 and 20 and was subject to various restrictions.[46]

The tensions between Lithuanians and Poles, combined with the economic turmoil, also strained relations between Poles and Jews. While few Jews in Vilnius spoke Lithuanian, the new authorities went out of their way to accommodate Jewish interests, which under these circumstances exacerbated fears among Poles of Jewish "betrayal."[47] At the same time, both Poles and Jews recognized that in this time of crisis all efforts should be made to continue a dialogue and to prevent disagreements from turning into clashes.[48] Unfortunately, this did not always work, as the Polish violence against Jews in Vilnius mere days after the handing over of power to the Lithuanians showed. On October 31, crowds of people waiting in line to purchase bread (the price of which had more than doubled in a matter of days) began to riot, attack passing Jews, and loot stores. In another part of town, Jews were attacked at a hotel. The Lithuanian police, taken by surprise, managed only with difficulty to curb the violence, but not before much property damage and many injuries were incurred.[49] Yitzhak Arad notes that after the October 31 violence, Jews formed self-defense squads.[50]

Another painful episode of late 1939, and one that continues to rankle for many Poles, was the closing of the Polish university in Vilnius (USB) by the Lithuanians. For the Poles closing down the university was nothing less than an attack on Polish culture tout court.[51] And it must be admitted that in a situation when Polish scholars and intellectuals were being arrested, murdered, or forced underground by the Nazis, the Lithuanian timing was at best unfortunate. The Lithuanians, however, saw matters differently.[52] It made no sense to have a foreign and often hostile university in their own capital city, especially when a primary goal of the Lithuanian government was to spread its culture in Vilnius.[53] In less stressful times a compromise might have been found—for example, having Polish and Lithuanian faculties or departments.

Instead, the Lithuanian ministry of education rather abruptly informed the rector of USB, Professor Stefan Ehrenkreutz, that the Polish university would cease operations at the end of the calendar year.[54] In particular the timing of the announcement, in the middle of the academic year and just before Christmas, was perceived as a calculated insult.[55] Student protests, petitions, and meetings were all to no avail.[56] On December 15, the end of the first trimester of the academic year, classes ended with a singing of "Boże coś Polskę" (God protect Poland).[57] When the university reopened, it was as a Lithuanian institution with faculty brought in from Kaunas and elsewhere, with the Lithuanian scholar Mykolas Biržiška serving as rector.[58]

## Vilnius as a Soviet Capital, Episode 1, 1940–1941

One reason for the Lithuanians' impatient and radical policies was, no doubt, fear that their grasp on Vilnius would soon be loosened. Such apprehensions were, of course, entirely justified. From spring 1940 the Soviet line toward the Lithuanian government became much more aggressive.[59] Under pressure from Moscow, the Lithuanian authorities legalized the communist party on April 25, 1940. Press and radio reports accused the Lithuanians of anti-Soviet attitudes and actions, in particular of endangering the Soviet troops stationed in Lithuania.

Lithuanian officials tried desperately to reassure Soviet authorities that they were neither planning nor tolerating provocations against Soviet troops, but of course, the Kremlin had already decided that the USSR's security required direct control over the Baltic states.

On June 14 the USSR issued an ultimatum to the Lithuanian foreign minister, Juozas Urbšys, that among other things demanded "free entry" for Red Army units into the country. It was made clear that whether or not the Lithuanian government agreed, the Red Army would enter the country. Under intense pressure and hoping against hope to salvage a modicum of sovereignty, the Lithuanian government acquiesced. Fearing arrest by the Soviet authorities, early on June 15 the Lithuanian president/dictator Antanas Smetona fled the country.[60]

From this point on, it makes little sense to see Lithuania as an independent country. Stalin sent his "viceroy," Vladimir Dekanozov, to Kaunas (most government agencies had not yet had time to move to Vilnius). Officially, Lithuanians were still in charge, but in fact the path toward integration into the USSR was being prepared. The journalist Justas Paleckis was made acting president, a position he would hold until early August (he would then remain, officially, as "head of state"—chairman of the LSSR's Supreme Soviet—until 1967). Paleckis, Dekanozov, and the Lithuanian Communist Party worked together to press for entry into the USSR. With their encouragement, agitators demanded elections to a "People's Parliament" (Liaudies seimas), which were duly held on July 14.[61] Unsurprisingly, given the atmosphere of intimidation and the electoral law that had been drawn up by the communists, the "People's Parliament" quickly assembled and requested entry into the USSR. On August 3, 1940, Lithuania was admitted to the USSR as its fourteenth republic.[62]

Few Westerners remarked on the absorption of Lithuania and the Baltic republics into the USSR; one who did was the left-wing journalist Anna Louise Strong. Her opinions, while heavily influenced by her ideological stance, reflected attitudes and perceptions not rare in the West. Specifically addressing the Vilnius question, Strong wrote strongly in favor of Lithuania's entry in the USSR. Speaking scornfully of the interwar period, she claimed that the city was "the cheapest place in Poland to live. Hordes of retired Polish officials on small government pensions moved here, where they could still be lords." As for the city's overall population, "Vilna contained seven nationalities. All lived in full separation and hated each other." When the Red Army arrived in Vilnius on September 19, she continued, "the common people met it with cheers," but when the Lithuanians took over, Smetona "set up a Lithuanian nationalism as exclusive and oppressive as the Polish had been." Now, however, under the "able Communist, Didzhulius," education in all languages would be made available, and special programs would be enacted to help the underprivileged of all nations.[63] Certainly Strong's account was informed in great part by her ignorance and ideology, but for all her one-sidedness, she correctly reported on the new Soviet authority's stated policy on developing the city and ending interethnic frictions.

In less than a year, Vilnius had gone through three major regime changes. The Soviet powers immediately set about establishing their own rule in the city. NKVD arrests started once again, sparing no nationality.[64] While some Lithuanian commentators speak of "genocidal" policies (against their nation) by the Soviets, Poles note that from June 1940 to at least the end of the year the NKVD worked hand-in-hand with the Lithuanian security forces (*saugumas*). In any case, thousands of Poles, Lithuanians, and Jews were arrested and exiled to the Soviet interior in this period.[65] At the same time nearly all private business was nationalized in an amazingly short period of time. Since business owners would have been almost entirely Jews and Poles, while the communists were Russians and Lithuanians (sometimes Jews by origin, but irreligious Russian- or Lithuanian-speaking Jews), this process also had a national element.[66]

Education was also a priority for the new regime. Already for the school year starting in autumn 1940, Soviet designations for schools and new educational programs were set in place. For practical reasons, most teachers remained at their posts, but the process already started by the Lithuanian government of replacing Polish teachers with Lithuanians continued apace (with, to be sure, somewhat different criteria for employment). A survey carried out in spring 1941 found that there were nearly 10,000 illiterate and barely literate inhabitants of Vilnius; courses were set up to help them learn to read and write. For adults wishing to learn practical skills (bookkeeping, typing, stenography, languages), special courses were held at the Vilnius "people's university."[67] The general Soviet discomfort with Jewish culture, even with secular Yiddish-based research, meant that YIVO was rapidly closed down by the Soviet authorities, its library and archives transferred to the Institute of Lithuanian Studies (Lituanistikos Institutas).[68]

Even more important for the future of Soviet rule was a reorganization of higher education. In a sign of the "flexibility" of the academic profession, mere weeks after the incorporation of Lithuania into the USSR, course plans in economics, history, anthropology, and other subjects had already been drawn up that duly reflected the importance of Lenin's and Stalin's teachings in these fields.[69] Initially the Lithuanian rector Mykolas Biržiška stayed on, though the faculty of theology was abolished, the teaching of Hebrew banned, and various faculty members fired.⁷⁰ Russian instruction was expanded, a department (*katedra*) of Marxism-Leninism was hastily created, along with a *rabfakas* (a Russo-Lithuanian sovietism referring to a special university course designed for workers).⁷¹ In November 1940, special festivities were held at the university to celebrate the twenty-third anniversary of the Great October Socialist Revolution.⁷² It seems likely that many of these reforms remained mainly on paper. A pamphlet published a year later by the Vilnius Pedagogical Institute insisted that the institute maintained its Lithuanian character during the academic year 1940–1941 and that "the Soviet gibberish directed by the Muscovites remained as plans on paper."⁷³ Obviously one cannot uncritically accept this statement (published under the Nazi occupation), but it seems likely to have had some validity in this case.

Almost immediately rumors began to circulate that a Nazi invasion was imminent. Mykolas Römeris wrote in his diary on October 12, 1940, that in particular Poles foresaw an armed conflict between Germany and the USSR, but that also a goodly number of Lithuanians agreed.⁷⁴ At the same time, the Soviet authorities attempted to establish some kind of normalcy in city life, trying to assure food supplies and opening the academic year at the university in October.⁷⁵

A Soviet Lithuanian capital could not, obviously, retain the street names inherited from the "bourgeois" Lithuanian Republic (and, in fact, even from Poland). During the first Soviet occupation (that is, 1940–1941) efforts were under way to remove inappropriate names (that had religious connotations or referred to the interwar Lithuanian Republic). With few exceptions, however, proposed name changes did not feature Russian socialist heroes (the exceptions are predictable enough: Stalin, Lenin, Gorkii, Voroshilov, Sverdlov, Kirov, Maiakovskii). On May 9, 1941, the Vilnius City Executive Committee and the presidium of the LSSR Supreme Soviet approved over 100 name changes of streets and squares. Thus "Archangel Way" was to become "The People's Way" (Liaudies), Church Street—Citizens Street (Baznyčios—Piliečių), Martyrs Street—Fighters Street (Aukų—Kovotojų), Muhammedan Street—Uzbek Street (Mahometanų—Uzbekų), St. Peter and Paul—Tractorists (Šv. Petro ir Povilo—Traktorininkų). Good Hope Street was to become Industry Street (Gerosios Vilties—Pramonės). Streets bearing the names of distinguished local Jews (Strašūno, Dr. Šabado, Gaono) were to receive the names of other distinguished Jews (Mendelės, Š. Aleichem, M. Antokolskio), only the last of whom had a direct connection to the city.⁷⁶ The great men Engels and Marx were also to be honored (Vokiečių and Domininkonų-Šv. Jono-Trakų, respectively).⁷⁷ The German invasion six weeks later prevented any of these name changes from being carried out.

The city was also to undergo significant reconstruction to make it a suitable site for a capital of a Soviet republic. In the plans for urban transformation, the specific national element is seldom emphasized but could be taken for granted. Already in early 1941, when Vilnius as the capital of the Lithuanian Soviet Socialist Republic was hardly six months old, a detailed report in Russian set down basic principles for the transformation of the city. First of all, all republican institutions (many of which continued to function in Kaunas) needed to be brought to Vilnius as one means of sweeping away its present condition as a "provincial city of lordly Poland [*Panskoi Pol'shi*] which continues to preserve its half-feudal character and a chaotic building muddle." The goal was to create a "well-built socialist city." Mincing no words, the report stated baldly that insisting on "'conservation' [*konservatsiia*] of the Old Town" was "entirely incorrect from the point of view of socialist city planning."

Denouncing the Polish city planners who apparently planned to build around rather than modernize the Old Town, it was concluded that this district needed a thorough and radical reconstruction. The idea of leaving the inhabitants of the Old Town "and in particular of the former Jewish 'ghetto' [*sic*]" in the terrible existing hygienic and transportational circumstances, like "some kind of bizarre museum exhibit," was unacceptable in a modern Stalinist world (or, "in light of Stalinist concerns [*v svete Stalinskoi zaboty*]"). In particular, city traffic should be modernized by the extension of Gedimino across Cathedral Square to the east (which, presumably, would have involved the destruction of the cathedral itself), linking Vilnius Street directly with the Green Bridge to the north and plowing a *magistral'* (a favorite word for Soviet enthusiasts) to the railroad station. The report also bewailed the lack of proper open spaces for demonstrations and called for the opening up of such large squares. All of these plans would have involved considerable damage to the Old Town. Tellingly, none of these ambitious projects was taken up again after the war.[78]

The Soviet occupation was accompanied by mass arrests and widespread fear, especially among middle-class elements and anyone involved in interwar Polish politics. At the beginning of 1941, according to the careful archival work of Liudas Truska, over a thousand (political) prisoners were in Vilnius jails.[79] Beginning on June 14, a major new wave of arrests and deportations began; thousands were arrested, loaded onto trains, and taken to the Soviet interior.[80] While most of the arrested in Vilnius were Poles and Jews, thousands of ethnic Lithuanians from the rest of the country were also taken away. This massive wave of repression was one reason that many Lithuanians welcomed the German invasion.

THE DESTRUCTION OF MULTINATIONAL VILNIUS, 1939-1955    167

## Nazi Occupation: June 1941–July 1944

Despite widespread rumors, the actual Nazi attack on the USSR early in the morning of June 22, 1941 caught everyone by surprise. Almost exactly one year after Soviet troops marched into Lithuania (June 15, 1940) the Nazi armies attacked the USSR in massive numbers. German airplanes attacked and bombed Vilnius throughout the night of June 22, and by the afternoon of June 23, Soviet troops had fled and were nowhere to be seen. Lithuanian flags appeared in the streets, and on the morning of June 24 German troops marched into the city.[81]

The Germans brought with them well-developed—and murderous—policies regarding national-racial hierarchy, and they rapidly put these into effect in Vilnius. All citizens were warned that any kind of resistance or disrespect would be met with severe, even fatal, punishment. Having already ruled over Polish territories for almost two years, the Nazis had very specific (and negative) ideas about Poles, based both on their ideology and on the practical experiences of occupation of the Generalgouvernement. The Nazis saw the Lithuanians as allies against the Russians and Poles and had a place for them in their future "New Europe." Poles were to be tolerated, barely, and Jews could expect the worst from the new rulers.

As soon as news of the Nazi attack reached Kaunas, an anti-Soviet uprising broke out throughout Lithuania, including in Vilnius.[82] Römeris wrote in his diary that Lithuanian soldiers who had been drafted into the Soviet army broke ranks and refused to leave the city.[83] On June 23 Radio Kaunas announced the formation of a provisional government made up mainly of Christian-Democrat politicians. At the same time a national uprising against the Soviets (and, by the same token, to assist the German invasion) was announced. The Lithuanians hoped thereby to persuade the Germans to treat them as allies. Unfortunately, the Germans had no intention of doing so; indeed, the Gestapo wanted simply to arrest the Lithuanian leaders but was dissuaded from doing so by the Wehrmacht. In the end, the provisional government recognized its own helplessness and disbanded itself on 5 August.[84]

The national uprising launched on June 23 also aimed to reassert Lithuanian nationhood. In the end, however, it was unable to achieve this goal due to the German unwillingness to see the Lithuanians as serious partners. The uprising was centered, as one would expect, in the central Lithuanian district and was of only secondary importance in Vilnius and its region.[85]

On the whole, Lithuanians regarded the German invasion favorably—at least at first. A longtime Polish resident of Vilnius and Kaunas recalled that when German troops entered Lithuania, Lithuanians pelted their tanks with flowers and then eagerly cooperated with the new German rulers, including in the repression and murder of Jews and Poles.[86] Reports from the Lithuanian security police corroborate much of these Polish memories. On June 28 the secret police reported that Lithuanians had enthusiastically greeted the Germans and hoped that with their entry in Vilnius a new "administration, truly Lithuanian and energetic" would be set up. Claiming to be speaking for "Lithuanian society," the report asserted that the first item of business should be to "liquidate/shoot or concentrate in labor camps the communists and especially Jews who were the first to join up with the communists." Jews and Poles should in any case be immediately fired from jobs in industry and commerce. Up to now, the report continued, the open enemies of Lithuanians (and, it implied, of Germans) had been treated too leniently. Henceforth if a Lithuanian patrol were shot at from a house, all Poles and Jews living there were to be instantly executed. All Jews were to be placed in work camps and have their property nationalized.[87]

The Germans and Lithuanian collaborators published a daily newspaper in Vilnius, *Naujoji Lietuva* (*New Lithuania*), which was full of enthusiastic articles on Lithuanians' role in the struggle to protect European culture against the Soviet menace. Young Lithuanians were called upon to join this struggle, in particular by volunteering to work in Germany.[88] An editorial on February 15, 1942 urged Lithuanians to work on independence day (the 16th) to do their part for the tremendous effort necessary to build the new Europe.[89] Other articles blamed Jews for both the NKVD and for the British war effort (through James Rothschild), chronicled the celebration of the Führer's birthday in Vilnius, and listed the names of Lithuanians who died "fighting bolshevism."[90]

Vilnius University continued to operate under Nazi rule though it was shut down in March 1943.[91] M. Biržiška continued on as rector until 1943 but—perhaps not surprisingly—ends his university war memoirs with the German invasion, noting that the Germans discovered a Soviet list with the names of many university officials, including that of the rector, who were to be evacuated to the Russian interior.[92] It appears that Biržiška did his best to behave in a humane way throughout the period, given the impossible circumstances.[93] Lithuanian culture developed normally—at least compared to Polish or Jewish culture—in the war years. The Lithuanian press, literature, and theater in Vilnius expanded under the Nazi occupation.[94] To be sure, the Nazis viewed Lithuanians merely as minor allies in the present struggle, but they allowed freer rein for Lithuanian culture than for Polish or Russian. The stress on "germanization" or even the word "genocide" in reference to Nazi policy toward Lithuanians is, to put matters very mildly, exaggerated. Such arguments ignore the far worse treatment of Poles, Russians, and Jews here during these terrible years.[95]

Nazi policy favored Poles less than Lithuanians, but at least in the first months after June 1941, Nazi terror concentrated on Jews and communists. There were, however, arrests of "suspect" Poles—in particular educated young men, scouts, and students. According to one Polish source, these arrests were carried out by Lithuanian activists who worked for the Nazi occupiers.[96] German policy actively played Lithuanians against Poles, exacerbating relations that were already bad enough. Mass arrests of Poles began in October 1942 with many taken to the nearby village Ponary (Paneriai) and executed. In principle, at least, these arrests were connected to the continued underground resistance activity among Poles.[97] At the same time, Polish priests were removed from their parishes—the new bishop, Mečislovas Reinys, seen by Poles as a Lithuanian nationalist, had been installed in the city already in early 1940 (though not confirmed by the Vatican). Reinys would remain bishop until arrested by the Soviet authorities in 1947.[98] Reinys exemplifies the difficulty of assessing figures from this period in a way free of national bias: Poles tend to portray him as a chauvinist, eager to replace Polish clergy with Lithuanians; Lithuanians stress his martyrdom under the Soviets (he would die in KGB custody) and insist that he condemned hatred among nations.[99]

Under the Nazi occupation, Poles had few rights but for the most part were not targeted for mass repression. Newspapers appeared in German and Lithuanian, but not in Polish. Thus the Polish press was forced underground. Throughout this period the Polish underground existed in Vilnius, though it avoided confrontations with the Germans, recognizing that overt resistance would bring massive and brutal retaliation. The Nazis favored Lithuanians for employment, but in many cases Polish workers were simply indispensable. All Poles knew, however, of the many arrests and executions of prominent Polish figures and recognized that they could well be next.[100] Nearly all Polish memoirs stress the cruelty of Lithuanians and their collaboration with the Nazis; the years of anti-Polish propaganda in the interwar period, combined with the brutalization wrought (and generally encouraged) by the Nazis bore bitter fruit.[101]

The tragic fate of the Vilnius Jewish community deserves special attention. The news of the Nazi invasion and the swift collapse of Soviet power in the city left the Jewish community in shock. Survivors recall a panic wave among Jews; many attempted to flee eastward, but all trains were packed with refugees, communists, and soldiers. Others continued eastward on foot but were turned back at the

Soviet border. Still others managed to get on trains that were destroyed by Nazi strafing.[102] In the end, very few Jews managed to escape Vilnius. Late on June 24, Herman Kruk wrote in his diary, "There are no words for my suffering. This day has turned me into an old man."[103]

On July 17 the Germans set up the administrative unit Ostland encompassing territory from the three Baltic republics and some parts of Belarus. Lithuanian territory was administered from Kaunas as Generalbezirk Litauen. On August 5, after six weeks of existence and under German pressure, the Lithuanian provisional government dissolved itself, though most offices and police forces in Generalbezirk Litauen, including Vilnius, continued to be staffed by ethnic Lithuanians.[104]

The issue of Lithuanian collaboration during the Nazi occupation and most especially the role of Lithuanians in the murder of Lithuania's Jews remains a controversial one.[105] In a joint article, Saulius Sužiedėlis and Christoph Dieckmann have stated starkly: "The persecution and killing of the Jews began within hours of the Nazi invasion of Lithuania. By the end of June, Jews already constituted a conspicuously large number of civilians killed." The authors also mention, as do memoirs, the widespread and egregious public humiliations and physical attacks to which Jews were subjected.[106] Jews were frequently attacked "as communists," but violence often took place with no political overtones, as in the most notorious incident, the beating and murder of dozens of Jews at the Lietūkis garage in downtown Kaunas on June 27, 1941. While both Germans and Lithuanians were involved in this atrocity, there is no evidence that the pogrom was organized or initiated by Germans. The most shocking aspect of the garage beatings and murders is that they took place in full sight of passers-by and no one—neither private citizen nor official—intervened to help the victims.[107]

In Vilnius, however, there were no large-scale attacks on Jews, possibly because of the larger numbers of Jews there (including thousands of refugees), the relatively small number of Lithuanians, and the uneasy position of Poles, who still constituted the majority of the population.[108] Throughout the period, indeed from late 1939 onward, the city administration remained largely Lithuanian; memoirs such as that of Herman Kruk refer frequently to Lithuanian policemen. Already on July 4 the Germans demanded that a *Judenrat* be formed; two days later all Jews were ordered to wear the Star of David. On July 10 Jews were prohibited from appearing on the main downtown streets (Didžioji, Vokiečių, Trakų, Pylimo, and Gedimino).[109] Other laws forbade Jews from using telephones, radios, or trains, and even from walking on the sidewalk.[110] As elsewhere, in Vilnius Jews were ordered to affix yellow stars on their exterior clothing.[111] In August a "contribution" of 5 million rubles was demanded of the Vilnius Jewish community. Despite the increasing numbers of laws against Jews, no ghetto was actually declared in Vilnius until early September.[112]

On August 31 in the middle of the city, at the corner of Stiklių and Didžioji Streets, there occurred an incident involving Lithuanian "partisans" (i.e., pro-Nazi irregular soldiers) who entered a building, shot from the window, then rushed out, claiming that Jews had fired at German soldiers standing nearby.[113] Two young Jews were hauled out of the building and shot, and the "provocation" gave the Germans an excuse for evicting Jews living nearby and sending them to Lukiškės prison (they would subsequently be transferred to Ponary and murdered there).[114] Several thousand Jews were thus arrested and taken away; as Kruk notes, 2000 Poles suffered the same fate. The remaining Jews, some 40,000 in number, were forced into two ghettos on September 6. Around 29,000 Jews crowded into the large ghetto ("First Ghetto") to the west of Niemiecka/Vokiečių, and around 11,000 were assigned to the small ghetto ("Second Ghetto") on the other side of the street (in the most traditional Jewish quarter of town, where the Old Synagogue was located).[115]

The first months of the ghetto's existence were extremely traumatic. By forcing Jews out of their homes and relocating them in the ghetto, the Germans destroyed neighborhood solidarity and lessened the possibility of resistance. As elsewhere, a ghetto police was set up, serving several purposes at once: to pass the dirty work of everyday surveillance and violence onto Jews, to break down solidarity within the ghetto, and to keep order.[116] In September and October it was clear that the Germans were also "culling" the Jewish population (though of course never openly admitting the fate of those taken away), reducing the number of mouths to feed, and in particular targeting the young and elderly for arrest and deportation. Mass arrests in October essentially emptied the "Second Ghetto," which was completely liquidated on October 21, 1941.[117] Further *Aktionen* took place in the ghetto in the following months, with the Germans issuing yellow and pink passes that protected the bearer from arrest, then hunting down anyone without the needed document. Thus by late 1941 only around 20,000 Jews remained in the Vilnius Ghetto, around one-third of the prewar Jewish population. A few days after the destruction of the Second Ghetto, Herman Kruk wrote in his diary, "The people in the ghetto, those who remained, stagger around—the community is once again diminished. . . . Is it really true that all those who are taken out of here are taken to the slaughter? Is it really that horrible?"[118]

With the initial killing over, the ghetto settled into an uneasy period of "stabilization."[119] As elsewhere, the Germans repeatedly assured the Jews that by working hard, they would earn the right to live on. The view that the best survival strategy required Jews to make themselves useful to the Germans was shared by the head of the Vilnius Ghetto from 1942, Jacob Gens. Unlike in Kaunas, there was no continuity of Jewish leadership nor any universally respected figure like Elkhanan Elkes.[120] The widely respected social activist Dr. Jacob Wygodzki had served on the earlier *Judenrats* (the first had been formed in early July), but he was arrested on August 24 and died (at age eighty-six) shortly thereafter.[121] After the death of Wygodzki there was no single individual who could serve as a rallying figure and inspiration in the way that Elkes did in Kaunas. Into this gap stepped Jacob Gens. Very unusually for Jews in Vilnius, Gens spoke Lithuanian well as he had been an officer in the Lithuanian army. He was not from the city, coming originally from Šiauliai and arriving in Vilnius only after the city passed to Lithuanian control. In the past he had been affiliated with the revisionist Zionist "Betar" movement; his instincts were those of a military man. Gens was also unusual in that his wife was Lithuanian and lived outside the ghetto. It would probably have been possible for him to hide his Jewishness, but he chose not to.

When the ghetto police was formed in September 1941, Gens was selected as its head. His organizational skills and military bearing impressed the Germans; when they abolished the Vilnius *Judenrat* in July 1942, he was named "ghetto representative," making him essentially the highest Jewish official in Vilnius.[122] Kruk, as a Bundist, despised Gens and even wrote sarcastically of him as "Il Duce of the ghetto."[123] For all this authoritarianism and lack of intellectual polish, however, Gens did try—as best he could according to his own judgment of the situation—to preserve the lives of as many Jews as possible. For this reason he maintained relations, if cool ones, with the ghetto underground, all the while making clear that he would strike hard against them if he felt that their activities endangered the ghetto as a whole. In September 1943, when Gens recognized his own failure, he allowed himself to be arrested by the Gestapo (though he had been warned in advance and could have escaped) and died at their hands.

Despite the horrible conditions, the cultural traditions of Vilnius Jewry continued even in the ghetto.[124] For example, the Germans were very interested in preserving some of the most unique books from Vilnius' libraries (especially the renowned Strashun Library). The so-called Einsatzstab Rosenberg hired a number of Jews, among them Herman Kruk, to go through and sort the books. While doing so, the Jewish staff attempted to spirit away and hide important material.[125]

Kruk described his misgivings at this task in this way, "Kalman[owicz] and I don't know if we are gravediggers or saviors. If we succeed in keep[ing the treasure] in Vilna, it could be our [great ser]vice to some extent, but if they take the [Strashun] library away, we [will have] had a hand in it."[126]

Cultural life in the Vilnius ghetto was amazingly rich. A recent collection of the posters announcing lectures, concerts, theater performances, and the like fills a book of several hundred pages.[127] Schools were created for the children who had survived the murderous *Aktionen* of 1941, public lectures on a variety of topics were organized, and—in an even more controversial move—musicians and actors were called upon to entertain the ghetto inhabitants. Kruk's reaction at the opening of the theater was one of personal offense: "you don't make theater in a graveyard"; he surmised (not quite fairly) that the theater had been allowed by the ghetto police for the purpose of ingratiating themselves with the Germans.[128] Most ghetto residents, however, appeared grateful for any kind of distraction from the grim reality surrounding them, and even Kruk later softened his disapproving stance. Theater performances began in January 1942 in a hall on Końska (Arklių); concerts were also held here. A ghetto library was set up at 6 Strashun Street, opening its doors not two weeks after the creation of the ghetto. By October 1942 the library had lent out over 100,000 books.[129] Religious life also continued, despite the ever more stringent restrictions coming from the Nazi authorities and the disruption caused by the loss of so many rabbis and traditional Jews in 1941.[130]

The non-Jewish population of Vilnius could not help but notice that the Jewish ghetto was set up in the middle of town and that groups of Jews left the ghetto daily to work in various enterprises. More research would be necessary to ascertain exactly which firms profited the most from the use of Jewish slave labor, but lists drawn up by the Nazis give well over one hundred firms, ranging from chemical enterprises to luggage manufacturers, who used Jewish labor. Judging from the names of these firms—though this could be deceptive—they were mainly Lithuanian-owned or at least "fronted" by Lithuanians.[131] In general, following Nazi policy of favoring Lithuanians as future participants in the Nazi-led "New Europe," Lithuanians held most administrative offices, including that of mayor, and Lithuanian names and companies dominated a type-written "telephone book" drawn up by the Nazi occupiers.[132]

Another way that local non-Jews profited from the misfortune of their Jewish neighbors was by taking over "abandoned" Jewish property, ranging from real estate to bedding and pillows.[133] The hundreds if not thousands of forms labeled *Anmeldung—Pranešimas—Zawiadomienie* in the archives document transfer of formerly Jewish property either "temporarily" (as a loan) or permanently (by sale, apparently for rather favorable prices) to non-Jews. These forms are almost exclusively filled out in German or Lithuanian, though at times ungrammatically (by Poles trying to "Lithuanize" themselves?).[134]

In the memoir literature and historiography, the resistance movement in the Vilnius ghetto has received a relatively large amount of attention.[135] This is only natural as many of the memoir writers survived because of their participation in the anti-Nazi underground and the partisan movement. And of course there is the psychological and political need to show Jews not only as victims but also as active resisters of evil. Abba Kovner's famous—or infamous—manifesto to Vilnius Jews (despite his name, Kovner was a Vilner, though born in Sevastopol): "Let us not be led like sheep to the slaughter" has sometimes been twisted into an accusation against the victims. Kovner's intent was quite different: now (January 1, 1942), he argued, we can see very clearly what was not so obvious earlier: "Ponar is no concentration camp. All were shot dead there. Hitler conspires to kill all the Jews of Europe."[136]

Despite its location in the middle of town, the Vilnius ghetto had active contact with the partisan organizations active in particular from 1943. Gens was well aware of the underground organization—the most famous group being the F.P.O. (United Partisan Organization)—and even assured their leaders that "at the proper time" he would make use of them. Meanwhile, however, Gens cautioned against any provocative or hasty actions that could push the Germans into fatal action against the ghetto as a whole.[137] Gens's unyielding position and growing unease with the underground is shown by his insistence that the F.P.O.'s head, Yitzak Witenberg, give himself up when the Gestapo sought him. Witenberg did turn himself in and, according to different stories, either died from poison given to him by Gens or was tortured to death by the Gestapo.[138] The F.P.O., now under the leadership of Abba Kovner, continued to operate until the very end of the ghetto.[139]

Himmler's order of June 21, 1943 to close all ghettos and transfer any remaining prisoners to concentration camps took some six weeks to affect Vilnius directly. In August several transports destined for Estonia removed thousands of Jews, including Herman Kruk, from the ghetto. It was becoming clear that the end was near but the underground and Gens differed on strategy: the F.P.O. held that they must strike now as the situation was desperate. Gens continued to hope for a reprieve and tried to put pressure on the underground in every way he could to avoid any provocative actions. On September 1 Jews were suddenly not permitted to leave the ghetto for work duties; all work was to be carried out within the ghetto. The F.P.O. decided that the time to strike was at hand and set up a barricade at their headquarters at 12 Strashun Street. Approaching Germans were fired upon, calling forth massive retaliation by the Germans.[140] On September 6 the F.P.O. decided that further resistance within the ghetto was suicidal and called on its members to leave the ghetto and join the partisans.[141] Gens was arrested and shot on September 14. On September 23 the Vilnius Ghetto was declared liquidated; remaining ghetto residents were loaded onto trucks and trains and deported, in part to Latvia and Estonia.[142] The Vilnius Ghetto was no more.

A few words need to be said about the place where most Vilnius Jews met their end, Ponar/Ponary (in Lithuanian Paneriai). A suburb of Vilnius some seven miles from downtown, before the war Ponary had been a place for picnics and weekend outings. Already in July 1941, however, the Nazis had transformed Ponary into a center for mass killings, first of political opponents, then for the wholesale slaughter of Vilnius' Jews.[143] A unique witness to these murders was the Pole Kazimierz Sakowicz, who described the killings of Poles and Jews (at the hands of both Lithuanians and Germans) that he witnessed from his nearby dwelling.[144] Sakowicz's sober descriptions, not without contempt for "Jewish passivity," show clearly that the large-scale murder in Ponary was no secret to inhabitants of Vilnius.[145]

By autumn 1943, when the ghetto was destroyed, the eventual defeat of the Germans could be foreseen. The question in most residents' minds was whether they would survive to see the end of the German occupation. The brutal liquidation of the ghetto made clear to all that the Nazis would not hesitate to slaughter civilian populations if it served their needs. Rations were increasingly tight and the Germans' desperate need for labor translated into roundups of citizens of various nationalities who had the bad luck to be on the street at the wrong time. In 1943 and the first months of 1944 thousands of Poles and Lithuanians were rounded up, treated like prisoners, and transported to work in Germany.[146] Both Poles and Lithuanians fled the city and joined the partisans in the forests in order to escape labor conscription.[147] The desperation of the moment was shown by negotiations between the Polish underground and the Nazis in Vilnius on possibly reaching an agreement with the Poles, in particular about cooperating against Soviet partisans/"Belarusian bandits." In the end, however, the Nazis could not countenance such a pact.[148]

In February 1944 Mykolas Römeris compared the current situation with the post-WWI period, noting however the crucial difference that the Soviets now were far stronger than the Bolsheviks who temporarily occupied Vilnius in 1919.[149] The

Red Army progressed steadily westward, and on July 13, 1944 German troops withdrew from Vilnius. At the same time the Polish underground Home Army (Armia Krajowa) launched its "Operation Ostra Brama." The operation aimed, by attacking the Germans, to show the Red Army that the Poles should be taken seriously as fighters. Unfortunately, Stalin and his army were entirely uninterested in dealing with the Poles who were not incorporated into the Red Army itself.[150] Anti-Soviet partisan activity continued for some time, first mainly Polish and then Lithuanian, and was put down with great brutality. The effects of the war on the city were also brutal: during the German occupation around one-third of the city had been destroyed along with a similar or greater percentage of its prewar population.[151]

## Sovietization and Population Transfer: 1944–1949

The entry of the Red Army into Vilnius on July 13, 1944 was greeted with mixed emotions. The very few surviving Jews emerged from their hiding places while Poles and Lithuanians for the most part perceived the "liberators" with fear and misgivings. Rumors about the city's future were bandied about and Poles still harbored the hope that Vilnius would once again be a Polish city. Most had great misgivings about the prospect of life under Soviet rule—in particular, memories of 1940-1941 were fresh and unpleasant—but the simple fact of having survived to see the Germans depart was cause for celebration.

When the Red Army once again entered the city in mid-July 1944, many of the city's buildings were in ruins and many of the prewar inhabitants dead or elsewhere as forced laborers. In the next months, a few hundred Jews made their way back to the city, coming out of hiding, from liberated concentration camps, or from the Soviet interior. Few Jews remained in the city, especially as local Soviet authorities showed themselves increasingly hostile to Jewish memories of the war, as the destruction in 1952 of the first Ponar monument demonstrated. According to NKVD figures, at the end of 1944, only 84,990 Poles and 7958 Lithuanians lived in Vilnius. The city's total population—106,500—was less than half of what it had been in 1939.[152]

While the percentage of Lithuanians in the city had increased during the war, Vilnius remained in 1944 a mainly Polish city by ethnicity—and this was a major problem and challenge for the new Lithuanian Soviet regime. It was, to say the least, problematic to have a Polish majority in the city, which had been proclaimed the capital of Soviet Lithuania. A solution was rapidly found. On September 22, 1944 an agreement was reached between representatives of the Lithuanian SSR and the Polish Committee of National Salvation (the so-called Lublin Poles, a pro-communist government formed under Stalin's auspices) for the voluntary evacuation of Poles from the LSSR and Lithuanians from Poland.[153] According to this agreement, transportation would be provided for anyone wishing to leave, and the evacuations would take place from December 1944 to June 1945. Evacuees would be allowed to take personal effects with them, with some exceptions (no automobiles, motorcycles, or furniture). Peasants could take with them tools, small livestock, and the like, and they would have land restored to them on the other side.[154]

Immediately upon the arrival of the Red Army, Poles were given many indications that their days in Vilnius were numbered. One such "hint" was the spelling of the city in the Polish-language communist newspaper, *Prawda Wileńska* in its first issue on July 17, 1944. Appearing in this issue were references to "Wilnius" (the transliteration of the Lithuanian, a form never used in Polish), along with positive references to the liberation of the city and fraternal relations with the Lithuanians.[155] The subtext could not have been clearer: the new masters would tolerate Poles who by the benevolence of the new Soviet Lithuanian authorities could continue to live in "Wilnius." However, continued residence in the capital of the Lithuanian Soviet Socialist Republic (LSSR) would be possible only by accepting this new order, both political and cultural-national. The September 22, 1944 accord, however, made clear that Vilnius Poles were expected to leave their native town and "repatriate," to use the contemporary term, to Poland.

The first mention of the signing of the accord was published in *Prawda Wileńska* on September 26 with a short informational notice. Over a week later a longer article interpreted and evaluated the agreement in entirely positive terms, calling it a "new historical phase" that would help wipe out "any kind of misunderstandings between Lithuanians and Poles." Rather than living as a minority in the other's country, now Lithuanians and Poles would join their national brethren in the two nation-states. No doubt anticipating an obvious objection and uncomfortable comparison, the article declared that this agreement was "the diametrical opposite" of Hitlerian policies of destroying nations and letting one rule over the others. Now, rather, members of each nation would live among their own kind; in this way both the countries and individuals would quickly be able to develop normal and positive relations. As for the practical matter of moving thousands of people (numbers are never mentioned), the "extremely favorable conditions for evacuees" was stressed several times. While the tone of the article was relentlessly upbeat and optimistic, it left no doubt that Poles were expected to leave Vilnius.[156]

In late 1944 and early 1945, arrests of Poles increased. To be sure, this was a rather grim period for anyone living in the LSSR, but Poles in Vilnius had the additional disability of being considered "foreign," middle-class, and quite possibly connected with the Polish underground that was being rooted out by the NKVD at that time. By the end of 1944, a full 8592 persons had been arrested by the NKVD in Vilnius. Polish residents, remembering the previous Soviet occupation of 1940–1941, had reason to fear worse. Different Polish historians cite figures between ten and twenty thousand arrests from July 1944 to early 1945.[157]

Whatever the exact figures, one thing was clear: the end for Polish Vilnius was approaching. Probably not realizing that the NKVD would be reading their letters—as we know from the secret police report of February 27, 1945—Poles expressed their fears that they would soon have to leave home. Anna Anasowicz (Vilnius, ul. Sadovskaia 3-3) wrote sadly, "We will have to abandon our beloved Wilno ... for Soviet power has given over Wilno to the Lithuanians and we Poles, like it or not, will be forced to leave." Around the same time Galja Dmitrowicz (Vilnius) wrote, "they're giving out new passports [i.e., identity cards, not travel documents], but only Russian and Lithuanians get them, not Poles, so they will be forced to leave for Poland. ... We Poles don't want to leave for Poland."[158]

Taking into consideration the enormous energy lavished on the evacuation effort by the Soviet authorities, it seems impossible not to agree with a Polish historian's assessment that "the Soviet authorities aimed at the quickest possible, most radical de-polonization of Vilnius." However, the second part of this same sentence seems quite incorrect: "and to give it the character of a Russian city."[159] On the contrary, the Soviet authorities wished to give the city a *Soviet* (which, to be sure, would include much that was Russian) and *Lithuanian* character. While Russian specialists did arrive in Vilnius in large numbers after World War II, even larger number of Lithuanians migrated to the city. From the late 1940s to the end of the century, the percentage of Russians among the Vilnius population declined steadily as the number of Lithuanians grew.

The most pressing single task for the Lithuanian communists upon liberation of Vilnius was to rid the town of its Polish population. As we have seen, the September 22, 1944 agreement between the Lithuanian SSR (nota bene: not the USSR) and the Lublin Polish committee cleared the way for just such a population transfer. As I have argued in some detail elsewhere, purging Vilnius of its former Polish population was a matter of primary importance for the new Lithuanian rulers.[160] Indeed, in a secret letter signed by the high Soviet officials A. Vyshinskii and A. Pavlov, addressed to foreign minister V. M. Molotov, the Soviet officials emphasized that the "Lithuanians are primarily interested in evacuating Poles living in Vilnius [Vil'no]."[161]

The evacuation was carried out by two separate sets of bureaucrats, Polish and Lithuanian, with frequent stresses and (verbal) clashes between them. The Poles were fundamentally interested in evacuating anyone who wanted to leave; the Lithuanians led by later Minister of Education of the LSSR A. Knyva consistently demanded a closer scrutiny of evacuees' nationality to prevent Lithuanians from emigrating. Of course nationality was not easy to ascertain in many cases, a fact tacitly acknowledged by the Poles' more lenient approach.[162] The Lithuanian side also pressed for the evacuation of Vilnius but devoted far less attention to rural areas populated by Poles. In the end, nearly all Vilnius Poles left for Poland. Of the 171,168 individuals who evacuated from the LSSR to Poland, over half (89,596) were from the Vilnius region (we have no figures for the city proper, but the city made up the bulk of the population in the "rajonas"). The disparity from other regions is even more striking when one compares numbers of those who registered to leave and the actual number of evacuees. In the Vilnius region over 80 percent of those who registered actually left (89,596 of 111,341). In the other regions put together, fewer than one-quarter of those who registered actually evacuated.[163] In short, the expulsion of Poles from the Lithuanian SSR amounted to "ethnic cleansing" only for the city of Vilnius.[164] To be sure, in time many Poles from nearby rural areas would come to Vilnius but their presence did not challenge the primary objective of creating a Soviet Lithuanian city. After 1947 the predominance of Lithuanian culture in Vilnius would never again be challenged by Poles.[165]

Street name changes also came with the new regime. Discussions in 1944–1947 continued to mention the 1940 names (like St. Stephen, Gaon, and the like). The Lithuanian historian (and later co-author of the most comprehensive city history to this day) Juozas Jurginis addressed a letter to the Vilnius City Committee dated May 16, 1947 urging that a number of local notables be honored by having streets named after them. Among the names Jurginis put forward were the writer Žemaitė, the poet Kazys Binkis, the Vilnius resident and "historian of Lithuania" Joachim Lelewel (his Polish nationality left unsaid), the "anti-tsarist Vilnius worker" [Hirsh] Lekert (his Jewish nationality and obviously Jewish first name left unmentioned), and others. In many cases these recommendations were accepted by the town council.[166] Remarkably, the main downtown street Gedimino retained its Lithuanian name until 1952, when it was renamed Stalino. Thus street names were to reflect both the international and socialist nature of the city but also its past (though without specific reference to non-Lithuanian nationality, including the spelling of names in the Lithuanian manner).

The most immediate considerations after the war were practical. According to the later city architect of Vilnius, some 40 percent of living space and 30 percent of industry in the city had been destroyed under the German occupation.[167] This impression is born out by photographs and drawings of major streets of the city, showing numerous burned-out and destroyed buildings.[168] The area of the former Jewish ghettos in the middle of the city remained a wasteland for several years after the final liquidation of the Vilnius ghetto in September 1943.[169] Despite the devastation, the principle monuments of non-Jewish Vilnius still stood (mainly, of course, churches). But the Soviet leadership had grand plans for the city.

According to the architect Vladislovas Mikučianis, who came to Vilnius in 1945, three basic principles were followed in drawing up a general city plan: (1) to open up the "picturesque Neris River scene," which previous architectural plans had neglected, (2) "to retain the rich silhouette of architectural monuments" found within the Old Town, and (3) in developing the city, to preserve its natural setting (hills and surrounding forests).[170] At the same time, Mikučianis and his colleagues wanted to develop the city's industry further, improve its profile as a Soviet capital with various prestigious architectural projects, and repair housing, infrastructure, and communications.[171] One of the earliest Soviet monuments to mark the downtown was the monument to Ivan Cherniakhovskii, the Soviet general who had liberated Vilnius and was killed in action shortly thereafter. The general's remains were interred and topped with a large obelisk in the downtown square that had previously borne Polish writer Eliza Orzeszkowa's name.[172] In this way one relic of the Polish past was erased and replaced with a Soviet (though not ethnically Lithuanian) site.

Other major construction projects of the early postwar included the "academicians' house" (*mokslininkų namas*), constructed on the banks of the Neris River. This building was to be in a sense Vilnius' answer to the famous "house on the embankment" in Moscow, but in this case it was intended for scholars, not high party officials. The impressive structure, topped with a pompous Stalinist tower, contained fifty apartments of five rooms (120 square meters each) and even included a small room for "home workers" (servants). The completion of this building in 1950 was a major event for Vilnius.[173] Around the same time, the Green Bridge over the Neris River was rebuilt and opened, adorned with four impressive statues representing students, the Red Army, industry, and agriculture.

The Railroad Station, devastated in World War II, was reconstructed in a pompous neoclassical/Stalinist style, and the "Victory" cinema in the same style was opened downtown.[174] These major architectural projects emphasized Vilnius' status as a republic capital of the USSR but can hardly be termed "Lithuanian." Rather, their architecture stressed the break with the past and Vilnius' present status within the USSR.

In their attempts to fashion a new Soviet Lithuanian capital in Vilnius, the Lithuanian communists also had to forget—and seek to blot out, at least rhetorically—many aspects of the city's past and present. The city's rich religious heritage, for example, was ignored or actively opposed as sites of religious practice or memory were transformed into secular uses, altered in appearance, or simply swept away. In Vilnius, religion and nationality had always gone hand in hand. Now the city's long multiethnic history (and the relatively small role played in it by ethnic Lithuanians) was also actively ignored or glossed over. While the friendship of nations within the USSR was trumpeted, mention of the now absent Polish and Jewish inhabitants of Vilnius might call into question the now unquestioned dominance of ethnic Lithuanians in the Soviet capital. In another attempt to create a kind of new Soviet Lithuanian patriotism, the postwar authorities also fashioned a one-sided and Manichaean "memory" of Lithuanians' experience in World War II.

For centuries, Vilnius had been an outpost of Catholicism in the east. But Catholicism had no role to play in the new Soviet Lithuanian patriotism. Catholic churches were shut down though seldom actually destroyed. The cathedral became a picture gallery and had statues and an enormous cross removed from its façade.[175] The Three Crosses monument, associated with the Polish 1830 rebellion against Russian authority (though originally commemorating far earlier martyrs to the faith), located on a hill next to the downtown Castle Hill, was destroyed in the middle of the night on May 30, 1950. Less dramatically, dozens of other churches were closed in the late 1940s. The city architect Mikučianis (who despite his Lithuanian name was quite russified and had only come to Vilnius after the war) recalled that after the "repatriation" of Poles it was argued that there were "too many churches" in the city (ignoring the inconvenient fact that most Lithuanian immigrants were just as Catholic as the Poles had been). Mikučianis also noted that the high Lithuanian communist official E. Ozarskis constantly complained that the church of St. Jacob and Philip clashed with the statue of Lenin on Lukiškės Square and should be destroyed (happily the church has outlived the statue).[176] Following normal Soviet practice, one of these (St. Kazimierz/Kazimieras) was converted into the Museum of Atheism in 1961. Other churches were turned into storehouses, offices, and in one case (the former Basilian Monastery near Ostra Brama) into the city's Technological Institute.[177]

The timing of these repressions of religious "monuments" is interesting. No major church was closed or destroyed (few were, in any case, actually destroyed) before 1948. In other words, the first order of business was to establish Soviet power (including putting the apparatus of repression in place),[178] expel the Poles (an action completed by September 18, 1946),[179] and assure the basic stability of the new Soviet order. It is surely no coincidence that the closing of churches came at the same time as the collectivization of Lithuanian agriculture (1948–1952).

Memory of Vilnius' multiethnic past was also a victim of the postwar remaking of Soviet Lithuania. Reading any of the three main party newspapers of the LSSR in these years, *Tiesa*, *Prawda Wileńska*, or *Sovetskaia Litva*, one is struck by the almost complete silence about the existence of non-Russian and non-Lithuanians in the city and region. To be sure, *Prawda Wileńska* did mention the opening of a Jewish museum in the city (at ul. Straszuna 6) by "comrades Markelsówna and Sz. Kaczergiński,"[180] but the same paper was capable of devoting an article to the "cruel past" of the Vilnius suburb Ponary (Paneriai) (where the majority of Vilnius' Jews had been murdered) without mentioning Jews at all.[181] Even in the Polish-language *Prawda Wileńska*, one finds enthusiastic articles extolling the great things being done by the USSR for "our Lithuanian nation" (*nasz naród litewski*) and its "capital Vilnius" (Wilnius).[182] In the late 1940s *Sovetskaia Litva* devoted remarkably little room to anything Lithuanian at all, addressing more frequently the Belarusian population (though using the Russian language). However, one article in March 1949 did breathlessly describe the forward "rapid rebuilding of the capital of Soviet Lithuania," with much about new buildings, landscaping, and decisions of the Soviet of Ministers of the USSR, and not a word about the actual inhabitants of the town.[183]

Not surprisingly, the most enthusiastic reports about the new Lithuanian Soviet capital appeared in the Lithuanian-language *Tiesa*. Here Lithuanian patriotism was inextricably intertwined with enthusiasm for Soviet construction, as in the article "Attention! Vilnius Speaking!" about the opening of radio broadcasts in Lithuanian from the city, already in 1940 and once again in 1944 after the Germans had been defeated.[184] A campaign in April 1945 called specifically on Lithuanians to move to Vilnius and repopulate the city, even calling it their patriotic duty.[185] At the same time the newspaper was full of articles about the "eternal friendship" between the Lithuanian and Russian peoples, enthusiastic *subbotniki* (*sekmadienio talka*; a Soviet institution to harness free labor for community service) to clear rubble and rebuild, and of course on the great benevolence and interest of the USSR in general and Stalin in particular for the prosperity and cultural development of the Lithuanian people.

In the late 1940s Poles are seldom mentioned as inhabitants (past or present) of Vilnius in the Lithuanian Soviet press, except in the context of their "repatriation." Similarly missing from press accounts is any mention of Vilnius' once large Jewish community. Given the Nazi obsession with Jews and their unspeakable crimes against this nation, one might have expected the Soviets to emphasize these black deeds of their adversaries. In fact, however, the murderous deeds are discussed but often without any mention of the main target of these mass murders. We have already seen an article on Paneriai, which failed to mention that over 90 percent of the tens of thousands of people murdered there were Jews. Indeed, an article in *Prawda Wileńska* in early November 1944 makes an even more egregious omission: when referring to the death camp at Auschwitz (Oswięcim), it mentions Jews only in passing, as "one of the nationalities" murdered there.[186] Four months later another article on Auschwitz lacked any mention of Jews whatsoever.[187]

Perhaps a few hundred Vilnius Jews had managed to survive to July 1944 in hiding; these were later joined by Jews who had fled to the countryside or Soviet interior. Once the survivors emerged, however, they found that neither the general population nor the Soviet leadership had much interest in them or their story. Within weeks of the Soviet liberation of Vilnius, the Yiddish poets Abraham Sutzkever and Shmerke Kaczerginski had founded in their apartment at Gedimino 15 a "Museum for Jewish Art and Culture" and called on all survivors to contribute any documents or artifacts they had that related to Jewish Vilnius.[188] In a short time they had collected hundreds of documents only a few of which, unfortunately, have come down to us.[189] The two poets who had survived as partisans also wrote their own accounts of the last days of Jewish Vilnius; Sutzkever's was published first in 1946 in Paris and Moscow (later also in Buenos Aires); Kaczerginski's appeared in 1947 in New York.[190]

By early 1945 the Jewish Museum had moved to the Strashun 6 (the previous location of the "paper brigade" employed by the Germans in ghetto times to sift through Jewish-language materials) but suffered from the unwillingness of the Lithuanian Soviet authorities to provide them with basic funding, office supplies, and furniture. Kaczerginski went to Moscow in March 1945 to complain about this neglect (to use a mild word) and there found out that thirty tons of material from the YIVO-Institute library and archives seized by the Nazi *Amt für Müllabfuhr* (the garbage disposal agency) had miraculously survived the war. Despite all of Kaczerginski's impassioned efforts, however, the material not destroyed by the Nazis was pulped by the Soviet authorities.

By mid-1945 the Jewish Museum was officially registered and had three paid employees but was forbidden to lend out any books without specific permission from Glavlit (the official censorship organ); the Moscow Yiddish journal *Einikayt* published an article on October 2, 1945 praising Kaczerginski's and Sutzkever's efforts. The poets, however, had had enough of the disinterest and even hostility of the Soviet authorities and left Vilnius in July 1946 for Paris. The Jewish Museum survived two more years before being shut down in 1949.[191]

The fate of other Jewish sites in Vilnius was similar. The area of the two Jewish ghettos set up by the Nazis (in the middle of the city) was a site of almost total ruin in 1944.[192] The city architect Mikučianis recalled that, despite the destruction, the walls of the Great Synagogue were intact and only the roof had been destroyed.[193] Surrounding buildings were damaged, but not gravely, and could have been repaired without enormous expense. In the end, however, the synagogue and surrounding buildings were razed and the entire former Jewish quarter essentially reconstructed, eliminating most of the small alleys, which, admittedly, had long presented a problem for hygiene and sanitation.[194]

German Street (Vokiečių), in the middle of the former ghetto area, was widened. A small park constructed in the middle of the street made it into something like a boulevard, but with the promenade in the middle rather than on the sides. The street was renamed "Muziejaus" (referring to the former town hall at its southern end, in Soviet times an art museum); "Jewish" Street (Žydų) was essentially eliminated by treating it as a mere extension of Stiklių (Glass) Street.[195] In this way the Jewish quarter of Vilnius, now devoid of Jews, also had most of its specifically Jewish character and sites of memory erased.

Perhaps the most egregious destruction of a Jewish site was the paving over of the old Jewish cemetery just across the Neris River from downtown.[196] Amazingly, this cemetery had survived the Nazi occupation almost intact.[197] Mikučianis mentions laconically that already before the war the Polish authorities had planned to develop this site (it is, after all, a very central location). In 1950 certain historically important graves (such as that of the Vilnius Gaon) were transferred to a new Jewish cemetery and the cemetery was razed to make way for a sports complex, pool, and athletic fields.[198] While such facilities may well have been welcomed by the residents of Vilnius, given other available plots in the vicinity it seems clear that the old Jewish cemetery was destroyed not primarily for practical reasons but to blot out an inconvenient memory of a population that no longer existed in the city.

THE DESTRUCTION OF MULTINATIONAL VILNIUS, 1939-1955   185

Actions taken by the Soviet leadership in Vilnius at the memorial site of Paneriai, where most of Vilnius' Jewish population had been murdered, also demonstrate this desire to remove Jewish traces. Soon after liberation a monument was erected at the site proclaiming in Yiddish and Russian eternal memory for the Jews of Vilnius and elsewhere who were murdered here. This monument was erected by Jewish survivors already in 1945. Seven years later it was dynamited and replaced by a more modest obelisk, which bore inscriptions in Lithuanian and Russian (but not in Yiddish) and mentioned only the "Victims of Fascism."[199] The fact that Jews had been singled out for extermination and subject to treatment far worse than that of ethnic Lithuanians was conveniently forgotten.

While the scars of war would long be visible in Vilnius—even in the early 1960s—concerted efforts at repair and construction got underway as soon as the war ended in May 1945. The population of Vilnius grew sharply in the next few years, from 110,000 in 1945 to 177,300 in 1951. The actual influx of new inhabitants was even higher, considering that around 80,000 Poles left the city in 1945-1947. These new inhabitants came from a variety of places. First of all, the party encouraged rural inhabitants to come to the city, in particular targeting nearby regions populated mainly by Lithuanians, Belarusians, and even Poles. Many thousands of former soldiers returned (or came for the first time) to Vilnius in this period. And thousands of specialists and industrial workers flowed to the city from different parts of the USSR, including the Russian Republic.[200] By 1951 the population was divided fairly evenly between Russians, Lithuanians, and "others." The largest ethnic group was Russians (33.3%), followed closely by Lithuanians (30.8%), then Poles (21.1%—probably very few of these had resided in the city in 1939), Belarusians (12.6%), Ukrainians (7.2%), and Jews (3.1%—again, probably mainly new arrivals). By 1959 the population had grown to 236,100, with Lithuanians the largest ethnic group (33.6%), Russians at 29.5 percent, and all others falling relatively, except for Jews, who now made up 7.0 percent of the population.[201]

Some Lithuanian commentators wish to see a "genocidal" plan in Soviet population policies after 1945, but this seems a very difficult charge to prove. The Soviets were going out of their way, after all, to appear pro-Lithuanian (at least "in form," while Soviet "in content," to paraphrase the old formula). It seems more likely that workers were taken where they could be found, and one should recall the geographical position of Vilnius in the extreme east of Lithuania, with Minsk and Grodno much closer than Klaipėda. Still, many thousands of Russians did settle in the city and continue in the early twenty-first century to make up a significant percentage of the population.

Vilnius University was reopened on October 16, 1945 with more than 800 students registered (the number would rise to 1359).[202] According to Soviet accounts, the historic central university building that houses (among other things) its library only barely escaped being put to the torch by the fleeing Nazis. By 1950 student numbers would reach nearly 3000. In 1955 the university was named after the Lithuanian communist Vincas Kapsukas, a name it would retain until the late 1980s. From the start Lithuanians made up the largest national group at the university, 86.4 percent of all students in 1945/1946, with 4.9 percent Russians (1945/1946). In 1951/1952 Lithuanians were down to 74.6 percent of the student body (their lowest percentage in the postwar period), with Russians constituting 11 percent. Jews made up around 7 percent of the student body throughout the period 1945–1951, but Poles never exceeded 3.7 percent, probably because most new Poles in Vilnius came from peasant backgrounds.[203] Elementary and secondary schools, which began to appear rapidly, were in all likelihood even more important for most residents. Already in fall 1944 nearly 8000 children were registered for classes.[204] For the most part, these schools used Lithuanian as the language of instruction though, of course, all pupils studied Russian as well.

By the mid-1950s, Lithuanians could be proud of their new Soviet capital city. A Russian-language guidebook published early that decade argued that "bourgeois Lithuania" had claimed Vilnius but only the USSR had delivered the capital to the Lithuanian people.[205] Writing a few years later, two Lithuanian historians agreed that "bourgeois Lithuania" had done little to get Vilnius "back." The USSR, however, with its concern for small nations, had been the only state to recognize the city as Lithuanian.[206] By 1955 most of the obvious ruins from the war period had been cleared away from the downtown, though empty patches continued to exist. Theaters, museums, the airport, and an intercity telephone center were already operating.[207]

By the mid-1950s Soviet Vilnius had, at least in the downtown area, assumed the shape it would retain with modest changes until the late 1980s. In 1955 the city's main street was still named after Stalin, but this would change to "Lenino" before long. Strolling down this main street from the cathedral (now closed), one passed the Central Post Office (then as now) and arrived at Cherniakhovskii Square. There the general's last remains rested, topped by a large statue on a granite pedestal.[208] Farther down Stalin Prospect was the huge statue of Lenin, completed in 1952. All along the Neris River construction continued.[209] By 1952 the destroyed Green Bridge over the Neris had been replaced and adorned by four sculptures (one at each corner) representing important segments of the Soviet population: "agriculture," "industry and construction," "students," "guardians of peace" (soldiers).[210] Recreation was also considered; "Pergalė" ("victory") movie theater opened in 1950 and was joined by the similarly opulent "Tėvynė" ("fatherland") theater in the next few years.[211] Not forgetting Lithuanian historical sensitivities, the Soviet authorities restored the castle atop Gedimino Hill.

Street names also reflected the city's Soviet character—most of these names would remain in place to the later 1980s. Some street names were obvious: Komunarų (Communards, now Jakšto), Komjaunimo (Komsomol, now Pylimo), Tarybinės Armijos (Soviet Army, now Savanorių), Tiesa ("Truth," that is, "Pravda," now Maironio). Other honored foreign and Lithuanian communists: Kapsuko, F. Dzeržinskio (now Kalvarių), L. Giros (Vilniaus). Many others streets, however, honored Lithuanian cultural or historical figures (Tallat Kelpšos, Paleckio, Vrublevskio, Basanavičiaus, Gedimino [though not the main street as today], B. Sruogos). Yet other streets continued to bear the same name as in late 1939 (that is, after having been Lithuanized)—Mėsinių, Rasų, Tilto, Universiteto, and others.[212] The city streets by the mid-1950s thus reflected the Lithuanian, Soviet, and historical past of Vilnius.

In a 1955 book entitled *Soviet Lithuania under Construction*, the engineer and party activist Juozas Maniušis wrote enthusiastically about the progress that had been made in rebuilding Vilnius since 1944. He particularly stressed capital construction, for example, of schools, industry, and large office buildings (for the Lithuanian Communist Party Central Committee, State Planning Commission, and Ministry of Agriculture, to name a few). Electricity had been restored and much expanded. Some 800 million rubles had been expended on capital construction in Vilnius in the decade after 1944, and since 1950 investment in construction had more than doubled. In proper Stalinist style, Maniušis ended his chapter on Vilnius with short, heroic biographical sketches of individuals who had improved building methods and efficiency in these years. One aspect of construction that seems strangely absent in Maniušis's account is housing. This is not by chance; in fact, housing conditions remained dire for most residents well into the 1960s (as we will see in the next chapter). Still, huge progress had been made by the mid-1950s.[213]

At the end of their 1956 book, Jurginis and Mikučianis took a look into the city's future. Here they spoke of the future effects that the sixth five-year plan would have on Vilnius. Industry was to be expanded, including production of cash registers and adding machines; trolleybuses were to be added to the increased number of buses used in public transport. Perhaps most exciting of all, a television center was planned that would beam both local and central TV programming to the local population. The authors mention several large-scale building projects, most of which do not appear to have been carried out. One that was realized, though, was a new central library for the Lithuanian SSR. (Completed in 1963, it is known today as the National Mažydas Library.)[214] Thus, not much more than a decade after the arrival of the Red Army in Vilnius, a new Soviet Lithuanian city had arisen from the ruins of the old Polish Jewish one.

• • •

By the mid-1950s, the most obvious war damage had been repaired or at least cleaned up and Vilnius' inhabitants had made impressive progress toward the construction of a modern, socialist capital. While the city core—with the obvious exception of the former Jewish ghetto—looked much the same as before the war, the population was almost entirely different from that of a generation earlier. Lithuanian was much more prevalent and the streets were marked with bilingual Lithuanian-Russian signs. For most people, however, while the mid-1950s did bring stability, everyday life remained very difficult indeed. Aside from a very small group of privileged individuals who received apartments in the new prestigious buildings such as the Scientists' House, almost no new housing was built in this period. In general everyday life remained difficult because of the Soviet state's emphasis on defense and capital investment to the neglect of light industry and consumer goods.

This short period was one of the most destructive in the city's history. Both human and material losses—buildings, libraries, art, monuments—were immense. The genocidal policies of the Nazis, followed by the postwar ethnic cleansing of the city's Polish community, radically altered the city's ethnic makeup. While no one ethnic group made up the majority of the city's population, Soviet culture—in both its Russian and Lithuanian guises—was unquestionably hegemonic here. Thus the multicultural, multireligious city that Vilnius still had been in 1939 was irretrievably lost ten years later. What remained was a city suffering from severe material deprivation and ruled by a repressive regime that demanded and codified selective historical memory, in both political and ethnic-national ways. As we will see in the next chapter, however, both material dearth and political repression would be somewhat mitigated—though by no means eliminated—in the next decades.

CHAPTER 7

# Socialist Normalcy in Vilnius, 1955–1985

A DECADE AFTER THE end of the Second World War, a new socialist Vilnius had arisen from the war-damaged city of 1944. Few of its residents remembered the Polish provincial city of 1939; the main languages heard on its streets were Russian and Lithuanian. Street and shop signs, historical placards, political exhortations ("The party and the people are one!")—all were bilingual. By the mid-1950s, overt political resistance had been almost completely repressed and it appeared that Soviet power was there to stay. At the same time, the extreme repression of the postwar decade gave way gradually to a political situation that remained repressive but in which the boundaries of tolerated behavior were broadened and the penalties for transgression reduced. A period of extreme, rapid, and often violent change was giving way to a less ideological and more humane—though hardly democratic—regime.

During this long generation, Vilnius grew rapidly, with the city's 500,000th resident born on November 22, 1980.[1] The city became steadily more Lithuanian in population during these years though a public bilingualism was still embraced and enforced. More than anything, this era was characterized by efforts to provide a reasonable material life for the city's residents by building new housing, cultural institutions, and retail outlets. Censorship remained and overt criticism of the Soviet system or public endorsement of Lithuanian independence would lead to significant penalties (generally arrest and possibly prison). Compared with the terrors of the 1940s and early 1950s, however, this was an era of relative political laissez-faire (i.e., "we will pretend to be reliable socialists, and the powers that be will pretend to trust us") and growing material prosperity.

I refer to this period, somewhat tongue in cheek, as one of "socialist normalcy." In contrast to the previous generation of enthusiasm, war, and ideology, the post-1955 decades emphasized material growth and pride in Soviet accomplishments. One may roughly date "socialist normalcy" from Nikita Khrushchev's secret speech denouncing Stalin's crimes (February 25, 1956) up to the death of Leonid Brezhnev (November 10, 1982), or perhaps until the election of Mikhail S.

Gorbachev as general secretary on March 11, 1985. During this period, to generalize somewhat, the Soviet leadership pulled back from extreme forms of repression and attempted to "win over" the populace not by projecting enthusiasm and ideology (though these continued to play an important public role) but by satisfying the needs and wants of everyday life.²

For an urban historian, one of the most important changes during this period was the huge boom in construction. As Geoffrey Hoskins points out, between 1955 and 1964 the housing stock of the USSR nearly doubled, and by 1980 it had doubled a second time.³ Throughout the Soviet Union, prefabricated construction methods were used to simplify and expedite the construction of large numbers of new apartments.⁴ In Vilnius, too, housing stock grew enormously in this period; one may even say that an entirely new city was constructed on the outskirts of the city that the Red Army liberated in July 1944.⁵ In urban development the construction of an appropriately grand socialist capital city continued to concern Vilnius architects, but the arguments and rationale for development tended to center on the population's needs rather than on the glorious march toward communism. Even more strikingly, increasing rhetorical emphasis and resources were devoted to developing the consumption sector: cafés, restaurants, shopping outlets, and recreation. This is not to say, of course, that before 1960 consumption had been totally neglected or completely disdained in the USSR: still, one may witness a considerable shift toward consumption as one part of a healthy, normal, and happy everyday life under developed socialism.⁶

In Vilnius socialist normalcy was complicated by the fact that the Soviet order had been brought to Lithuania by Red Army bayonets. As we have seen, the first year of Soviet rule (1940–1941) and the immediate postwar years were marked by a great deal of violence, repression, and—for Lithuanian patriots—national humiliation.⁷ The period of Nazi occupation had to be remembered selectively by both Soviet authorities—not wishing to stress the widespread welcome given the Wehrmacht by ethnic Lithuanians—as well as Lithuanians themselves, who wished to see themselves as victims rather than collaborators during those murderous years.

This was the era of "peaceful coexistence" and "developed socialism." The term "normalcy" is justified, I believe, because in the 1960s and 1970s life in Vilnius became more predictable and for many, more pleasant on an everyday level. For the average resident in 1960, still living in crowded rooms or a communal apartment, there was at least a good chance of obtaining an individual apartment over the next decades—nearly a quarter of a million did so. Educational opportunities expanded, new cultural institutions such as libraries, theaters, and movie houses were built.

In this period, the city grew steadily and entire new residential districts were planned and constructed. Prestigious new buildings went up in the city center while serious efforts were made to preserve the old city's fabric and to integrate new architecture as needed into it. For all the weaknesses visible in hindsight in this spurt of new construction, at the time Soviet Vilnius was touted as a model for other cities in the USSR. Similarly, an expanding consumer sphere made everyday life more pleasant. While the availability (and quality) of consumer goods lagged far beyond that expected in the West, new shops selling everything from bicycles to flowers opened up.

A greater attention to consumer needs was, however, just one element of socialist normalcy. The post-Stalinist period witnessed a shift away from zealous public avowals of ideology and toward a compromise between public orthodoxy (dissent was still severely punished, though now rarely by death) and private life. Much could not be said, certainly, and publicly challenging Soviet truths could result in severe punishment. Among these "truths"—perhaps foremost among them—was a historical narrative of class struggle and, in the specific case of Vilnius, an emphasis on the city's Lithuanian essence despite its multicultural past.[8]

If in the decade following World War II radical change and ideological repression were the norm, during these decades predictability set in. The vast majority of the population learned to live with, if not necessarily to love, the USSR. Only under Soviet rule, after all, had Vilnius become a truly Lithuanian city—despite its mixed population. Population statistics are somewhat misleading in this respect. While Poles and Russians continued to make up sizable minorities in the city, the hegemony of Lithuanian language and culture (at the university, in the academy of sciences, in the majority of research institutes, and in the mass press) was not in question.[9] Most Poles in Vilnius, descendants of immigrants from the countryside, in any case spoke Lithuanian fairly well. The same could not be said, of course, of Russian residents. Soviet Lithuanian culture and identity were understood as participating in wider Soviet concerns for which fluency in the Russian language was a prerequisite. On a daily level, however, one could avoid Russian much of the time—even if one worked as a teacher or otherwise belonged to the "intelligentsia." Despite the post-1990 rhetoric of some Lithuanian patriots, the bilingual signs on Vilnius streets did not represent an effort to stamp out Lithuanian culture in the city.

Vilnius changed enormously during these decades and on the whole in a positive way (at least when compared with another thirty-year period, 1915–1945). In the mid-1950s the city's population stood at around 200,000 (in 1950 it was 176,300 and in 1959 it was about 236,100); thirty years later it had more than doubled, passing the half-million mark.[10] A 1988 guidebook proudly pointed out that the current population of 577,500 represented a five-fold increase since the war and that three-quarters of the city's inhabitants lived in apartments constructed after 1945.[11] In fact, as we will see, nearly all of those new apartments were built from 1960 on.

## City Administration

The city was divided into four administrative districts (*rajonai*), rather unimaginatively named after the October Revolution (until the early 1960s named after Stalin), Lenin, Dzierżyński, and the USSR (Sovetskii/Tarybų). The city lacked elected representation. Each of the four *rajonai* had its own administration with an executive committee looking after the needs of the city as a whole. The chairman of the city's executive committee functioned, more or less, as the city's mayor. In Vilnius this position was held from 1974 to 1990 by the same man: Algirdas Vileikis. Vileikis's career in city administration reached back to 1965, when he became chairman of the October Rajonas executive committee. In interviews conducted some twenty years after the collapse of the USSR, this "last Soviet mayor" of Vilnius shares a great deal of specific information about practical issues and problems facing the city while saying almost nothing about politics or ideology.[12]

Certainly party organizations were also integrated into the city administration. While Vileikis's nonideological memories may have been colored by the fact that he was being interviewed long after the collapse of the USSR, it seems reasonable to assume that many administrators were more concerned with real urban problems than with ideological issues. At the same time, dealing with economic and social issues was always cloaked—this was the USSR, after all—in ideological language. As elsewhere in the Soviet Union, party cells were active in factories, institutes, workshops, schools, and institutions of higher education. In 1970, over 25,000 Vilnans were active in the city's party organization.[13]

A look at some of the published "decisions" of the Vilnius City Soviet corroborates the assumption that everyday concerns of hygiene, economic development, and keeping order dominated the administration. The very organization of the committee's work (at least in this published form) reflects these practical issues. The report of the "most important decisions" of the city council for 1958 shows decisions grouped under ten headings: Organizational-mass work; Public order and administrative questions; Accounting and allocation of building space (for living or other purposes); Local economy (and infrastructure, also including many decisions on the use of buildings); City transport, building, and architecture; Education, social care, culture, physical culture, and health care; Commerce and finances; and Veterinary oversight, parks, and gardens. Here we find a wide variety of practical rulings, inter alia, on obliging visitors and new residents to register with the local police station, on reducing street noise, on combating pigeons, on installing television antennas, on specific traffic rules for major streets, on improving ambulance service, and on rules for keeping pets and other small animals within city limits. Budgets were approved for building more than 250,000 square meters of living space, as well as for improving opportunities for after-school activities for children seven to eighteen years of age.[14] In short, aside from a few references to "socialist justice" and "improving mass organizational work," there is little here that one would not find in the proceedings of city councils anywhere.

A bilingual "short informational" guide from 1970 tells the same story. Work of the city council continues here along similar lines—building, living space, industry, public transport, education, culture and sport, health care, trade, finances, but with a few new categories: "legality" (decisions having to do with criminality, incorrect fulfillment of previous city council decisions, and the like) and consideration of letters and complaints sent by citizens. Here we also get a month-by-month list of activities sponsored by the city council (e.g., a seminar for workers at clubs and libraries, a conference of pediatricians on preventative measures to improve children's health, and meetings of representatives of various city agencies). A number of pedagogical and informational meetings were dedicated to the life and thought of V. I. Lenin in this centenary of his birth.[15]

Three years later a shorter collection of important decisions followed similar lines. The collection detailed rules concerning the following: the maintenance of clean public streets, prohibitions on keeping animals other than dogs and cats in the downtown areas of most cities, the days on which the Soviet and Lithuanian SSR flags should be displayed (and how), a prohibition on fishing in city rivers (specifically in polluted areas), and detailed requirements for dog and cat owners. This small digest of new regulations was, like the 1970 collection, published in both Russian and Lithuanian, though the 1973 publication was considerably shorter (with a total of only eight new rulings).[16]

Obviously, political decisions, censorship, and police matters were not considered (at least not publicly) in the city council and executive committee. For all that, the decisions reached here and policies carried out reflected concerns not specific to Soviet cities. Unfortunately we still know very little about the actual inner workings of city administration in these years, but it seems reasonable to conclude from existing evidence that it was primarily concerned with practical, everyday matters while larger issues—including the building of large-scale objects and housing areas—were decided upon at other levels of government.

## Creating a Socialist City: Urban Planning and Ideology

While the city Soviet and administrators were dealing mainly with day-to-day matters, large-scale changes were planned and carried out during this period. The city expanded outwardly into new satellite communities, and the downtown area too changed quite noticeably. While the basic core remained intact, new buildings filled the holes left by war damage—and most radically, the entire former ghetto area (on both sides of Vokiečių Street), still mainly undeveloped in the mid-1950s, was entirely rebuilt. The main east-west axis, from the early 1960s no longer Stalino but Lenino, also changed noticeably with new constructions and major remodelings of buildings such as the State Academic Dramatic Theater, Central Post Office, Central State Statistical Administration, and State Planning Commission Building. The city was ringed with new housing areas, and new sites for recreation, relaxation, and consumption (theaters, cafés, restaurants, and shops) popped up throughout Vilnius during these decades.

What was this city of developed, "normal" socialism to look like? Discussions of city planning in this period tended to emphasize comfort, beauty, and utility—not ideology per se. Part of a Soviet citizen's birthright, so to speak, was a comfortable, pleasant lifestyle. At the same time, arguments about urban planning and city development typically noted the advantage of rational planning over "wild" development based on the capitalist profit motive.

A pamphlet of 1965 entitled *Vilnius Architecture Today and Tomorrow* places the present-day architectural achievements in the perspective of past and future goals. After the war, it notes, the primary task was to rebuild the city as quickly as possible. But now that the "wounds of war" have been healed, architects and city planners can think about filling in empty plots and expanding the city. Since 1958, it continues, broad new possibilities in construction have been opened up by the production of prefab concrete slabs in Vilnius at the "Vilniaus gelžbetoninių konstrukcijų gamykla Nr. 1" (Vilnius Factory No. 1 for reinforced concrete). New housing estates (*mikrorajonai*) using this construction type were going up in the districts of Antakalnis and along Raudonosios Armijos prospektas (Red Army Avenue—today's Savanorių). And in the near future a "new city" housing a population of some 120,000 would be constructed on the northwest edge of town. The efficacy of this new style of construction can be summed up, the pamphlet enthused, in the statistic that in 1963 alone 3000 new apartments were completed.

New possibilities in housing construction encompassed just one aspect of the pamphlet's survey. Equally important were new buildings for recreation, sport, culture, administration, and learning. New downtown movie theaters like the "Vilnius" and "Lietuva" were to be built; a large sports center was to rise on the north side of the Neris and somewhat downstream from it, a large complex including hotels, office buildings, and a shopping center. The Central Post Office would be entirely reconstructed (but in the same place on Lenino). In the near future a new opera and ballet theater, bus station, and party executive committee building (*vykdomojo komiteto pastatas*) would all be constructed with "a great deal of attention ... paid to functionality and the modern appearance of the buildings." Thus new architecture in the socialist Lithuanian capital had to be at the same time practical and modern. All of this new construction would also require investment in infrastructure: new roads, public transport lines, and bridges would allow citizens to make their way quickly from one part of the city to the other. The pamphlet ended enthusiastically: "Thus the mutual effort of architects, builders, building material industry workers will help the Vilnius of tomorrow grow. The capital of Soviet Lithuanian will grow rapidly, becoming more beautiful and youthful [*auga, gražėja ir jaunėja*]."[17]

## "Prestige Objects": Culture, Administration, and Communism

The new building in Vilnius served many functions relating to administration, education, sports, recreation, culture, housing, and consumption. We may divide the types of buildings into three broad categories: "prestige buildings" of a public nature that required considerable investment, housing, and construction for the purpose of consumption and recreation. Obviously these are categories of convenience, which could overlap. In the first category one can place prominent buildings that house administration and bureaucracies, government agencies, and cultural/educational institutions. The primary purpose of this construction was, of course, to house offices and bureaucrats but the architecture and placing of these buildings reflected a desire to create a proper, modern, Soviet capital.

The new prestige objects were not built in the Old Town but in the adjacent nineteenth-century city and in particular along and near its main thoroughfare, Lenino Prospektas. While the Central Post Office had been on this avenue's first block (coming from the cathedral) much earlier, the building's interior was entirely gutted and rebuilt (a process common enough in the USSR to have its own immediately understandable Russian phrase: "kapital'nyi remont") in 1969. A few steps further on was the headquarters of the Lithuanian Communist Party Central Committee, until 1982 housed in a repaired prewar building and after that in a new complex just north of the Cherniakhovskii monument, only a few steps from Lenino.[18]

Other prominent administrative buildings along Lenino included the Ministry of Health (housed in a building dating from the 1930s), two main buildings of the Central Statistical Administration, and the city party headquarters. The Statistical Administration's buildings were (and remain) particularly interesting: the main building was a pre–World War I (1913) apartment building that underwent a "kapitalinis remontas" in the years 1964–1966 that allowed its interior to be transformed for administrative purposes while retaining the striking facade. Next door, an entirely new computation center was constructed in 1977 whose newly constructed facade on Lenino echoed the vertical sweep of the 1913 building.[19] These buildings show clearly the desire of Vilnius architects to preserve the past while modernizing the city's infrastructure.

A short walk from Lenino, on a hill leading to the new city (Naujamiestis) constructed in the late nineteenth century, two buildings characteristic of the Soviet style (both in function and in architecture) were constructed in this period. One, a neo-classical building perched atop Tauro Hill, housed the Union (profsąjungų) administration for the Lithuanian SSR while the other, close by across Tauro Street, was the modernist Palace of Weddings, completed in 1974 and awarded the USSR Council of Ministers' architectural prize for 1976.[20]

Cultural institutions were also thick on the ground along and near Gedimino. At the cathedral end of the avenue, across the street from the Central Post Office, was the State Dramatic Theater, reconstructed and adorned with a statue of the three muses.[21] At the other end of the avenue was the Lithuanian SSR "republican library," a neoclassical, very Stalinist-looking building that (astonishingly) was completed fully ten years after the Soviet dictator's death.[22] In between, overlooking the Neris River, stood the large, entirely new, and very Soviet-modern opera and ballet complex, opened in late 1974.[23] All three of these institutions, and most especially the main library, with its stately Grecian facade and the impressive glass and concrete modernism of the Ballet and Opera Theater, proclaimed

SOCIALIST NORMALCY IN VILNIUS, 1955-1985    197

the Lithuanian Soviet Republic's (and, by extension, the USSR's) commitment to culture.

The builders of new Soviet Vilnius were careful to emphasize their desire to preserve the best of the city's architectural past. The simple location of these new buildings—outside the pre-nineteenth-century historical core of the city—attests to this effort to retain the architecture of the early modern and medieval periods. There were, however, some (though not many) new buildings in the Old Town, most notably the regrettable cinema "Moscow" (the name could not have been better chosen), constructed in 1977 across from an equally unfortunate apartment building in the very center of the Old Town.[24] While these two buildings were apparently built on vacant sites, they do clash with the surrounding architecture. It is notable that very few such buildings were put up in the Old Town. Indeed, considerable interest and effort was put into avoiding further development of the Old Town and preserving its architectural beauty and integrity.[25]

Perhaps the most obvious prestige construction of them all, certainly the most noticeable on Vilnius' skyline even in the twenty-first century, is the Television Tower, built between 1974 and 1980. The tower, even in the twenty-first century the tallest structure in Lithuania, was constructed at around the same time as similar towers in Tallinn and Riga—it is probably not by chance that the latest of the three, in Riga, is a few dozen meters higher than the other two. When construction started in the mid-1970s, only the towers in Moscow and Berlin were taller. The ostensible purpose of the tower was to transmit radio and television signals, but one wonders whether the prestige value of the object was not more important still.[26] After all, why were so many of these impressive television towers constructed in the USSR and not elsewhere? (By the time the Vilnius tower was completed, it was so to speak in the shadow of towers in Kiev and Tashkent.)[27] The television tower in Vilnius, like those in other Soviet republics' capitals, aimed to symbolize the technological prowess of the USSR. Ironically, however, they most likely simply revealed misplaced values and ambitions.

## Urbanistika and Housing Socialist Vilnius

Putting up a single building is complex enough, but for a city to function optimally, the building must also fit into the larger urban fabric, both in style and function as well as infrastructure. The overall vision of the direction in which a city should properly develop is the business of *urbanistika*, or urban planning.

In a planned economy like the USSR's, urban planning could have a far greater influence on the shape of a city's future than in the capitalist world.[28] The gap between the urban architect's intentions and the actual plans carried out after cost considerations and political wrangling was probably no smaller—and possibly far greater—than such divergence between ideal and reality in the capitalist world. In any case, Soviet Lithuanian architects were certainly interested in and aware of trends in urban planning and architecture around the world. At the same time, there remained a practical political imperative to acknowledge the leading role of Moscow even while noting new developments in Paris, New York, Stockholm, and Helsinki.[29] Developments in Soviet Lithuania were paralleled, it would seem, by those in other Soviet republics—unfortunately, research on this topic is only just beginning.[30]

Urban planning in Vilnius, as elsewhere, started with the city's topography. In the late nineteenth century the city had expanded from the Old Town core to the south, where the railroad station was located, and from there to the west— the so-called New Town. Hills to the east made large-scale expansion in that direction impractical, though the neighborhoods of Užupis and Antakalnis (Zarecze and Antokol in Polish) already existed during the Russian period.[31] Even in 1939, most of Vilnius remained south and east of the Neris River: to the northwest was the "suburb" of Žverynas, characterized by wooden "summer cottages." North of the Neris River from downtown were barracks and a motley assortment of buildings. If Vilnius was to grow three- or four-fold in population, as postwar plans foresaw, the large new population would have to be housed north and west of the Neris River.

Up to 1960, new housing had been located mainly in Antakalnis and the New City (along Red Army Prospect)—that is, still contiguous with the nineteenth-century city. The scale of housing construction in the 1950s remained fairly modest.[32] In 1960 over 90 percent of all housing in Vilnius was one or two stories high and a mere twenty buildings had been constructed of prefab blocks (compared with over 4260 wooden and 2819 brick structures).[33] From the late 1950s, however, in part because of the new possibilities for large-scale housing estates built with prefab concrete slab methods, ambitious plans for entire new satellite settlements were proposed and carried out.

The rapid shift from more solid but far more expensive housing to prefab techniques can be seen, not just in the Vilnius landscape but also in writings about the Lithuanian SSR's industrial development. Taking three works of a single (prolific) engineer, Juozas Maniušis, we see this shift very clearly. In his 1955 book, *Soviet*

*Lithuania under Construction*, Maniušis dedicated a chapter to Vilnius, praising the heroic progress that had been made in improving the city's buildings since the end of World War I. But he mentioned housing only in passing—noting the use of prefab techniques for a dormitory and for the building that housed a musicians' organization (*muzikos fondo pastatas*). The book's only illustrations depict an impressive, large school building and the new, equally prestigious construction along the Neris River.[34] A somewhat longer pamphlet issued the following year lacked a specific section on Vilnius but emphasized the increased resources dedicated to improving housing in the Sixth Five-Year Plan (1956–1960). However, the pamphlet's only illustration of an apartment building shows a construction of the old-fashioned, non-prefab type.[35] Only the third publication, a Russian-language book by the same author published in 1960, features rows of (now familiar) prefab apartment buildings under construction in Vilnius. The latter book also includes a model for a large-scale housing area with dozens of apartment buildings that were planned but apparently never built in Antakalnis.[36]

The year after Khrushchev's declaration of a new Seven-Year Plan (1960) marked a new era of large-scale housing construction in Vilnius. In this year one could already see a number of the new prefab apartment buildings but as yet these were not built together as a planned unit—but this was about to change with the creation of the "mikrorajonas," a term I am translating as "housing estate." The architectural press was full of articles discussing the new type of large-scale housing area, constructed using prefab methods.[37]

The first major housing estate in Vilnius using these new methods was located north and west of the Neris in Žirmūnai (the river makes a sharp turn to the north at Castle Hill). Housing construction in the Žirmūnai district may be seen as an intermediate step between the smaller, piecemeal construction of the late 1950s and early 1960s and the massive new neighborhoods of the 1970s. Located due north of the Old Town and to the east, just across the river from Antakalnis, Žirmūnai was contiguous with the existing city and not separated from it by a park or forest. The district was constructed along the Neris River in three adjacent mikrorajonai, which included stores and two multipurpose shopping and "service centers" ("Minskas" and "Žirmūnai"). In the end some 45,000 people lived here. Žirmūnai district went up between 1962 and 1967; in 1965 a new bridge was constructed across the Neris to facilitate access between the new housing estate and Antakalnis.[38]

Žirmūnai shared many of the characteristics of later Vilnius housing areas: it was planned to be more or less self-contained for everyday purposes, with child care, schools, clinics, and shopping integrated with the housing. The housing estate consisted mainly of five-story buildings, but there were also twelve-story towers. The most important difference between Žirmūnai and later estates like Lazdynai or Fabijoniškės was its location. Unlike later developments, Žirmūnai was within easy walking distance of the Old Town: it represented an extension of the existing built-up area of Vilnius, not a "satellite" built a few kilometers from the main city core.

In the mid-1960s it was still not quite clear just what direction Vilnius' development would take. The city's topography and the desire to preserve the Old Town (including much of the nineteenth-century town) made clear that expansion would have to take place north of the Neris River. The city's general plan of 1965 set down the main outlines of this direction, including a major housing area at Viršuliškės to the northwest of the city, as well as improvements in roads and bridges to make this region more accessible to the center.[39] A new "town center" was planned just north of the river with a "universal" (department) store, a hotel, and other buildings, the hope being that this new center would relieve congestion and enable the transformation of Lenino Avenue into a pedestrian zone.[40] The new town center was completed in the 1970s, but it was only in the post-Soviet period that this area, enhanced by several skyscrapers, would truly take off as an alternative to the downtown area south of the Neris.[41] Interestingly, already in the 1960s the growth of interest in private automobiles (and the possibility of acquiring them) was reflected in an article on multistory garages in *Statyba ir architektūra*. However, little provision was made for automobile parking in the large housing areas constructed in Vilnius (or elsewhere in the USSR) in the 1970s and 1980s.[42]

In the mid-1960s it was still unclear, however, just where the main housing estates would be built. The general plan mentioned Viršuliškės, several kilometers from the city center, but sites closer to the downtown, more like Žirmūnai, were also put forth.[43] On the occasion of the twentieth anniversary of Vilnius' liberation, an enthusiastic article showed the "rebirth" of "Old Vilnius." The article featured images of the monument to the city's Red Army liberator Cherniakhovskii, construction on large-scale prefab housing areas, and the factory that produced the concrete slabs used for this massive housing project.[44] At that point (1964), it was not clear that future mikrorajonas would be located at a considerable distance from the center. No doubt a more thorough study in the archives would reveal exactly why the close-in alternatives were ultimately rejected in favor of large satellite communities, but the resounding success of Lazdynai quite possibly made more modest apartment complexes closer to the center seem outdated and uninteresting—or even backward and reactionary.

Unlike previous housing estates, Lazdynai was not part of a contiguous accretion to the city—rather, it constituted an entirely new complex. The site, some eight kilometers from the city, was selected in part because it was entirely devoid of buildings and thereby allowed the architects to create an architectural whole using the gently sloping landscape. The result was very successful, and even today most residents express contentment with the area, its layout, and (to a lesser extent) its buildings. Like Žirmūnai but on a larger scale, Lazdynai combined buildings of a variety of heights (5, 9, 12, and 16 stories high). The rajonas included a shopping center, recreation area, cinema, schools, and other such amenities. Lazdynai was also used as an example for the architectural principle that every housing complex should have its own "face" rather than rise up in a sea of identical structures. The latter failing, characteristic of most Brezhnev-era Soviet housing, was parodied in the classic film "Irony of Fate" (1975), in which the vodka-befuddled hero could not tell a residential area in Leningrad apart from one in Moscow because the street names, buildings, apartments, and even keys were exactly alike.[45] The architects of Lazdynai were awarded the Lenin prize, and the housing area became a centerpiece and model for Soviet urban planners, despite the fact that the model was never really followed.[46]

The success and prestige of Lazdynai probably made it difficult for Vilnius architects to propose more modest, even if more practical, housing alternatives. The uniformly positive descriptions in contemporary journals and guidebooks should not blind us to the fact that in real life stores were often empty, "service centers" frequently closed or useless, and for most residents everyday life included an exhausting commute to the city center in crammed-full public transport.[47] By the early 1980s, Vilnius was ringed (to the west and northwest) by a semi-circle of housing estates—Karoliniškės, Viršuliškės, Justiniškės, Pasilaičiai, and Fabijoniškės—in which the majority of the city's population resided. In the post-Soviet period these housing areas (largely with the exception of Lazdynai) have been criticized as gray, uniform, and of low quality construction. It needs to be admitted, however, that for all the distance between enthusiastic plans and cold reality, these new housing areas provided hundreds of thousands of Vilnius residents with living quarters that were a huge improvement over what they had previously had.[48] In that sense the prefab mikrorajonai, for all their weaknesses, may be seen as one of the major accomplishments of "socialist normalcy."

## Lithuanian Socialist Architecture

Lithuanian Soviet architects were influenced by concepts and trends from outside the USSR, as a glimpse at their monthly organ, *Statyba ir architektūra* (Building and architecture), shows. The title of the periodical is also its program: it sets out to bring together both actual building workers and the architects who design those structures. Thus in its pages one finds stories about especially effective workers and "collectives" next to historical articles about architects and buildings from Lithuania's past or proposals for new buildings and for new city planning. In nearly every issue one also finds information about the latest architectural ideas from around the world, whether they pertain to new suburban planning in Stockholm or skyscrapers in the USA and East Asia. At the same time, given the importance of Vilnius for the Lithuanian SSR, that city's development, past, and future are frequently discussed.

Choosing more or less at random a half-dozen years of the monthly to leaf through, one finds a mixture of articles that remains more or less constant throughout the 1960s to early 1980s. Articles from 1960 consider the new large-scale concrete apartment buildings going up in some neighborhoods (at this point, mainly in Antakalnis but also along "Red Army Avenue") and projects for new opera and theater buildings. The soon-to-be-legendary Neringa Café is also mentioned. Different versions of the mikrorajonas are discussed. At the beginning of the 1960s the large-scale residential areas that made use of mass construction and prefab materials were still a novelty in Soviet Lithuania. Later they became the basic form of housing development in Vilnius and throughout the USSR.[49]

The following year, 1961, a number of articles tackled the issue of Soviet consumption. To be sure, they did not develop this idea directly but, rather, took for granted that reasonable leisure and retail opportunities must be available for Soviet citizens. This idea is developed in articles about cafeterias and other food-service establishments in Vilnius, new movie theaters, flower shops, and a newly opened Intourist hotel. The latter would, of course, not cater to local customers or, indeed, to many Soviet customers at all. (This fact, obvious to any Soviet reader, remains unstated.) It would appear that the status of the republic's capital demanded reasonable accommodation for foreign guests, and for this reason locals could take pride in the opening of this hotel. The last issue of 1961 addresses the problems associated with growth, and the article's authors concede, at least partially, that the Soviet obsession with expansion and production could also have its negative side.[50]

By mid-decade, *Statyba ir architektūra* articles reflected the progress made both in new housing construction and in large-scale prestige buildings (which, however, remained at this point mainly in the planning stage). Plans for the new sports complex across the Neris from Castle Hill were discussed, and a model (*maketa*) of the skyscraper "Hotel Lietuva" adorned the pages of the April issue. By this point, concrete-slab constructed apartment buildings were being constructed along Red Army Avenue; a story entitled "Fragments of Vilnius' New Everyday Life" appeared in the July issue with pictures of these new apartment buildings. In autumn an article on Le Corbusier implied that some of the famous French architect's theories could well be applied to Soviet reality.[51]

In 1970, a major story was the planned new shopping area north of the Neris, across from downtown. This complex, including the Lietuva hotel mentioned earlier and a new history of the revolution museum, was to be part of city planners' efforts to shift the city center away from the traditional core south of the Neris. Another major project being mooted was for a new Supreme Soviet building for the Lithuanian SSR, to be built at the end of Lenin Avenue. At this point large-scale housing estate construction was also starting: one article described plans for the future Baltupio mikrorajonas. Difficulties (and achievements) of public transport and efforts to spruce up the Old Town (while retaining its historical aspect) were also discussed in the journal's pages. Architectural matters outside Lithuania also received attention, for example the Lenin Museum in Tashkent, the new Coronado Bridge in San Diego, and the international architectural congress in Buenos Aires.[52]

By 1975, several large-scale housing estates were under construction or complete. The most famous of these, Lazdynai, is discussed in that year's January issue. Another estate, Karoliniškės (so to speak the "next in line"), also figures in articles. By this point the larger plan to place Vilnius' population mainly in these estates several kilometers from the city center was taking clear shape. In the middle of town, the new "civil metrification office" (where one would go, for example, for civil marriage) had been completed on Tauro Hill. Even more impressively, the television tower in the aforementioned Karoliniškės housing area was taking shape in the Vilnius skyline.[53]

In 1980, at the beginning of the decade that would bring enormous changes to Eastern Europe and the USSR, *Statyba ir architektūra* showed little sign that major shifts were imminent. True, this year one notices a significantly larger number of advertisements in the journal than earlier, though many of these were aimed at building cooperatives rather than individual consumers. By 1980 the Vilnius television tower had been completed and was the seventh highest in the world. The new mikrorajonas Šeškinė was now going forward, one of the final large-scale housing estates to be completed in the Soviet period. An article in the December issue considered the future of Vilnius' downtown, praising the newly completed buildings of the Finance Ministry, the Presidium of the Lithuanian SSR Supreme Soviet, and the Council of Trade Unions. To these would soon be added the new Supreme Soviet building (a model appears in the article) and plans for a more thoroughgoing reconstruction of the Lukiškės quarter were also mooted (although, happily, not carried out).[54]

It is easy to criticize the architects and their buildings from this period. The construction was often of poor quality: the Lietuva Hotel survived barely two decades before being totally gutted and rebuilt; the sports complex, an eyesore on the banks of the Neris, has lasted a bit longer; and Vilnius has its share of the gray, decaying concrete buildings familiar throughout the former USSR. However, the architects should not shoulder the blame for the generally miserable level of quality in Soviet construction (which simply reflected the overall low standards in manufacturing and customer service). Many buildings erected during the Soviet period continue to serve their purpose and have become part of the Vilnius cityscape. One wonders whether the flashy and vulgar architecture of the first post-Soviet generation will age better or worse.[55]

## Soviet Consumer Culture

In the period of socialist normalcy, Soviet citizens were allowed to express their desire to live well, not just to work hard and fulfill the plan. Recreation and consumption became a quite acceptable part of life, not a sign of "shirking." Already in 1957 an informational address book (*adresno-spravochnaia kniga*) for Vilnius residents ended with nearly thirty pages of advertisements, for seven movie theaters, a department store (*univermag*), and a number of different types of store ("Citizens! Buy food products at the 'Gastronom' stores!").[56] The Soviet commitment to increasing living standards was reflected in the huge resources dedicated to housing, as we have seen, but also to the expansion of retail opportunities, restaurants, and other leisure-time activities. The present-day emphasis on political repression or economic stagnation during this period should not blind us to the fact that for individuals who lived through the 1960s and 1970s in the USSR—in particular those of a generation old enough to remember World War II—these were years of stability and economic prosperity.

The Soviet regime had never condemned a comfortable life entirely, but in the Stalinist years other priorities predominated.[57] In the decades after the dictator's death, the open, confident, and unabashed embrace of material comforts as a central part of a healthy, developed Soviet society represented a major ideological shift. In an interview in 1973, Vilnius' chief architect stated that "modern comforts" were an essential part of city planning that he and his colleagues were working to create.[58] While Comrade Valiuškis did not spell out exactly what "modern comforts" entailed, from his comments one may imagine that among them were decent housing, public spaces for recreation, and access to goods.

Sports fit uneasily between ideology and recreation in the Soviet experience. While sports had always played an important role in Soviet ideology, as a pastime and recreational activity they grew during the period of socialist normalcy. Indeed, the USSR first competed in the Olympic games in Helsinki in 1952, obviously as much for ideological-propaganda reasons as for any other.[59] Sports as everyday activities of healthy Soviet citizens had long been given lip service, and from the later 1950s noncompetitive sports—for the citizen, not just for the athlete—became increasingly important. In Vilnius, the most obvious symbol of this shift was the construction of the Sport Center just across the Neris River from Gedimino Hill, which was completed in 1971.[60] Indeed, among the "great challenges/tasks" facing architects discussed by the president of the LSSR architects' union was the construction of leisure-time sport facilities (a mock-up of one appears as an illustration to his article).[61] For the most part, however, it must be admitted that sports continued to appear in Lithuanian Soviet publications more as spectator activities (including basketball, of course) than as everyday leisure for the healthy Soviet citizen.[62]

The growth of consumption in various forms also characterized the period of Soviet normalcy. This is reflected on the pages of *Jaunimo Gretos*, the organ of the Lithuanian young communists (Komsomol). The monthly, whose title—roughly translated as "the ranks of youth"—harks back to a more ideological, even Stalinist period, clearly wanted to avoid seeming overly strident regarding ideology by the 1960s. The frequent features on fashion that appeared in *Jaunimo Gretos*, including photos, drawings, and even dress patterns, indicate that even Young Communists were not immune to the attractions of up-to-date and attractive clothing. In general Soviet consumers, including the inhabitants of Vilnius, shared these desires and demanded more and better retail outlets. The incorporation of shopping centers in the suburban housing estates reflected these demands, and the large department store in the planned "new city center" on the north bank of the Neris served as an acknowledgment that shopping was not only a necessary everyday task but also a pleasure.[63]

The Vilnius city executive committee also concerned itself with the opening of retail stores in the early 1970s. Besides opening food and other types of stores in Žirmūnai and other housing areas, the committee "improved the quality" of products sold in a number of other stores, opened a vegetable kiosk on Dariaus ir Girėno Street, and had department stores built in Žvėryne and on Ukmergės Street. As if all this activity were not enough, the committee forbade the selling of alcoholic beverages at a shish-kabob eatery (šašlikinė) on Gorky Street (present-day Didžioji).[64] While these achievements hardly constitute a consumer revolution, they do show that the primary Soviet organ of local government in Vilnius concerned itself actively with citizens' everyday consumption habits.

Describing "the Vilnius of today and tomorrow," Algirdas Motulas proudly pointed out that in 1979 the city boasted 687 small-scale shops, 31 restaurants, 375 cafeterias (valgyklos), 35 cafés, and 9 beer-drinking establishments (uluus barai). While the present-day reader is likely to be shocked at these small numbers for a city of nearly one-half million, the contemporary Soviet reader was more likely to be impressed with another statistic cited by Motulas: that the value of goods sold in Vilnius per capita had shot up six-fold since 1945.[65] In his fairly detailed discussion of retail trade (prekyba), Motulas takes nearly all his examples of large shopping centers from the 1970s, often constructed as part of the new housing complexes created in that decade. Like other Soviet cities, Vilnius had a specific child-centered department store named—inevitably—children's world (vaikų pasaulis) as well as numerous specialty stores selling everything from bicycles to consumer electronics (televisions, tape recorders, radios). While admitting certain problems (training staff in these stores, supplying goods in the summer season), Motulas's (obviously highly optimistic and one-sided) portrayal shows a Soviet Lithuanian consumer culture, sure of its own rights and confident of future positive development.

Another aspect of Soviet consumption was the development of cafés and restaurants. As the statistics proudly cited by Motulas indicate, a visit to a café or restaurant was a rare special occasion in the life of a citizen of Vilnius (after all, there was only one café or restaurant for every 10,000 inhabitants). On a more everyday basis, citizens were far more likely to visit a cafeteria or an eatery like the šašlikinė on Gorky Street mentioned above (where they, no doubt, would have been annoyed by the City Executive Committee's decision to forbid the sale of alcoholic beverages). Still, for special occasions and as one available (albeit not always affordable) consumer lifestyle option, restaurants and cafés filled an important niche. This is a topic that has almost not been researched at all and is deserving of serious scholarly attention. For present purposes, let us look briefly at the opening of the prestigious Café Neringa on Lenino Prospect, an eating and drinking establishment that—possibly uniquely among Vilnius Soviet establishments—is still in business well into the twenty-first century.

The Neringa was opened in late 1959 in a nineteenth-century building on what was then still known as "Stalino prospektas." The café instantly became a Lithuanian cultural icon, in particular for its innovative and attractive interior, which included a large painting depicting the Lithuanian legend of Neringa and Naglis. The café's interior is notable for its curving lines, with suitably modern furniture.[66] In the 1960s and 1970s, the Neringa would become famous also as a gathering place for Lithuanian intellectuals, including those associated with the dissident movement. Most likely the prices and a gruff Soviet doorman would have kept most Vilnius residents away, but for special occasions and for the lucky or well-connected, the Neringa provided an atmosphere, service, libations, and cuisine at least comparable (or imaginably comparable for Soviet citizens) to those in Western Europe. And that, too, would constitute an achievement of socialist normalcy in Vilnius.[67]

One occasion that highlighted for non-Lithuanian Soviet and foreign visitors the progress Vilnius made under Soviet rule was the 400th anniversary of Vilnius University, celebrated in 1979. The anniversary was marked by numerous ceremonies, guests from throughout the USSR and from abroad, and a flurry of publications. A number of books on the history of Vilnius University appeared in both Russian and Lithuanian, all attempting in one way or another to fit the university into the narrative of the Lithuanian Soviet capital. The most interesting of these works is the three-volume history edited by Vytautas Merkys, the last volume of which appeared in the jubilee year.[68] A volume of scholarly essays on the university's history also appeared in Cracow, though the touchy interwar period was passed over in silence.[69]

In other, less scholarly, histories of the university aimed at broader audiences, one finds much that is characteristic for the Soviet Lithuanian discourse on the city's history. Here the closing of the Polish "University of Stefan Batory" and the establishment of the Lithuanian University in late 1939/early 1940 is portrayed as simply the putting-right of a historical injustice. The account notes that during the years of Nazi occupation several professors were forced to flee to the Soviet interior while others were arrested, but collaboration is not discussed. Once reopened in 1944 with the help of Russian and other Soviet scholars, the university quickly succeeded in becoming a cultural focus for the city and the republic. Since the 1960s, the university has had exchanges with various foreign universities, especially those in Greifswald, Erfurt (Vilnius' "sister city" in the GDR), Prague, Cracow, Lublin, and Brazzaville. The university has enjoyed "frequent" visits from foreign scholars and students from a variety of countries, from Japan to Finland to the USA.[70]

The university's primary task was, of course, to train specialists and scholars. For Soviet educators, however, "to cultivate personalities" was a no less crucial goal. That is, the university aimed not only to spread knowledge but also to instill communist ideals of patriotism (both Soviet and Lithuanian), civic responsibility, and pride in Soviet achievements. To this end, the party organization of the university organized appropriate activities. Song festivals and athletics also contributed to this formation of a complete Soviet Lithuanian personality.[71]

Such sentiments are echoed in books on Vilnius University published in 1979 by the longtime educational bureaucrat Andrius Bendžius. A richly illustrated and well-published trilingual (Polish, Russian, and Lithuanian) documentary history of the institution (*Academia et universitas vilnensis*), while not ignoring Polish influences there in the nineteenth century, entirely omits any document from the interwar period.[72] A Russian-language history of the university, edited by Bendžius, described the interwar period as a time of stewardship under "bourgeois landowners' Poland," when unjust Polish "occupation" of the city also led to an unimpressive scholarly level at the university. As one would expect, the real flourishing of scholarship and teaching here came only after 1944 (after the initial start in 1940–1941, cut short by the Nazi invasion). The book's final paragraph extols the university's accomplishments over several centuries and "with confidence looks into the future." This confidence, the final sentence notes, is based on the unceasing work and concern of the Communist Party and the Soviet government for the development of science and education, the right of every Soviet citizen.[73]

## Conclusion: Lithuanian and Soviet Identities

The brief period beginning with de-Stalinization and ending with the naming of Mikhail Sergeevich Gorbachev as general secretary of the Soviet Communist Party was not long enough to create a durable Soviet Lithuanian identity. Many would argue, of course, that the endeavor was in any case doomed from the start.

We should not, however, view the past entirely through the lens of subsequent major events of world historical importance (i.e., the collapse of the USSR in late 1991). From the late 1950s to the 1980s, most residents of Vilnius managed to create a personal identity that included different components that expressed themselves with different levels of intensity: aspects of Lithuanian, Soviet, Russian, Polish, and Jewish cultures. The city, too, showed a mixed identity, primarily Lithuanian and Soviet, but also Russian inasmuch as the Soviet Union presupposed Russian and Lithuanian bilingualism. The Jewish and Polish identities of the citizenry were publicly suppressed but persisted in understated ways.

Soviet and Lithuanian identities coexisted uneasily in Vilnius. The cityscape was relentlessly bilingual, with everything from street signs to historical plaques appearing in both Russian and Lithuanian. Many aspects of Lithuanian high culture did, of course, develop rapidly in this period: never before had there been so many periodicals, book publications, or Lithuanian university students. At the same time, certain core aspects of traditional Lithuanian identity as it had developed from the nineteenth century had to be avoided or denied, in particular the link to the Catholic Church. There always existed a tension between the desire for autonomous Lithuanian cultural development and the need to embed this culture in an accepted Soviet framework. Worse yet, general Soviet culture for most Lithuanian intellectuals not only failed to impress when compared with Western examples but always threatened to shift into pure efforts at russification.

The city in 1985 was very different from that of thirty years earlier. It had expanded greatly in size as well as in the percentage of ethnic Lithuanians making their home there. Entire new housing estates went up and the downtown was full of buildings constructed or renovated since the war. While Russians and their language were present in large numbers, the city appeared—at least to an outsider—a mainly Lithuanian one (unlike initial impressions of, say, Riga in these years). Few Lithuanians were enthusiastic about Soviet power, but even fewer could conceive of any real alternative to it, at least not in the foreseeable future. Furthermore, even the most anti-Soviet citizen had to admit that the city had come to Lithuania through the agency of the Red Army and that the city had indeed developed for the better in the past generation. Next to no one, of course, could foresee that in a few years Soviet certainties would be swept aside and the city would embark on an entirely new history as the capital of independent Lithuania.

CHAPTER 8

# Building a Lithuanian Capital City, 1985–2000

IN THE EARLY 1980S, the inhabitants of Vilnius were materially better off than ever before. Despite a repressive government and inefficient bureaucracy, everyday life for most was noticeably more agreeable than a generation or—for the very few who could remember—two generations earlier. No one would have predicted that the system ruling the city and the entire USSR would collapse and dissolve within a few years.

In hindsight we now recognize that by the end of the Brezhnev years (1964–1982), the USSR faced an economic crisis. The computer revolution and widespread use of personal computers in the West left the USSR far behind. Loans from the West and inefficient investments threatened the balance of payments. The astonishing birth and development of the Polish labor union Solidarność in 1980–1981 brought to the fore grievances that many non-Russians had felt under communist rule. The repression of Solidarność merely made the communists seem inept and vacillating. To paraphrase Adam Michnik, they were like a vicious dog with bad teeth. Educated Lithuanians in the Vilnius area could often read Polish and were well informed about events across the border.

The leaders of the Soviet communist party—and its Lithuanian branch—no doubt recognized the need for significant change, but the doddering old men at the top were simply incapable of taking action. Even the election of the lifelong party functionary Mikhail Sergeevich Gorbachev in March 1985 to the post of general secretary of the Soviet communist party did not at first seem to portend any radical shift in policy. In the next few years, however, Gorbachev astonished Soviet citizens and the world by launching a reform program under the buzzwords "glasnost'" (openness) and "perestroika" (restructuring). In turn, Soviet citizens by the late 1980s surprised Gorbachev by dismissing him as yesterday's news and an overly timid leader. The unceremonious collapse of the USSR after a comic-opera coup in August 1991 took everyone by surprise.[1]

Non-Russians, including Lithuanians, played a role in the downfall of the USSR, but not a principal one. The economic chaos engendered by Gorbachev's muddled reform efforts and internal Russian politics, in particular the rise of Boris Yeltsin, were vastly more important than Baltic protests in bringing down the USSR. On a more profound level, the cynicism and ebbing of any kind of real enthusiasm for communism made mobilization for the regime exceedingly difficult—as Gorbachev (a true believer, by all indications) soon found out. In any case, by 1990 it seemed inevitable that the Baltic countries, including Lithuania, would split off from the USSR—unless Gorbachev or conservatives in Moscow wished to risk major bloodshed. And the center of Lithuanian resistance to Soviet rule was, of course, in the "Soviet Lithuanian capital," Vilnius.

For all the heroic historiography regarding events in Vilnius 1990–1991— and heroism was indeed one part of the story—from a broader perspective it makes more sense to see the end of communist rule here as a collapse of the center. That collapse allowed Lithuanian leaders, many of them ex-communists (most famous among them Algirdas Brazauskas), to play the nationalist card, though, to their credit, not in a chauvinist or vicious way. After real independence was achieved in late 1991 (with the dissolution of the USSR), Vilnius experienced major changes over a decade, partly in the economic sphere (more or less unchecked market capitalism either fueled a renaissance or savaged the economy, depending on one's point of view) and partly in the ethno-linguistic sphere. While non-Lithuanian culture continued to be tolerated in the city, the bilingual street signs vanished quickly, streets were renamed mainly for Lithuanian figures and events, and it became immediately clear that Lithuania perceived itself first and foremost as the homeland of ethnic Lithuanians. Happily, little ethnic tension existed (at least compared to the situation in the other two Baltic republics) because non-Lithuanians constituted a relatively small and nonthreatening minority, and the Lithuanian leadership from the start adopted a conciliatory policy toward the most important ethno-linguistic minorities, the Russians and the Poles. This mild (and wise) policy was aided by the fact that both Russians and Poles refrained from making any large demands on the state or, most pertinent for us, on Vilnius. Unlike in Tallinn, where Russians protested the moving of World War II monuments, no one seemed at all interested when the obelisk honoring General Cherniakhovskii, the city's "liberator" in 1944, was dismantled and carted away. The process of creating a Lithuanian capital city—along with the larger process of putting in place a (relatively) functioning democratic Lithuanian republic—may be seen as symbolically completed by 2004, when the republic was accepted into both NATO and the European Union.[2]

## Vilnius in the 1980s

In 1980 Vilnius had reached a population of around a half-million, remaining one of the smallest capitals in one of the smallest Soviet republics. Alongside Gothic and Baroque churches, many newer, recognizable Soviet buildings had risen and from Castle Hill by the picturesque Old Town one could see satellite *mikrorajonai* of stark concrete blocks.[3] On the streets—where all street signs and important notices were posted in bilingual form, Lithuanian and Russian—Russian was nearly as prevalent as Lithuanian. Compared to Moscow and Leningrad (not to mention smaller provincial cities), Vilnius' stores and restaurants were noticeably better stocked. Considerable numbers of Russians—and individuals of various other Soviet nationalities—made their home in the city, but Lithuanians were the largest and most prominent group here. In short, this was a pleasant Soviet provincial town that in 1985 celebrated Soviet Lithuanian's forty-fifth anniversary.[4]

In the 1970s Vilnius had grown considerably, from 372,000 inhabitants in 1970 to 535,000 in 1983. As we have seen, much of this new population was housed in the new high-rise satellite suburbs Lazdynai, Viršuliškiai, Šeškinė, and Karoliniškės. The largest single employer was industry, with nearly 38 percent employed in that branch in the early 1980s, followed by education and culture (including the arts) with 15.7 percent. Building trades employed 7.5 percent of the population, transportation 8.9 percent, and trade, restaurants, and other services made up 8.8 percent of Vilnius' workers. The average size of a Vilnius family in 1970 was 3.4 persons and had slipped to 3.3 by decade's end. In 1979 14.1 percent of the population had higher education (up from 9.9% nine years earlier), and in the same year 62 percent of Vilnius inhabitants had completed at least secondary education (up from 54.4% in 1970). As throughout its history, Vilnius remained a multiethnic city, with no one ethnicity making up the majority of the population in 1979. However, Lithuanians were very nearly half of the population (47.3%), and 22.2 percent were Russians, 18.0 percent were Poles, and 6.4 percent were Belarusians.[5] Among the 6.1 percent of the population made up of "other nationalities" were a significant number of Jews, nearly all of whom had arrived in the city after 1944, and many of whom spoke Russian rather than Lithuanian as their primary language.

By the 1980s, most Vilnans lived in new housing areas that had been constructed in the previous two decades. As we have seen, using prefab concrete construction allowed a boom in apartment construction quite unprecedented in the city's history. The new mass-produced apartments often suffered from poor workmanship and planning, but few would have traded the concrete-block apartment buildings for their previous housing. The general plan was to ring the city, in particular to the north, with new satellite communities. Architects had designed these settlements to be largely self-sufficient, with stores, industry, schools, and entertainment. In reality, living in these new districts often entailed long rides on crowded buses to get to work and to obtain the necessities of life.

Residents of Soviet Vilnius could also point proudly to the many public buildings that had been erected since the early 1970s. Besides the entirely new housing estates, numerous public institutions had received new quarters, dotting the downtown area with new buildings. Among these were a new building for art exhibitions (1970), a "palace of sport" (1971), a bus station (1973), a "marriage palace" (1974), the Opera and Ballet Theater (1974), the new Supreme Soviet of the Lithuanian Soviet Socialist Republic (1978), and the Academic Drama Theater (1981).[6] The Old Town remained on the whole untouched by new construction and efforts were made to conserve "architectural monuments." However, many of the innumerable churches in the city—as well as the one remaining synagogue—seldom benefited from state conservation efforts. In general it may be said that new construction was a higher priority than upkeep or restoration. At the same time, Vilnius architects made an effort to blend old and new styles in new construction, several examples of which arose along the city's principal thoroughfare, Lenino prospektas/Leninskii prospekt (now Gedimino).

In 1985 the city was dotted with monuments emphasizing its communist present and liberation from fascism by the Red Army. Primary among these was the large central monument to General Cherniakhovskii, standing where one now finds a rather awful would-be modernist monument to the author of the Lithuanian national anthem, Vincentas Kudirka. The Cherniakhovskii monument itself could be called typically Soviet, a heroic and resolute bronze figure at approximately double life size (upon a granite and bronze base of similar height) but, remarkably, the square also contained the general's mortal remains. An inscription (bilingual, of course) explained that Cherniakhovskii had died fighting German fascists on February 18, 1945 (he was buried in this spot two days later). The base of the statue contained bas reliefs showing soldiers (presumably Cherniakhovskii himself) greeting and being hailed by men and women in peasant and worker garb.[7] A ten-minute walk further along Lenin Prospect brought one to Lenin Square, in the middle of which Lenin towered to a height of some eleven meters on a base of red granite. The monument itself was a copy of a sculpture by the Russian Soviet artist Nikolai Tomskii; the copy was cast and placed in the square in 1952.[8]

Other monuments honored political, cultural, and historical figures. In front of the art museum (now the town hall) stood a statue of V. Mickevičius-Kapsukas, founder of the Lithuanian Communist Party. Kapsukas was joined by Lenin in another statue, this one near the new student city toward the north of town. A statue of the Polish Bolshevik Feliks Dzierzyński, who attended secondary school in Vilnius, stood near his childhood home, which had been transformed into a museum. Possibly the best-known statues of the postwar period were those adorning the main bridge across the Neris—in 1985 still officially called "Černiavskio" (after the general). On each corner of the bridge stood a pair of figures representing four key groups of the Soviet Lithuanian nation: peasants, industry and construction, students, and "defenders of the peace" (Red Army soldiers). Interestingly, women appeared in only two of these statues (as peasants and students) and in both cases were slightly smaller and standing demurely somewhat behind their male companions.[9]

Of course, not all (probably not even most) Vilnius monuments were dedicated to Soviet people and themes. Mickiewicz, who of course came from "Lithuania" (speaking geographically, not ethnographically) and attended university in Vilnius (Wilno, for him), was given a monument near St. Anne's Church in 1984. The monument bore only the poet's name "Adomas Mickevičius" (i.e., in Lithuanian orthography) and gave no indication that he had penned his works in Polish. Other monuments commemorated Lithuanian writers and scholars such as Žemaitė, Kristijonas Donelaitis, and Liudas Gira.[10] Foreign artists were represented by a monument to Pushkin (interestingly, in the same place where up until 1914 another similar bust had stood) and the Polish composer Stanisław Moniuszko (this monument from 1922 amazingly survived in its original place).[11]

It is fair to say, however, that most residents and visitors to the city paid far less attention to these monuments—whether to Pushkin or Cherniakhovskii—than to the beautiful Gothic and Baroque churches dotted throughout the city. Even after two generations of Soviet rule there were few views of the downtown area that did not include a church. Some of these, like the cathedral, had been converted from their original purposes. For example, St. Kazimieras had been turned into the museum of atheism.[12] Many others, both Catholic and Orthodox, remained in use. An exhaustive scholarly guide to architectural monuments in Vilnius published in 1988 lists several dozen churches, which are described in great detail. More general works on Soviet Vilnius, however, avoided mention (or depiction) of churches. Algirdas Motulas's book on "past and present Vilnius" (1980) does not specifically identify a single church in dozens of photographs.[13] Writing in the mid-1980s, Vileikis mentions only five churches under the heading "important historical and architectural monuments." And while his book contains dozen of photographs of the university, streets, new districts of town, monuments, parades, sports facilities, and the like, only one church is specifically depicted and labeled as such, the stunning brick Gothic masterpiece, St. Anne's.[14]

## Glasnost' in Lithuania, 1985–1988

At first the selection of M. S. Gorbachev as first secretary of the Communist Party of the Soviet Union seemed to make little impact on life in socialist Lithuania. Reading through the 1986 issues of *Jaunimo Gretos* ("Ranks of the Youth"), the monthly organ of the Lithuanian young communists, one finds no reference to any major shift in policy. As in 1981—or earlier, for that matter—the monthly described in enthusiastic terms the activities of communist youth in the Lithuanian SSR and in other parts of the Soviet Union, as well as demonstrations by "progressive youth" in the West.

By 1988, however, certain changes can be discerned in *Jaunimo Gretos*. In the year's first issue, a long article was dedicated to denying that February 16 (1918) was Lithuania's true independence day. This date, commemorating the signing of a declaration of independence (in Vilnius) by the Lithuanian patriot Jonas Basanavičius and others, had been the interwar independence day for the "bourgeois republic."[15] In Soviet Lithuania, however, an alternate date was celebrated: December 29, 1918, when the Lithuanian communist Vincas Mickevičius-Kapsukas issued a resolution against the "counterrevolutionary" Taryba government and declared a revolutionary workers' and peasants' government. In essence, the article contained nothing new; both the arguments and the language ("bourgeois Lithuania," "the imperialist powers") could have been written decades earlier. What *was* new is the simple fact that the organ of the communist youth league had decided to enter into this historical argument at all, in that sense validating the importance of other versions of Lithuanian history by arguing publicly in favor of February 16 as the date of commemoration.[16]

What is more, by the end of the year the tone of the periodical had changed almost completely. Rather than focusing on visits to Soviet cities, as in the past, it now included descriptions of Brussels (April, p. 20) and Geneva (October, pp.

28–29). Where earlier the periodical featured pictures of earnest-looking Soviet *sportsmena*, it now boasted pictures of buff male bodybuilders (February, pp. 20–21) and naked women in arty poses (March, pp. 30–31). More seriously, articles addressed unpleasant aspects of life and—in contrast to a short period earlier—admitted that such problems existed in the USSR and Soviet Lithuania. Examples of these serious issues include AIDS (February, pp. 26–27), prisons (April, pp. 30–31), pollution (June, pp. 4–5), and drug addiction (November, pp. 24–25). Uncomfortable topics from Soviet history were also discussed, such as the pseudo-scientist and Stalin protégé Trofim Lysenko's baleful influence on Soviet Lithuanian biology (May, pp. 15–18) and individuals unjustly convicted under Stalinism (June, pp. 18–19). In September an interview with the musicologist and future oppositional leader Vytautas Landsbergis appeared (p. 21). The November and December issues published photos of demonstrators and police, with obvious sympathy for the former. By the end of the year, *Jaunimo Gretos* had become Lithuanian—rather than Soviet—in its themes and approach. This tendency would only increase in the next years, reflecting changes within Soviet Lithuania and in the city of Vilnius.

## Disputing Soviet History: Vilnius, 1988–1991

Historians often complain that their research and teaching are dismissed as irrelevant by the younger generation. In the late 1980s in the Soviet Union, however, history was a topic of burning interest and controversy. Throughout the union there was great interest in new revelations about the Stalin era, among other things denigrating Stalin's role as military leader during World War II.[17] Previously unmentionable names like Nikolai Bukharin and Lev Trotsky were openly discussed as having provided possible alternative models for revolution. Even the untouchable, semi-sacred figure of Lenin was now challenged, though cautiously, by historians and journalists. Books that had long been banned, most famously Aleksander Solzhenitsyn's *Gulag Archipelago* and Leonid Pasternak's *Dr. Zhivago*, which had been published only abroad, were now published in Soviet editions. The Baltic republics of Estonia, Latvia, and Lithuania also participated in these discussions of Stalinism. But here historical interest focused far more on one specific historical period: the early 1940s, when these independent republics had been incorporated into the USSR.[18]

Previous Soviet Lithuanian historiography had explained the incorporation of Lithuania into the USSR in summer 1940 as reflecting the demands of Lithuanian workers. History books emphasized the many petitions from enterprises and organizations asking for Lithuania to be allowed into the USSR and the mass demonstrations demanding the same. To take one example, from a 1972 history of Vilnius since 1917, describing the incorporation of the city into the USSR: "The working people of Vilnius in their meetings and demonstrations approved the work of the Lithuanian SSR's Supreme Soviet. They welcomed the adoption of the Lithuanian SSR's constitution which created the organs of rule for the new republic."[19] No mention was made of intimidation, arrests, or deportations that accompanied the events of June and July 1940.

By 1988 certain important institutional changes had occurred within the Lithuanian historical establishment, which was located mainly in Vilnius. In 1986 Vytautas Merkys became the director of the Lithuanian Academy of Sciences' Institute of History. Merkys had published extensively, both traditional Soviet-style works on the development of the proletariat and workers' movement in Lithuania and, since the 1970s, works on the development of the Lithuanian national movement in the late nineteenth and early twentieth centuries.[20] Merkys was clearly no radical, but his interest in the beginnings of Lithuanian national politics may have indicated an openness to a less Moscow-centered historiography.[21]

While some public demonstrations had occurred in 1987 to mark (interwar) Lithuanian holidays such as February 16 (independence day), it was only in 1988 that such demonstrations assumed large proportions. Besides these demonstrations, several other key events occurred in 1988. On June 3 a reform group came into being calling itself Lietuvos persitvarkymo sąjūdis (Lithuanian reform [or "perestroika"] movement). This loosely organized public group came to be known internationally simply as Sąjūdis and played a part akin to Solidarity in Poland or Rukh in Ukraine in bringing down the Soviet order.[22] During 1988 the interwar Lithuanian flag (a tricolor of red-yellow-green) and the interwar national anthem were also legalized (August 17). By the end of the year the Lithuanian—not Soviet—flag was flying over Gediminas castle tower on the hill overlooking downtown Vilnius, and a reform-minded, explicitly Lithuanian communist, Algirdas Brazauskas, headed the Lithuanian Communist Party.[23]

Three public gatherings of 1988 (or demonstrations, depending on one's interpretation) in Vilnius helped push along the process toward a Lithuanization of the city and republic. First there was the demonstration in commemoration of the 1918 Declaration of Independence on February 16. In May (21–22) there were demonstrations calling attention to the purges and deportations of Lithuanians that had taken place in the late 1940s and early 1950s. On August 23 a public gathering in Vilnius' Vingis Park commemorated the Molotov-Ribbentrop Pact of 1939 that paved the way for Lithuania's incorporation into the USSR. Finally, police attacks on peaceful demonstrators in Gediminas Square on September 28 helped polarize public opinion on the present Soviet order.

One of the key points of contention between pro-Soviet and, to simplify somewhat, pro-Lithuanian forces was the choice between December 29 or February 16 as Lithuanian independence day. In 1988 the Lithuanian forces felt strong enough to publicly celebrate the interwar ("bourgeois") holiday with a demonstration in Vilnius. Interestingly, these demonstrations were almost entirely ignored in the official press. Looking at two major periodicals published in Vilnius, the daily *Sovetskaia Litva* (Soviet Lithuania) and monthly *Jaunimo Gretos*, one would never know that any such demonstration in support of February 16 had occurred. While the January *Jaunimo Gretos* issue did contain an article arguing against the February 16 anniversary, no mention is made of any demonstration. *Sovetskaia Litva* took a different tack. One searches in vain for a mention of demonstrations or even "disturbances" in the February 17, 1988 issue, though one does find three letters directed against the American president (Reagan), Western "bourgeois" interference in Soviet Lithuania's internal affairs, and those who "lead our youth astray."[24]

More interesting is the previous day's issue, which under the headline "Resolute Protest of Vilnius Workers" describes a rally of 15,000 workers on Gediminas Square to protest "bourgeois nationalists living abroad and local extremists" who aimed "to inflame hatred against Soviet power," "to speculate in the national sentiments of the Lithuanian people and to falsify history." Led by the president of the Vilnius city executive committee (*ispolkom*), Algirdas Vileikis (whose 1986 book on Vilnius was cited above), those assembled called for "friendship among nations" and a correct view of history. In particular the article emphasizes that "in 1918 and 1919 the reactionary forces of Lithuania in league with the Kaiser's occupiers and foreign powers [*interventy*] drowned the young Soviet power in [Lithuania] blood." Furthermore, in summer 1940 the "bourgeois yoke was thrown off" in Lithuania with the establishment of Soviet power, an obviously positive step welcomed by most Lithuanians. The article has a photograph showing a large crowd (though no landmarks to connect it specifically with Gediminas Square or any other point), with four signs visible—all in Lithuanian. The signs read "We are for the USSR and friendship among nations," "USSR: Friendship among nations,"

"Unity between Nations—the Lithuanian SSR's Strength!" and "Our knowledge is necessary for Soviet Lithuania!"[25]

In spring another major demonstration took place in Vilnius. On May 21 at the monument to Zigmas Angarietis a large crowd of several thousand people assembled to honor him and other victims of Stalinism.[26] Angarietis, a Lithuanian communist, had been deported to Moscow when Lithuania was incorporated into the USSR and "unjustly repressed," dying on May 22, 1940. In *Sovetskaia Litva*, the gathering was front page news, with a headline reading "Memory of Victims of the Cult of Personality Honored." According to this article, the ceremony had been organized by "the creative unions of Soviet Lithuania—writers, artists, journalists, architects," and a large crowd of "workers, white-collar workers, representatives of the creative intelligentsia, youth" gathered. A long list of dignitaries, including winners of Lenin prizes, attended. The article was full of condemnation for Stalin and his "hangmen," and it noted that "as the decisions of the XVIIth congress of the CPSU are carried out the errors of the past . . . will be discussed openly [*predaiutsia glasnosti*]." In other words, the communist party was itself leading the way in a healthy discussion about these tragic events. To be sure, the article does state that "communists, komsomols, and *bezpartiinye* [noncommunists] suffered" but the very wording suggests that noncommunists only incidentally suffered. In any case, actual persons named in the article are overwhelmingly either past or present party members or somehow part of the Lithuanian Soviet establishment (including writers and scholars).[27]

Each demonstration, it appeared, attracted more people. In part this can be explained by the better organization of noncommunists, in particular in the form of Sąjūdis ("the movement"), which was established on June 3 and began publishing its own—uncensored—newspaper, *Sąjūdžio Žinios* (Sąjūdis news) on June 13, using a dot-matrix printer and copy machines.[28] For the anniversary of the Molotov-Ribbentrop Pact a huge gathering was planned in Vilnius Vingis Park. Despite the stormy weather, thousands of Lithuanians from all over the country came to remember the fateful date. *Sovetskaia Litva* published a sympathetic article under the headline "For an Honest and Open Study of History." Unlike two months earlier, the article did not portray the demonstration as entirely organized and carried out by communists. To be sure, the article bristles with names of communist dignitaries who took part and spoke, but it admits that the demonstration was organized by "the Lithuanian movement for reform [perestroika]"—a Russian translation for "Sąjūdis"—and that the first speaker was Professor Vytautas Landsbergis.

The article engages in some soul-searching, admitting that "it would be unjust not to recall that a year ago an attempt was made to commemorate [*otmetit'*] this date." The article's author did not have to specify what the authorities' reactions had been only a year earlier, noting simply that "now that all seems strange: they sort of allowed it, sort of condemned it" (*kak budto razreshili, kak budto-osudili*). Once again the piece places local communists center stage (e.g., A. Šepetys, the secretary of the Lithuanian Communist Party, is named) but it is a stage they share with others, among them even a priest, father E. Atkočiunas.

Unfortunately, the article continues, the gathering was marred by "incidents." After the end of the speeches, some 300 persons marched through town to Gediminas Square (this is quite a long walk, probably taking forty minutes to an hour), wishing to continue the rally there. "Among them were persons in a drunken state, behaving like hooligans [*v netrezvom sostoianii, nastroennye po-khuliganski*]." Unable to penetrate into the square, which had been cordoned off by police, the crowd moved on to the MVD (ministry of the interior) and KGB building (another 10–15 minute walk), attempting to enter there, again unsuccessfully. At this point both the minister of the interior and representatives of Sąjūdis (the Lithuanian name is mentioned here for the first time), "citizens Skučas and Kubilius," were allowed to speak to the crowd with a megaphone, appealing to them to maintain order. However, "it was necessary" to arrest one G. Anskis, who was sentenced (already) to two months "corrective labor." The article ends on a sober, if not provocative, note: "The organs of internal affairs will in the future continue unwaveringly to assure public order in any and all situations, carefully observing [*strogo sobliudaia*] legality, faithfully protecting the constitutional rights and freedoms of citizens."[29]

*Sąjūdžio Žinios* had a somewhat different tack on the events, speaking of hundreds of thousands of participants and mentioning the speeches of communist officials with some degree of irony. As for the "incident" afterward, the blame for any friction was assigned to the authorities who called out large numbers of military and police in order to prevent peaceful demonstrators from continuing their speeches on Gediminas Square. Furthermore, as several articles pointed out, the communist press (in particular *Tiesa* and *Komjaunimo Tiesa*) published false and misleading information about these events, attempting to blacken the reputation of Sąjūdis.[30]

The significance of the Vingis Park assembly can hardly be overstated. Alfred Senn, who arrived in Vilnius precisely at this time, later stated, "In just three hours on August 23, 1988 Sajudis changed Lithuania."[31] From this point onward, the popularity of the Lithuanian reform movement would grow steadily, affecting even the Lithuanian communists.

A final key event of the crucial year 1988 was the police beating of demonstrators on Gediminas Square (now Cathedral Square) on September 28, 1988. With this brutal attack the communist authorities discredited themselves gravely, completely underestimating the power and popularity of Sąjūdis—and the profound unpopularity of the communist party among the Lithuanian public. *Sąjūdžio Žinios* printed several petitions expressing anger and disgust at the "vandal-like treatment" (*vandališkas susidorojimas*) meted out to peaceful citizens who had gathered to remember the supplementary Soviet-Nazi agreement of that date in 1939 (in the original Molotov-Ribbentrop Pact, Lithuania was placed in the German, not Soviet, sphere of influence).[32] An indication of internal dissent within the Lithuanian Communist Party is reflected by the condemnation of this violence in the young communists' organ, *Jaunimo Gretos*, and the rather different views expressed in *Sovetskaia Litva*.[33]

*Sovetskaia Litva*, unlike the Lithuanian-language Komsomol monthly, seemed to harden against the Lithuanian movement. The day after the violence on Gedimino Square, several letters appeared on the organ's front page expressing unhappiness about recent trends. One, with the headline "I Unfortunately Do Not Speak Lithuanian" complained that Russian speakers in the republic were being made to feel like "emigrants" in Lithuania, in particular because television programs were now entirely in Lithuanian with the exception of "10–15 minutes of news." Another much longer letter signed by several party members and "participants in the Great Fatherland War" (WWII) was entitled "Do not confuse hangmen with victims." Here the four letter writers (all of whose names, by the way, were Lithuanian, not Russian) demanded that the postwar Lithuanian partisans be remembered not as freedom fighters but as murderers and fascists. They expressed indignation that at the August 23 meeting much had been said about the Molotov-Ribbentrop Pact and Stalinist atrocities, but "nobody spoke of the hundreds of thousands tortured [to death] during the years of the Hitlerite occupation and the tens of thousands killed in the postwar years." The letter ended with a by-now-obligatory bow to perestroika ("as necessary as air and bread") and a warning that democracy does not give "extremists" an unbridled right "to pour filth over the honest people" (*polit' pomoiki na chestnykh liudei*) who built socialist Lithuania.[34] As for the actual events of September 28 in Vilnius, they receive no mention at all.[35]

Thus already a year before the historic autumn of 1989, the signs of serious change were visible in Vilnius. Taboos of the past had been openly discussed,

Lithuanian national feelings publicly aired in a way impossible just a few years earlier, and demands for further, more sweeping reform had been expressed. Gorbachev's glasnost' had opened the path for vastly more far-reaching changes than the first secretary could have imagined.

## The End of Soviet Vilnius, 1989–1991

During 1989 Gorbachev attempted to hold the line on perestroika, navigating between furious party conservatives and "democrats" demanding even more far-reaching reforms, including the dismantling of one-party rule and creation of a multiparty political system. The Lithuanian communist leader Algirdas Brazauskas spent the year trying to get the necessary concessions from Moscow to forestall a complete break in relations between Vilnius and Moscow.[36] At least in the short run, Gorbachev was successful and Brazauskas was not. But the amazing events of summer and fall 1989, when from Berlin to Bratislava to Budapest to Bucharest, even to Sofia, the entire Soviet bloc collapsed with no intervention from Moscow, sounded the death knell for perestroika—though of course few recognized this at the time. Perhaps the single most striking event in the Baltic region that year was the attempt to form a human link from Lithuania to Estonia on August 23. *Jaunimo Gretos* published a photo of this event among images of Lithuanians gathered around crosses and participating in (religious) processions—in what was a rather remarkable editorial decision for a communist organ.[37]

Relations between Lithuanians and Russians in Vilnius were tense by 1990. While Sąjūdis called for unity among all inhabitants of the republic, inevitably the concepts "Russian" and "Soviet occupier" were not always easy to keep apart. In an attempt to reassure (and woo) Russian speakers, Sąjūdis published from January 13, 1989 a Russian-language supplement entitled *Soglasie* ("Agreement"). The first few issues even bore the Polish slogan (though in Russian, of course) "For Our Freedom—and Yours" on the masthead.[38] The paper encouraged Russian speakers to think of Lithuania as their homeland and to defend its freedoms. Articles by such luminaries as Tomas Venclova and Czesław Miłosz were included.[39] Despite the significant numbers of Poles in and around Vilnius (judging from the main language they spoke, but also according to the Soviet understanding of nationality), within the city itself their voice was not much heard in the period 1988–1992. In part this may be explained by their relatively small numbers but perhaps also by the fact that within Vilnius Poles tended to be trilingual, speaking Lithuanian and Russian almost as well as (and sometimes better than) Polish.[40]

Sąjūdis was certainly not a nationalistic or chauvinist movement. It was, however, *Lithuanian*, and naturally demanded greater rights for Lithuanian language and culture. Many local Russians—like the individual lamenting, "I unfortunately do not speak Lithuanian" in *Sovetskaia Litva*—were surprised and even outraged at the possibility that their language would be relegated to second place, or even not used at all. On a more practical level, the relative advantage that Russians had enjoyed as native speakers of what could be called the "mother tongue of the Soviet motherland" threatened to disappear. If they wished to live and prosper in an independent Lithuanian republic, Russian speakers would have to learn the Lithuanian language. While some recognized this early on, many others found this basic fact hard to accept. Of course, those interested in preserving the USSR and the status quo did what they could to encourage and foment this dissatisfaction. In Soviet Lithuania the most significant pro-Soviet and anti-reform grouping called itself (typically) *Edinstvo*, or "unity."

After the fall of the Berlin Wall in November 1989 and the quick collapse of communist rule in Eastern Europe, Gorbachev's position was considerably weakened. Party conservatives (and Russian nationalists—not necessarily two separate groups) accused him of "losing the gains of World War II." And economically the country was in disastrous shape. Thus Gorbachev was in no mood to make significant concessions to Lithuania or other republics. In January 1990 Gorbachev visited Vilnius and expressed his hope that Lithuanians would move forward along the lines of perestroika, not forgetting their "living connections—human, economic, social, scientific" with the rest of the USSR.[41] But his anodyne phrases made it clear that the Soviet leader had not grasped the seriousness of the Lithuanian movement. Only days after Gorbachev left Lithuania, Algirdas Brazauskas was elected chairman of the LSSR's Supreme Soviet's presidium. An astute politician—as can be seen by his success in becoming the first president and later prime minister of the independent republic—Brazauskas calculated that the only way for Lithuania's communists not to be swept away was to exert their independence from Moscow.[42] And what better way to do that than to cancel the act that incorporated Lithuania into the USSR? Under Brazauskas's leadership, on February 7, 1990 the Supreme Soviet passed a resolution declaring the treaty of July 21, 1940 between Lithuania and the USSR null and void.[43]

From here it was only a small—and logical—step to independence; this step was soon taken. On March 11, 1990 the Supreme Soviet of the Lithuanian SSR, now fashioning itself as the parliament of the Lithuanian Republic, declared that despite the destruction of Lithuanian sovereignty in 1940, the declaration of independence of January 16, 1918 had never lost its legal force. Hence Lithuania declared its state sovereignty on the basis of the Helsinki Final Act of 1975.[44] *Sovetskaia Litva*, which had gone from calling itself the "newspaper of the Central Committee of the Communist Party of Lithuania" to a "Social-political newspaper of the Supreme Soviet/Council [the words are identical in Russian and Lithuanian] and Council of Ministers of the Lithuanian USSR" on March 2, now changed its title to *Echo of Lithuania* (*Ekho Litvy*) on March 16.[45] In the next few weeks, speeches by the chairman of the Supreme Council (as the governing body now preferred to be known), Vytautas Landsbergis, appeared in nearly every issue (following Soviet journalistic practice). Very soon the "supreme council" would adopt the name "seimas," referring back to the interwar parliament. Also in spring 1990 Vilnius elected its first city council since the interwar period. The majority of council members were supported by Sąjūdis. In the midst of the next few turbulent years of Soviet boycott and establishing independent Lithuanian democratic institutions, the Vilnius city council—and a directly elected mayor—would take up their duties.[46]

Meanwhile, relations between Vilnius and Moscow had reached the breaking point. Gorbachev reacted to the Lithuanian declaration of independence by blockading the republic (in particular, keeping out energy supplies) beginning on April 18, 1990. During this period the government began publishing its own newspaper (at first twice weekly, later daily), *Lietuvos Aidas* ("Echo of Lithuania"). The newspaper's title was identical to the Lithuanian government's official organ that had ceased publication in 1940. Significantly, the renewed periodical bore the number 1 (5548), indicating a continuation with the daily of a half century earlier. Until early July, every issue's front-page header gave a reminder of how long the blockade had lasted (e.g., "27th day of blockade" in no. 6 [5552] for May 25, 1990).

Not all residents of Vilnius were happy with the political changes taking place. On May 18 a "no confidence" rally took place outside the parliament building, calling on the present Lithuanian government to step down and complaining of a reduction of rights for non-Lithuanians (*inoiazychnoe naselenie*). Part of the outrage, one supposes, lay simply in the fact of being (for once) the *other*, the "second language," and not the hegemonic cultural-linguistic group. According to the pro-Sąjūdis Russian-language newspaper *Soglasie*, around four to five thousand people gathered, "a considerable number of whom were military men." The rally took place peacefully, ending with a discussion—heated but peaceful—between supporters of the current parliament and its detractors (such as the leaders of "Edinstvo," one of the organizers of the rally).[47]

The blockade was lifted on June 29 when the Lithuanian government "temporarily suspended" the declaration of March 11.[48] Thereafter natural gas and petroleum began to flow once again from Russia into the republic. But the main issue of contention, Lithuania's political status, remained unresolved. The rest of the year played out in Vilnius under tense uncertainty. The Lithuanian government continued to act as if it were independent (at least in its public statements), while Moscow uneasily treated the republic as part of the USSR. One very worrying element was the continued presence in Lithuania of Red Army units—could these be used to reestablish Soviet rule? Meanwhile, Soviet monuments were being taken down and hauled away already in summer 1990.[49] In Vilnius plans for a new monument dedicated to the medieval Lithuanian Grand Duke Gediminas were proposed.[50]

In December 1990 Landsbergis traveled to Washington, where he met with the American president, George H. W. Bush.[51] Bush was polite but noncommittal, but it was hoped that the very fact that the Lithuanian leader had visited the White House would make aggressive Soviet action less likely. Gorbachev, meanwhile, had been awarded the Nobel Peace Prize for 1990. At the end of the year *Lietuvos Aidas* published pictures of the year's main events, including a picture of Red Army soldiers with the caption "They demonstrated crude force and intolerance towards us. We are not afraid. We will stand fast."[52]

The violent events of January 1991 were thus long anticipated and feared. Perhaps the most surprising thing about Soviet power (whether exercised by Gorbachev himself or though officialdom at another level) is not that it attempted to restore itself in Vilnius but, rather, that it took so long to take this step. Some of the tension in the air at that time comes through in the New Year's wish printed in *Ekho Litvy*: "May 1991 be a year of building [*sozidanie*], the fulfillment of wishes, the triumph of reason and mutual understanding among people."[53] A mere week later the Russian pro-Soviet movement "Edinstvo" organized a rally to protest price increases; an angry crowd numbering in the thousands attempted to push into the parliament building.[54] The attempt to storm the parliament building called forth crowds who assembled there to protect it. Rallies and counter-rallies continued for the next few days. Meanwhile, on January 11 and 12 Soviet troops moved in and occupied key installations throughout Lithuania, including the Vilnius train station, the Police Academy, and the press center.[55] Tanks and troops moved to surround the television tower in the Vilnius neighborhood Karoliniškės.[56]

On January 12 the situation seemed grave enough for *Lietuvos Aidas* to print an appeal with the headline, "People of Lithuania! The Republic Is in Danger."[57]

As is well-known, thirteen Lithuanians, ranging in age from fifteen to fifty-three, lost their lives on January 13, 1991.[58] With this bloodshed ended any possibility of a compromise solution between Moscow and Vilnius. *Ekho Litvy* published a photograph of thousands of people standing in line in snowy Vilnius to pay their last respects; *Lietuvos Aidas* published photos of the parliament behind metal barriers, tanks in the streets, and the dead and wounded (with the caption "red terror").[59] At this point, Gorbachev had the choice of an all-out war with the Lithuanians or attempting a dignified retreat. To his credit, he chose the latter course.[60] After the events of January 1991, full Lithuanian independence was merely a matter of time, a process considerably sped up by the ill-fated Moscow putsch of August 1991. Of course, no one could know this at the time; fear of a full-scale military invasion continued until August.

With the August events in Moscow, the Soviet Union for all practical purposes ceased to exist (and officially gave up the ghost on December 25, 1991). Almost immediately the face of Vilnius changed when on August 23 the statue of Lenin was removed from the eponymous downtown square, now again known as Lukiškių.[61] The first foreign embassy, Sweden's, opened at Jogailos No. 10, on August 29.[62] To commemorate the first state to recognize Lithuania's regained independence, a street in the downtown was given the name "Iceland Street."

## Creating a Lithuanian Capital, 1991–2004

The transition from "Soviet" to "Lithuanian" Vilnius began a couple of years before the actual collapse of the USSR. Antanas Čaplinskas, a prolific city historian and one of the leaders in the Vilnius city council of the early 1990s, notes that already before 1990 several downtown streets got their historical names back. Totorių (Tatar) Street returned in 1987 after a mere seven years as "Paleckio" (named after one of the communist collaborators in 1940), Gorky Street went back to its old designation (Pilies/Didžiojo), and by late 1988 Aušros Vartų Street got back its old name (in a Lithuanian version, to be sure, of "Ostra Brama"). The following year witnessed the return of Vokiečių (Muziejaus; prewar Niemiecka), Pylimo (Komjaunimo; prewar Zawalna), and L. Sapiegos (Suvorov) Streets.[63]

After the official reestablishment of independence in March 1990, many streets reverted to (Lithuanian versions of) pre-Soviet names. To be sure, already before that date several important streets—such as Kalvarijų (no longer named after the Polish Soviet communist Feliks Dzierżyński), Gedimino (Lenin), and Savanorių (Red Army)—returned to their 1940 designations.[64] One entirely new name was given the street running by the KGB/district court building: "Aukų," in honor of that building and the institution's victims. Many streets regained their traditional religious names (St. Michael's, St. Nicholas's, etc.), and two important downtown squares lost their Soviet designations: Lenino went back to the prewar name, Lukiškių, while the square known after Polish writer Eliza Orzeszkowa in the interwar and bearing the name of Vilnius' Red Army "liberator" after World War II (Cherniakhovskii) got the neutral name "Savivaldybės," referring to the offices of the city self-government nearby.[65] In 2009, when a monument honoring the Lithuanian patriot Vincas Kudirka was unveiled in the square, it was renamed Kudirka Square. By the mid-1990s, Vilnius streets bore new, monolingual Lithuanian designations (the bilingual Soviet street signs were replaced with surprising speed), most of which would have been familiar to the city's 1940 residents.

Much more changed quickly in the city. The detested Soviet *militsiia* was reorganized as a Lithuanian police force (*policija*) in summer 1991.[66] Politically, it took barely two years for the Lithuanian electorate to sour on Sąjūdis and its leader Landsbergis: in October 1992 the reformed communists (LDDP) swept elections, bringing the longtime Lithuanian communist leader (now turned social democrat) Algirdas Brazauskas to the presidency in the following year. In 1997, toward the end of Brazauskas's (first) term as president, the former bishop's/governor's palace, newly renovated, was opened as the presidential palace (his office, not his residence).[67] In late June 1993 the interwar Lithuanian currency, the *litas*, was introduced, replacing an interim medium of exchange, the *talonas*. The new bills bore images of Lithuanian cultural figures and iconic places, including Vilnius University (on the 100 litas bill). The new currency further emphasized the resurrection of the Lithuanian nation-state.

In Vilnius, the cityscape also continued to change and develop. While population gains leveled off before independence, one last large-scale housing area—Pilaitė—went forward. More common, however, was smaller-scale, privately financed apartment construction. Ownership of automobiles increased dramatically, bringing with it significant traffic problems. A new bridge connecting Antakalnis and Žirmūnai was opened in 1993, but gridlock continued at rush hour.[68] International recognition of the historical-cultural value of Vilnius' Old Town was achieved when Unesco declared the entire area a World Heritage Site (no. 427). Nearby, but on a rather different cultural plane, the Soviet-era bakery and sweet-shop Svajonės was shut down and reopened in July 1996 as Vilnius' first downtown McDonald's. Two months later, on September 22, a monument to the city's fourteenth-century founder, Grand Duke Gediminas, complete with howling iron wolf, was unveiled in Cathedral Square. While Russian and Polish could still be heard on Vilnius' streets, by the later 1990s the cityscape reflected the city's new role as capital of a Lithuanian nation-state.

As for the future, in 1999 a glossy "general plan" for Vilnius' future development was published. This plan addressed in some detail such matters as the direction of future expansion of commerce and housing in the city, socioeconomic change, the continued development of parks and other such cultural and recreational areas, and the direction that public and personal transportation should take in the near future (the main target for planning being 2015).[69] By that date, it was hoped, Vilnius would resemble in most ways other European capitals (Lithuania would join the EU in 2004). Looking forward into the new century, Vilnius town planners aimed to preserve the city's cultural heritage while allowing it to develop economically and physically to meet new challenges.

A matter of particular concern was historical preservation of the Old Town. An analysis of the issues facing city administrators set down four main sets of "actions required" to preserve and enhance the value of this important cultural resource: (1) private owners of property must take responsibility for its upkeep, with the government possibly offering tax incentives toward this end; (2) particularly neglected or abandoned buildings should be restored by public or combined public-private action, including possible sale, lease, or development; (3) data must be gathered and kept up-to-date regarding present usage of properties in the Old Town, among other things to ascertain whether housing is being converted into commercial space and/or being "gentrified"; and (4) the city administration must cooperate with religious authorities regarding the "restoration or conversion to new uses" of properties owned by different religious communities.[70] In general city authorities seemed open to private investment as the only way to make up for decades of infrastructure neglect under Soviet rule.

Most inhabitants of Vilnius agreed that it was a pleasant place to live, though opinions differed sharply—not surprisingly—among correspondents from different neighborhoods. Polls conducted in the mid-1990s found that most residents were "satisfied" with life in Vilnius (54%), but only 4 percent were "entirely satisfied," and 16 percent were "very dissatisfied."[71] Among the positive features of living in the Lithuanian capital named by those polled were the beauty of the city, the Old Town, the presence of relatives in the city, and interesting possibilities for leisure activities. As for negative aspects, pollution came in first (46% of those polled), followed by the presence of different nationalities (30%), complaints about poor service, and general agreement that life in Vilnius was too expensive.[72]

The assessment of Vilnius' multinational population as a negative factor runs counter, of course, to the official position embracing cultural diversity. One wonders whether this negative opinion was based on simple chauvinism or is connected, rather, to the post-Soviet perception of a link between crime and Russian speakers in the Baltic. However, this would be speculation as the interviewers did not choose to follow up on that question. Certain neighborhoods, especially Antakalnis and Žvėrynas (characterized by a higher than average percentage of single-family and semi-detached residences, with few large-scale apartment buildings), were considered the most prestigious, while others (e.g., Vilkpėdė and Fabijoniškės, on the outskirts) were considered the least attractive as residential areas.[73] Most residents termed themselves "middle class" (60%) or "lower class" (28%), but the poll did not specify further (e.g., intelligentsia, worker, professional, service industry). In most ways, it seems, Vilnius residents were concerned with issues universal throughout Europe and beyond: pollution, noise, the expense of everyday life, and traffic.

A Lithuanian sociologist working in Germany corroborated many of these findings in a doctoral dissertation of the early twenty-first century. Since the 1990s, she points out, foreign investment in Vilnius has far outstripped investment in all other Lithuanian cities combined.[74] This has had the effect of adding to Vilnius' tax income but has also led to a significant levels of income polarization. Another problem was that many industrial plants in and near the city ceased operation when the USSR and its planned economy collapsed, and as a result many were out of work. Some of the displaced workers, to be sure, then found work in the city's growing service sector, but in 2000 some 13 percent of the city's households were frequently behind in rent and utilities payments.[75]

Pensioners and the unemployed figured largely among the poorest inhabitants of Vilnius; younger, university-educated professionals were prominent in the upper-income group. Russian and Polish speakers were disproportionately found in the poorest quarter of the city.[76] Unsurprisingly, income differences were paralleled by differences in size and location of household apartments. The wealthier residents (who tended to be ethnic Lithuanians) tended to live in prestigious neighborhoods (both on the edge of town and in the center) while the poor, among whom ethnic Poles and Russians were overrepresented, lived mainly in the less attractive neighborhoods.[77] Interestingly, the early large-scale housing estates of Žirmūnai and Lazdynai continued to be perceived as attractive to residents. One cannot generalize either positively or negatively about the large housing estates built from the 1960s and 1970s: some were viewed positively, and others were not. Clearly, the specific location and circumstances of each estate were more important than any global, generalized feelings about such large housing areas.[78]

As we have seen, even after Lithuania regained independence, non-Lithuanians continued to make up a large proportion of Vilnius inhabitants. Poles remained the largest and most important non-Lithuanian group. In Vilnius county, Poles made up a full quarter of the population (according to 2001 figures) though this percentage would be somewhat lower in the city itself.[79] We can better appreciate the imperfect view of a complex situation that these statistics afford us if we consider that 20 percent of Lithuanian Poles declared a language other than Polish (usually, Russian or Lithuanian) as their native tongue. No reliable statistics seem to exist on how many of these Poles were comfortable in Lithuanian, but it seems likely that bilingualism (or something approaching it) is far from rare and has been increasing since the 1990s. Various experts agree that Poles were on the whole less likely to have attended university than Lithuanians or Russians in the republic and were generally poorer than the average citizen.[80] This fact may be a function of the social origins of many Vilnius Poles: most were the descendants of peasants from nearby rural areas who moved into the city after the Second World War.[81] After independence, Vilnius Poles had more than a dozen clubs and associations focused on everything from aviation to billiards to education in Polish.[82] Russians also made up a significant percentage of the population (14% in 2001),[83] though this group was more disparate and less organized than local Poles. Neither Poles nor Russians seemed very interested in challenging the Lithuanian cultural hegemony in the city (and republic), though certain frictions occasionally arose regarding native-language education.

A fairly large Jewish community also made its home in Vilnius. Few of these individuals, however, were direct descendants of the Jews living here in 1939. As we have seen, more than 90 percent of that population was murdered, and most survivors preferred not to return to the ruined city after the war. In the first postwar census, carried out in 1959, nearly 30 percent of Vilnius Jews were native speakers of Russian and another 69 percent were native Yiddish speakers. Just over 1 percent were native speakers of Lithuanian.[84] The bulk of the postwar Jewish community came to Vilnius from other parts of the USSR in the years and decades after 1945. Like most Soviet Jews, they were on the whole neither particularly religious nor very interested in Jewish culture and history. In the post-1990 period, however, interest in the city's Jewish past increased noticeably.

Perhaps the most emblematic project "marking" Vilnius as capital of the Lithuanian nation-state was the reconstruction of the lower castle near the cathedral in the heart of town. This palace had already been in ruins at the beginning of our period (i.e., in the late eighteenth century) and soon after Russia occupied the city, Catherine the Great gave orders that the vestiges of the palace be eliminated.[85] Because of the complete destruction of the lower castle and the dearth of historical documentation that could help assure a historical reconstruction, most historians opposed plans to re-create the lower castle. The quibblings of specialists had little effect, however, on the enthusiasm of those who dreamed of resurrecting the Grand Duke's Palace as a symbol of the Lithuanian past. A public subscription to this end was begun, and in the early years of the new millennium, tourists could visit the partially completed new palace.[86]

## Rewriting Vilnius History

Rebuilding a centuries-old structure is one way of claiming a city's past. Another method, less dependent on public and private funds, is simply to write. Since 1990 a number of new publications indicate an upswing of interest in the history of Vilnius, though primarily not among professional historians. Some of the publications are nonetheless of high quality, and on the whole their approach is liberal and multicultural in the American sense of the word. At the same time, certain blind spots and one-sided attitudes remain. (This state of things is probably inevitable and not terribly regrettable.) All historical accounts reflect to some extent the cultural and political views of those who are writing them. By the early twentieth-first century, Lithuanians had produced a number of works that portrayed Vilnius both as Lithuanian and as "other," both as their own capital and (to cite the title of an excellent work) as a "City of Strangers."

Immediately after independence, some emphasized the city's Lithuanian character and past. The Soviet Lithuanian linguist and post-independence minister of education Zigmas Zinkevičius exemplifies this patriotic approach, which (happily) was fairly short-lived. In his interesting work *Eastern Lithuania in the Past and Now*, Zinkevičius advances the view that the Slavic (and especially Polish) element in Vilnius and the surrounding region either came from outside or consisted of polonized Lithuanians. To be sure, many other historians have pointed out that polonization was a constant force in the region for centuries, thanks in part to the efforts of the Catholic Church. Zinkevičius goes a bit further than this, however. He wishes to argue for the eternal Lithuanian nature of the region, a viewpoint that no historical or linguistic methods seem likely to support.[87]

This "eternal Lithuanian" essence of Vilnius comes through even more strongly in the rather less scholarly pamphlet issued in conjunction with an exhibition at the Lithuanian National Museum entitled "Lithuania's Capital 1904–1939: Lithuanian Social and Culture Activities in Vilnius." In the introduction to this catalogue, Zinkevičius underscores the heroic struggle of Lithuainian culture in Vilnius despite Polish influences since the sixteenth century and pressure toward "denationalization" (*nutautinimas*). In the late nineteenth century, he argues, polonization and "brutal russification" nearly wiped out Lithuanian culture in the city and its environs. Even worse was the interwar period, when Polish policy consistently stymied Lithuanian education, publications, and cultural development. All of this is more or less true, but the specific assertions are undercut by the underlying assumption that actual ethnographic data or feelings of national identity matter little compared to the unchanging Lithuanian nature of the region. This assumption takes political form in the charge that Vilnius was "occupied" by Poles in the interwar period. To be sure, General Żeligowski's "rebellious" taking of the city was a bit of a farce, but it was a farce supported by most local residents (for better or worse). Another striking aspect of Zinkevičius's conception is the absence of the city's Jewish population: essentially the narrative unfolds between Poles and Lithuanians, with no room for other groups. Following his logic (and minimizing the importance of 1939–1940, not to mention 1941–1944), the events of 1990 represent the long-delayed fulfillment of a historical teleology—a moment in time when historical verities played themselves out.[88]

Zinkevičius's historical-linguistic ethnocentrism cannot be dismissed as insignificant. Most professional historians in Lithuania, to be sure, avoid such crass nationalism, but many popular historical works (which are by no means without scholarly value) follow a similar Lithuanian-centric approach. However, most historical works on the city of Vilnius do not pursue such an overt patriotic agenda. Instead of directly arguing against would-be Polish pretensions to the city (at least in the past), they tend to emphasize a Lithuanian story line and integrate the city's multicultural past into a primarily Lithuanian narrative. Two modest collections aimed at helping students and teachers enhance their knowledge of Lithuanian literature and history follow this pattern, organizing their material as a series of walks through the city.[89] More ambitious in scope but also aiming to provide texts and documents on Vilnius city history are the two large volumes edited by Eugenijus Manelis and Romualdas Samavičius, which were useful resources for this study.[90] Altogether these sources contain a wealth of information on Vilnius history, presented through primary sources and historiography, with a significant amount of material on non-Lithuanian cultural and religious communities (despite the emphasis on Lithuanian culture and interpretations). Perhaps the weakest aspect of these collections is their coverage of the Soviet period, which is portrayed almost exclusively as an era of repression, with very little discussion of the economic growth, cultural development, and major physical changes in Vilnius during these four and a half decades. The destruction of buildings and monuments during the Soviet period was also covered in a one-volume study whose scope goes beyond Vilnius to include the entire republic.[91]

The most indefatigable writer on Vilnius city history in the post-1990 period was Antanas Čaplinskas, who served on the first elected city council. Beginning with his lively history of Vilnius streets, their changing names and histories, Čaplinskas then concentrated his considerable energy on various specific downtown streets, describing them in great historical detail building by building. One year before he died, he published a large, beautifully illustrated history of the city, aimed at a broad audience. Čaplinskas's preference for the city's early history and his tendency to lump together the very disparate periods of the modern era are discernible in the way he divides up his study: in this tome of nearly 600 pages, he devotes only the shortest of four sections to "The Period of Wars and Occupations, 1914-1990." Despite this weakness, Čaplinskas's work has made a major contribution to the Vilnius city historiography.[92]

A major contribution to our understanding of Vilnius' history, especially its architectural and art history, is Vladas Drėma's lavishly illustrated, trilingual (Lithuanian, Russian, and English) volume, *Vanished Vilnius*. An art historian, Drėma lived in Vilnius as a young man (during the Polish years), graduated from USB, and beginning in 1945 served as an administrator and instructor in ethnographic and art historical institutions in the city. When his book *Vanished Vilnius* was published in 1991—a kind of homage to the city's past—Drėma was already an elderly man.[93]

The city's Jewish past has not been neglected in the post-1990 historiography. A large-scale illustrated guidebook was published in 2011 and instantly sold out. Reflecting its authors' and anticipated readers' language preferences, the book appeared in Russian. Despite an obvious demand for the book, discord between the publisher, the authors, and the city Jewish Museum have prevented this valuable work from being reprinted or published in Lithuanian.[94] At the same time, important earlier works focusing on Vilnius' Jewish past such as Herman Kruk's diary and Lucy Dawidowicz's memoirs have been published in Lithuanian translation.[95] Foreign scholars have also produced valuable work on Jewish Vilnius; particularly noteworthy is Anna Lipphardt's study of Vilnius Jews after 1945 in Israel, New York, and even Vilnius itself.[96]

Increasingly, the patriotic paradigm that characterized the 1990s has become less relevant in a more self-confident and less complex-ridden Lithuania. As a result, more scholars and students of Vilnius are focusing on the city's rich, diverse, and multicultural past. The poet and professor of Slavic literature at Yale Tomas Venclova has produced some extremely interesting and informative books on the city in which he grew up. Venclova's own story parallels that of many Vilnius inhabitants of the interwar period. Born just before the war in Klaipėda, Venclova arrived in Vilnius in 1944 as a young boy, the son of one of the most famous (or infamous, depending on one's politics) cultural figures of the Soviet Lithuanian period, the writer Antanas Venclova. Quite unlike his father, Venclova rebelled against the Soviet system and was obliged to emigrate in 1977, arriving first at the University of California at Berkeley and getting close to another émigré from the city, Czesław Miłosz.[97]

In Miłosz, Venclova found a kindred spirit. The two men shared an intense interest in the city of their respective youths, and both despised narrow nationalism while at the same time recognizing the extent to which their perspectives had been formed by their eras and their native cultures and languages. Their different perspectives on Wilno/Vilnius took literary shape in an exchange of "letters" that they published in Venclova's *Vilties Formos* (*Forms of Hope*) and Miłosz's *Zaczynając od moich ulic* (*Beginning with My Streets*).[98] Miłosz recalled a provincial city with memories of the Polish romantics and a present day dominated by Polish nationalists. One could not imagine that city without the Jews, living in the densely populated "medieval" city center.

Venclova, on the other hand, felt that he had grown up in another city altogether—sharing many of the same old buildings, to be sure, but little else. Venclova recalled a city half destroyed by the war, bearing many traces of the previous inhabitants, both Jewish and Polish. "Everything was done [in the postwar period] to eradicate the past and implant a new mentality." Possibly connected with this postwar desire on the part of the Soviet regime to blot out the past (or at least great parts of it), Venclova also remarks, "In Vilnius I often had the nagging feeling that the present inhabitants somehow did not belong to that city." The authorities played with Lithuanian nationalism, allowing it a certain legitimacy (as in praising the Lithuanian Grand Dukes and restoring Gediminas's Castle in Vilnius) but were always careful to put Lithuanian patriotism where it belonged: in second place, after Soviet ideology. For Venclova, recovering the past meant dealing with Polish Lithuanian frictions and also with the even more troubling issue of Lithuanians' involvement in the Holocaust. In the end, Vilnius belongs to its residents—past and present—not to a single nation or culture.

The complexity of Vilnius' past and the mixture of diverse religions and cultures inform Venclova's works on the city. Indeed, one could say that he delights in this cultural diversity, viewing the presence of various religious and cultural groups there not as a threat to its Lithuanian present but as a fascinating aspect of its makeup. Probably most influential, at least in terms of copies sold, is his guidebook that has appeared in Polish, Lithuanian, English, German, and Esperanto. Within the boundaries of this genre, this "guide to the city" presents an admirable history of the city as a whole and its various sights.[99]

Venclova's "personal history" of Vilnius, published in somewhat different forms in English, Polish, German, and Lithuanian, delves more deeply into the city's past. Presenting an overview of the city from its very beginnings, Venclova weaves together his own memories with perceptions of the city's long history. The book's German title, *Vilnius. Eine Stadt in Europa,* reflects on Venclova's approach. No longer does the city's history need to be written from a national or ideological perspective. Rather, it can be considered—like Trieste, Prague, or Helsinki—as a European city where different cultural and political actors have left their mark over the centuries. Venclova's latest Vilnius book, *Vilnius Names,* is a miniencyclopedia arranged by era (e.g., the Middle Ages, the Baroque era, the age of Totalitarianism) and featuring the kinds of actors who shaped Vilnius' history. Among these are priests, poets, religious leaders, and . . . hangmen.[100] Venclova's works on the city of his youth reflect a cultural confidence and cosmopolitan perspective that stem from not needing to "claim" the city for a specific nation. He is a poet who is free to revel in the cultural complexities and peculiarities of the past.[101] It is heartening to see that a similar approach is now being adopted by professional historians in some very interesting recent work.[102]

It is perhaps fitting that a Vilnius native who emigrated to Canada as a teenager—Laimonas Briedis—should provide a quite new approach to the city's past. As both an insider (by birth and initial upbringing) and an outsider (by residence and citizenship), Briedis has a unique perspective on the city. His perspective is made clear in the first and final pages of the book, where he places Vilnius—as various geographers have also done—at the center of Europe. Thus, rather than telling a story about a Lithuanian city diverted from its proper historical path under Polish, Russian, and Soviet rule, Briedis portrays a city in which nobody was entirely at home, a "city of strangers."[103] Drawing on literature, travel accounts, and guidebooks among other sources, Briedis shows convincingly that the "reality" of Vilnius was nearly entirely in the eyes of the beholder. While this book may make a historian, even a postmodern one, a bit uneasy, its impressionistic and frankly subjective approach has much to commend it. After all, as the present, more pedestrian history has suggested, throughout the modern period Vilna/Wilno/Vilnius existed on at least two planes: on the hilly terrain on the eastern edge of what is now the Republic of Lithuania and in the minds of its residents, visitors, and exiles. And who is to say whether the historical/geographical or the imagined Vilnius is in the end the true one?

CONCLUSIONS

VILNIUS WAS, AND IS, an extraordinary city. Even today, with a single cultural-linguistic group dominating, the mix of languages and architecture remains a fascinating attraction. Poles make pilgrimages to Ostra Brama and tour the city where their grandparents were born; Jews visit on "heritage tours" and learn of the Gaon, Bund, and Yiddish literature written here. For present-day inhabitants—in particular the younger generation—the frictions between Poles and Russians and the anti-Jewish violence are vestiges of an era that has little connection to them. The positive side of this indifference to history is the lack of interest in chauvinistic squabbles about "whose city this is"; the negative side, however, can be a failure to comprehend the difficulties and attractions of a truly multicultural city.

When Vilnius found itself by chance incorporated into the Russian Empire, at the outset of this book, the situation was vastly different. The city was much smaller and its population far more Jewish than at present. On a broader level, the world of 1795—at least in this part of Europe—could hardly be termed "modern." The Russian Empire did not view its own political legitimacy or policy toward "minority nationalities" (the very term is anachronistic) as twentieth-century states have done. Indeed, the cultures resident in Vilnius at this early date tended to live their own lives, parallel to other groups living only a stone's throw away.[1] One could compare—though inexactly—the religious and linguistic groups inhabiting the city to castes in other world history contexts. And, for the most part, the Russian Empire was quite content to allow these cultures to live their separate lives. It was concerned only with maintaining political stability and public order, though it struck hard (as Poles could attest) when any non-Russian nation seemed to threaten the status quo.

In the twentieth century and beyond, the situation is radically different. Nearly all states wish to see themselves as nation-states or at least pay homage before the altar of nationality. This notion of nationality is often constructed as a semi-sacred combination of historical memory, linguistic unity, and other factors such as religion or "race." In the twentieth century nationality became (and remains) vastly more central to political legitimacy and to everyday governance than ever before. The hypertrophy of nationality as a source of identity and political legitimacy meant that on the one hand states had to emphasize and nurture "their own" culture but also, frequently, were obliged to adopt active policies (whether aggressive or tolerant) toward citizens not belonging to the dominant culture. "Solutions" to this political conundrum run the gamut from extensive autonomy and funding of parallel cultural institutions (e.g., Finland) to ethnic cleansing and genocide. In twentieth-century Vilnius different political entities carried out various forms of such policies, both benevolent and deeply evil, toward resident cultures.

While the most radical changes took place in the twentieth century, the long period of Russian rule also belongs in a story about national cultures in an urban space. While the Russian Empire remained mainly premodern in its governance—at least until the opening of the Duma after the 1905 Revolution—many elements of modernity developed in the nineteenth century. In particular after the period of the Great Reforms/November Uprising—that is, from the 1860s—the Russian Empire struggled to remake itself in a modern guise. Part of this attempted transformation involved industrialization (the railroad connecting Petersburg with Warsaw, through Vilna). Another important aspect of tsarist modernization was an increasing emphasis on the Russian language and a growing suspicion of non-Orthodox and non-Russian subjects. Here the Jews and Poles, who made up together the great majority of Wilno's population, played a special role in the mentality, even demonology, of the tsarist state. The Polish university in Wilno was shut down after the first Polish Lithuanian uprising of 1830–1831, and increased measures of russification followed the second uprising in 1863. Still, even on the eve of World War I, Russians in Vilna were a small community that had roots mainly in distant provinces. As for the Lithuanians, their numerically small presence in Vilnius was offset by the city's centrality in their national ideology.

World War I changed much in Vilnius. The three-year-long German occupation, followed by another three years of war and uncertainty, dealt the city's population a painful blow. When the dust settled in the early 1920s, it was clear that barring outside intervention, Poles would rule the city. The newly formed Lithuanian Republic refused to acquiesce to what they termed an illegal occupation and continued to claim the city as its capital throughout this period. Economically interwar Wilno was a poor provincial town, but its culture was rich and varied. The university produced impressive scholarship; the local press published in several languages; writers in Yiddish and Polish made their mark. One of the first radio stations in Poland was located here. For non-Poles, however, all was not well. The Polish Republic saw itself as a nation-state of Poles that tolerated other nationalities. Thus Belarusians, Lithuanians, Jews, and others were subjected to forces of polonization far stronger than russification had ever been under the tsars. Partly, to be sure, this was simply a function of the forward march of modernity: children of any nationality were much more likely to attend school in the 1930s than a generation earlier. The sharpening antagonism between Poles and Jews in the later 1930s makes optimism difficult, but perhaps a solution here could have been found had not the catastrophe of 1939 occurred.

The half-dozen years starting with the Soviet invasion of September 1939 (Lithuania had allied itself with Nazi Germany) can only be termed a catastrophe for the inhabitants of Vilnius. Poles were humiliated in their national pride and pushed aside in employment by Lithuanian and Soviet authorities; arrested and killed in the thousands by both Soviets and Nazis; and finally deported ("repatriated") after the wars. The fate of Vilne's Jewish community is known only too well: only a tiny percent of the tens of thousands of Jews living there in 1939 survived to 1945, and most of the survivors left the devastated city. In the years 1939-1947, the city was nearly emptied of its original population and repopulated—in part by entirely new people (although the city would take some time to recover its 1939 population): Belarusians, Russians, and Lithuanians, for the most part (but also Jews from the Russian interior). Connected to this population shift, the Soviet authorities placed their stamp on Vilnius' development, attempting to build a city that was simultaneously Soviet-socialist and Lithuanian, with the first term implying a great deal of russification.

From today's perspective, the decades of Soviet rule are widely regarded as dominated by repression, economic impoverishment, and the grinding process of russification. These generalizations are only partially accurate. Certainly the USSR was no liberal state, and Moscow in the 1950s and 1960s regarded Catholic Lithuanians with the same suspicion that the St. Petersburg authorities had shown toward Catholic Poles a century earlier. Still, it is necessary to keep certain nuances in mind. The Soviet regime always supported and emphasized Lithuanian culture in the Lithuanian Soviet Socialist Republic—to be sure, in tandem with the "fatherland culture" of Russian. Demographically, the Lithuanian population in Vilnius grew steadily from the late 1940s. Economically, too, the city developed considerably during these decades, though one can certainly argue that the growth would have been more rapid under a liberal democratic government.

Beginning in the late 1980s, Lithuanian opposition to Soviet rule rapidly gained strength. The impetus for this push for independence was the power vacuum created as an unintended consequence of Mikhail Gorbachev's reforms in Moscow. Gorbachev, like many Russians, appeared incapable of appreciating the extent to which non-Russian regions of the USSR detested and resented Soviet power for subjecting them not only to repression and economic backwardness but also to national humiliation. The tragic events of January 1991 in Vilnius, whether or not actually sanctioned by the Soviet leader, brought the situation to a stark choice: either employ massive violence to bring the Lithuanians to heel or acquiesce in their desire to leave the USSR. To Gorbachev's credit, in the end he refused to agree to the first choice and thus opened the way for the second.

From the time of the "redeclaration" of independence in March 1990, Lithuanian politicians (including many, like Algirdas Brazauskas, who had spent their life as Soviet politicians and administrators) have worked to re-create Vilnius as the capital of a Lithuanian nation-state. Happily, the relatively small numbers of non-Lithuanians in the republic and the generally moderate demands on the part of local Poles and Russians have allowed for a transition to a Lithuanian state that has avoided overtly chauvinistic tendencies. (The other two Baltic republics to the north, with larger Russian populations, have had a more difficult time reconciling national identity with their demographic makeup.) Still, there was no doubt after 1991 whose city this was: Vilnius had become a place that privileged Lithuanian culture and historical memory while merely tolerating Polish and Russian culture. The revival of Jewish culture in Vilnius since 1990 deserves its own book: suffice it to say that, as in other cities of Lithuania, Poland, and Ukraine, this process has been more like the birth of a new culture than the revitalization of an existing culture. In the early twenty-first century, Vilnius had become a "normal" European city, proud of its multicultural past (often understood in a peculiarly Lithuanian way) and tolerant of local non-Lithuanians, but in the end a Lithuanian city in a globalized world.

What are the lessons from this two-century voyage through empires, nation-states, wars, and demographic catastrophes? I would cautiously suggest at least two. One is confirmation that diverse cultures are entirely capable of flourishing side-by-side, even if they despise each other, if they avoid significant clashes. A second lesson is this: while cultural diversity is at present almost universally praised, in fact the modern state tends to value uniformity and monocultural hegemony far more than variety. While we may look back nostalgically to earlier periods in Vilnius' history when the city was a center of Polish, Jewish, and even

Muslim culture, at present we should be content that vestiges of these cultures remain—and are in need of economic and political protection. Looking at the history of any multicultural city, the outsider is struck by the starkly different narrative told by, say, a Jew or a Pole or a Lithuanian. There is nothing wrong with this. As the Spanish say, "Every dog loves his own backyard." Still, as modern citizens in a globalized world, we do need to recognize the extra effort, both mental and financial, that preserving cultural diversity demands. The peculiarly mixed and complicated cultural-political history of Vilnius is worth keeping in mind as we work toward advancing the cause of tolerance and diversity.

# Notes

## Notes to Introduction

1. On capital cities and their national functions, see John Taylor, Jean G. Lengellé, Caroline Andrew, eds., *Capital Cities: International Perspectives = Les Capitales. Perspectives internationales* (Ottawa: Carleton University Press, 1993); and David L. A. Gordon, ed., *Planning Twentieth-Century Capitals* (London: Routledge, 2006).

2. *Rocznik statystyczny Wilna 1937* (Wilno: Zarząd miejski w Wilnie, 1939), section 4, p. 9 claims that in 1931, nearly 66% of the city's population was Polish, 28% was Jewish, less than 5% was Russian or Belarusian, and less than 1% was Lithuanian. Most likely the figure for Poles is at least somewhat inflated and the others are correspondingly reduced.

3. Statistics cited in Jolita Lenkevičiūtė, *Vilnius im Wandel. Wohnsegregation in einer ostmitteleuropäischen Hauptstadt* (Berlin: Wissenschaftlicher Verlag, 2006), 142.

4. For various statistics on nationality-ethnicity in Vilnius in the second half of the nineteenth century, see VMI, 1:303–304.

5. Dangiras Mačiulis, Alvydas Nikžentaitis, Vasilijus Safronovas, "L'appropriation symbolique d'une ville multiculturelle. Les cas de Kaunas, Klaipeda et Vilnius," *Revue germanique internationale* 11 (2010), 41–60.

6. Theodore R. Weeks, "Vilna, Wilno, Vilnius 1863-1939. Une étude de cas sur les cultures parallèles et sur «l'Autre» invisible" in *Revue germanique internationale*, 11 (2010), 79–102.

7. Yael Zerubavel, *Recovered Roots: Collective Memory and the Making of Israeli National Tradition* (Chicago: University of Chicago Press, 1995).

8. To cite one example of this tendency, the linguist Zigmas Zinkevičius steadfastly insisted that "Poles" in the Vilnius region are in fact simply "polonized Lithuanians" who need only to be "relithuanized." See, e.g., his *Rytų Lietuva praeityje ir dabar* (Vilnius: Mokslo ir enciklopedijų leidykla, 1993).

9. Emily Greble, *Sarajevo, 1941–1945: Muslims, Christians, and Jews in Hitler's Europe* (Ithaca: Cornell University Press, 2011), 14.

10. I do not, of course, deny the physical proximity of different cultures and a certain degree of interchange between them. I would argue, however, that for most people and at most times in Vilnius before the 1930s, the "national other" was perceived—if at all—in a distorted way that reflected a lack of everyday relations. David Frick has convincingly demonstrated the porous boundaries between cultural-religious groups in an earlier period (in particular between Christian denominations) in his marvelous *Kith, Kin, & Neighbors: Communities and Confessions in Seventeenth-Century Wilno* (Ithaca: Cornell University Press, 2013).

11. Catherine Evtuhov, *Portrait of a Russian Province: Economy, Society, and Civilization in Nineteenth-Century Nizhnii Novgorod* (Pittsburgh: University of Pittsburgh Press, 2011).

12. Theodore R. Weeks, *Nation and State in Late Imperial Russia: Nationalism and Russification on the Western Frontier, 1863–1914* (DeKalb: Northern Illinois University Press, 1996).

13. For the importance of World War II in Soviet and Russian history, see Nina Tumarkin, *The Living and the Dead: The Rise and Fall of the Cult of World War II in Russia* (New York: Basic Books, 1994); and Stephen Lovell, *The Shadow of War: Russia and the USSR, 1941 to the Present* (Chichester, West Sussex [U.K.]: Wiley-Blackwell, 2010).

## Notes to Chapter 1

1. Joachim Tauber and Ralph Tuchtenhagen, *Vilnius. Kleine Geschichte der Stadt* (Cologne: Böhlau, 2008), 15-16. For a twentieth-century retelling of the legend, see Władysław Zahorski, *Podania i legendy wileńskie* (Wilno: Zawadzki, 1925), 22-24.

2. For discussions of Vilnius as a political and economic center in these early years, see Eugenijus Manelis and Romaldas Samavičius, eds., *Vilniaus miesto istorijos skaitinai* [henceforth: VMIS] (Vilnius: Vilniaus knyga, 2001), 17-30; documents from this period are to be found in Manelis and Samavičius, *Vilniaus miesto istorijos dokumentai. Vilniaus miesto istorijos skatinių chrestomatij* [henceforth: VMID] (Vilnius: Vilniaus knyga, 2003), 22-30.

3. On this early period, see Marceli Kosman, "Wilno dawne i współczesne. Główne kierunki rozwoju XIV-XX w." in Feliksiak-1992, 1:35-58; Vytautas Daugudis, *Iš Vilniaus miesto praeitis* (Vilnius: Mokslo ir enciklopedijų leidykla, 1993).

4. For a fair overview of the period, see Zigmantas Kiaupa, Jūratė Kiaupienė, Albinas Kuncevičius, *The History of Lithuania before 1795* (Vilnius: LII, 2000). An example of "nationalized historiography"—although also providing a good deal of useful information—is Florian N. Dobrianskii, *Staraia i novaia Vil'na*, 3rd ed. (Vil'na: A. G. Syrkin, 1904), 1-121. Dobrianskii goes out of his way to stress the closeness and affinity of Gediminas and Lithuanians to their Russian neighbors.

5. On the spread of the city from the twelfth to twentieth century, see A. Jankevičienė, ed., *Vilniaus architektūra* (Vilnius: Mokslas, 1985), 6-12 ("Urbanistinė raida").

6. For a discussion of the castle and city wall defenses, see Napoleonas Kitakauskas, Vytautas Levandauskas, Adolfas Tautavičius, "Vilniaus pilys" in VMIS, 61-65, which includes an interesting image showing how the wall may have looked at the end of the fourteenth century.

7. On this crucial battle—and the subsequent historiographical battle between Poles and Lithuanians over "who won it"—see Darius Staliūnas, Dangiras Mačiulis, Rimvydas Petrauskas, *Kas laimėjo Žalgirio mūšį? Istorinio paveldo dalybos Vidurio ir Rytų Europoje* (Vilnius: Mintis, 2012).

8. The figure of 30,000 inhabitants (for the late fourteenth century) is given in Tauber and Tuchtenhagen, *Vilnius*, 50.

9. Israel Klausner, *Vilnah, Yerushalayim de-lita. Dorot rishonim 1495-1881* (Tel Aviv: Bet lohame ha-getaot, 1988), 3-6.

10. Algė Jankevičienė, *Vilniaus Didžojo Sinagoga—Great Synagogue of Vilnius* (Vilnius: Savastis, 1996).

11. Marceli Kosman, "Wilno w dobie rozkwitu (XVI-połowa XVII w.)" in Feliksiak-2002, 31-46.

12. Ludwik Abramowicz, *Cztery wieki drukarstwa w Wilnie 1525-1925* (Wilno: Ludwik Chomiński, 1925), 14-86, 115; on the Jewish press see Genrikh Agranovskii, *Stanovlenie evreiskogo knigopechataniia v Litve* (Vilnius: "Academia," 1994).

13. David Frick, "The Bells of Vilnius: Keeping Time in a City of Many Calendars" in *Making Contact: Maps, Identity and Travel* (Edmonton: University of Alberta Press, 2003), 27-28.

14. One indication of the university's importance is the fact that a post-Soviet bibliography of Vilnius is divided into two volumes: one on the university (1579-1939) and the other on "the city": Henryk Baranowski, *Bibliografia Wilna. 1: Uniwersytet Wileński 1579-1939. 2: Miasto* (Toruń: Wydawnictwo Uniwersytetu Mikołaja Kopernika, 1996, 2000). On the academy's early years, see Ludwik Piechnik, *Początki Akademii Wileńskiej 1570-1599* (Rome: apud Institutum Historicum Societatis Jesu, 1990).

15. For an good overview of the university's early history, see Marceli Kosman, *Uniwersytet Wileński 1579-1979* (Wrocław: Ossolineum, 1981), 12-21; or in English, Domas Butėnas et al., eds.,

*Academia et universitas Vilnensis. Vilniaus universiteto steigimo dokumentai* (Vilnius: Kultūra, 2004), 31–36. The latter volume also contains a beautiful reproduction of the original *privilegia* by which the university was established (89–91).

16. There is an enormous body of literature on Piotr Skarga, mainly in Polish. See, for example, Janusz Tazbir, *Piotr Skarga. Szermierz kontrreformacji* (Warsaw: "Wiedza Powszecna," 1983).

17. On the union, see Mečislovas Jučas, *Unia polsko-litewska* (Toruń: Europejskie Centrum Edukacyjne, 2003).

18. Ryszard Łużny, Franciszek Ziejka i Andrzej Kępiński, eds., *Unia brzeska. Geneza, dzieje I konsekwencje w kulturze narodów słowiańskich* (Kraków: Universitas, 1994).

19. On the unique position of Uniates between Russians and Poles, see Barbara Skinner, *The Western Front of the Eastern Church: Uniate and Orthodox Conflict in Eighteenth-Century Poland, Ukraine, Belarus, and Russia* (DeKalb: Northern Illinois University Press, 2009).

20. David Frick, ed., *Wilniane. Sywoty siedemnastowieczne* (Warsaw: Studium Europy Wschodniej, 2008); Frick, *Kith, Kin, & Neighbors: Communities and Confessions in Seventeenth-Century Wilno* (Ithaca: Cornell University Press, 2013).

21. For more detail, see Frick, *Kith, Kin, & Neighbors*, Chapter 2: "Neighbors"; and David Frick, "Jews and Others in Seventeenth-Century Wilno: Life in the Neighborhood," *Jewish Studies Quarterly* 12 (2005), 8–42.

22. The Karaites are Jews (at least, by most definitions) who accept only the *Tanakh* (Hebrew Bible) but not the Talmud.

23. Frick, "The Bells of Vilnius."

24. Maria Łowmiańska, *Wilno przed najazdem moskiewskim 1655 roku* (Wilno: Magistratu m. Wilna, 1929), 47–55 (religious establishments), 71–78 (population), 91–105 (culture).

25. On this period of chaos and decline see, for example, Robert I. Frost, *After the Deluge: Poland-Lithuania and the Second Northern War, 1655–1660* (Cambridge: Cambridge University Press, 1993).

26. On disasters but also continued cultural activities, see the articles in VMIS, 235–305.

27. Michał Baliński, *Historya miasta Wilna*, 2 vols. (Wilno: A. Marcinkowski, 1836). This work is available online at www.polona.pl.

28. Józef Ignacy Kraszewski, *Wilno od początków do roku 1750*, 4 vols. (Wilno: Józef Zawadzki, 1840–1842).

29. Ibid., 1:15ff.

30. Vytautas Berenis, introduction to Mykolas Balinskis, *Vilniaus miesto istorija* (Vilnius: Mintis, 2007).

31. Romuald Naruniec, *Michał Baliński jako mecenas polsko-litewskich więzi kulturowych* (Warsaw: Semper, 1995).

32. Michał Baliński, *Historya miasta Wilna* (Wilno: A. Marcinkowski, 1836), 2: 70ff.

## Notes to Chapter 2

1. This, of course, does not prevent most Polish and Lithuanian accounts from portraying the period 1795–1915 precisely as one of more or less unremitting repression and russification. For a recent example of such a historical view, see the otherwise very helpful and interesting chapters on this period in Antanas Rimvydas Čaplinskas, *Vilniaus istorija. Legendos ir tikrovė* (Vilnius: Charibdė, 2010), 284–447. Čaplinskas sums up the political history of the period as "struggles for freedom" (*laisvės kovos*), 284–293.

2. On this towering figure, his life, and thought, see Eliyahu Stern, *The Genius: Elijah of Vilnius and the Making of Modern Judaism* (New Haven: Yale University Press, 2013).

3. On early Lithuanian culture in the city, see VMIS, 241–305.

4. Lietuvos Valstybės Istorijos Archyvas (LVIA), f. 458, ap. 1, b. 374, l. 8. This entire file contains hundreds of such documents arranged, apparently, by the location of the house in question.

## 246 NOTES TO CHAPTER 2

5. However, see Vytautas Jogėla, Elmantas Meilus, Virgilijus Pugačiauskas, *Lukiškės. Nuo priemiesčio iki centro (XV a.-XX a. pradžia)*. *Kolektyvinė monografija* (Vilnius: Diemedžio leidykla, 2008), esp. 93–97 for some interesting conclusions, derived in part from this 1795 survey ("rewizja") on the suburb of Lukiškės.
6. Leonid Żytkowicz, *Rządy Repnina na Litwie w latach 1794–7* (Wilno: Nakładem Towarzystwa Przyjaciół Nauk w Wilnie, 1938), 305.
7. VMI, 1:214.
8. Romuald Naruniec, *Michał Baliński jako mecenas polsko-litewskich więzi kulturowych* (Warsaw: Semper, 1995); Reda Griškaitė, *Mykolas Balinskis. Kova dėl istorijos?* (Vilnius: Eugrimas, 2005).
9. Michał Baliński, *Opisanie statystyczne miasta Wilna* (Wilno: Józef Zawadzki, 1835), 36.
10. Ibid., 37–39.
11. Ibid., 64.
12. Ibid., 60.
13. Ibid., 62–63.
14. LVIA, Vilnius, f. 458, ap. 1, b. 567. The houses are listed with their owners' names, arranged by streets beginning from Ostra Brama.
15. Baliński, *Opisanie statystyczne*, 44–46.
16. Ibid., 61.
17. Ibid., 112–118. See also VMI, 1:205–229 on the city's population and economy in the first half of the nineteenth century.
18. Baliński, *Opisanie statystyczne*, 136–138.
19. Ibid., 130–131.
20. Ibid., 61.
21. Adam Mickiewicz's famous evocation of *Litwa* in *Pan Tadeusz* runs parallel to Baliński's usage. It should be noted that the two were near contemporaries. Mickiewicz was born five years after Baliński, and the two most likely had many of the same teachers at the university in Vilnius.
22. Baliński's figure seems reasonable. A contemporary official document about numbering properties in the city gives the figure of 1546 properties. LVIA, f. 381, ap. 24, b. 105777 (1833).
23. Baliński, *Opisanie statystyczne*, 44–51. According to Baliński, there were a total of 142 streets in the entire city, including suburbs like Antakalnis. For more information on the history of street names in Vilnius, see Jonas Jurkštas, "Vilniaus senamiesčio gatvėvardžiai," *Lietuvos TSR Mokslų Akademijos darbai. A serija* (1979), vol. 2 (67), 97–122.
24. Baliński, *Opisanie statystyczne*, 22.
25. LVIA, f. 381, ap. 24, b. 12134, ll. 1–3, 52.
26. LVIA, f. 937, ap. 1, b. 1519 (1833–1848); ibid., b. 9399 (1851–1853).
27. LVIA, f. 378, ap. 121, b. 204A.
28. LMI, 1:275–276.
29. VMID, 270. The telegraph office was opened on November 22, 1859.
30. LMI, 1:214 gives a population figure of 56,226 for 1860, derived apparently from the voluminous statistics contained in LVIA, f. 388, ap. 1, b. 287.
31. On the struggles against the Russians and the first years of Russian occupation, see the somewhat novelistic treatment in Maria Babnis, *Nad Wilią i Wilenką. Szkice wileńskie z lat 1791–1825* (Gdańsk: Pelplin, 2011).
32. Żytkowicz, *Rządy Repnina*, 57–87.
33. Ibid., 186–187 (confiscations of estates), 279–280 (Uniates). For more on the Uniates in this period, see Barbara Skinner, *The Western Front of the Eastern Church: Uniate and Orthodox Conflict in Eighteenth-Century Poland, Ukraine, Belarus, and Russia* (DeKalb: Northern Illinois University Press, 2009).
34. VMID, 249, letter of Lithuanian civil governor Jan Friesel to governor general of August 21, 1799.
35. Leonid Żytkowicz, *Zburzenie murów obronnych Wilna* (Wilno: Wydaw. Magistratu m. Wilna, 1933).
36. For an excellent recent overview of this key period in European history, see Dominic

Lieven, *Russia against Napoleon: The Battle for Europe, 1807 to 1814* (London: Penguin, 2010).

37. F. A. Kudrinskii, *Vil'na v 1812 godu* (Vil'na: Izdanie Vilenskago Uchenago Okruga, 1912), 26–37; N. Bernatskii, *Sobytiia v Vil'ne vo vremia Otechestvennoi voiny* (Vil'na, 1912), 12–88.

38. M. Lavrinovich, "Vil'na v 1812 godu," *Istoricheskii vestnik*, 70 (1897), 873–880.

39. Virgilijus Pugačiauskas, *Napoleonas ir Vilnius. Karinio gyvenimo kasdienybės bruožai* (Vilnius: Arlila, 2004), 26.

40. "Kamienice pamiątkowe z roku 1812-go," *Litwa i Ruś*, no. 5–6 (1912), 170–172.

41. Władysław Zahorski, *Z roku 1812-go w Wilnie* (St. Petersburg?, 1901?), 3–4. This pamphlet, without clear indication of place or date of publication, is at the University of Warsaw library.

42. J. Balčiūnas, "Napoleonas ir Vilnius," *Mūsų Žinynas* 21, no. 79 (1931), 358–359.

43. A frequently cited source that I have been unable to locate is F. Grzymała, "Entrée de Napoléon à Wilna," in *Souvenirs de la Pologne* (Paris, 1833), 185–186.

44. For a copy of this act, see K. Voenskii, *Akty, dokumenty i materialy dlia istorii 1812 goda* (St. Petersburg: Tip. A F. Shtol'tsenburga, 1909), 1:103–104.

45. Janusz Iwaszkiewicz, *Napoleon w Wilnie w 1812 r.*, 454–456.

46. "Jak obchodziła Litwa Imieniny Wielkiego Napoleona 15 sierpnia 1812 r.," *Litwa i Ruś*, zesz. 5–6 (1912), 135–141.

47. In general on the situation in Lithuania during this fateful year, see Janusz Iwaszkiewicz, *Litwa w roku 1812* (Kraków: L. Anczyc, 1912).

48. Lavrinovich, "Vil'na v 1812 godu," 871–909.

49. Kudrinskii, *Vil'na*, esp. 35–141.

50. Jan Obst comments on contemporary documents he published in *Litwa i Ruś*, zesz. 5–6 (1912), 177–183; Israel Klausner, *Vilnah, Yerushalayim de-Lita. Dorot rishonim 1495–1881* (Tel Aviv: Bet lohame ha-geta'ot, 1988), 134–6. A Lithuanian specialist also speaks of Jewish hostility toward the French and help for the Russians, Bronius Dundulis, *Napoléon et la Lituanie en 1812* (Paris: Alcan, 1940), 192.

51. See Kudrinskii, *Vil'na*, 20 (on Jews helping the Russian cause by offering intelligence on French movements), but also p. 110 that "only Jews got rich" from provisioning the French. An apologetic but still useful work on the Jews in 1812 is S. M. Ginzburg, *Otechestvennaia voina 1812 god i russkie evrei* (St. Petersburg: "Razum," 1912), 47–48 on the situation in Vilnius and the Lithuanian area. For some interesting contemporary documents, see Sh[lomo] Pozner, "Vilner yidn unter der napoleonischer okupatsie (a bintl nay-gefundene dokumentn)," *YIVO-bleter*, no. 3 (1934), 278–286.

52. More generally on Napoleon's effect on Jews in Europe, see Franz Kobler, *Napoleon and the Jews* (New York: Schocken, 1976).

53. Daniel Beauvois, "Les Français à Vilna en 1812," *Annales historiques de la Révolution Française*, t. 53, no. 246 (1981), 560–571, esp. 562–564.

54. Pugačiauskas, *Napoleonas ir Vilnius*, 63–64.

55. Kudrinskii, *Vil'na*, 83–85.

56. For an admirable military and political account of these events, see Lieven, *Russia against Napoleon*, 174–214, 242–252.

57. Kudrinskii, *Vil'na*, 105–114. On the last months of French occupation in Vilnius, esp. from the military point of view, see "Iz vospominanii generala Godara, byvshago frantsuzskago voennago gubernatora v Vil'ne v 1812 godu" in Konstantin Voenskii, *Istoricheskie ocherki i stat'i, otnosiashchiesia k 1812 godu* (St. Petersburg: Sel'skii Vestnik, 1912), 358–364.

58. Kudrinskii, *Vil'na*,115–119; Iwaszkiewicz, *Litwa w roku 1812*, 272–308.

59. Pugačiauskas, *Napoleonas ir Vilnius*, 97–107. A very detailed history of Vilnius' six months under French occupation (in Polish) can be found in the archives (LVIA, f. 1532, ap. 1, bb. 1–10).

60. On the devastations caused by the military (mainly by the French) in 1812, see LVIA, f. 937, ap. 1, b. 165 (1812–1814).

61. Jörg Ganzenmüller, "Russische Staatsgewalt und polnischer Adel. Staatsbau und Elitenintegration in den Westgouvernements des Zarenreiches (1772–1850)" (Habilitation dissertation, Friedrich-Schiller-Universität Jena, 2010), 98–105.

62. Robert Frank Leslie, *Polish Politics and the Insurrection of November 1830* (London: Athlone Press, 1956); and Edward C. Thaden, *Russia's Western Borderlands 1710-1870* (Princeton: Princeton UP, 1984), 63-79. For events in Lithuania, including Vilnius, see Feliksas Sliesoriūnas, *1830-1831 metų sukilimas Lietuvoje* (Vilnius: Mintis, 1974).

63. On the events leading to the rebellion and the November Insurrection of 1831 itself, see Marian Zgórniak, *Polska w czasach walk o niepodległość* (Kraków: Oficyna wydawnicza, 2001), 85-148.

64. Leslie, *Polish Politics*, 120-123.

65. Sara Rabinowiczówna, *Wilno w powstaniu roku 1830/31* (Wilno: Wydawnictwo Magistratu, 1932), 8, 12-13.

66. Ibid., 9. The tsar's manifesto was dated December 7/19, 1830 and published in *Kurjer Litewski*, no. 151-153, in 1830. The marshals of the nobility's response appeared in the same newspaper, no. 155-156.

67. Rabinowiczówna, *Wilno w powstaniu*, 10. Rabinowiczówna does, however, express some skepticism as to this account's reliability, calling it "possible, but not certain."

68. Józef Bieliński, *Uniwersytet Wileński (1579-1831)* (Kraków: W. L. Anczyc, 1899-1900), 3:551.

69. Sliesoriūnas, *1830-1831 metų sukilimas*, 170-189.

70. Gabriela z Güntherów Puzynina, *W Wilnie i w dworach litewskich. Pamiętniki z lat 1815-1843* (Wilno: Józef Zawadzki, 1928; reprint Kraków, 1990), 143-147.

71. Eugenjusz Gulczyński, *Rok 1830-1831 w Wilnie* (Wilno: Druk "Lux," 1933), 40-50.

72. Stanisław Szumski, *W walkach i więzieniach. Pamiętniki Stanisława Szumskiego 1812-1848* (Wilno: Józef Zawadzki, 1931), 58-73.

73. Gulczyński faults the Komitet Centralny for not taking advantage of anti-Russian and pro-insurrection sentiments, in particular among Vilnius students and artisans, to attack the Russians in March and early April 1831. *Rok 1830-1831*, 56-60.

74. This is Rabinowiczówna's basic position. Instead of faulting Vilnius for passivity in the national cause, she takes another tack, arguing that while an uprising in the city itself was impossible, the city provided many fighters for the cause. *Wilno w powstaniu*, 133-142. She admits the "bezczynność" of the Komitet Centralny but dismisses this as a secondary factor.

75. See the tsarist regulations on punishing rebels (of March 22, 1832 and July 25, 1833) reprinted in *TSR istorijos šaltiniai* (Vilnius: Valstybinė politinės ir mosklinės literatūros leidykla, 1955), 1:427-428.

76. "Chetyre politicheskie zapiski grafa Mikhaila Nikolaevicha Murav'eva Vilenskogo," *Russkii arkhiv* (April 1885), 161-175. This document was drawn up just after the beginning of the Polish insurrection, on December 22, 1830.

77. I agree with Ganzenmüller that the 1830-1831 uprising was transformational in its effect on Russian attitudes toward the possibility of integrating the Polish elite into a kind of supra-national imperial ruling class. However, the actual measures taken—at least in the Lithuanian provinces—before 1863 did little to challenge Polish domination (with the significant exception of the closing of Vilnius University). Ganzenmüller, "Russische Staatsgewalt und polnischer Adel," esp. 297-314.

78. Leslie, *Polish Politics*, 267.

79. "Russians" included many individuals who by modern definitions would be considered "Belarusians." Unfortunately extant written sources make it very difficult to distinguish between the two groups. In any case, the history of Belarusians in Vilnius is a topic that deserves study.

80. David Althoen, *That Noble Quest: From True Nobility to Enlightened Society in the Polish-Lithuanian Commonwealth 1550-1830* (Ann Arbor: DMA, 2001; this is a revised and self-published version of the author's 2000 dissertation at the University of Michigan), esp. chapters 6 ("'We Don't Need Books!' The Paradox of Polish Reading Culture: A Literate Society, a Lack of Readers, and the Lack of a Market for Books") and chapter 7 ("'Besides, What Could a Pole Write That Was Any Good!' Polish Contempt for Polish Literature at the Beginning of the 19th Century"). Althoen notes (541) that, even in Zawadzki's celebrated Wilno bookstore, "the room with foreign books was the centerpiece of the store."

81. This act is included in VMID, 290–293.
82. Daniel Beauvois, *Wilno. Polska stolica kulturalna zaboru rosyjskiego, 1803–1832* (Wrocław: Wydawnictwo Uniwersytetu Wrocławskiego, 2010). This work is a translation of Beauvois's *Lumières et société en Europe de l'Est. L'Université de Vilna et les écoles polonaises de l'Empire Russe 1803–1832* (Paris: H. Champion, 1977).
83. Wacław Sobieski, *Uniwersytet Wileński w roku 1812* (Kraków: Głos Narodu, 1915), 25–28. On Jan Śniadecki as scholar and rector of the university, see Michał Baliński, *Pamiętniki o Janie Śniadeckim, jego życiu prywatnem ir publicznem, i działach jego* (Wilno: Józef Zawadzki, 1865); and Mark Francis O'Connor, "Cultures in Conflict: A Case Study in Russian-Polish Relations. The University at Wilno" (Ph.D. diss., Boston College, 1977), 195–240.
84. For an overview of the university from 1804 to 1832, see *Vilniaus universiteto istorija 1579–1994* (Vilnius: Valstybinis Leidybos Centras, 1994), 127–168. For more details, see Beauvois, *Lumières et société* 2; and *Vilniaus universiteto istorija 1803–1940* (Vilnius: "Mokslas," 1977), 9–113.
85. *Vilniaus miesto istorija*, 246.
86. Joseph Frank also left an invaluable memoir of his years in Vilnius (1804–1823), originally written in French. Józef Frank, *Pamiętniki* (Wilno: "Lux," 1923), 3 vols.
87. VMI, 1:228.
88. On both Franks, their appointments and careers at Vilnius University, see LVIA, f. 721, ap. 1, b. 383.
89. For an overview of the Filomaci and related groups, their activities and thought, see Aleksander Kamiński, *Polskie związki młodzieży* (Warsaw: PWN, 1963), 276–480.
90. Zofja Jabłońska-Erdmanowa, *Oświecenie i romantyzm w stowarzyszeniach młodzieży wileńskiej na początku XIX w.* (Wilno: Nakładem Towarzystwa Przyjaciół Nauk, 1931), 156.
91. See, for example, the essays collected in Ludwik Janowski, *W promieniach Wilna i Krzemieńca* (Wilno: Józef Zawadzki, 1923).
92. Ignacy Domeyko, "Filareci i filomaci" in Henryk Mościcki, *Ze stosunków wileńskich w okresie 1816–1823. Z Filareckiego świata* (Warsaw: "Biblioteka polska," 1924), 78–91.
93. On the Decembrists, see Ludmilla A. Trigos, *The Decembrist Myth in Russian Culture* (New York: Palgrave-Macmillan, 2009).
94. Writing considerably later, Gabriela Puzynina z Güntherów described Wilno during the 1821 "season" as "full of officers" who danced at the local casino and were present at balls. *W Wilnie i w dworach litewskich*, 27–29.
95. These clashes often seem to parody the "contests" of Dostoevsky's "underground man" in *Notes from the Underground*. See the accounts, for example, in Stanisław Pigoń, *Z dawnego Wilna. Szkice obyczajowe i literackie* (Wilno: Wydawnictwo Magistratu, 1929), 49–53; and Otto Ślizień, "Z pamiętnika (1821–1824)" in Mościcki, *Ze stosunków wileńskich*, 127–128.
96. Pigoń, *Z dawnego Wilna*, 55–58.
97. For somewhat contradictory accounts of Jankowski's behavior and motives, see the different memoirs in Mościcki, *Ze stosunków wileńskich*, esp. 100–103, 129, 167, 286–288.
98. It should be remembered that the Russian Empire was on the whole more lenient toward youthful political offenders than twentieth-century regimes were. Mickiewicz, for example, was indeed exiled to the Russian interior, but he worked there as a secretary to various military and civilian authorities. For a short sketch, see Theodore R. Weeks, "Adam Mickiewicz (1798–1855)" in Stephen M. Norris and Willard Sunderland, eds., *Russia's People of Empire: Life Stories from Eurasia, 1500 to the Present* (Bloomington: Indiana University Press, 2012), 138–147.
99. Puzynina's memoirs pass over the Filareci/Filomaci trials in silence. Puzinina, *W Wilnie*, 44–58 (1823).
100. Stanisław Małachowski-Łempicki, *Wolnomularstwo na ziemiach dawnego wielkiego księstwa Litewskiego 1776–1822. Dzieje i materiały* (Wilno: Towarzystwo przyjaciół nauk, 1930), esp. 10–60; S. F. Dobrianskii, *Ocherki iz istorii masonstva v Litve* (Vil'na: Tip. Iosifa Zavadzkago, 1914).
101. In particular on the reasons for *Tygodnik Wileński*'s closure (mainly, it would appear, for offending [Catholic] religious sensibilities), see Pigoń, *Z dawnego Wilna*, 29–42.

102. Józef Bieliński, *Szubrawcy w Wilnie (1817–1822)* (Wilno: Nakładem Korwina, 1910).
103. Jadvyga Kazlauskaitė, *Vilniaus periodiniai leidiniai 1760–1918* (Vilnius: "Mintis," 1988), 31–32.
104. Personal files on Zawadzki and his printing business are located at LVIA, f. 1135, ap. 7. For a good overview of the man, his life, and his importance for Polish culture in Vilnius, see Radosław Cybulski, *Józef Zawadzki. Księgarz, drukarz, wydawca* (Wrocław: Ossolineum, 1972).
105. For more on Vilnius University's involvement with printing houses and publishing, see Daniel Beauvois, *Szkolnictwo polskie na ziemiach litewsko-ruskich 1803–1832* (Rome-Lublin: Fundacja Jana Pawła II/Wydawnictwo KUL, 1991), 1:177–203.
106. Ludwik Abramowicz, *Cztery wieki drukarstwa w Wilnie. Zarys historyczny (1425–1925)* (Wilno: Tłocznia "Lux," 1925), 86–95. An invaluable source on the Zawadzki publishing house is Tadeusz Turkowski, *Materiały do dziejów literatury i oświaty na Litwie ir Rusi. Z archiwum drukarni i księgarni J. Zawadzkiego w Wilnie z lat 1805–1865* (Wilno: Nakł. Towarzystwa przyjaciół nauk w Wilnie, 1935), 3 vols.
107. Jerzy Czarnecki (pseud. for Tadeusz Turkowski), *Wilno w dziejach książki polskiej* (Wilno: Józef Zawadzki, 1928), 14.
108. Abramowicz, *Cztery wieki*, 99–103; statistics on numbers of books printed from Estreichera, *Bibljografii Polskiej*, cited in Czarnecki, *Wilno*, 23. See also Althoen (*That Noble Quest*, 442–498) more generally on reading publics, publishers, and bookstores throughout Poland-Lithuania in the eighteenth and early nineteenth centuries.
109. Piotr Chmielowski. *Liberalizm i Obskurantyzm na Litwie i Rusi (1815–1823)* (Warsaw: Drukarnia artystyczna Saturnina Sikorskiego, 1898).
110. Alina Witkowska, *Rówieśnicy Mickiewicza* (Warsaw: Wiedza Powszechna, 1962), 35.
111. Andrzej Romanowski, *Pozytywizm na Litwie. Polskie życie kulturalne na ziemiach litewsko-białorusko-inflanckich w latach 1864–1914* (Kraków: "Universitas," 2003).
112. Małgorzata Stolzman, *"Nigdy od ciebie miasto . . ." Dzieje kultury wileńskiej lat międzypowstaniowych (1832–1863)* (Olsztyn: Wydawnictwo Pojezierze, 1987), 34–36; *Vilniaus universiteto istorija*, 169–176.
113. Dr. Maciej Łowicki, *Duch Akademji Wileńskiej. Z czasów Szymona Konarskiego pamiętnika ucznia wileńskiej akademji medyczno-chirurgicznej*, ed. Wacław Gizbert-Studnicki (Wilno: Książnica Atlas, 1925).
114. Puzyna, *W Wilnie*, 270–271.
115. Szumski, *W walkach*, 80–116.
116. Władysław Zahorski, *Zarys dziejów Cesarskiego Towarzystwa Lekarskiego w Wilnie (1805–1897)* (Warsaw: K. Kowalewski, 1898).
117. See, for example, David Fajnhauz, *Ruch konspiracyjny na Litwie ir Białorusi 1846–1848* (Warsaw: PWN, 1965).
118. Egidijus Aleksandravičius, *Kultūrinis sąjūdis Lietuvoje 1831–1863 metais. Organizaciniai kultūros ugdymo aspektai* (Vilnius: "Mokslas," 1989). Unfortunately Aleksandravičius considerably weakens his argument by failing to distinguish between ethnic and geographic "Lithuania" and Lithuanians.
119. Ibid., 34–64; Stolzman, *"Nigdy . . .,"* 55–7, 96–9. On the founding of an "museum of antiquities" in Vilnius by the archaeological commission, see LVIA, f. 567, ap. 3, b. 12 (1851–1865).
120. Ryszard Mienicki, *Wileńska Komisja Archeograficzna (1864–1915)* (Wilno: Nakładem Towarzystwa Przyjaciół Nauk w Wilnie, 1925).
121. LVIA, f. 378, BS 1832, b. 2826.
122. Stolzman, *"Nigdy . . .,"* 79.
123. Małgorzata Stolzman, *Czasopisma wileńskie Adama Honorego Kirkora* (Kraków: Nakładem UJ, 1973).
124. Władysław Syrokomla, *Wycieczki po Litwie w promieniach od Wilna* (Wilno: A. Ass, 1857–1860); A. H. Kirkor, *Przewodnik historyczny po Wilnie i jego okolicach* (Wilno: J. Zawadzki, 1880).
125. Stolzman, *"Nigdy .."*, 105–232.
126. Leszek Zasztowt, *Szkolnictwo na ziemiach litewskich i ruskich dawnej Rzeczpospolitej (Kresy*

NOTES TO CHAPTER 2    251

*1832-1864)* (Warsaw: Tow. Nauk. Warszaw. Instytuta Historji PAN, 1997), esp. 151–160, 376–377.

127. Daniel Beauvois, "Powstanie listopadowe a szkolnictwo na ziemiach litewsko-ruskich" in Jerzy Skowronek and Maria Żmigrodzka, eds., *Powstanie listopadowe 1830–1831. Geneza, uwarunkowania, bilans, porównania* (Wrocław: Ossolineum, 1983), 45–54.

128. Ignacy Myślicki, "Zarys historii walk o oświatę polską w Wileńszczyźnie i Mińszczyźnie" in Bogdan Nawroczyński, ed., *Nasza walka o szkołę polską* (Warsaw: Wydawnictwo Komitetu Obchodu 25-lecia walki o szkołę polską, 1934), 327–369.

129. This tendency can be seen, for example, in the monumental and still very useful two-volume work by Israel Klausner, *Vilnah, Yerushalayim de-Lita* (Tel Aviv: Bet lohamei ha-getaot, 1983, 1988).

130. LVIA, f. 381, ap. 24, b. 6523, ll. 10–18 (notes street names and the thirty Jews officially allowed to reside here); ll. 156–7 (Gordon petition); ll. 249, 466a (maps).

131. For more on attempts to prohibit Jewish residence on certain streets in Vilne, see "Zapreshchenie evreiam zhit' na glavnykh ulitsakh gor. Vil'ny," in S. A. An-skii et al., eds., *Perezhitoe. Sbornik posviashchenyi obshchestvennoi i kul'turnoi istorii evreev v Rossii* (St. Petersburg: Tip. I. Fleitmana, 1910), vol. 2.

132. For a sophisticated analysis of this movement—and its "enlightened" opponents—in this period, see Marcin Wodziński, *Haskalah and Hasidism in the Kingdom of Poland: A History of Conflict* (Portland, Oregon: Littman Library of Jewish Civilization, 2005).

133. S. L. Zitron, "Geschichte der Wilnaer jüdischen Gemeinde," *Neue jüdische Monatshefte* 2 (1918), 565.

134. Klausner, *Vilnah, Yerushalayim de-Lita*, 86, 133 and *passim*.

135. Genrikh Agranovskii, *Stanovlenie evreiskogo knigopechataniia v Litve* (Vilnius: "Academia," 1994), 17–42; Klausner, *Vilnah, Yerushalayim de-Lita*, 134, 150–152; Pinchas Kon, *Dos ershte poylish-yidshe verterbuch und zayn mehaber levin liondor* (Wilno: B. Kletskin, 1926).

136. More work needs to be done on the social/economic history of Vilna Jews. Klausner's excellent work, for example, barely touches on this topic. One interesting source from the period is A. K. Korev, "Evrei Vilenskoi gubernii" in *Pamiatnaia knizhka Vilenskoi gubernii* (1860, part 2), 37–88.

137. Pinchas Kon, *Dawny Uniwersytet Wileński a Żydzi* (Wilno: Lux 1926), 7–8.

138. E. Aleksandravičius, "Hebrew Studies at Vilnius University and Lithuanian Ethnopolitical Tendencies in the First Part of the 19th Century," *Lituanus* 37, no. 2 (1991), 5–22.

139. Verena Dohrn, "Das Rabbinerseminar in Wilna (1847–1873). Zur Geschichte der ersten staatlichen höheren Schule für Juden im Russischen Reich," *Jahrbücher für Geschichte Osteuropas* 45, no. 3 (1997), 379–401.

140. Verena Dohrn, *Jüdische Eliten im Russischen Reich. Aufklärung und Integration im 19. Jahrhundert* (Cologne: Böhlau, 2008).

141. On the "Rabbi school," see also Mordekhai Zalkin, "Beit hamidrash lerabanim bevilnah—bein dimui lematsiut," *Gal-Ed*, 14 (1995), 59–71 (Hebrew numeration).

142. Theodore R. Weeks, "Between Rome and Tsargrad: The Uniate Church in Imperial Russia" in Robert P. Geraci and Michael Khodarkovsky, eds., *Of Religion and Empire: Missions, Conversion, and Tolerance in Tsarist Russia* (Ithaca: Cornell University Press, 2001), 70–91.

143. David Frick, *Kith, Kin, & Neighbors: Communities and Confessions in Seventeenth-Century Wilno* (Ithaca: Cornell University Press, 2013).

144. Flavian Nikolaevich Dobrianskii, *Staraia i novaia Vil'na*, 3rd ed. (Vil'na: A. G. Syrkin, 1904), 53. Dobrianskii, in his zeal to prove Vilnius' Russianness, states, "The mass of permanent residents in Vilna was purely Russian." At the same time he notes the presence of 30,000 Catholics, 30,000 Orthodox, and 15,000 Jews.

145. Adomas Honoris Kirkoras, *Pasivaikščiojimai po Vilnių ir jo apylinkes* (Vilnius: Mintis, 2012), map on end flyleaf. This work was originally published in Polish in 1859.

146. Lev Savitskii, *Pravoslavnoe kladbishche gor. Vil'no. K stoletiiu kladbishchenskoi tserkvi sv. Evfrosinii 1838–1938 gg.* (Vil'no: E. Kotliarskii, 1938).

147. Iu. F. Krachkovskii, *Istoricheskii obzor deiatel'nosti upravleniia Vilenskogo uchebnogo okruga* (Vil'na: Syrkin, 1903).

148. M. V. Serebiakov, *Istoricheskii ocherk stoletnego suchchestvovaniia Vil'niusskoi I-ii gimnazii (1803-1903)* (Vil'na: Syrkin, 1903).

## Notes to Chapter 3

1. For more detail, see Theodore R. Weeks, *Nation and State in Late Imperial Russia: Nationalism and Russification on the Western Frontier, 1863-1914* (DeKalb: Northern Illinois University Press, 1996). Recent research has shown that there were, indeed, more activist proposals for conversions and russification, but this research also confirms that in the end such policies either were not implemented or were implemented on a very small scale. See, e.g., Darius Staliūnas, *Making Russians: Meaning and Practice of Russification in Lithuania and Belarus after 1863* (Amsterdam: Rodopi, 2007); Mikhail Dolbilov, *Russkii krai, chuzhaia vera. Etnokonfessional'naia politika imperii v Litve i Belorussii pri Aleksandre II* (Moscow: Novoe literaturnoe obozrenie, 2010).
2. Dawid Fajnhauz, *1863. Litwa i Białoruś* (Warsaw: Neriton, 1999), esp. 27-56.
3. The literature on 1863 in Polish and Lithuanian is enormous, though much less impressive in English. For a classic, enormously detailed account, see any of the dozens of works of Stefan Kieniewicz. A recent discussion is Jerzy Jedlicki, *Droga do narodowej klęski* (Warsaw: IH PAN, 2013). The only full treatment is English is Robert F. Leslie, *Reform and Insurrection in Russian Poland 1856-1865* (London: Athlone Press, 1963). More specifically on the insurrection in the Northwest Provinces (which included, of course, Vilnius), see V. D'iakov et al., *Revoliutsionnyi pod''em v Litve i Belorussii v 1861-1862 gg.* (Moscow: Nauka, 1964); A. F. Smirnov, *Vosstanie 1863 goda v Litve i Belorussii* (Moscow: Izdatel'stvo Akademii nauk SSSR, 1963); Vida Girininkienė, ed., *1863-1864 metai Lietuvoje. Straipsniai ir dokumentai* (Kaunas: Šviesa, 1991).
4. Murav'ev was lionized by Russian society in 1863; even the radical poet Nikolai Nekrasov sang his praises (Kornei Chukovskii, *The Poet and the Hangman (Nekrasov and Muravyov)* (Ann Arbor, Mich.: Ardis, 1977 [originally published in 1922]). For the writings of some Murav'ev supporters see A. N. Mosolov, *Vilenskie ocherki 1863-1865 gg. (Murav'evskoe vremia)* (St. Petersburg: Tip. A. S. Suvorina, 1898); A. I. Milovidov, "Deiatel'nost' grafa M.N. Murav'eva po narodnomu prosveshcheniiu v Severo-Zapadnom krae (1863-1865 gg.)," *Zhurnal ministerstva narodnogo prosveshcheniia* (July 1905), 30-100; *Podvig Murav'eva - Nastol'naia kniga praviteliam i pravitel'stvam* (St. Petersburg: A. Porokhovshchikov, 1898). Murav'ev's memoirs were published in 1882-1883 in *Russkaia starina* and later as a book. Mikhail Dolbilov analyzes the different images of the "mutiny" in "Konstruirovanie obrazov miatezha. Politika M.N. Murav'eva v Litovsko-Belorusskom krae v 1863-1865 gg. Kak ob''ekt istoriko-antropologicheskogo analiza," *Actio Nova* (2000), 399-408.
5. Zita Medišauskienė, *Rusijos cenzūra Lietuvoje XIX a. viduryje* (Kaunas: Vytauto Didžiojo universitetas, 1989), 204-216, 262-271.
6. This period in Lithuanian history is sometimes called "knygnešių laikai"—"the time of the book-pedlars"—after the individuals who would illegally transport books into the Russian Empire from East Prussia. On different aspects of these restrictions, see Vytautas Merkys, ed., *Bor'ba litovskogo naroda za svobodu pechati v 1864-1904 gg.* (Vilnius: Litovskii natsional'nyi muzei, 2004); and Darius Staliūnas, ed., *Raidžių draudimo metai* (Vilnius: LII leidykla, 2004).
7. On preparations for this census and the methods to be used, see LVIA, f. 378, BS 1874, b. 66.
8. N. Zinov'ev, *Vil'na po perepisi 18 aprelia 1875 g.* (Vil'na: Syrkin, 1881), 16-23, 29, 32, 42.
9. VMI, 2:304; for more detail on the city, including the population figure of 167,959 for 1903, see I. I. Goshkevich, ed., *Vilenskaia guberniia. Polnyi spisok naselennykh mest so statisticheskimi dannymi o kazhdom poselenii* (Vil'na: Gubernskaia tipografiia, 1905), 24-27.
10. Michael F. Hamm, ed., *The City in Late Imperial Russia* (Bloomington: Indiana University Press, 1986), 3.
11. Vytautas Jogėla, Elmantas Meilus, Virgilijus Pugačiauskas, *Lukiškės. Nuo priemiesčio iki centro (XV a.-XX a. pradžia)* (Vilnius: Diemedžio leidykla, 2008), 84-85, 132-133, 161-182.

12. On the Lutheran cemetery in the nineteenth century, see Antanas Čaplinskas, *Vilniaus istorija. Legendos ir tikrovė* (Vilnius: Charibdė, 2010), 375.

13. Map from A. H. Kirkor, *Przewodnik historyczny po Wilnie i jego okolicach*, 3rd ed. (Wilno: J. Zawadzki, 1889).

14. Nijolė Lukšionytė-Tolvaišienė, *Istorizmas ir modernas Vilniaus architektūroje* (Vilnius: Vilniaus Dailės Akademija, 2000), 113-115.

15. A thick file on prostitution in Vilnius from the early twentieth century has a number of specific references to houses in this area: LVIA, f. 383, ap. 1, 1903, b. 402.

16. Lukšionytė-Tolvaišienė, *Istorizmas ir modernas*, 126-128.

17. See, for example, ibid., 93-115; Darius Osteika and Jūratė Tytlytė, eds., *Vilnius 1900-2005. Naujosios architektūros gidas* (Vilnius: Architektūros fondas, 2005), B1-C17.

18. Map from Wacław Gizbert-Studnicki, *Wilno. Przewodnik ilustrowany po mieście i okolicy* (Wilno: A. Żukowski i W. Borkowicz, 1910).

19. Lukšionytė-Tolvaišienė, *Istorizmas ir modernas*, 137-155; Lukšionytė-Tolvaišienė, "Istorizmo architektūros daugiabučiai nuomojamieji namai Vilniuje," *Vilniaus TSR architektūros klausimai*, 8 (1986), 70-82.

20. YdL, 1:113.

21. For another, famous example of this sort of new-style apartment building of the late nineteenth century, built for the upper-middle class, see Carl E. Schorske, *Fin-de-Siècle Vienna: Politics and Culture* (New York: Vintage, 1981), 24-115 ("The Ringstrasse, Its Critics, and the Birth of Urban Modernism").

22. Lukšionytė-Tolvaišienė, *Istorizmas ir modernas*, 115-126.

23. On other cities in the empire at this time, see Daniel Brower, *The Russian City between Tradition and Modernity, 1850-1900* (Berkeley: University of California Press, 1990); Michael F. Hamm, ed., *The City in Late Imperial Russia* (Bloomington: Indiana University Press, 1986); and Jeff Sahadeo, *Russian Colonial Society in Tashkent, 1865-1923* (Bloomington: Indiana University Press, 2007).

24. Nijolė Lukšionytė-Tolvaišienė, "Vilniaus architektai (1850-1914)" in *Europos dailė. Lietuviškieji variantai* (Vilnius: Leidybos centras, 1994), 227-269; see also the essays on this period in A. Butrimas, ed., *Vilniaus architektūros mokykla XVIII-XX a.* (Vilnius: Vilniaus darbės akademija, 1993).

25. Erich Amburger, *Geschichte der Behördenorganisation Rußlands von Peter dem Großen bis 1917* (Leiden: Brill, 1966), 392-393. The two longest-serving governors general in this period were A. L. Potapov (1868-1874) and P. P. Al'bedinskii (1874-1880).

26. Aleksei Gene, "Vilenskie vospominaniia," *Russkaia starina*, kn. 5-6 (May-June 1914), 418-434, 580-610.

27. As always, matters are a bit more complicated. While Russian (*russkii*) and Orthodox (*pravoslavnyi*) were indeed almost inevitably equated, some administrators recognized Catholic Belarusians as "ours" (Russians), despite their religion. It was to prevent polonization of this group that efforts were made to introduce Russian into Catholic churches in mainly Belarusian areas (and not, as is sometimes implied, to russify Poles). And even this effort ended in a fiasco. See Theodore R. Weeks, "Religion and Russification: Russian Language in the Catholic Churches of the 'Northwest Provinces' after 1863," *Kritika: Explorations in Russian and Eurasian History* 2, no. 1 (Winter 2001), 87-110.

28. Images of the monastery's stately gate appear in A. A. Vinogradov, *Pravoslavnye sviatyni g. Vil'ny* (Vil'na: Gubernskaia tipografiia, 1906), 13-14.

29. Ibid., 16-19.

30. Ibid., 19-27; O. V. Shcherbitskii, *Vilenskii prechistenskii sobor. Istoricheskii ocherk v sviazi s tserk.-rel. zhizn'iu g. Vil'ny* (Vil'na: Russkii pochin, 1908).

31. Vinogradov, *Pravoslavnye sviatyni*, 33-37.

32. Florian Dobrianskii, *Putevoditel' po Vilenskoi publichnoi biblioteke* (Vil'na: I. Ia. Ialovtser, 1879), 24-33.

33. Stanisław Lisowski, "Uniwersytecka Bibljoteka Publiczna za czasów rosyjskich" in Adam Łysakowski, ed., *Bibljoteki wileńskie* (Wilno: "Znicz," 1932), 11-36.

34. Eglė Tamulevičienė, *Rusijos geografų draugijos Šiaurės Vakarų krašto skyrius (1867-1915)* in *Mosksło draugijos Lietuvoje* (Vilnius: "Mokslas," 1979), 32-65; *Vil'na* (Vitebsk: Gubernskaia tipografiia, 1910).

35. *Russkaia Vil'na. Prilozhenie k puteshestviiu po sv. mestam russkim* (Vil'na: A. Syrkin, 1865).
36. V. G. Vasil'evskii, *Ocherk istorii goroda Vil'ny*, in P. N. Batiushkov, ed., *Pamiatniki russkoi stariny zapadnykh gubernii*, vyp. 5–6 (St. Petersburg: Tip. A. Transhelia, 1872).
37. As Anna Komzolova points out, Batiushkov was fired in 1869 in part due to his overly zealous russifying measures in local schools and churches, but he was essentially "kicked upstairs" to serve as a high official in the Ministry of Education in Petersburg. A. A. Komzolova, *Politika samoderzhaviia v Severo-Zapadnom krae v epokhu Velikikh reform* (Moscow: Nauka, 2005), 251–252, 362.
38. P. N. Batiushkov, *Belorussiia i Litva. Istoricheskie sud'by Severo-Zapadnogo kraia* (St. Petersburg: "Obshchestvennaia pol'za," 1890). It is worth noting that the book was published "s vysochaishago soizvoleniia . . . pri ministerstve vnutrennikh del," that is, with the support of the Ministry of Internal Affairs.
39. A. I. Milovidov, *K 50-letiiu russkoi Vil'ny* (Vil'na: "Russkii pochin," 1914).
40. "Slukh obo mne proidet po vsei Rusi velikoi / I nazovet menia vsiak sushchii v nei iazyk . . . / I doliu budu tem liubezen ia narodu, / Chto chuvstva dobrie ia liroi probuzhdal." See the description of the Pushkin monument in Vinogradov, *Putevoditel'*, 195–196.
41. A. A. Vinogradov, ed., *Kak sozdalsia v Vil'ne pamiatnik grafu M.N. Murav'evu* (Vil'na: Komitet po sooruzheniiu pamiatnika, 1898), 29–49.
42. A. T., "Zakladka pamiatnika v Vil'ne grafu Mikhailu Nikolaevichu Murav'evu," *Vilenskii Kalendar'—1898* (Vil'na: Tip. Vilenskogo Pravoslavnogo Sv.-Dukhov. Bratstva, 1897), 230–234.
43. Quoted in "Torzhestvo osviashcheniia i otkrytiia grafu M. N. Murav'eva v Vil'ne," *Vilenskii kalendar'—1899*, 332. In general on the opening of the monument: LVIA, f. 380, ap. 55, 1898, b. 692.
44. "Torzhestvo osviashcheniia i otkrytiia grafu M. N. Murav'eva v Vil'ne," *Vilenskii kalendar'—1899*, 287. For more on the Murav'ev monument, see Theodore R. Weeks, "Monuments and Memory: Immortalizing Count M. N. Muraviev in Vilna, 1898," *Nationalities Papers* 27, no. 4 (December 1999), 551–564.
45. For more detail, see Theodore R. Weeks, "Reconciliation or Treason: The Catherine Monument in Wilno/Vilna and Polish Society, 1904" in Andrzej Nowak, ed. *Ofiary imperium. Imperia jako ofiary. 44 spojrzenia. / Imperial Victims. Empires as Victims. 44 Views* (Warsaw: IPN / IH PAN, 2010), 283–295.
46. Batiushkov, *Belorussiia i Litva*, esp. 315–325.
47. Roman Jurkowski, "Edward Ropp jako biskup wileński 1903–1907 (w 50-tą rocznicę śmierci)," *Studia Teologiczne* 8 (1990), 232.
48. Szpoper, following *Głosy prasy polskiej* . . ., lists sixty names (Szpoper, *Sukcesorzy*, 11). Czesław Jankowski, however, mentions forty-nine names (*O uroczystości*, 51–52). To further complicate matters, *both* lists include the name of Hipolit Korwin-Milewski, who insists in his memoirs that he did *not* attend. In any case, references to the "sixty Polish nobles" who attended rapidly became the norm in press coverage of the event.
49. For images of the monument, see the above-cited *Niva* article, Szpoper, *Sukcesorzy*, 12, Jelena Karpowa, "Dziewiętnastowieczne pomniki na północno-zachodnich rubieżach Imperium Rosyjskiego. Idee, losy, artyści" in Dariusz Konstantynów and Piotr Paszkiewicz, *Kultura i polityka. Wpływ polityki rusyfikacyjnej na kulturę zachodnich rubieży Imperium Rosyjskiego (1772–1915)* (Warsaw: Instytut Sztuki PAN, 1994), 192; and *Vil'na v karmane* (Vil'na: Tip. Artel' Pechatnago Dela, 1912), 18.
50. St. Budrys and A. Budrienė, "Piešimo mokykla Vilniuje 1866–1915 metais" in *Iš lietuvių kultūros istorijos* (Vilnius: Valstybinė politinės ir mokslinės literatūros leidykla, 1959), 2:333–337.
51. Konstantynów and Paszkiewicz, *Kultura i polityka*; Inessa I. Svirida, *Mezhdu Peterburgom, Varshavoi i Vil'no. Khudozhnik v kul'turnom prostranstve XVIII–seredina XIX vv. Ocherki* (Moscow: O.G.I., 1999).
52. Medišauskienė, *Rusijos cenzūra Lietuvoje*, 204–216.
53. Teresa Nowak, "Firma wydawniczo-księgarska Zawadzkich w Wilnie w latach 1839–1865," *Księgarz* 24, no. 3 (1980), 47.
54. Figures cited in Jerzy Czarnecki (pseud. for Tadeusz Turkowski), *Wilno w dziejach książki polskiej* (Wilno: Józef Zawadzki, 1928), 23.

55. Andrzej Romanowski, *Pozytywizm na Litwie. Polskie życie kulturalne na ziemiach litewsko-białorusko-inflanckich w latach 1864-1904* (Kraków: Universitas, 2003), 148-164.

56. On Orzeszkowa as a "cultural institution" in this region, see Kwiryna Handke, "Eliza Orzeszkowa jako kresowa instytucja narodowa i kulturalna" in Feliksiak-1996, 2:101-124.

57. Ibid., 165-171.

58. Stefan Rosiak, *Księgarnia 'E. Orzeszkowa i S-ka' w Wilnie 1879-1882* (Wilno: Wydawnictwo magistratu m. Wilna, 1938), 18-19, 28-29.

59. On methods of getting Polish books to Wilno (amusingly, the books were often published in Petersburg), see Zygmunt Nagrodzki, *Ze wspomnień oświatowca* (Wilno: "Kurjer Wileński," 1929).

60. Stefania Walasek, *Polska oświata w gubernii wileńskiej w latach 1864-1915* (Kraków: "Impuls," 2003), 75-101; Leszek Zasztowt, "Nielegalne szkoły w Wileńskim Okręgu Naukowym w latach siedemdziesiątych XIX wieku," *Rozprawy z dziejów oświaty* 37 (1996); Ignacy Myślicki "Zarys historii walk o oświatę polską w Wileńszczyźnie i Mińszczyźnie" in Bogdan Nawroczyński, ed., *Nasza walka o szkołę polską* (Warsaw: Wydawnictwo Komitetu obchodu 25-lecia walki o szkołę polską, 1934), 327-355; Ludwika Życka, *Krótki rys dziejów tajnej oświaty polskiej na Ziemi Wileńskiej od 1880 do 1919* (Wilno: Lux, 1932).

61. Ludwik Czarkowski, *Wilno w latach 1867-1875 (z wspomnień osobistych)* (Wilno: "Pogoń," 1929), 39-43.

62. I will cite just one of the long files on "secret schools" in Vilnius and the province: LVIA, f. 378, PS 1893, b. 17.

63. For a chatty but informative memoir of Polish culture in Vilnius in the late tsarist period, see Mieczysław Jałowiecki, *Dawne Wilno i ludzie zapomniani* (London: Wydawnictwo Klubu Londyńskiego Społeczności Akademickiej Uniwersytetu Stefana Batorego, 1955).

64. On this figure and his description of Vilnius in 1878, see Tadeusz Bujnicki, "Oczyma Galicjanina. Mickiewiczowskie i realne Wilno Stanisława Tarnowskiego" in Bujnicki, *Szkice Wileńskie. Rozprawy i eseje* (Kraków: Collegium Columbinum, 2002), 27-50.

65. The mass would, of course, have been in Latin. However, hymns, prayers, homilies, and the like (so-called supplemental service) could be pronounced in local languages such as Polish or Lithuanian.

66. Stanisław Tarnowski, *Z Wilna* (Kraków: "Czas," 1879), quotations from 16, 43, 60.

67. "German Street," translated into Lithuanian, becomes today's Vokiečių. However, as we will see, that street bears little resemblance to the prewar *Daytshe gos* and not just because of the dearth of Jews there.

68. N. Zinov'ev, *Vil'na, po perepisi Aprelia 1875 goda* (Vil'na: Tipografiia A. G. Syrkina, 1881), 30.

69. According to the 1875 census, 3134 Jews worked in fields requiring physical labor ("fizicheskii trud") while there were 5491 Catholics in that category: Zinov'ev, *Vil'na . . . 1875*, 44.

70. Ibid., 45.

71. Ibid., 55. According to Zinov'ev, sixty of the prostitutes were Jewish, ten Orthodox, and forty-three Catholic.

72. LVIA, f. 383, ap. 1, b. 402 (1903). To be sure, this impression (of the frequency of Jewish madams) could be mistaken as I have not done thorough research on the topic. And, it should be noted, a certain Shtabs-Kapitan Vasilii Vasiliev is also mentioned in this large file (ll. 96-97) as the proprietor of a "public house" on Bol'shaia Pogulianka.

73. Sch. Gorelik, "Wilna vor 40 Jahren," *Jüdische Rundschau*, no. 45/46 (June 13, 1929), 289-290.

74. Mojżesz Heller, "Wilno jako ośrodek żydowskiego życia kulturalnego" in *Wilno i ziemia wileńska. Zarys monograficzny* (Wilno: Wydawnictwo wojewódzkiego komitetu regjonalnego, 1930), 263; and Israel Klausner [Kloizner], *Vilnah, Yerushalayim de-Lita. Dorot rishonim, 1495-1881* (Tel Aviv: Bet lohame ha-geta'ot, 1988), 330-346.

75. Hirsz Abramowicz, *Profiles of a Lost World: Memoirs of East European Jewish Life before World War II*, trans. Eva Zeitlin Dobkin (Detroit: Wayne State University Press, 1999), 117-125. Here Abramowicz describes Joshua Steinberg, *maskil*, government censor, graduate of the Rabbinical

School, and later teacher there; and Samuel Gozhanski, later a founder of the Bund who ironically called Abramowicz to task for speaking Yiddish.

76. Zinov'ev, *Vil'na*, 33. The exact statistics were 21.4% literate, 5.0% *polugramotnyi* or "half-literate" among Jews; 37.7% and 7.3% among Catholics; and 66.4% and 5.3% among Orthodox.

77. On the *heder* in the East European context, see Shaul Stampfer, "*Heder* Study, Knowledge of Torah, and the Maintenance of Social Stratification in Traditional East European Jewish Society," *Studies in Jewish Education* 3 (1988), 271–289.

78. Leyzer Ran, *Jerusalem of Lithuania* (New York: Laureate Press, 1976), 2: 283.

79. Zinov'ev, *Vil'na*, 50.

80. O. N. Shteinberg, "Graf M. N. Murav'ev i ego otnosheniia k evreiam g. Vil'ny v 1863–1864 gg. (Iz zapisok ravvina)," *Russkaia starina* 3, no. 2 (February 1901), 305–319.

81. Russian State Historical Archive (St. Petersburg; RGIA), f. 1284, op. 70, 1882, d. 176, l. 11.

82. John Doyle Klier, *Russians, Jews, and the Pogroms of 1881–1882* (Cambridge: Cambridge University Press, 2011); Jonathan Dekel-Chen, David Gaunt, Natan M. Meir, Israel Bartal, eds., *Anti-Jewish Violence: Rethinking the Pogrom in East European History* (Bloomington: Indiana University Press, 2011).

83. Lietuvos Valstybinis Istorijos Archyvas, Vilnius (LVIA), f. 378, PS 1881, b. 52, ll. 10–13.

84. It does need to be noted that Totleben's colleague in Kiev, A. R. Drentel'n, while personally antisemitic, also attempted to prevent attacks on Jews. Why exactly Drentel'n was unsuccessful in preventing pogroms while Totleben had better luck has not yet been satisfactorily explained. On Drentel'n and the situation in Kiev, see Michael F. Hamm, *Kiev: A Portrait, 1800–1917* (Princeton: Princeton University Press, 1993), 123–126.

85. For a small map showing the layout of the main synagogue's courtyard, see YdL, 1:105.

86. Dr. J. Rülf. *Drei Tage in Jüdisch-Russland. Ein Cultur- und Sittenbild* (Frankfurt a/M: Verlag von J. Kauffmann, 1882), 4–6.

87. Ibid., 26–43.

88. A. P. Subbotin, *V cherte evreiskoi osedlosti. Otyvki iz ekonomicheskikh issledovanii v zapadnoi i iugo-zapadnoi Rossii za leto 1887 g.* (St. Petersburg: Izdanie red. "Ekonomicheskago zhurnala," 1888), 1:57, 70–71, 82.

89. Ibid., 1:61, 85–90.

90. Ibid., 1:63–64.

91. Ibid., 1:58. It is difficult to say just how many Vilnius Jews actually knew Russian but figures from a generation later (1911) show that more than half of the books taken from the OPE (Organization for the Spread of Enlightenment) society library were in Russian. Jeffrey Veidlinger, *Jewish Public Culture in the Late Russian Empire* (Bloomington: Indiana University Press, 2009), 81.

92. Henri Minczeles, *Vilna, Wilno, Vilnius. La Jérusalem de Lituanie* (Paris: Editions la découverte, 1993), 92–93; Gottfried Schramm, "Wilna und die Entstehung eines ostjüdischen Sozialismus 1870–1900" in Shulamit Volkov, ed., *Deutsche Juden und die Moderne* (Munich: R. Oldenbourg, 1994), 129–140.

93. LVIA, f. 378, PS 1875, b. 193; Pinchas Kon, "Razgrom pervogo evreiskogo revoliutsionnogo kruzhka v Vil'ne v 1875 g. (Po materialam arkhiva byv. Vilenskogo Gub. Zhand. Upravleniia)," *Evreiskii vestnik* 1 (1928), 143–154.

94. LVIA, f. 446, a1, b. 249.

95. Minczeles, *Vilna*, 99–100. For a more personal account, see Abramowicz, *Profiles*, 132–142. Lekert's assassination attempt occurred on May 6, 1902 (old style); he was hung on May 28.

96. RGIA, f. 1284, op. 194, 1904, d. 52, l. 5.

97. Minczeles, *Vilna*, 97–98; Pinchas Kon, *Geheimberichte über Herzls Besuch in Wilno im Jahre 1903* (Vienna, 1928).

98. RGIA, f. 1284, op. 190, 1903, d. 101, l. 1.

99. Pahlen blamed Jewish interest in radical politics and Zionism on economic misery. Israel Klausner [Kloizner], *Vilnah, Yerushalayim de-Lita. Dorot aharonim, 1881–1939* (Tel Aviv: Bet Lohame ha-geta'ot, 1983), 67–69.

100. This is the only presently functioning synagogue in Vilnius, the so-called Choral Synagogue, known in Hebrew as "Taharat ha-Kodesh." G. Agranovskii and I. Guzenberg, *Litovskii Ierusalim. Kratkii putevoditel' po pamiatnym mestam evreiskoi istorii i kul'tury v Vil'niuse* (Vilnius: Lituanus, 1992), 35.

101. For the fascinating autobiography of one such Jew, born near Vilna in 1860, see Abraham Cahan, *The Education of Abraham Cahan* (Philadelphia: Jewish Publication Society of America, 1969).

102. Laimonas Briedis, *Vilnius: City of Strangers* (Vilnius: Baltos Lankos, 2008), 125–160.

103. Flavian Nikolaevich Dobrianskii, *Staraia i novaia Vil'na*, 3rd ed. (Vil'na: A. G. Syrkin, 1904), 10.

104. Ibid., 76.

105. Along similar lines, see A. Murav'ev, *Vilna russe* (Vilna: n.p., 1865); A. A. Vinogradov, *Putevoditel' po gorodu Vil'ny i ego okrestnostiiam* (Vil'na: Tip. Shtaba Vilenskago voennago Okruga, 1908); and *Vil'na v karmane* (Vil'na: Izd. M. Tassel'krauta, 1912).

106. On this important figure, see Michał Brensztejn, *Adam-Honor Kirkor, wydawca, redaktor i właściciel drukarni w Wilnie od roku 1834 do 1867* (Wilno: Wydawnictwo Towarzystwa pomocy naukowej im. E. i E. Wróblewskich, 1930).

107. Adam-Honory Kirkor, *Przewodnik historyczny po Wilnie i jego okolicach* (Wilno: J. Zawadzki, 1880), 39. David Frick (personal communication) notes that Kirkor is not quite accurate: "[Jews] were supposed to live primarily above German Street, in a triangle formed by Jewish Street, Meat Shop Street, and a few houses on German Street, plus a few more houses below German Street on St. Nicholas Street."

108. Kirkor, *Przewodnik historyczny*, 11–65.

109. Ibid., 102–181 (Catholic churches), 181–188 ("non-existent" Catholic churches), 188–199 (Orthodox churches and monasteries), 199–201 (Protestant churches).

110. Gizbert Studnicki, *Wilno. Przewodnik ilustrowany*, 9.

111. Wacław Gizbert-Studnicki, *Wilno. Przewodnik ilustrowany po mieście i okolicy* (Wilno: A. Żukowski i W. Borkowicz, 1910), 8–15.

112. Wacław Gizbert-Studnicki, *Wilno. Przewodnik ilustrowany po mieście i okolicy* (Wilno: A. Żukowski i W. Borkowicz, 1910), 27.

113. There was an elected town council in the city, but very few could vote, and even of those wealthy men with the right to elect this council, few were interested.

114. Grigori Aronson et al., *Di geshikhte fun Bund* (New York: Farlag Unzer tsayt, 1960), 2:176. Vilnius governor Pahlen's report to the governor general of Vilnius, dated February 12, 1905, in Iu. I. Zhiugzhda [Juozas Žiugžda] et al., eds., *Revoliutsiia 1905-1907 gg. v Litve. Dokumenty i materialy* (Vil'nius: Gos. Izd. Polit. i nauchnoi literatury, 1961), 94. For the original document, see LVIA, f. 378, PS-1905, b. 2, ll. 37–38.

115. E. V. Grishkunaite [Griškūnaitė], "Zabastovki rabochikh Litvy v ianvare 1905 g." *Lietuvos TSR Mokslų Akademijos darbai, serija A*, no. 2/11 (1961), 171–173.

116. LVIA, f. 378, PS-1905, b. 2, l. 39.

117. *Vilniaus Žinios* 1, no. 12 (January 15/28, 1905), 1.

118. LSDP manifesto of January 25, 1905, first published in *Darbininkų balsas*, 1905, 41–48, cited in Kipras Bielinis, *Penktieji metai. Revoliciuno sąjūdžio slinktis ir padariniai* (New York: Amerikos Lietuvių Socialdemokratų sąjunga, 1959), 45–46. See also Leonas Sabaliunas, *Lithuanian Social Democracy in Perspective 1893–1914* (Durham: Duke University Press, 1990), 48–49.

119. Juozas Jurginis, *1905 metų revoliucijos įvykiai Vilniuje* (Vilnius: Politinės ir Mokslinės Literatūros Leidykla, 1958), 26–29.

120. On 1905 in Russian Poland, see Robert Blobaum, *Rewolucja. Russian Poland 1904–1907* (Ithaca, NY: Cornell University Press, 1995).

121. For official reports and correspondence about the spread of illegal brochures and other propaganda, see LVIA, f. 419, ap. 1, b. 42 (1905–1906).

122. Flyer of Vilnius group of RSDRP, February 19, 1905, reprinted in Zhiugzhda, *Revoliutsiia*, 103–104.

123. Pahlen letter to Vilnius governor general Freze, March 23, 1905 in Zhiugzhda, *Revoliutsiia*, 108–110; original document: LVIA, f. 378, PS-1905, b. 25, ll. 4–6.
124. Zhiugzhda, *Revoliutsiia*, 112–114.
125. Jurginis, *1905*, 40–44.
126. Abraham Ascher, *The Revolution of 1905* (Stanford: Stanford University Press, 1988), 1:211–242.
127. See the account in Sidney Harcave, trans. and ed., *The Memoirs of Count Witte* (Armonk, NY: M. E. Sharpe, 1990), 479–491. For a copy of the actual manifesto, see *Sobranie uzakonenii i rasporiazhenii pravitel'stva*, no. 190, otdel pervyi (October 17, 1905). "Vysochaishii Manifest. 1658. Ob usovershenstvovaniia Gosudarstvennogo poriadka."
128. B. Glik, "Pod"em revoliutsionnogo dvizheniia v Litve osen'iu 1905 g.," *Lietuvos TSR aukštųjų mokyklų mokslo darbai, Istorija* 3 (1961), 115–146.
129. For an overview of the period October–November 1905 in Vilnius, see VMIS, 326–330; and Jurginis, *1905*, 60–146.
130. M. I. Vasilevskaja-Žebrovskaja, "Visuotinis geležinkelininkų streikas Vilniuje" in *Komunistas*, no. 12 (December 1955), 25–26. See also in the same issue the memoirs of Jefimas Černuchinas, "Rūsčiaisiais 1905 metais," 30–33.
131. *Vilniaus Žinios*, no. 249 (October 13/27, 1905), 1; no. 250 (October 25/November 7, 1905), 1.
132. Document no. 183 in Zhiugzhda, *Revoliutsiia*, 177.
133. Bielinis, *Penktieji metai*, 147–8.
134. Emilija Griškūnaitė, *Darbininkų judėjimas Lietuvoje 1895–1914* (Vilnius: Mintis, 1971), 164–165; Report of Colonel Fediai to Nicholas II (October 17, 1905) in Zhiugzhda, *Revoliutsiia*, 179–180.
135. Telegram of Rotmistr Shebeko to the Department of Police in St. Petersburg (October 18, 1905), in Zhiugzhda, *Revoliutsiia*, 180.
136. Resolution of commission of representatives of political parties, unions, and aldermen (*glasnye*) of the Vilnius City Duma (October 20, 1905), published in *Severo-Zapadnoe slovo*, no. 2424 (October 23, 1905).
137. *Severo-Zapadnoe slovo*, no. 2427 (October 27, 1905).
138. Ibid., no. 2426 (October 26, 1905), in Zhiugzhda, *Revoliutsiia*, 186–187.
139. For example, the Vilnius group of the Russian SD issued a flyer on November 19 calling on all secondary school students of the city to join in the revolutionary struggle. Reprinted in Zhiugzhda, *Revoliutsiia*, 209–210.
140. Jurginis, *1905*, 40–41, 83–88.
141. Bielinis, *Pienktieji metai*, 181–202.
142. "Zajścia w Wilnie," *Kraj*, no. 43, 44, 45 (November 24/11, 1905), 33.
143. For appeals by middle- and upper-class persons for the government to protect them and their property, see LVIA f. 378, PS 1905, b. 73.
144. "Krwawe hasła," *Kraj*, rok 24, no. 1 (July 14, 1905), 3–6.
145. On the Moscow uprising and its suppression, see Laura Engelstein, *Moscow 1905: Working-Class Organization and Political Conflict* (Stanford: Stanford University Press, 1982); and Ascher, *Revolution*, 1:304–336.
146. *Vilniaus Žinios*, no. 290 (December 20, 1905/January 2, 1906), 1.
147. Report of Colonel Isarlov to Nicholas II about the events of December 13, 1905, in Zhiugzhda, *Revoliutsiia*, 223.
148. See the flyers issued on December 15 by the unified Vilnius RSDPRP and Bund (ibid., 226–227) and by the SDPL and PPS (ibid., 227–228).
149. The rise of the Lithuanian national movement is well documented in Lithuanian and Polish historiography, but unfortunately much less so in English. For a contemporary sympathetic source, see Michał Römer, *Litwa. Studium o odrozeniu narodu litewskiego* (Lwów: Polsk. Tow. Naukowe, 1908). In English, see Tomas Balkelis, *The Making of Modern Lithuania* (New York: Routledge, 2009), which also provides a good bibliography.

150. The conflict between Lithuanian and Polish priests and parishes is vividly reflected in *Vilniaus vyskupijos lietuvių katalikų butis ir panpolonistų išdykimas*. *Lietuvių kunigų memorialas/Die Lage der katholischen Litauer im Bistum Wilna und die Ausschreitungen des Panpolonismus. Denkschrift des katholischen Klerus Litauens* (Tilžė: "Lithuania," 1913).

151. Piotr Łossowski, "Litewski ruch narodowy w polskiej myśli politycznej (1883–1914)" in *Polska myśli polityczna XIX ir XX wieku* (Wrocław: Ossolineum, 1975), 1:119–157.

152. For an overview of the early Lithuanian national movement, see Egidijus Aleksandravičius, "Political Goals of Lithuanians, 1863–1918," *Journal of Baltic Studies* 23, no. 3 (1992), 227–238; and Jerzy Ochmański, *Litewski ruch narodowo-kulturalny w XIX wieku* (Białystok: PWN, 1965).

153. On definitions of "Lithuanian" and "Lithuania" in this period, see Egidijas Aleksandravičius, "Kas buvo Lietuva ir lietuviai XIX amžiuje?" in Aleksandravičius, *XIX a. profiliai* (Vilnius: Lietuvos rašytojų sąjungos leidykla, 1993), 133–136.

154. Alma Lapinskienė, "Vilniaus Žinios—pirmasis lietuvių dienraštis" in Donata Linčiuvienė, ed., *Vilniaus kultūrinis gyvenimas ir Petras Vileišis* (Vilnius: Lietuvių literatūros ir tautosakos institutas, 2001), 20–27.

155. Egidijus Motieka, *Didysis Vilniaus seimas* (Vilnius: Saulabolis, 1996).

156. Jonas Basanavičius (J. S-lius, pseud.), *Iš didžiojo Vilniaus Seimo istorijos* (Vilnius: "Ruch," 1925), 3.

157. Dr. J. Basanavičius, "Atsišaukimas į Lietuvių tautą," *Vilniaus Žinios* 1, no. 254 (October 29/November 11, 1905), 1.

158. Basanavičius, *Iš didžiojo Vilniaus Seimo istorijos*, 12–13.

159. "Pirmojo Lietuvių Tautos Atstovų susivažiavimo nutarimai," *Vilniaus Žinios* 1, no. 276 (November 24/December 7, 1905), 1–2.

160. Basanavičius, *Iš didžiojo Vilniaus Seimo istorijos*, 19–21. A translation of these decisions can be found in Jonas Dainauskas, "Prelude to Independence: The Great Conference of Vilnius, 1905" *Lituanus* 11, no. 4 (Winter 1965), 56–57.

161. Jadvyga Kazlauskaitė, *Vilniaus periodiniai leidiniai 1760–1918* (Vilnius: Mintis, 1981), 96.

162. Edvardas Vidmantas, *Lietuvos darbininkų periodinė spauda 1895–1917* (Vilnius: Mintis, 1979), 45–59; and Emilija Griškunaitė, "Legali darbininkų spauda Lietuvoje 1906–1908 m. ('Naujoji gaudynė', 'Skardas', 'Žarija')" in Juozas Jurginis et al., eds., *Spauda ir spaustuvės (Iš lietuvių kultūros istorijos* 7) (Vilnius: Mintis, 1972), 111–141.

163. For a list of these periodicals (and also of Lithuanian clubs and organizations), see *Lietuvos ukininko Vilniaus kalendorius devinti 1914 metai* (Vilnius: Spaustuvė J. Zavadzkio, 1913), 131–132.

164. See, for example, the documents on such "arrests" of newspapers and journals in this period in LVIA, f. 378, BS 1908, b. 318; and f. 601, ap. 1, b. 1.

165. Compare, for example, the general inability of Polish newspapers in the city—which had a far greater potential readership—to achieve solvency. See the memoirs of Czesław Jankowski (editor and publisher of the conservative *Kurjer Litewski*), *W ciągu dwóch lat. Przyczynek do dziejów prasy polskiej na Litwie* (Warsaw: Nakł. Autora, 1908); and Roman Jurkowski, "'Gazeta Wileńska' i 'Głos Kijowski' (Z dziejów polskiej prasy radykalno-liberalnej na Litwie i Ukrainie w 1906 roku)" *Kwartalnik Historii Prasy Polskiej* 26, no. 4 (1987), 59–84.

166. Anelė Butkuvienė, "Lietuviška spauda" in VMIS, 390–393.

167. In general on the cultural developments of this decade, see Matas Šalčius, *Dešimt metų tautiniai-kulturinio darbo Lietuvoje 1905–1915* (Chicago: Spauda "Lietuvos," 1915); and M. Biržyszka (Mykolas Biržiška), *Skrót dziejów Piśmiennictwa Litewskiego* (Wilno: "Głos Litwy," 1919), esp. 63–66. This process is also emphasized—perhaps overly so—in Zigmas Zinkevičius, *Lietuvos sostinė 1904–1939. Visuomeninė ir kultūrinė veikla Vilniuje, paroda 1994.10.20–1995.02.17* (Vilnius: Lietuvos nacionalinis muziejus, 1994).

168. Vladas Žukas, *Marijos ir Jurgio Šlapelių lietuvių knygynas Vilniuje* (Vilnius: Mokslo ir enciklopedijų leidybos institutas, 2000); Julius Butėnas, *Lietuvių teatras Vilniuje 1900–1918* (Kaunas: Spaudos fondas, 1940); Laima Laučkaitė, *Vilniaus dailė XX amžiaus pradžioje* (Vilnius: Baltos Lankos, 2002); Laima Laučkaitė, ed., *Vilniaus dailės draugija, 1908–1915. Parodos katalogas* (Vilnius: Sapnų sala, 1999).

169. Insight into the activities of the city Duma may be gained from perusing *Zhurnaly Vilenskoi gorodskoi Dumy*, which was published from 1910 to 1913, covering the period 1907-1912.
170. Napoleonas Dūdas, "Vilniaus miesto transportas. Nuo vežimų iki taip ir nejrengto tramvajaus" in VMIS, 360-362; Čaplinskas-2010, 341-346. In 1912 the city collected 1053 rubles from automobile registrations—but 4651 from the tax on pet dogs. *Otchet goroda Vil'na za 1912 g.* (Vilnius: "Promen", 1913), 10-11.
171. Čaplinskas-2010, 358-360.
172. A. V. Tupal'skii, *K voprosu o blagoustroistve goroda Vil'no. Doklad vilenskoi gorodskoi dume chlena upravy A.V. Tupal'skogo* (Wilno: Tip. "Promen," 1913).
173. On Lithuanian politics in the Duma period, see Steponas Kairys, *Tau, Lietuva* (Boston: Lietuvių enciklopedijos Sp., 1964), 207-212; *Vilniaus kalendorius* (Brooklyn: n.p., 1909), 13-15 lists Lithuanian representatives in the 4th Duma as Andrius Bulota, Pranys Keinis, Ignotas Požela, Pranys Kužma.
174. On Jewish participation in the four Dumas, see Vladimir Levin, "Hapolitika hayehudit beimperiah harusit beidan hariaktsiia" (Ph.D. diss., Hebrew University of Jerusalem, 2007), in Hebrew with English summary.
175. Dariusz Szpoper, *Sukcesorzy Wielkiego Księstwa. Myśl polityczna ir działalność polityczna konserwatywistów polskich na ziemiach litewsko-białoruskich w latach 1904-1939* (Gdańsk: Arche, 1999). On two specific conservative brothers from the region, see Theodore R. Weeks, "Political and National Survival in the Late Russian Empire: The Case of the Korwin-Milewski Brothers," *East European Quarterly* 33, no. 3 (September 1999), 347 369.
176. Walerian Meysztowicz, *Gawędy o czasach i ludziach* (London: Nakładem Polskiej Fundacji Kulturalnej, 1973), 2:236-240; Roman Jurkowski, "Edward Ropp jako biskup wileński," 1903-1907 (w 50-tą rocznicę śmierci)," *Studia Teologiczne* 8 (1990), 205-280; Jurkowski, "Stronnictwo Konstytucyjno-Katolickie na Litwie ir Białorusi w 1906 r. (Szkic do dziejów)," *Acta Baltico-Slavica* 18 (1996), 93-118.
177. But for an overview of parties and politics, see Jan Jurkiewicz, *Rozwój polskiej myśli politycznej na Litwie ir Białorusi w latach 1905-1922* (Poznań: Wydaw. Nauk. UAM, 1983).
178. Jan Sawicki, "'Przegląd Wileński' w latach 1911-1915," *Zapiski Historyczne* 59, no. 4 (1994), 41-56; Roman Jurkowski, "'Gazeta Wileńska' i 'Głos Kijowski' (Z dziejów polskiej prasy radykalno-liberalnej na Litwie i Ukrainie w 1906 roku," *Kwartalnik Historii Prasy Polskiej* 26, no. 4 (1987), 59-84.
179. Czesław Jankowski, *W ciągu dwóch lat. Przyczynek do dziejów prasy polskiej na Litwie* (Warsaw: Nakład autora, 1908); Roman Jurkowski, "Czesław Jankowski jako dziennikarz," *Kwartalnik Historii Prasy Polskiej* 23, no. 3 (1984), 15-51; Irena Fedorowicz, *W służbie ziemie ojczystej. Czesław Jankowski w życiu kulturalnym Wilna lat 1905-1929* (Kraków: Collegium Columbinum, 2005).
180. Leszek Zasztowt, "Wileńscy miłośnicy 'starożytności' w latach 1899-1914," *Kwartalnik Historii Nauki i Techniki* 30, no. 2-3 (1990), 259-283; Roman Jurkowski, "Życie kulturalne Wilna w latach 1899-1914," *Zapiski Historyczne* 55, no. 1 (1990), 59-88.
181. Helena Romer-Ocheńkowska, *Dwudziestopięciolecie wskrzeszonego Teatru Polskiego w Wilnie* (Wilno: Nakładem Komitetu Obchodu, 1932); Fedorowicz, *W służbie ziemie ojczystej*, 72-82.
182. Irena Fedorowicz, "W hołdzie Mickiewicza. O projektach uczczenia w Wilnie 50. rocznicy śmierci Adama Mickiewicza (na podstawie publikacji 'Kuriera Litewskiego' 1905-1906)" in Katarzyna R. Łozowska and Ewa Tierling, eds., *Literackie Kresy i bezkresy. Księga ofiarowana profesorowi Bolesławowi Hadaczkowi* (Szczecin: Wydawnictwo US, 2000), 49-62.
183. Andrzej Romanowski, Roman Włodek, "Kino pradžia Vilniuje (iki 1915 m.)," *Naujoji Romuva*, no. 2/522 (1998), 60-64; Andrzej Romanowski, *Młoda Polska Wileńska* (Kraków: Universitas, 1999), 336-343. In general, Romanowski's book is the best guide to Polish culture in Vilnius in the 1905-1914 period.
184. On multicultural life in Vilnius after 1905, see the documents and readings in VMIS, 453-472; and VMID, 301-312. On Jewish press in these years, see Susanne Marten-Finnis, *Vilna as a Centre of the Modern Jewish Press, 1840-1926* (Oxford: Peter Lang, 2004).

185. Theodore R. Weeks, *From Assimilation to Antisemitism: The "Jewish Question" in Poland, 1850-1914* (DeKalb: Northern Illinois University Press, 2006), 129-169.
186. Edvardas Vidmantas, *Religinis tautinis sąjūdis Lietuvoje XIX a. antrojoje pusėje-XX a. pradžioje* (Vilnius: Katalikų akademija, 1995), 158-169.
187. On Polish-Lithuanian relations before World War I, see the texts collected (in Polish or in Polish translation) in Marian Zaczyński and Beata Kalęba, eds., *W kręgu sporów polsko-litewskich na przełomie XIX i XX wieku. Wybór materiałów*, 3 vols. (Kraków: Wydawnictwo Uniwersytetu Jagiellońskiego, 2004, 2009, 2011); and the essays in Ryšardas Gaidis and Jaroslav Volknovski, eds., *Lietuvių-lenkų santykiai amžių tėkmėje. Istorinė atmintis—Stosunki polsko-litewskie na przestrzeni wieków. Pamięć historyczna. Straipsnių rinkinys* (Vilnius: Vilniaus universiteto leidykla, 2009), esp. 103-178.
188. The literature on the *krajowcy* is fairly extensive (in Polish), but there is a crying need for a synthesizing volume on the movement. Meanwhile, see Jan Jurkiewicz, "Demokraci Wileńscy w latach 1905-1914 (Zarys działalności ir myśli politycznej)," *Acta Baltico-Slavica* 15 (1983), 157-173; Rimantas Miknys, "Stosunki polsko-litewskie w wizji politycznej krajowców," *Zeszyty Historyczne*, tom 104 (1993), 123-129; Dariusz Szpoper, "Stronnictwo Krajowe Litwy i Białej Rusi. Przyczynek do dziejów 'koncepcji krajowej' w polskiej myśli konserwatywnej," *Myśl Konserwatywna* (1997), 53-69; Darius Staliūnas, "Grazhdanin Velikogo Kniazhestva Litovskogo," *Vil'nius*, no. 2/141 (1995), 122-143 (about Tadeusz Wróblewski); Jan Sawicki, "'Krajowość'—idea czy metoda (Z dziejów polskiej myśli politycznej na Litwie i Białorusi)," *Lithuania*, no. 1/6 (1992), 279-282; Jan Jurkiewicz, *Krajowość—tradycje zgody narodów w dobie nacjonalizmu. Materiały z międzynarodowej konferencji naukowej* (Poznań: Instytut Historii UAM, 1999); Jan Sawicki, "Od dwuszczeblowości do dwoistości litewsko-polskiej. Świadomość narodowa Michała Römera" in Feliksiak 1996, 1:127-138.
189. The humane political-cultural ideas of *krajowość* and these individuals deserve a fresh look. Two interesting recent studies make a start: Zbigniew Solak, *Między Polską i Litwą. Życie i działalność Michała Römera 1880-1920* (Kraków: Arcana, 2004); Darius Szpoper, *Gente lithuana, natione lithuana. Myśl polityczna i działalność Konstancji Skirmuntt (1851-1934)* (Sopot: Arche, 2009).

## Notes to Chapter 4

1. The Russians did, of course, occupy Galicia for a significant period of time: Mark Von Hagen, *War in a European Borderland: Occupations and Occupation Plans in Galicia and Ukraine, 1914-1918* (Seattle: University of Washington Press, 2007).
2. Despite a number of excellent new monographs covering World War I and the Eastern Front, we still lack an up-to-date synthetic work on the topic. Meanwhile, see the still useful Norman Stone, *The Eastern Front, 1914-1917* (New York: Scribner, 1975).
3. Andrzej Chwalba, *Samobójstwo Europy. Wielka wojna 1914-1918* (Kraków: Wydawnictwo Literackie, 2014), 190-194.
4. Karen Petrone, *The Great War in Russian Memory* (Bloomington: Indiana University Press, 2011); Katja Bruisch and Nikolaus Katzer, eds., *Bol'shaia voina Rossii. Sotsial'nyi poriadok, publichnaia kommunikatsiia i nasilie na rubezhe tsarskoi i sovetskoi epokh* (Moscow: Novoe literaturnoe obozrenie, 2014).
5. See, for example, Pranas Čepėnas, *Naujųjų laikų Lietuvos istorija* (Vilnius: Lituanus, 1992), 2:25ff.
6. Petras Klimas, *Dienoraštis 1915-1919* (Chicago: AM & M Publications, 1988).
7. Hubertus F. Jahn, *Patriotic Culture in Russia during World War I* (Ithaca: Cornell University Press, 1995).
8. Wiktor Sukiennicki, *East Central Europe during World War I: From Foreign Domination to National Independence* (Boulder: East European Monographs, 1984), 100-111.
9. Stanisław Cywiński, *Kartki z pamiętnika (1914-1920)* (Wilno: Odbitka z "Dziennika Wileńskiego," 1931), 10-12.

10. Wanda Dobaczewska, *Wilno i Wileńszczyzna w latach 1914–1920* (Wilno: Dziennik Urzędowy Kuratorjum Okr. Szk. Wileńskiego, 1934), 12.

11. On these forcible evictions by the Russian military of thousands of Jewish civilians from their homes near the front lines, see Peter Gatrell, *A Whole Empire Walking: Refugees in Russia during World War I* (Bloomington: Indiana University Press, 1999), esp. 16–23. In general on the tragic position of East-European Jews during World War I, see Frank Schuster, *Zwischen allen Fronten. Osteuropäische Juden während des Ersten Weltkrieges (1914–1919)* (Cologne: Böhlau, 2004).

12. "Poufny memoriał Michała Römera z sierpnia 1915" edited and published by Wiktor Sukiennicki under the title "Wilno na schyłku rządów carskich," *Zeszyty Historyczne* (1970), 119.

13. Semion Goldin, "Deportation of Jews by the Russian Military Command, 1914–1915," *Jews in Eastern Europe* 41, no. 1 (2000), 40–73.

14. Czesław Jankowski, *Z dnia na dzień. Warszawa 1914–1915 Wilno* (Wilno: Wydawnictwo Kazimierza Rutskiego, 1923), 20–68.

15. Petras Ruseckas, ed., *Lietuva Didžiajame Kare* (Wilno: Wydawnictwo "Vilniaus Žodis," 1939), 12; Cywiński, *Kartki z pamiętnika*, 19 (entry for August 12–15): "Zdjęto w Wilnie pomniki Katarzyny ir Puszkina. Murawjew stoi jeszcze. Ach, żeby Moskali stąd wyszli I nigdy już nie wrócili!"

16. "Wilnas Leidenzeit im Krieg" in *Das Litauen-Buch. Eine Auslese aus der Zeitung der 10. Armee* (N.p. [Wilna]: Druck und Verlag Zeitung der 10. Armee, 1918), 116–117. This account ends with the German entry into the city; unfortunately Vilnius' sufferings were far from over at that point. On the military operations from the German point of view, see Erich von Ludendorff, *Ludendorff's Own Story* (New York: Harper & Brothers, 1919), 1:197–202.

17. Hirsz Abramowicz, *Profiles of a Lost World: Memoirs of East European Jewish Life before World War II* (Detroit: Wayne State University Press, 1999), 177–178.

18. Peliksas Bugailiškis's diary in Klimas, *Dienoraštis*, 18–25.

19. Wanda Dobaczewska, "Nastroje Wileńskie w latach wojny" in Stefan Burhardt, *P.O.W. na ziemiach W.X. Litewskiego 1919–1934. Szkice i wspomnienia* (Wilno: Wydawn. Wileńsko-Nowogródzkiego okręgu związku peowiaków, 1934), 16.

20. Jankowski, *Z dnia na dzień*, 235–237.

21. Graf Pfeil's announcement "An die Einwohnerschaft von Wilno!" (German version) in Stefan Glaser, *Okupacja niemiecka na Litwie w latach 1915–1918. Stosunki prawne* (Lwów: Wydawnictwo Wschód, 1929), 159–160.

22. Abramowicz, *Profiles*, 180–181.

23. Lietuvos Mokslo Akademijos Biblioteka, Rankraščių skyrius (Lithuanian Academy of Sciences Library, Manuscript Division, Vilnius; LMAB), f. 23–23, l. 9. The German text is much more expressive: "Den Frauenzimmern wird es verboten, sich deutschen Soldaten feil zu bieten." (The admonition appeared also in Polish and Lithuanian, along with the warning that those [presumably prostitutes] with venereal disease would be arrested.)

24. Ibid., ll. 10–25.

25. Ludendorff, *Ludendorff's Own Story*, 1:221–222.

26. An excellent account of Polish Wilno in the first months of the German occupation is Andrzej Pukszto, "Wilno pod koniec roku 1915–na początku 1916. Polskie czy niepolskie?" *Przegląd Wschodni*, 8, no. 1 (2002), 39–56. For a general cultural-social history of the city in this period, see A. Pukszto, *Między stołecznością a partykularizmem. Wielunarodowościowe społeczeństwo Wilna w latach 1915–1920* (Toruń: Adam Marszalek, 2006).

27. L. A. [Ludwik Abramowicz], ed., *Litwa podczas wojny. Zbiór dokumentów* (Warsaw: Wydawnictwo Departamentu Spraw Politycznych, 1918), 7–12.

28. Jankowski, *Z dnia na dzień*, 277–283.

29. Ibid., 279–280.

30. Abramowicz, *Profiles*, 186–202. Another excellent source on Jewish life in Vilnius during World War I is Sh. An-ski, ed., *Pinkas far der geshikhte fun vilne in di yorn fun milhome un okupatsie* (Vilne: n.p., 1922).

31. "Lietuvių atstovų pareiškimas Vilniaus miesto vokiečių valdžiai dėl gyventojų surašymo"

(dated March 19, 1916) in Edmundas Gimžauskas, ed., *Lietuva vokiečių okupacijoje pirmojo pasaulinio karo metais 1915-1918*. Lietuvos nepriklausomos valstybės genezė (Vilnius: LII, 2006), 64-65.

32. Dr. J. Basanavičius, *Iš lietuvių gyvenimo 1915-1917 m. po vokiečių jungu* (Vilnius: "Švyturio" spaustuvė, 1919).

33. LMAB, F23-23, ll. 62-64.

34. LMAB, F23-23, ll. 16, 153. In general on the currency policies of the period, see Borys Paszkiewicz, "'Ostrubel' i 'Ostmarka.' O pieniądzu okupacji niemieckiej na Litwie," *Biuletyn Numizmatyczny* 7 (1982), 130-134.

35. On the economic policy of the Germans, see Gerd Linde, *Die deutsche Politik in Litauen im ersten Weltkrieg* (Wiesbaden: Otto Harrassowitz, 1965), 52-68; and Glaser, *Okupacja niemiecka*, 131-142 ("Rekwizycje i kontrybucje").

36. LMAB, F23-23, ll. 120-124; in general on the legal situation of schools under German occupation, see Glaser, *Okupacja niemiecka*, 143-148 ("Szkolnictwo").

37. Pukszto, "Wilno pod koniec roku 1915," 50-52.

38. Abramowicz, *Profiles*, 203.

39. Klimas, *Dienoraštis*, 79, 88.

40. The order forbidding any kind of university course in Vilnius was issued on February 19, 1916. The document is given in Lithuanian translation in *Lietuvos TSR istorijos šaltiniai* (Vilnius: Mintis, 1965), 558.

41. Vejas Liulevicius, *War Land on the Eastern Front* (Cambridge: Cambridge University Press, 2000), 127.

42. Christoph Westerhoff, *Zwangsarbeit im Ersten Weltkrieg. Deutsche Arbeitskräftepolitik im besetzten Polen und Litauen, 1914-1918* (Paderborn: Schöningh, 2012).

43. Ruseckas (ed.), *Lietuva Didžiajame Kare*, 16-23.

44. Cemach Szabad, "Ruch naturalny ludności żydowskiej w Wilnie w ciągu ostatnich lat 18-tu (1911-1928)," *Księga pamiątkowa I Krajowego Zjazdu Lekarskiego 'TOZ-u'* (Warsaw: Nakładem Centralu Tozu, 1929), 83-85.

45. "Referat o ogólnem położeniu miasta" (spring 1917) in *Litwa za rządów ks. Isenburga* (Kraków: Nakładem Krakowskiego Oddziału Zjednoczenia Narodowego, 1919), 42-54.

46. Liudas Gira, "Vilniaus gyvenimas po Vokiečiais, 1917 m.," *Mūsų senovė* 2, no. 3 (1922), 410-422.

47. Haikl Lunsky, *Me-hageto havilnai. Tipusim ve-tslalim* (Vilna: Agudat ha-sofrim veha-zhurnalistim ha'ivriyim veVilna, 1921), 7.

48. Marija Urbšienė, *Vokiečių karo meto spauda ir Lietuva* (Kaunas: Spaudos fondas, 1939), 41-43.

49. Liulevicius, *War Land*, 151-175.

50. "Kraus und wirr ziehen Strassen und Gassen durcheinander, vergeblich sucht das Auge die ordnenden Linien, die den Sinn des ganzen städtischen Organismus irgendwie logisch und sinnvoll darstellen." Paul Monty, *Wanderstunden in Wilna*, 3rd ed.(Wilna: Verlag der Wilnaer Zeitung, 1918), 9.

51. "Eigentlich nur Material zu einem Platz, mit einer echt russischen Raumvergeudung ohne jede Raumgestaltung hingelegt, ohne Beziehung auf die umliegenden Gebäude, mehr ein unbebautes Stück als ein lebendiger Teil der Stadt." Ibid., 12-15.

52. Ibid., 19, 30.

53. Ibid., 59, 61-67.

54. Ibid., 29.

55. A shorter and rather less poetic guidebook to the city for German soldiers concentrated more on practical advice, giving two walking tours with the admonition "Die Heimat kann dir Wilna nicht ersetzen; trachte jedoch, es kennen zu lernen, halt die Augen offen, so wirst du dich heimischer fühlen." *Ich weiß Bescheid. Kleiner Soldatenführer durch Wilna* (Wilna: Verlag Zeitung der 10. Armee, 1918).

56. Paul Listowsky, *Neu-Ost. Unser Zukunftsgrenzgebiet um Ostpreussens Ostrand. Fahrten durch Polen und Litauen unter deutscher Kriegsverwaltung* (Königsberg: Hartungsche Zeitung, 1917).

57. Max Friedrichsen, *Landschaften und Städte Polens und Litauens. Beiträge zu einer regionalen Geographie* (Berlin: Gea Verlag, 1918), 32. "Stadt und Land [sind] von einer mit größtem Erfolg arbeitenden deutschen Verwaltung in sorgsame Pflege genommen.... Die Stadt ist damit in die jüngste Phase ihrer kulturellen Entwicklung eingetreten, welche die früheren Perioden des litauischen, dann des polnischen und schließlich des russischen Einflusses abgelöst hat."

58. Albert Ippel, *Wilna-Minsk. Altertümer und Kunstgewerbe. Führer durch die Ausstellung der 10. Armee* (Wilna: Zeitung der 10. Armee, 1918).

59. Bruno Steigueber, ed., *Wilna im Bilde. 20 Kunstblätter nach Lichtbildern* (Wilna: Verlag der Zeitung der 10. Armee, 1918).

60. Paul Weber, *Wilna. Eine vergessene Kunststätte* (Wilna: Verlag der Zeitung der X. Armee, 1917), 10 and *passim*.

61. Tomas Balkelis, *The Making of Modern Lithuania* (New York: Routledge, 2009).

62. An excellent short collection of Polish memoirs from the war years is Andrzej Rosner, ed., *Teraz będzie Polska. Wybór z pamiętników z okresu i wojny światowej* (Warsaw: Instytut Wydawniczy Pax, 1988).

63. This memorandum and the Lithuanian response were published together (in the original German) in *Litauen und die Polenfreunde* (Wilno: n.p., 1917); for a Lithuanian translation, see Gimžauskas, ed., *Lietuva vokiečių okupacijoje*, document 20, 134–138.

64. This memorandum is printed (in Lithuanian) in Gimžauskas, ed., *Lietuva vokiečių okupacijoje*, document 21, 139–147.

65. Petras Klimas, "Lietuvos Valstybės Kūrimas 1915-1918 metais Vilniuje" in *Pirmasis Nepriklausomos Lietuvos dešimtmetia 1918-1928* ([originally published 1930] London: Nida, 1955), 7–16; Steponas Kairys, *Tau, Lietuva* (Boston: Lietuvių enciklopedijos spaustuvė, 1964), 249–251.

66. For the most important decisions of this conference, see "Lietuvių Vilniaus konferencijos 1917 m. rugsėjo 18–22 d. posėdžių protokolo ištrauka" in Gimžauskas, *Lietuva vokiečių okupacijoje*, document 21, 159–161. An excellent study of the relations between Germans and the Lithuanian national movement is A. Strazhas, *Deutsche Ostpolitik im Ersten Weltkrieg. Der Fall Ober Ost 1915-1917* (Wiesbaden: Harrassowitz Verlag, 1993).

67. Alfred Erich Senn, *The Emergence of Modern Lithuania* (New York: Columbia University Press, 1959), 25.

68. Andrzej Pukszto, "Postawy wileńskich Polaków pod niemiecką okupacją w latach 1915–1918," in Tadeusz Bujnicki and Krzysztof Stępnik, *Ostatni obywatele Wielkiego Księstwa Litewskiego* (Lublin: Wydawnictwo Uniwersytetu Marii Curie-Skłodowskiej, 2005), 281–286. Some Polish political groupings took a more positive stance toward the Lithuanian movement but often made vague references to the close connections previously existing between the Kingdom of Poland and the Grand Duchy of Lithuania, e.g., "Lenkijos politinių judėjimų ir organizacijų deklaracija Lietuvos klausimu" (May 19–22, 1917), in Gimžauskas, ed., *Lietuva vokiečių okupacijoje*, document no. 19, 126–128.

69. Obviously Zawadzki was taking the normal Lithuanian ethnonym, *lietuvas/lietuvai* (sing./pl.) and spelling it according to Polish orthography.

70. Wiktor Sukiennicki, ed., "Memoriał o sprawie litewskiej złożony przez Władysława Zawadzkiego w Warszawie w listopadzie 1917," *Zeszyty Historyczne*, 30 (1974), 77–85; the original text of this memorandum can be found in *Litwa podczas wojny* (Warsaw: Wydawnictwo Departamentu Spraw Politycznych, 1918), 55–58.

71. See, for example, the discussion in Wilhelm Gaigalat, *Litauen. Das besetzte Gebiet, sein Volk und dessen geistige Strömungen* (Frankfurt: Frankfurter Vereinsdruckerei, 1917), *passim* and especially the pages on Lithuanians and Poles, 120–130.

72. Cywiński, *Kartki*, 84.

73. "Lietuvos Taryba skelbia aktą dėl Lietuvos valstybės atkūrimo 1918 02 16" in VMID, 342; on the discussions leading up to this declaration, see Klima, "Lietuvos Valstybės Kūrimas," 19–25.

74. "Lietuvos Taryba skelbia aktą dėl Lietuvos valstybės atkūrimo 1918 02 16" in VMID, 342. See also Jonas Basanavičius, "Dėl vasario 16 dieną paskelbtos Lietuvos nepriklausomybės" in VMIS, 478–488.

75. Senn, *Emergence*, 32–38. Aside from Senn's classic work, this crucial period for the creation of independent Lithuania is very poorly researched in Western languages. For more information by two of the most important diplomatic actors of the period, see Juozas Gabrys, *Vers l'Indépendance Lituanienne. Faits, Impressions, Souvenirs 1907-1920* (Lausanne: Librarie Centrale des Nationalités, 1920) and Petras Klimas, *Der Werdegang des Litauischen Staates von 1915 bis zur Bildung der provisorischen Regierung im November 1918* (Berlin: Pass & Garleb G.m.b.H., 1918).

76. On the exceedingly complicated diplomatic wrangling over Wilhelm von Urach's election as Lithuanian king, see the documents collected in Gimžauskas, *Lietuva vokiečių okupacijoje*, 340–404.

77. Senn, *Emergence*, 61–68; Liulevicius, *War Land*, 214–219.

78. Alfred Erich Senn, "Die bolschewistische Politik in Litauen 1917–1919," *Forschungen zur osteuropäischen Geschichte* 5 (1957), 93.

79. B. Vaitkevičius and Z. Vasiliauskas, *Lithuania in 1918-1919: First Soviets* (Vilnius: Mintis, 1979), 38–40, 56–60.

80. Algirdas Grigaravičius, "Vilnius. 1918 metų gruodžio 20–24 dienos" in VMIS, 496–505.

81. Władysław Wejtko, *Samoobrona Litwy ir Białorusi. Szkic historyczny* (Wilno: Nakładem Związku Organizacyji B. Wojskowych w Wilnie, 1930).

82. *Wilnas Auslieferung an die Polen. Denkschrift des zurückgetretenen Soldatenrats der 10. Armee* (Stuttgart: Jung u. Sohn, 1919).

83. "April 1919" in Abramowicz, *Profiles*, 209–218.

84. Bolesław Waligóra, *Walka o Wilno. Okupacja Litwy i Białorusi w 1918-1919 roku przez Rosję Sowiecką* (Wilno: Wydawnictwo Zarządu Miejskiego, 1938). On the taking of the city by the Polish troops, see Tadeusz Piskor, *Wyprawa wileńska* (Warsaw: Księgarnia wojskowa, 1919).

85. For contemporary accounts of the retaking of Vilnius from the Soviets, see Juliusz Kaden-Bandrowski, *Wyprawa wileńska* (Warsaw: Żolnierz polski, 1920); and Zygmunt Nagrodzki, *Wyprawa wileńska roku 1919 we wspomnieniach cywila (Kartki z pamiętnika)* (Wilno: Kurjer Wileński, 1933).

86. Edward Małachowski, ed., *Wilno 1919.IV.19–1934. Wydawnictwo poświęcone 15-ej Rocznicy odzyskania Wilna* (Wilno: Politechnika robotnicza w Wilnie, 1934).

87. For a political-military history with documents, see Grzegorz Łukomski, Rafał E. Stolarski, *Walka o Wilno. Z dziejów samoobrony Litwy i Białorusi 1918-1919* (Warsaw: "Adiutor," 1994).

88. On the Vilnius pogrom of April 19–22, 1919, see Schuster, *Zwischen allen Fronten*, 445–448; Frank Golczewski, *Polnisch-jüdische Beziehungen 1881-1922. Eine Studie zur Geschichte des Antisemitismus in Osteuropa* (Wiesbaden: Franz Steiner, 1981), 229–232; "Report on the Occurrences in Vilna. Presented to the Polish Government by the Jewish Committee of Vilna" (1919) in Šarūnas Liekis, Lidia Miliakova, Antony Polonsky, eds., "Three Documents on Anti-Jewish Violence in the Eastern Kresy during the Polish-Soviet Conflict," *Polin* 14 (2001), 138–149.

89. Jakub Wygodzki, *In shturm. Zikhroynes fun di okupatsye-tsaytn* (Vilna: B. Kletskin, 1926), 152–166. Wygodzki stresses cooperation between soldiers and civil (presumably Polish) population in robbing and committing atrocities from April 20–22 (154–156).

90. On efforts within the Jewish community to organize itself in this chaotic period, see Samuel Kassow, "Jewish Communal Politics in Transition: The Vilna *Kehile*, 1919-1920," *YIVO Annual* 20 (1991), 61–91.

91. Neal Pease makes the point that initial reports about the pogroms were much exaggerated and the actual level of violence was lower than was thought at the time—or is often imagined. However, at the time, Polish Jews were convinced that hundreds or thousands of Jews had been slaughtered by Polish antisemites and this belief—however false—influenced their attitudes. N. Pease, "'This Troublesome Question': The United States and the 'Polish Pogroms' of 1918–1919" in M. Biskupski, ed., *Ideology, Politics and Diplomacy in East Central Europe* (Rochester: University of Rochester Press, 2003), 58–79.

92. Even in the late twentieth century, memory of the Wilno pogrom remained divided: see Stefan Bergman, "W sprawie pogromu w Wilnie w kwietniu 1919 roku," *Odra* 32, no. 2-3 (1992), 126–127.

93. Česlovas Laurinavičius, "Aus der Geschichte des provisorischen litauischen Komitees von Wilna (April bis Juni 1919)," *Nord-Ost Archiv* 2, no. 2 (1992), 361–376.

## NOTES TO CHAPTER 4

94. Joanna Gierowska-Kałłaur, *Zarząd cywilny ziem wschodnich (19 lutego 1919-9 września 1920)* (Warsaw: Wyd. Neriton IH PAN, 2003).
95. Andrzej Pukszto, "Kultura polska Wilna w okresie Zarządu Cywilnego Ziem Wschodnich w latach 1919-1920," *Zapiski Historyczne* 68, no. 4 (2003), 69-88.
96. Adam Wrzosek, *Wskrzeszenie Uniwersytetu Wileńskiego w r. 1919* (Wilno: Zawadzki, 1919). For the full text of this decree, see Józef Piłsudski, "Dekret Naczelnego Wodza Wojsk Polskich o otwarciu U.S.B. w Wilnie" in Feliksiak-1992, 3:57-58. This volume contains several articles connected with USB and other schools in Wilno.
97. M. Siedlecki, "Wspomnienia z pierwszych dwóch lat organizacji Uniwersytetu Wileńskiego" in *Księga pamiątkowa ku uczczeniu 350 rocznicy założenia Uniw. Wileńskiego* (Wilno: Uniwersytet Stefana Batorego, 1929), 2:60-80.
98. Vygintas B. Pšibilskis, *Iš Lietuvos XX a. kultūros istorijos* (Vilnius: "Arlila," 1997), 37-64.
99. On the development of the Lithuanian army in these years, see Vytautas Lesčius, "Lietuvos kariuomenė 1918-1920 metais," in VMIS, 506-517.
100. On the complicated military and diplomatic maneuvers of July 1920, see Erich Senn, "Lithuania's Fight for Independence: The Polish Evacuation of Vilnius, July 1920," *Baltic Review* 23 (1961), 32-39.
101. Some years later Piłsudski was reported to have remarked that he "chose" Żeligowski to retake Wilno (Grzegorz Łukomski, *Wojna domowa. Z dziejów konfliktu polsko-litewskiego 1918-1920* [Warsaw: Adiutor, 1997] 36). On Żeligowski's "revolt," see Zenon Krajewski, "'Bunt' generała Żeligowskiego i zajęcie Wilna," *Wojskowy przegląd historyczny* 46, no. 1 (1996), 56-71. In general on this interesting figure, see Dariusz Fabisz, *Generał Lucjan Żeligowski (1865-1947). Działalność wojskowa i polityczna* (Warsaw: DiG, 2007).
102. On these battles, see Andrzej Żak, *Wilno 1919-1920* (Warsaw: Bellona, 1993); Bolesław Waligóra, *Zajęcie Wilna przez Gen. Żeligowskiego* (Warsaw: Wojskowe biuro historyczne, 1930); and Piotr Łossowski, *Stosunki polsko-litewskie w latach 1918-1920* (Warsaw: Książka i Wiedza, 1966), 319-367. Anger against Żeligowski and the general apathy of the Western powers is reflected in the contemporary articles collected in Mich. Birżiszka [Mykolas Biržiška], *Na posterunku wileńskim* (Wilno: "Głos Litwy," 1922), 4: 59-94 (articles from October to December 1920).
103. On "Middle Lithuania," see Zenon Krajewski, *Geneza i dzieje wewnętrzne Litwy Środkowej* (Lublin: Ośrodek Studiów Polonijnych ir Społecznych PZKS, 1996); Beata Kolarz, *Ustrój Litwy Środkowej w latach 1920-1922* (Gdańsk: Wydaw. Uniwersytetu Gdańskiego, 2004).
104. For a good example of the Lithuanian point of view, see Mykolas Biržiška, *Spalių 9 diena (1920-1927)* (Kaunas: Vilniui vaduoti sąjunga, 1927); for pro-Polish rhetoric, see "Niema Litwy bez Polski, niema Polski bez Litwy" in *Zorza wileńska na rok 1920. Kalendarz* (Wilno: Księgarnia Jurkiewicza i Szalkiewicza, 1920), 17-31.
105. For a sampling of Polish and Lithuanian arguments claiming the city, see (Polish): *Poland and Lithania: The Question of Wilno* (Warsaw: Straż Kresowa, 1921); *O Wilno. Memorjał delegacji polskiej przedłożony Konferencji Brukselskiej* (Lwów: Komitet dni wileńskich, 1921); Georges Moresthes, *Vilna et le problème de l'Est européen* (Paris: Bossard, 1922); Karl Bögholm, *Von Wilno bis Memel. Betrachtungen über die litauische Frage* (Danzig: Verlag der Danziger Zeitungsverlaggesellschaft, 1928); and (Lithuanian): Juozas Bagdonas, *Wileńszczyzna pod względem kulturalnym i politycznym* (Wilno: "Dzwon Litewski," 1921); Zigmas Žemaitis, *Przyszłe losy Wilna I Wileńszczyzny* (Kaunas: Valstybės spaustuvė, 1922); Zigmas Žemaitis, *Vilnius Lietuviai ir Lietuva Vilniui* (Kaunas: S-ga Vilniui vaduoti, 1928); Vytautas Bičiūnas, *Tiesa apie Vilnių* (Kaunas: Lietuvos Šaulių sąjungos leidinys, 1931); Adolfas Šapoka, *Vilnius in the Life of Lithuania* (Toronto: Lithuanian Association of the Vilnius Region, 1962).
106. The document, "Exposé des considérations relatives aux droits des Lithuaniens sur Vilna et sur territoire, présenté à S. E. M. Le Président de la Conférence de la Paix, par S. E. M. A. Voldemar, Président de la Délégation de Lithuanie" is printed in *Conflit polono-lithuanien. Question de Vilna 1918-1924. Documents diplomatiques* (Kaunas: République de Lithuanie Ministère des affaires étrangères, 1924), 8-11.

107. Ibid., 8-9. "Vilna est la capital historique de l'État lithuanien et elle est située dans une région qui, de temps immémorial fait partie intégrante du domaine ethnographique purement lithuanien."
108. Ibid., 9. "L'histoire de la ville de Vilna est l'histoire de la Lithuanie et inversement."
109. Ibid. "La ville de Vilna constitue, actuellement, le centre économique, politique et intellectuel du pays, ainsi que le noeud principal des voies de communication. Elle se nourrit des forces vives du peuple lithuanien."
110. Ibid. "[s]éparer Vilna de la Lithuanie, ce serait porter une atteinte des plus graves au pays et un coup de grâce à la ville elle-même."
111. Ibid., 9-10.
112. The *rapport* by Simonas Rozenbaumas [Shimshon Rosenbaum] is included in ibid., 11-12.
113. On the Jews and the Vilnius plebiscite of January 8, 1922, see Theodore R. Weeks, "Between Poland and Lithuania: Jews and the Vilnius Question, 1918-1925" in Vladas Sirutavičius and Darius Staliūnas, eds., *A Pragmatic Alliance: Jewish-Lithuanian Political Cooperation at the Beginning of the 20th Century* (Budapest: Central European University Press, 2011), 207-227.
114. On Hymans and his plan, see Alfred Erich Senn, *The Great Powers, Lithuania, and the Vilna Question 1920-1928* (Leiden: E. J. Brill, 1966), 66-82. For a contemporary critique by a Pole sympathetic to the Lithuanians, see Tadeusz Wróblewski [Juodvarnis, pseud.], *Uwagi o projekcie p. Hymansa* (Wilno: "Nowiny Wileńskie," 1921).
115. For the Polish memorandum, see *Conflit polono-lithuanien*, 195-214.
116. Ibid., 197.
117. Ibid.
118. Ibid., 198.
119. Ibid.
120. The peace accord reached between Bolshevik Russia and Lithuania recognized the latter's claim on Vilnius. Regina Žepkaitė, "Lietuvos-Tarybų Rusijos taikos sutartis ir Vilniaus klausimas," *LTSR MA darbai. Serija A*, tomas 2, 107-122. In general on Lithuanian diplomacy regarding the Vilnius question, see Audronė Veilentienė, ed., *Vilniaus klausimas Lietuvos respublikos diplomatijoje (1918-1940)* (Kaunas: "Jumena," 2003).
121. Ran, *Yerushalayim de Lita*, 1:30.
122. See, for example, Klausner, *Vilna, Yerushalayim de-Lita. Doroth Ahronim 1881-1939*, 166-171. Also see the official reports on Jews in Middle Lithuania from early 1921 in LCVA, f. 22, ap. 1, b. 57.
123. Liudas Truska, *Lietuviai ir Žydai nuo XIX a. pabaigos iki 1941 m. birželio. Antisemitizmo Lietuvoje raida* (Vilnius: Vilniaus pedagoginis universitetas, 2005), 57-77. For a more general account, covering the entire interwar period, see Ezra Mendelsohn, *The Jews of East Central Europe between the World Wars* (Bloomington: Indiana University Press, 1983), 213-240.
124. On the Lwów pogrom, see William W. Hagen, "The Moral Economy of Popular Violence: The Pogrom in Lwów, November 1918" in Robert Blobaum, ed., *Antisemitism and Its Opponents in Modern Poland* (Ithaca: Cornell University Press, 2005), 124-147.
125. One sign of Wygodzki's support for the Lithuanians was the fact that he agreed to serve as Minister of Jewish Affairs in the Lithuanian Taryba without, however, leaving Vilnius. (Wygodzki, *In shturm*, 199-200.) Wygodzki does admit that the Lithaunians made mistakes in Vilnius, including a tendency to favor Lithuanians for state jobs and an overly hasty attempt to introduce the Lithuanian language in the city (203). See also Šarūnas Liekis, "On Jewish Participation in the *Taryba* in 1918," *Lithuanian Historical Studies* 4 (1999), 62-82.
126. Lietuvos Centrinis Valstybės Archyvas, Vilnius (LCVA), f. 22, ap. 1, b. 27 (Sprawozdanie z życia politycznego społeczeństwa żydowskiego w Wilnie).
127. See, for example, the rather different portrayals of Jewish attitudes by two serious scholars: Liekis, *A State within a State?*, 157-166; and Jarosław Wolkonowski, *Stosunki polsko-żydowskie w Wilnie i na Wileńszczyźnie 1919-1939* (Białystok: Wydawnictwo Uniwersytetu w Białymstoku, 2004), 96-108.

128. LCVA, f. 383, ap. 7, b. 251, l. 120 (typed article "The Attitude of Jews toward the Plebiscite in Vilna" dated February 10, 1921, labeled as translation of article from *Evreiskaia Tribuna*, February 4, 1921).

129. LCVA, f. 19, ap. 1, b. 68, l. 64 (document entitled "Delegacja żydowska u P. Meysztowicza").

130. In his memoirs, Wygodzki is much more openly critical of the Poles, writing that the elections were not regarded as legitimate and accusing the Poles of electoral fraud. According to Wygodzki, trains filled with "voters" arrived from Warsaw just before the elections. Wygodzki, *In shturm*, 263–265.

131. LCVA, f. 21, ap. 1, b. 12 ("Sprawy dotyczące Sejmu Wileńskiego"), l. 24.

132. *Wybory do Sejmu w Wilnie, 8 stycznia 1922. Oświetlenie akcji wyborczej i jej wyników na podstawie źródeł urzędowych* (Wilno: Generalny Komisarjat Wyborczy, 1922), 164–165.

133. Ibid., 102–104, 137; on the election results, see also LCVA, f. 19, ap. 1, b. 92 ("Sprawozdanie - raport o przebiegu i wynikach głosowania do Sejmu Wileńskiego w dniu 8 styczniu 1922 r.").

134. *Wybory do Sejmu w Wilnie*, 33.

135. *Wybory do Sejmu w Wilnie*, 94–95 contains the text of this *Uchwała Sejmu Wileńskiego* (February 20, 1922), bearing the title "Uchwała w. przedmiocie przynależności państwowej Ziemi Wileńskiej."

136. Kolarz, *Ustrój Litwy Środkowej*, 67–85. On the Vilnius Sejm, see also Aleksander Srebrakowski, *Sejm wileński 1922 roku. Idea i jej realizacja* (Wrocław: Wydawnictwo Uniwersytetu Wrocławskiego, 1993).

## Notes to Chapter 5

1. See, for example, Halina Kobeckaitė, *Lietuvos Karamai* (Vilnius: Baltos Lankos, 1997); Stanisław Kryczyński, *Tatarzy litewscy. Próba monografii historyczno-etnograficznej* (Warsaw: Wyd. Rady Centralnej Związku Kulturalno-Oświatowego Tatarów Rzeczypospolitej Polskiej, 1938); M. Ivanou, "Problema prynalezhastsi Vil'ni ir belaruskae natsyianal'nae pytanne u 1939 h.," *Belaruski historychny chasopis*, no. 1 (1994), 37.

2. *Rocznik statystyczny Wilna 1937* (Wilno: Zarząd miejski, 1939), 9.

3. Władysław Studnicki, *Ziemia wileńska, jej stan gospodarczy i pożądany statut* (Wilno: Ludwik Chomiński, 1922).

4. *Wileńszczyzna w latach 1926–1930* (Warsaw: Wydaw. Bezpartyjnego Bloku Współpracy z Rządem, 1930). This brochure argues that Warsaw's policy changed in 1926—in part due to this political grouping's support—but this seems more election propaganda than reality.

5. These buildings were located across from the main post office (one housed the Post Office Bank). Darius Osteika and Jūratė Tytlytė, eds., *Vilnius 1900–2005. Naujosios architektūros gidas/A Guide to Modern Architecture* (Vilnius: Architektūros fondas, 2005), D2D3.

6. Ibid., D11, D4, D10.

7. On the early years of YIVO in Vilnius, see Stefan Schreiner, "Die Wissenschaft des Ostjudentums—Eine Erinnerung an die Gründung des YIVO vor 70 Jahren," *Judaica* 51, no. 4 (December 1995), 209–221.

8. Marian Morelowski, *Co będzie z placem katedralnym, co ze starym Wilnem? Niebezpieczeństwa modernistycznej urbanistyki w głównych centrach wielkiej przeszłości* (Wilno: Znicz, 1937).

9. Stanisław Lorentz, *Album wileńskie* (Warsaw: PIW, 1986), esp. 13–45.

10. Leon Kryczyński, *Historia meczetu w Wilnie (Próba monografii)* (Warsaw: "Przegląd Islamski," 1937).

11. Henryk Jensz, "Elektryfikacja, siły wodne a rozwój gospodarczy Wileńszczyzny," *Rocznik Ziem Wschodnich* 5 (1939), 152–161; Jensz, *Wodociągi i kanalizacja miasta Wilna* (Wilno: Wydawnictwo Magistratu, 1932).

12. Similar budget problems limited efforts to improve child welfare in the city. Aleksandra Siedlaczek, *Wileńskie Towarzystwo Opieki nad Dziećmi w latach 1901–1940* (Częstochowa: Wy-

dawnictwo WSP, 1998).
13. *Vilniaus autobusai* (Vilnius: Transporto pasaulis, 2003), 14–17. A ride on an "Arbon" is described by a visitor in Jonas Vytautas Narbutas, "Vilnius 1936" in VMIS, 576–577.
14. Čaplinskas-2010, 480, 518–519.
15. VMI, 2:84; Čaplinskas-2010, 540.
16. Czeslaw Milosz, *Beginning with My Streets* (New York: Farrar Straus Giroux, 1991), 20–21.
17. LCVA, f. 64, ap. 25, b. 77; LCVA, f. 64, ap. 25, b. 89.
18. Maciej Kwiatkowski, *Narodziny polskiego radia. Radiofonia w Polsce w latach 1918–1939* (Warsaw: PWN, 1972), 270–278.
19. Čaplinskas-2010, 534–535; LCVA, f. 923, ap. 1, b. 1068; Adam Berwaldt, ed., *10 lat rozgłośni wileńskiej. Radio dla miasta i wsi (Wilno 1928–1938)* (Wilno: Referat Prasowo-Propagandowy rozgłośni wileńskiej, 1938).
20. See, for example, the marvelous advertisement for Elektrit radio receivers (manufactured in Vilnius) for 1939–1940 in Henryk Berezowski, *Towarzystwo Radiotechniczne Elektrit. Wilno 1925–1939* (Warsaw: Nakładem autora, 2011), 104.
21. J. Kobzakowski and A. Wasilewski, "O planie zabudowy Wilna. Rozmowa Urbanisty z Laikiem" in *Wilno. Kwartalnik poświęcony sprawom miasta Wilna* 1, no. 1 (March 1939), 36–42. For a more specific discussion of "the Wilno of the future," see Witold Bańkowski, *Wilno przyszłości. Rozważania na tematy urbanistyczne* (Wilno: Dru. A. Zwierzyńskiego, 1937).
22. Wiktor Sukiennicki, *Legenda i rzeczywistość. Wspomnienia i uwagi o dwudziestu latach Uniwersytetu Stefana Batorego w Wilnie* (Paris: Instytut Literacki, 1967). On many of the same people and events of the early 1930s, but from a quite different point of view, see Eugeniusz Filipajtis, *Lewica akademicka w Wilnie 1930–pocz 1935* (Białystok: Białostockie Towarzystwo Naukowe. Komisja Historii Najnowszej, 1965).
23. R. Maliukiavichius [Maliukevičius], *Vil'niusskoe podpol'e* (Vilnius: Vaga, 1966); Maliukiavichius, ed., *Revoliutsionnoe dvizhenie v Vil'niusskom krae 1920–1940. Dokumenty i materialy* (Vilnius: Mintis, 1978). For a rather exciting, if exaggerated, account by a Lithuanian communist active in interwar Vilnius, see Jonas Karosas, *Mówią kamienie Wilna* (Warsaw: Książka ir Wiedza, 1968). Far less gripping as a narrative, though also mentioning Karosas, is Boris Samuilovich Klein, *Ruch rewolucyjny na Wileńszyźnie w latach 1920–1939* (Wilnius [sic]: Państwowe Wydawnictwo Literatury Politycznej i Naukowej, 1961).
24. More generally on this periodical and its views in the period, see Janusz Osica, *Politycy anachronizmu. Konserwatyści wileńskiej grupy "Słowa" 1922–1928* (Warsaw: PWN, 1982).
25. On Mackiewicz's entire career, see Jerzy Jaruzelski, *Stanisław Cat Mackiewicz 1896–1966. Wilo-Londyn-Warszawa* (Warsaw: Czytelnik, 1987). More generally on politics and political concepts in interwar Wilno, see Przemysław Dąbrowski, *Rozpolitykowane miasto. Ustrój polityczny państwa w koncepcjach polskich ugrupowań działających w Wilnie w latach 1918–1939* (Gdańsk: Arche, 2012).
26. On the university as a key element of Polish culture and national identity in this region, see A. Gołubiew, "Znaczenie Uniwersytetu Stefana Batorego dla Ziem Północno-Wschodnich," *Rocznik Ziem Wschodnich* 4 (1938), 145–154.
27. A. Wrzosek, "Wskrzeszenie Uniwersytetu Wileńskiego" in *Księga pamiątkowa ku uczczeniu 350 rocznicy założenia Uniw. Wileńskiego* (Wilno: Uniwersytet Stefana Batorego, 1929), 2:21.
28. Ibid., 24. For the full text of this decree, see Józef Piłsudski, "Dekret Naczelnego Wodza Wojsk Polskich o otwarciu U.S.B. w Wilnie" in Elżbieta Feliksiak, ed., *Wilno-Wileńszczyzna jako krajobraz i środowisko wielu kultur* (Białystok: Towarzystwo Literackie im. Adama Mickiewicza, 1992), 3:57–58. This volume contains several articles connected with USB and with other schools in Wilno.
29. M. Siedlecki, "Wspomnienia z pierwszych dwóch lat organizacji Uniwersytetu Wileńskiego" in *Księga pamiątkowa*, 2:60–80.
30. M. Siedlecki, "Wspomnienia," 89–92.
31. J. Kublius, ed., *A Short History of Vilnius University* (Vilnius: Mokslas, 1979), 132; on the university's structure, see also Kosman, *Uniwersytet Wileński*, 57–60.
32. Ryszard Mienicki, "Pierwsze dziesięciolecie Uniwersytetu Stefana Batorego w Wilnie" in

*Księga pamiątkowa*, 2:115-158.

33. For a very detailed statistical account of students at USB in its first decade, see Kazimierz Karaffa-Korbutt, "Działalaność naukowa i pedagogiczna U.S.B. z lat 1919-1929 w świetle zestawień statystycznych" in *Księga pamiątkowa*, 2:577-594. Figure for 1938/1939 from Kosman, *Uniwersytet Wileński*, 62.

34. There was at the university, for example, a specific "Association for Mutual Aid for Jewish Students," and, following stereotypes, Jews dominated in the USB Esperanto Circle. LCVA, f. 175, ap. 15, b. 9 (Stowarzyszenie wzajemnej pomocy stud. Żydów USB); ibid., b. 35 (Akademickie koło Esperantystów USB).

35. For a report on the activities of student organizations of all kinds at USB, see *Alma Mater Vilnensis* (every issue contains such a "sprawozdanie"), e.g., zeszyt 6 (1927), 29-34; zeszyt 7 (1928), 70-79.

36. An exception to this rule, however, is Wiktor Sukiennicki, *Legenda i rzeczywistość. Wspomnienia i uwagi o dwudziestu latach Uniwersytetu Stefana Batorego w Wilnie* (Paris: Instytut Literacki, 1967). Sukiennicki's very valuable work is part memoir and part historical overview and is unique in its analysis (in some ways typical for the Cold War) of the links between USB students and Moscow.

37. See, for example, the memoirs of student life in Anna Kiezuń, ed., *Kultura międzywojennego Wilna* (Białystok: Towarzystwo Literackie im. Adama Mickiewicza, 1994), 35-128. On the study of Polish language and literature at USB, see Teresa Dalecka, *Dzieje polonistyki wileńskiej 1919-1939* (Kraków: Towarzystwo Naukowe Societas Vistulana, 2003).

38. Irena Sławińska, "Z życia naukowego akademików USB w Wilnie" in Elżbieta Feliksiak and Antoni Mironowicz, eds., *Wilno i kresy północno-wschodnie* (Białystok: Towarzystwo Literackie im. Adama Mickiewicza, 1996), 2:283-296.

39. Maria Znamierowska-Prüfferowa, *Wilno. Miasto serce najbliższe*, edited by Krystyna Jakowska (Białystok: Towarzystwo Literackie im. Adama Mickiewicza, 1997), 285.

40. Many files from the interwar Uniwersytet Stefana Batorego are housed at Lietuvos Centrinis Valstybinis Archyvas, Vilnius (LCVA), f. 175. Of particular interest are the files on student groups (including Esperantists, Jewish students, and Zionists) in f. 175, ap. 15. Some personal files of USB professors ended up at Lietuvos Valstybės Istorinis Archyvas, Vilnius (LVIA), whose collections generally concentrate on the period before 1914. See, e.g., LVIA, f. 1135, ap. 12, personal archive of architect and art historian Juljus Kłos (1881-1933); f. 1135, ap. 13, personal archive of historian Stanisław Kościałkowski (1881-1960); f. 1135, ap. 16, archive of law professor Alfons Parczewski (1849-1933).

41. S. Januszewicz, *Skorowidz ważniejszych gmachów m. Wilna oraz spis uic z uwzględnieniem ostatnich zmian, uchwalonych przez radę miejską w roku 1920* (Wilno: Zawadzki, 1922); and the city map by the same author *Plan miasta Wilna* (Wilno: Józef Zawadzki, 1933).

42. St. Bogorja, *Co każdy Polak powinien wiedzieć? (O Wileńczyźnie)* (Wilno: Nakładem komitetu zjednoczenia kresów wschodnich z Rzecząpospolitą, 1921).

43. Stanisław Kutrzeba, *La Question de Wilno* (Paris: Librairie de la cour d'appel et de l'ordre des avocats, 1928).

44. Witold Malczyk, *Zabytki Wilna a nauka historii w szkole powszechnej* (Wilno: Nakładem Dziennika Urzędowego Kuratorium Okr. Szk. Wileńskiej, 1936), esp. 88-92 (Klasa III).

45. For example, Stefan Burhardt, ed., *P.O.W. na ziemiach W.X. Litewskiego 1919-1934. Szkice i Wspomnienia* (Wilno: Wydaw. Wilensko-Nowogródzkiego okręgu peowiaków, 1934); Edward Małachowski, ed., *Wilno 1919.IV.19-1934. Wydawnictwo poświęcone 15-ej Rocznicy odzyskania Wilna* (Wilno: Politechnika robotnicza, 1934).

46. Neal Pease, "God's Own Patriot: Jerzy Matulewicz as Bishop of Vilna, 1918-1925," *East Central Europe* 18, no. 1 (1991), 69-79.

47. Neal Pease, *Rome's Most Faithful Daughter: The Catholic Church and Independent Poland, 1914-1939* (Athens: Ohio University Press, 2009).

48. See, for example, Vincas Martinkėnas, "Lenkinimas Vilniaus Vyskupijos Bažnyčiose 1897-1939 m.," *Voruta* (June 1994), no. 21, p. 5; no. 23, p. 5. This work contains useful information but the author's rather strident anti-Polish tone indicates the need to use it with caution.

49. The latter is, of course, Tadeusz Bujnicki. Among his important works on literary and

cultural life (and not just of Poles) in Wilno, see *Życie literackie i literatura w Wilnie XIX–XX wieku*, edited with Andrzej Romanowski (Kraków: Collegium Columbinum, 2000); *Poezja i poeci w Wilnie lat 1920–1940. Studia*, edited with Krzysztof Biedrzycki (Kraków: Universitas, 2003); and *W Wielkim Księstwie Litewskim i w Wilnie* (Warsaw: DiG, 2010).

50. On Żagary, see Filipajtis, *Lewica akademicka*, 25–34; Andrzej Zieniewicz, *Idące Wilno. Szkice o Żagarach* (Warsaw: PIW, 1987); Stanisław Bereś, *Ostatnia wileńska plejada. Szkice o poezji kręgu Żagarów* (Warsaw: Wydawnictwo PEN, 1990); Tadeusz Bujnicki, *Szkice Wileńskie. Rozprawy i eseje* (Kraków: Collegium Columbinum, 2002), 89–110 and 133–140.

51. Jagoda Hernik Spalińska, *Wileńskie Środy Literackie (1927–1939)* (Warsaw: Instytut Badań Literackich, 1998).

52. Two of the most famous historical-literary periodicals, now in part available online, were *Ateneum Wileńskie* and *Tęcza* (the Rainbow). For an idea of the spectrum of Polish periodicals published in the city in the later 1920s, see Stefan Rygiel, *Polskie czasopiśmiennictwo wileńskie w r. 1928* (Wilno: "Lux," 1928).

53. Mirosława Kozłowska, ed., *Wilno teatralne* (Warsaw: Ogólnopolski klub miłośników Litwy, 1998); Irena Pikiel, "W szopkowym zwierciadle. Ze wspomnień o wileńskich szopkach akademickich (1921–1933)," *Pamiętnik teatralny*, no. 2–3 (1986), 383–407.

54. On the Mickiewicz monuments in Kraków and Warsaw (respectively), see Patrice Dabrowski, *Commemorations and the Shaping of Modern Poland* (Bloomington: Indiana UP, 2004), 133–156; and Theodore R. Weeks, "A City of Three Nations: Fin-de-Siècle Warsaw," *Polish Review* 49, no. 2 (2004), 747–766.

55. Józef Poklewski, "Projekty pomnika Mickiewicza w Wilnie w okresie międzywojennym w świetle ówczesnych krytyk i polemik prasowych," *Lituano-Slavica Poznaniensia. Studia Historiae Artium* 5 (1991), 258–260. See also Piotr Szubert, "Pomnik Mickiewicza w Wilnie," *Blok-Notes Muzeum Literatury im. Adama Mickiewicza* 9 (1988), 195–236.

56. Józef Poklewski, "Organizacje artystyczne i instytucje opieki nad sztuką w międzywojennym Wilnie" in Anna Kieżuń, ed., *Kultura międzywojennego Wilna* (Białystok: Towarzystwo Literackie im. Adama Mickiewicza, 1994), 173–174.

57. Juljusz Kłos, *Wilno. Przewodnik krajoznawczy (szkic monografii historyczno-architektonicznej)* (Wilno: Wydaw. Oddz. Wileńskiego Pol. Tow. Krajozawczego Touring-Klubu, 1929), 262. For an image of the model that was apparently located at the foot of Castle Hill (on the Wilia/Neris side), see Poklewski in Kieżuń, ed., *Kultura*, 176.

58. Czesław Jankowski, *Wystawa projektów konkursowych pomnika Adama Mickiewicza w Wilnie, otwarta 14 listopada 1926 r. w byłej ujeżdżalni przy placu Orzeszkowej* (Wilno: Wydawnictwo Wileńskie, 1926). Jankowski would become a vociferous, even vicious, opponent of the artist finally chosen, Henryk Kuna.

59. Poklewski, "Projekty pomnika Mickiewicza," 262–269; Katrin Steffen, "Ein 'jüdisches Denkmal' in Wilna? Das Denkmalprojekt von Henryk Kuna und der Gedächtnisort Adam Mickiewicz im Fokus der polnisch-jüdischen Beziehungen" in Marina Dmitrieva and Heidemarie Peterson, eds., *Jüdische Kultur(en) im Neuen Europa. Wilna 1918–1939* (Wiesbaden: Harrassowitz Verlag, 2004), 34–49.

60. Poklewski claims, based on press accounts, that the statue of Mickiewicz was actually cast in bronze in April 1939 but remained in the workshop and was destroyed during the Second World War ("Projekty pomnika Mickiewicza," 265). Steffen, who does not use Poklewski's article (but does use archives in Vilnius), makes no mention of the casting of the statue.

61. *Ferdynand Ruszczyc. Życie i dzieło* (Wilno: "Grafyka," 1939). The artist's diary also provides interesting information: Ferdynand Ruszczyc, *Dziennik* (Warsaw: Secesja, 1994–1996); the second volume covers the interwar period.

62. Józef Poklewski, "'Szkoła wileńska' i jej ocena przez międzywojenną krytykę artystyczną," *Acta Universitatis Nicolai Copernici. Nauki humanistyczno-społeczne. Zabytkoznawstwo* 25 (1994), 251–266.

63. Poklewski, *Życie artystyczne*, 68–73.

64. Jerzy Malinowski, Michał Woźniak, Rūta Janonienė, eds., *Kształcenie artystyczne w Wilnie*

*i jego tradycje/Vilniaus meno mokykla ir jos tradicijos* (Toruń: Wydawnictwo Uniwersytetu Mikołaja Kopernika w Toruniu, 1996), 329–408; Darius Konstantynów, *Wileńskie towarzystwo artystów plastyków 1920-1939* (Warsaw: Instytut Sztuki PAN, 2006).

65. Helena Obiezierska, *Jedno życie prywatne na tle życia narodu polskiego w wieku XX* (Bydgoszcz: Towarzystwo miłośników Wilna, 1995), 35, 82–85, 100–119.

66. Ibid., 198, 217.

67. Ibid., 303, 333–335.

68. Janusz Dunin-Horkawicz, *Wilna—verlorene Heimat. Jugenderinnerungen eines polnischen Bibliotekars* (Hannover: Laurentius, 1998), 5–7. The memoir was originally published as Janusz Dunin-Horkawicz, *Co było a nie jest—czyli kilka lat młodości mojej w Wilnie* (Łódź: "Poprzeczna Oficyna," 1992).

69. Stanisław Mianowski, *Świat, który odszedł. Wspomnienia Wilnianina 1945-1895* (Warsaw: Oficyna wydawnicza Rytm, 1995), 11–12, 22, 28, 64–71.

70. Ibid., 91–92.

71. Ibid., 172–173.

72. Krzysztof Mianowski, *Dwadzieścia młodych lat w Wilnie* (Bydgoszcz: Tow. miłośników Wilna, 2001), 13–15, 23, 33.

73. Ibid., 35, 108–115.

74. Tadeusz Łopalewski, *Czasy dobre i złe* (Warsaw: Czytelnik, 1966), 102–106.

75. Ibid., 136, 144.

76. On the early years of radio in Wilno, see Maciej Józef Kwiatkowski, *Narodziny polskiego radia* (Warsaw: PWN, 1972), 270–293.

77. Łopalewski, *Czasy dobre i złe*, 211–212.

78. For pioneering essays on tourism in this region, see Diane Koenker and Anne E. Gorsuch, eds., *Turizm: The Russian and East European Tourist under Capitalism and Socialism* (Ithaca: Cornell UP, 2006). Unfortunately there are no specifically Polish case studies among the pre–World War II essays here.

79. Among pre-1914 guidebooks, see A. H. Kirkor, *Przewodnik historyczny po Wilnie i jego okolicach*, 2nd ed. (Wilno: Józef Zawadzki, 1880); Wacław Gizbert-Studnicki, *Wilno. Przewodnik ilustrowany po mieście i okolicy* (Wilno: A. Żukowski i W. Borkowicz, 1910); and Ludwik Życka, *Wilno* (Warsaw-Kraków: Gebethner i spółka, 1912).

80. For a short biography of the author, see W. Zahorski, *Przewodnik po Wilnie*, 5th ed. (Wilno: Józef Zawadzki, 1935), iii–v.

81. Zahorski, *Przewodnik*, 1910, 53.

82. Zahorski, *Przewodnik*, 1935, 75–77.

83. Ibid., 73–75. Czesław Miłosz, *Zaczynając od moich ulic* (Wrocław: Wyd. Dolnośląskie, 1990), 24: "Niemiecka była ulicą wyłącznie żydowską..."

84. Jerzy Remer, *Wilno* (Poznań: Wydawnictwo Polskie, 1934), 58.

85. Ibid., 82–86.

86. Kłos, *Wilno* (1937), 3.

87. Ibid., 28–44.

88. Ibid., 196.

89. *Rocznik statystyczny Wilna 1937* (Wilno: Zarząd statystyczny w Wilnie, 1939), table IV, p. 9.

90. The six short films looked at Warsaw, Vilna, Lwów, Kraków, Białystok, and Łódź. The Łódź film has been lost.

91. Frank Schuster, *Zwischen allen Fronten. Osteuropäische Juden während des ersten Weltkrieges (1914-1919)* (Cologne: Böhlau, 2004).

92. This is a very controversial issue that deserves more serious, impartial research. Meanwhile, see the pioneering work of Jerzy Tomaszewski, e.g., *Ojczyzna nie tylko Polaków* (Warsaw: Młodziejowa Agencja Wydawnicza, 1985).

93. LCVA, f. 21, ap. 1, b. 12, l. 24.

94. Jarosław Wołkonowski, *Stosunki polsko-żydowskie w Wilnie i na Wileńszczyźnie 1919-1939* (Białystok: Wydawn. Uniwersytetu w Białymstoku, 2004).

95. Samuel D. Kassow, "Jewish Communal Politics in Transition: The Vilna Kehile, 1919–

1920," *YIVO Annual* 20 (1991), 61-91.
    96. See, for example, *Barikht fun der Yidisher Kehile in Vilne 1923-1933* (Vilna, 1934).
    97. Arcadius Kahan, "Vilna—The Socio-Cultural Anatomy of a Jewish Community in Interwar Poland" in Kahan, *Essays in Jewish Social and Economic History* (Chicago: University of Chicago Press, 1986), 150-156 (quotation 156).
    98. Cemach Szabad, "Ruch naturalny ludności żydowskiej w Wilnie w ciągu ostatnich lat 18-tu (1911-1928)" in *Księga pamiątkowa Pierwszego Krajowego Zjazdu Lekarskiego "TOZu"* (Warsaw, 1929), 81-87.
    99. J. Lestschinski [Leshchinskii], "Wilna, der Niedergang einer jüdischen Stadt," *Jüdische Wohlfahrtspflege und Sozialpolitik* 2 (1931), 21-33. For a less pessimistic description of Vilna commerce, see A. Kavenoki, "Yidishe miskher in Vilne" in Isaac Kowalski, ed., *Vilner Almanakh/Vilna Almanac* (Vilna: Overt Kuryer, 1939), 173-182. For a comparative overview of economic-demographic factors in Poland's main Jewish cities, see Yankev Leshchinski, "Yidn in di gresere shtet fun poyln 1921-1931," *YIVO-Bleter* 21 (1943), 20-45.
    100. Cecile Kuznitz, "On the Jewish Street: Yiddish Culture and Urban Landscape in Interwar Vilna" in Leonard Greenspoon, ed., *Yiddish Language and Culture: Then and Now* (Omaha: Creighton University Press, 1998), 65-92.
    101. On this institution, see the recent well-researched monograph: Cecile Esther Kuznitz, *YIVO and the Making of Modern Jewish Culture: Scholarship for the Yiddish Nation* (Cambridge: Cambridge University Press, 2014).
    102. *Das Jiddische Wissenschaftliche Institut (1925-1928)* (Berlin: n.p., 1929); Mojżesz Heller, "Żydowski instytut naukowy," *Miesięcznik Żydowski* 1, no. 2 (1931), 345-351; Stefan Schreiner, "Die Wissenschaft des Ostjudentums—eine Erinnerung an die Gründung des YIVO vor 70 Jahren," *Judaica* 51, no. 4 (December 1995), 209-221. See also photos of the YIVO headquarters and exhibits there in YdL, 2:357-359.
    103. Anke Hilbrenner, "'Simon Dubnow war eine Art intellektueller Pate'. Das YIVO in Wilna und Dubnows Aufruf zur Arbeit am nationalen Gedächtnis" in Dmitrieva and Peterson, eds., *Jüdische Kultur(en)*, 147-162.
    104. On Jewish cultural life, see, for example, Daniel Kac, *Wilno Jerozolimą było. Rzecz o Abrahamie Sutzkeverze* (Sejny: Pogranicze, 2004); Joanna Lisek, *Jung Wilne. Żydowska grupa artystyczna* (Wrocław: Wydawnictwo Uniwersytetu Wrocławskiego, 2005); Mojżesz Heller, *Wilno jako ośrodek żydowskiego życia kulturalnego* (Wilno: "Lux," 1930); Elias Schulman, *Yung Vilne 1929-1939* (New York: Getseltn, 1945); Nachmanas Šapira, *Vilnius naujojoj Žydų poezijoj* (Kaunas: Vilniui vaduoti sąjungos leidinys, 1935); Justin Cammy, "Tsevorfene Bleter: The Emergence of Yung Vilne," *Polin* 14 (2001), 170-191; and essays in Hebrew and Yiddish, in part by contemporaries, on various aspects of Vilna culture and education: Yisrael Rudnitski, ed., *Vilner zamlbukh/Me'asef vilnah* (Tel Aviv: Igud olami shel yotsei Vilnah vehasvivah be'Israel, 1974).
    105. N. Weinig, "Piętnaście lat 'Trupy Wileńskiej,'" *Miesięcznik Żydowski* 1 (1931), 359-364.
    106. Susanne Marten-Finnis, "The Jewish Press in Vilna: Traditions, Challenges, and Progress during the Inter-War Period" in Dmitrieva and Petersen, *Jüdische Kultur(en)*, 138-139. See also Susanne Marten-Finnis, *Vilna as a Centre of the Modern Jewish Press, 1840-1926* (Oxford: Peter Lang, 2004).
    107. Yefin Yeshurin, *Vilne. A zamelbukh gevidmet der shtot Vilne* (Vilna: Vilner brentsh 367 Arbeyter Ring, 1935), 267-752.
    108. Kahan, "The University of Vilna" in Kahan, *Essays in Jewish Social and Economic History*, 166.
    109. LCVA, f. 175, ap. 15, b. 9 (Jewish mutual aid society); ibid., b. 35 (Esperanto club).
    110. Jack Jacobs, "Jews and Sport in Interwar Vilna" in Larisa Lempertienė and Jurgita Siaučiūnaitė-Verbickienė, eds., *Jewish Space in Central and Eastern Europe: Day-to-Day History* (Newcastle-upon-Tyne: Cambridge Scholars Publishing, 2007), 165-173.
    111. See, for example, the posters announcing matches at the Makabi field in the late 1920s in LCVA, f. 64, ap. 25, b. 89, ll. 10, 37, 38.
    112. Moritz Grossmann, *Yidishe vilne in wort un bild* (Vilne: Farlag drikeray "Hirsh Mats,"

1925); Mojżesz Worobiejczyk, *Ein Ghetto im Osten (Vilna)* (Zürich/Leipzig: O. Füssli, 1931).
113. Israel Klausner, *Vilnah, Yerushalayim de-Lita. Doroth ahronim, 1881-1939* (Hotsaath kibutz hameuhad: Bet lohame ha-getaʾot, 1983), 291-306; see also Ran, *Jerusalem of Lithuania*, 1:40-43.
114. For two Polish reactions to the 1931 incident and the growth of antisemitic feeling in the city, see Bronisław Żongołłowicz, *Dzienniki 1930-1936* (Warsaw: Fontes, 2004), 255-258; Wileńczuk, "Antysemityzm wileński," *Przegląd Wileński* 20, no. 1 (1937), 4-5.
115. Kahan, "University of Vilna," 168.
116. There were, however, Polish statesmen and officials who argued for a less repressive policy toward East Slavs. For one interesting example, see Timothy Snyder, *Sketches from a Secret War: A Polish Artist's Mission to Liberate Soviet Ukraine* (New Haven: Yale University Press, 2005).
117. Mykolas Biržiška, *Na posterunku wileńskim* (Wilno: Głos Litwy, 1920-1922), 5 vols. For one example of this historical argumentation, see his article from *Głos Litwy* of May 16, 1919, reprinted here in 1:6-7.
118. Biržiška, *Na posterunku* (article in *Głos Litwy*, no. 9, May 24, 1919), 1:20-22.
119. Mykolas Biržiška, *Vilniaus Golgota. Okupuotosios Lietuvos lietuvių ir kančių dienoraštis* (Kaunas: Vilniui vaduoti s-ga, 1930).
120. Ibid., 409-413, 437.
121. Mykolas Biržiška, *Spalių 9 diena (1920-1927)* (Kaunas: Vilniui vaduoti sąjungos leidinys, 1927); Mykolas Biržiška, *Dėl mūsų sostinės. Iš Vilniaus darbo atsiminimų* (London: Nida, 1960, 1962), vols. 1-2. Vol. 3 published by Viktoras Biržiška in 1967 after his brother's death: Mykolas Biržiška, *Per Vilnių į lenkus 1928 m.* (Kaunas: "Vilniaus" sp., 1939).
122. VMI, 2:43-44, 46-52, 77-86.
123. On Lithuanian culture in Vilnius during these years, see Valentinas Šiaudinis, "Vilniaus krašto lietuvių pasipriešinimas Lenkijos okupacijai" in K. Garšva und L. Grumadienė, eds., *Lietuvos Rytai. Straipsnių rinkinys* (Vilnius: Valstybinis leidybos centras, 1993), 179-206; and VMID, 368-396, 403-433.
124. Vytautas Steponaitis, *Vilniaus lietuvių spauda 1919-1928* (Kaunas: Vilniui vaduoti sąjunga, 1931); Danielius Alseika, *Vilniaus krašto lietuvių gyvenimas 1919-1934 metais* (Vilnius: Zorzos spaustuvė, 1935); Vincas Martinkėnas, *Vilniaus krašto lietuviškos mokyklos ir skatyklos 1919-1939 metais* (Vilnius: Mokslas, 1989); Vladas Žukas, *Marijos ir Jurgio Šlapelių lietuvių Knygynas Vilniuje* (Vilnius: Mokslo ir enciklopedijos leidybos institutas, 2000); Julius Būtėnas, "Lietuvių teatras Vilniuje," *Mūsų senovė* 2, no. 2 (1937), 214-236.
125. For reflections of two very different segments of Vilnius Lithuanian society ("high" and "low," so to speak), see Rapolas Mackonis, *Amžiaus liudininko užrašai. Atsiminimai* (Vilnius: Vilniaus rašytojų sąjungos leidykla, 2001); and *Vilniaus kalendorius 1926 metams* (Vilnius: "Ruch" spaustuvė, 1925).
126. Petras Klimas, *Mūsų kova dėl Vilniaus 1322/23-1922/23* (Kaunas: A. ir P. Klimų leidinys, 1923); Vytautas Bičiūnas, *Tiesa apie Vilnių* (Kaunas: Lietuvos Šaulių sąjungos leidinys, 1931); Kazys Pakštas, *Vilniaus problema ir kaip ją spręsti* (Kaunas: Žaibas, 1935).
127. Nastazija Kairiūkštytė, *Vilniaus vadavimo sąjunga 1925 04 26-1938 11 25* (Vilnius: LII, 2001). See also *Vilniaus geležinis fondas* (Vilnius: Vilniaus sp., 1934). For an example of LVV's propaganda/education efforts, see *Vilniaus kraštas nuo amžių lietuviškas* (Kaunas: Vilniui vaduoti sąjungos leidinys, 1936).
128. See, for example, *Vilnius ir Vilniaus kraštas. Krašto pažinimo pradai* (Kaunas: Vilniui Vaduoti Sąjunga, 1932).
129. J. V. Narbutas, *Vadovas po Vilnių* (Kaunas: Mokytojų knygynas, 1939); Mykolas Biržiška, *Apie lietuviškus Vilniaus miesto gatvėvardžius. Dėl J.V. Narbuto Vadovo po Vilnių ir jo gatvėvardžių* (Kaunas: sp. "Vilnius," 1939).
130. On the events leading to opening diplomatic relations and the situation afterward, see Stanisław Sierpowski, *Piłsudski w Genewie. Dyplomatyczny spór o Wilno w roku 1927* (Poznań: Instytut Zachodni, 1990); Stanisław Łossowski, *Stosunki polsko-litewskie, 1921-1939* (Warsaw: Instytut Historii PAN, 1997), 283-375.
131. On the importance of 1939 for Lithuania, see Šarūnas Liekis, *1939: The Year that Changed*

*Everything in Lithuanian History* (Amsterdam: Rodopi, 2010).
132. "Moda 1939," *Kurjer Wileński*, no. 78 (4754), March 19, 1939, 4.
133. Lucy Dawidowicz, *From that Place and Time: A Memoir, 1938-1947* (New York: W. W. Norton, 1989), 186.
134. "Na darmo trafi się p. Ribbentrop," *Kurjer Wileński*, no. 232 (4908), August 24, 1939, 1. The article wondered sardonically whether Ribbentrop would be greeted by the politburo member Lazar' Kaganovich (who was, of course, Jewish) upon his arrival in Moscow.
135. On the pact from a Lithuanian point of view, see Nerijus Šepetys, *Moltovo-Ribbentropo paktas ir Lietuva. Teorinės, istoriografinės ir istorinės problemos* (Vilnius: Vilniaus universitetas, 2002).

## Notes to Chapter 6

1. Stanisław Mianowski, *Świat, który odszedł. Wspomnienia Wilnianina 1945-1895* (Warsaw: Oficyna wydawnicza Rytm, 1995), 196.
2. Stanisława Lewandowska, *Wilno 1921-1944. Czasy i ludzie* (Warsaw: Neriton, 2009), 133-135.
3. On the military operations taking Wilno, see Czesław Grzelak, *Wilno 1939* (Warsaw: Bellona, 1993).
4. Mianowski, *Świat*..., 196-197.
5. Longin Tomaszewski, *Wileńszyzna lat wojny i okupacji 1939-1945* (Warsaw: Rytm, 2001), 32-40.
6. See, for example, the sober but despairing short article by Stanisław ("Cat") Mackiewicz, "Wilno," *Słowo* (September 18, 1939), reprinted in Stanisław Cat-Mackiewicz, *Teksty* (Warsaw: Czytelnik, 1990), 363.
7. Daniel Boćkowski, "'Za pierwszego sowieta'—okupacja radziecka Wilna jesienią 1939 r." in Feliksiak-2002, 2:229-240.
8. The literature on the AK (Armia Krajowa) and other forms of armed resistance is enormous. See, for example, the memoirs of seven young men from Wilno in the fateful month of September 1939: Lech Iwanowski et al., *Wilnianie we wrześniu 1939 r. (Prolog epopei)* (Bydgoszcz: Tow. Miłośników Wilna, 2000). For very detailed description of operations in the Wilno region, see Jarosław Wołkonowski, *Okręg Wileński Związku Walki Zbrojnej Armii krajowej w latach 1939-1945* (Warsaw: Adiutor, 1996). An excellent overview is provided in Bernhard Chiari and Jerzy Kochanowski, eds., *Die polnische Heimatarmee. Geschichte und Mythos der Armia Krajowa seit dem Zweiten Weltkrieg* (Munich: Oldenbourg, 2003).
9. Herman Kruk, *The Last Days of the Jerusalem of Lithuania: Chronicles from the Vilna Ghetto and the Camps, 1939-1944* (New Haven: Yale University Press, 2002), 23, 28-31.
10. Stanisława Lewandowska, *Życie codzienne Wilna w latach II wojny światowej* (Warsaw: Wydawnictwo Neriton, Instytut Historii PAN, 1997), 17.
11. Aleksander Wat, *My Century* (New York: New York Review Books, 2003); on this important figure, see Tomas Venclova, *Aleksander Wat: Life and Art of an Iconoclast* (New Haven: Yale University Press, 1996).
12. Dov Levin, "The Jews of Vilna under Soviet Rule, September 19-October 28, 1939," *Polin*, 9 (1996), 107-137.
13. For a pro-Lithuanian—and anti-Polish—version of the events of autumn 1939 to early 1940 by an eyewitness, see Jeronimas Cicėnas, *Vilnius tarp audrų* (Vilnius: Mokslo ir enciklop. leidykla, 1993), 231-290. For a balanced and scholarly Lithuanian account of this entire period, see Liudas Truska, *Lietuva 1938-1953 metais* (Kaunas: Šviesa, 1995).
14. On Lithuanian neutrality and the internment of Polish soldiers, see Piotr Łossowski, *Litwa a sprawy polskie 1939-1940* (Warsaw: PWN, 1985), 9-54.
15. Lietuvos Centrinis Valstybės Archyvas, Vilnius (LCVA), f. 377, ap. 10, b. 429. (1939) (Visuomenės komiteto pasitarimo, įvykusio 1939 m. rusgsėjo 18 d., dėl susidariusios vidaus padėtis išaiškinio visuomenei, dėl santykių su Tarybų Sąjunga ir kitomis didžiosiomis valstybėmis, dėl Vilniaus krašto

problemos protokolas). On the Lithuanian government between Germany and USSR in September 1939, see also LCVA, f. 923, ap. 1, bb. 1080, 1082, 1084.

16. LCVA, f. 317, ap. 1, b. 14. These lists were drawn up later in the year and in early 1940, mainly by the Lithuanian authorities and interested parties (families, colleagues, etc.) trying to get these individuals released from Soviet prisons.

17. Piotr Niwiński, *Garnizon konspiracyjny miasta Wilna* (Toruń: Wydaw. Adama Marszałka, 1999).

18. Regina Žepkaitė, *Vilniaus istorijos atkarpa, 1939 m. spalio 27 d.-1940 m. birželio 15 d.* (Vilnius: Mosklas, 1990), 27.

19. Bronisław Krzyżanowski, *Wileński matecznik 1939-1944 (z dziejów "Wachlarza" ir armii krajowej)* (Paris: Instytut literacki, 1979), 11.

20. Lewandowska, *Wilno 1921-1944*, 143-144.

21. On the negotiations and the contents of the pact, see Žepkaitė, *Vilniaus istorijos atkarpa*, 32-39; and Łossowski, *Litwa...*, 55-59.

22. On the takeover of Vilnius in the larger Lithuanian context, see Šarūnas Liekis, *1939: The Year that Changed Everything in Lithuanian History* (Amsterdam: Rodopi, 2010), 115-176.

23. Longin Tomaszewski, *Kronika Wileńska, 1939-1941* (Warsaw: Pomost, 1994), 44-47.

24. See, for example, the special issue of *Naujoji Romuva* dedicated to the occasion (no. 42-43 [October 22, 1939], 455-456).

25. LCVA, f. 496, ap. 2, d. 7. For a Lithuanian memoir of those days, see Bronius Aušrotas, *Sunkių sprendimų metas* (Vilnius: Vyriausioji enciklopedijų redakcija, 1990 [originally published Chicago, 1985]), 99-107.

26. "Sveikiname Lietuvos kariuomenę, įžygiavusią į sostinę Vilnių," *Vilniaus balsas*, no. 1 (October 28, 1939). This newspaper, published by the government as a "Lithuanian Vilnius newspaper," is a good source for official attitudes during the period October 1939 to June 1940.

27. LCVA, f. 923, ap. 2, b. 10.

28. Krzysztof Woźniakowski, "Wileńskie jednodniówki polskojęzykowe z października 1939 roku" in Woźniakowski, ed., *Prasa—Kultura—Wojna. Studia z dziejów czasopismiennictwa, kultury literackiej i z artystycznej lat 1939-1945. Seria druga* (Kraków: Wydaw. Naukowe WSP, 2005), 206-218.

29. Remarkably, even much later commentators tend to present the October 1939 events in an entirely positive light, e.g., Julius Butėnas, "Kaip grįžo mūms Vilnius," *Literatūra ir menas*, no. 35 (August 31, 1974), 13; Antanas Martinionis, *Žygis į Vilnių 1939 m. spalio 29-27 d.* (Vilnius: Kardas, 1995).

30. Mykolas Römeris, "Vilnius ir tarptautinė teisė," *Naujoji Romuva*, no. 42-43 (October 22, 1939), 749-750.

31. Lithuania was, of course, in no way unusual for favoring ethnic Lithuanians. Such policies were more or less universal in the mid-twentieth century (and, unfortunately, beyond). The rosy view of the "nation-state" as benevolent and liberating has recently—and very justifiably—been questioned in recent historiography, e.g., Phillip Ther, *Die dunkle Seite der Nationalstaaten. "Etnische Säuberungen" im modernen Europa* (Göttingen: Vandenhoeck & Ruprecht, 2011).

32. J. V. Narbutas, *Vadovas po Vilnių* (Kaunas: Mokytojų knygynas, 1939). The street name changes were based on suggestions by Professor M. Biržiška, which originally appeared in the periodical *Mūsų Vilnius*, no. 23-24, 1938 and were published as a pamphlet the following year: *Apie lietuviškus Vilniaus miesto gatvėvardžius* (Kaunas, 1939). It should be noted that not all suggestions were in fact taken up by the Lithuanian authorities.

33. Łossowski, *Litwa...*, 103.

34. *Vilniaus miesto gatvių sąrašas / Spis ulic miasta Wilna* (Vilnius: Spaustuvė "Neris," 1940).

35. A number of excellent archival documents from the (first) Lithuanian occupation of Vilnius can be found in VMID, 466-522.

36. Lewandowska, *Życie codzienne*, 28-44, 178-188. Lewandowska points out that, before the arrival of the Lithuanian troops, Poles were much more likely to know German or French than Lithuanian.

37. The Catholic clergy in Vilnius was notoriously pro-Polish (or, to put it another way, anti-Lithuanian). Łossowski, *Litwa*, 277–297; Žepkaitė, *Vilniaus istorijos atkarpa*, 132–139. Here as elsewhere the two historians differ strikingly in tone and interpretation.

38. LCVA, f. 401, ap. 6, b. 4 (October–December 1939), Valstybės saugumo policijos Vilniaus Apygardos biuleteniai. One police report (l. 2, October 30) stated that Poles were angered by the warm reception afforded the Red Army by some Jews, who then often were friendly with the Soviet authorities.

39. Tomaszewski, *Wileńszczyzna*, 70–109.

40. For one attempt to make sense of the catastrophe, see P. Kownacki, *"Gdyby Dziadek żył"* (Wilno: Spaustuvė "Bendras Darbas," 1940).

41. Danuta Ciesielska, "Strajk młodzieży szkolnej w Wilnie w grudniu 1939 r. Wspomnienia uczennicy gimnazjum im. Elizy Orzeszkowej" in Elżbieta Feliksiak and Marta Skorko-Barańska, eds., *Wilno jako ognisko oświaty w latach próby. Świadectwa o szkole (1939–1945)* (Białystok: Towarzystwo literackie im. Adama Mickiewicza,1994), 287–294.

42. Michał Römer, "O stosunkach polsko-litewskich w Wilnie na początku 1940 roku. Wybrane fragmenty 'Dziennika,'" *Lituanica*, no. 1 (1991), 64–69.

43. Lewandowska, *Życie codzienne*, 73.

44. LCVA, f. 401, ap. 6, b. 4, ll. 31–32. By law, either the Lithuanian (litas) or Polish (złoty) currencies could be accepted until the currency reform.

45. The conversion of złoty to litas was a constant story in Vilnius newspapers in November 1939. See, for example, "Dėl zlotų likimo," *Vilniaus balsas*, no. 13 (November 11, 1939), 3; and "Lit i złoty," *Kurjer Wileński*, no. 263 (4939), November 8, 1939, 1. See also Vladas Terleckas, "Vvedenie lita v vil'niusskom krae" in Alfonsas Eidintas, ed., *Novyi vzgliad na istoriiu Litvy* (Kaunas: Šviesa, 1991), 112–117.

46. Žepkaitė, *Vilniaus istorijos atkarpa*, 82–83; Lewandowska, *Życie codzienne*, 74–77.

47. Šarūnas Liekis, "The Transfer of the Vilna District into Lithuania, 1939," *Polin* 14 (2001), 212–213.

48. Andrzej Friszke, "Dialog Polsko-Żydowski w Wilnie 1939–1940," *Więź* 30, no. 4 (April 1987), 88–90.

49. I am following the account given by Liekis, *1939*, 265–269. As his source he cites LCVA, f. 401, ap. 6, bb. 1 and 4. While Liekis's description is rather confused, other sources also mention "pogroms" on October 31 and November 1.

50. Yitzhak Arad, "The Concentration of Refugees in Vilna on the Eve of the Holocaust," *Yad Vashem Studies* 9 (1973), 207–208. Arad mentions that one young Jew died in the violence and 200 were injured but these figures must be used with caution.

51. "Uniwersytet Wileński," *Kurjer Wileński*, no. 276 (4952), 1.

52. "Vilniaus universitetas," *Vilniaus balsas*, no. 42 (December 16, 1939), 1; and "Lietuvos universitetų įstatymas" in the previous day's issue.

53. In a secret memorandum (undated but probably late October 1939) on the "normalization of life in the Vilnius region" the very first matter mentioned is the need to transfer at least two faculties (humanities and law) from Kaunas to Vilnius University as soon as possible. LCVA, f. 317, ap. 1, b. 19, l. 1.

54. Archiwum Polskiej Akademii Nauk (APAN), Materiały Stefana Ehrenkreutza, syng. III/108, T.73.

55. The bitterness felt over this episode still comes through very clearly in the annotated document collection put together by one of Poland's most important historians of Lithuanian, Piotr Łossowski, *Likwidacja Uniwersytetu Stefana Batorego przez władze litewskie w grudniu 1939 r. Dokumenty i materiały* (Warsaw: "Interlibro," 1991). For a personal recollection of these events, see Leonid Żytkowicz, "Uniwersytet Stefana Batorego w ostatnich miesiącach swego istnienia. Wspomnienia asystenta" in Feliksiak-1992), 3:121–152.

56. LCVA, f. 401, ap. 6, b. 4, ll. 122–125, 141–144, 215–220.

57. Ibid., 232–240. On the transfer of property and hiring (mainly staff, not faculty), see LCVA, f. R856, ap. 1, b. 16.

58. Algirdas Augustaitis, "Kaip buvo atkurtas Vilniaus universitetas" in VMIS, 724–727, originally published in *Vakarinės naujienos* (February 2, 1990). See also Mykolas Biržiška, *Vilniaus universitetas, 1940-1941 m.* (Memmingas: "Mintis," 1948).

59. For documents on the establishment of Soviet rule in Lithuania, see E. Jacovskis, ed., *Tarybų valdžios atkūrimas Lietuvoje 1940-1941 metais* (Vilnius: Mintis, 1965).

60. Alfred Senn, *Lithuania 1940: Revolution from Above* (Amsterdam: Rodopi, 2007), 85–118.

61. For diametrically opposed portrayals of the events of summer 1940 in Lithuania, see V. Kancevičius, *1940 metų birželis Lietuvoje* (Vilnius: Mintis, 1973); Algirdas Budreckis, *Soviet Occupation and Annexation of the Republic of Lithuania June 15–August 3, 1940* (New York: Amerikos Lietuvių Tautinė Sąjunga, 1968). For all its Soviet rhetoric ("collapse of the fascist regime," "the great achievement of the Lithuanian Communist Party"), Kancevičius actually provides considerable useful information and sources. See the Soviet story told in documents in *Lietuvos TSR istorijos šaltiniai* (Vilnius: Valstybinės ir mokslinės literatūros leidykla, 1961), IV: 749–777.

62. On this process by a contemporary observer, Mykolas Römeris (Michał Römer), *Lietuvos Sovietizacija 1940-1941. Istorinė Lietuvos sovietizacijos apžvalga ir konstitucinis jos įvertinimas* (Vilnius: Lituanus, 1989). Römeris wrote this pamphlet during the war years. It remained in manuscript after his death (February 1945) and was only published during the perestroika period.

63. Anna Louise Strong, *Lithuania's New Way* (London: Lawrence & Wishart, 1941), 24–30.

64. Tomaszewski, *Kronika Wileńska*, 153–158; Genrikas Shadzhius, "Litva v 1940–1941 gg." in A. Eidintas et al., *Novyi vzgliad*, 155–177.

65. Lewandowska, *Życie codzienne*, 54–56; Arvydas Anušauskas, *Lietuvių tautos sovietinis naikinimas 1940-1958 metais* (Vilnius: Mintis, 1996), 16–140. The Anušauskas book is particularly valuable because of its extensive use of Russian and Lithuanian archives.

66. Henrikas Šadžius, *Socialistinio Vilniaus darbininkai (Pereinamuoju iš kapitalizmo į socializmą laikotarpiu)* (Vilnius: "Mokslas," 1980), 1–79. This works is very useful for the data it provides, despite its complete failure to deal with the national issue and its unquestioning acceptance of Soviet historiographical teleology (i.e., the belief that "building the working class" outweighs all else).

67. VMI, 2:146–151.

68. Israel Lempert, "Der goral fun YIVO in historishn iberbroch (1939–1941)," *YIVO-Bleter* 3, new series (1997), 9–42.

69. LCVA, f. R856, ap. 1, b. 134.

70. On the (initial) Soviet period and Vilnius University, see Mykolas Biržiška, *Vilniaus universitetas 1940-1941 m.* (Iš 'Minties') (Memmingen: 'Mintis," 1948). See also the articles in Pranas Čepėnas, ed. *Lietuvos universitetas 1579-1803-1922* (Chicago: Leidėjas Lietuvių Profesorių Draugija Amerikoje, 1972), 657–696.

71. P. Žostautaitė, "Darbininkų ir valstiečių kursai prie Vilniaus Valstybinio Universiteto 1941 ir 1944-1950," *LTSR MAD, serija A*, no. 1 (14) (1963), 183–188.

72. Vygintas Bronius Pšibilskis, *Mykolas Biržiška ir Vilniaus universitetas. Veiklos studija ir atsiminimų publikacija* (Vilnius: Vilniaus universiteto leidykla, 2008), 98–157.

73. *Vilniaus pedagoginis institutas* (Vilnius: Švyturys, 1942), 6.

74. M. Römeris, "Dienoraštis" in *Kultūros barai*, no. 9 (September 1991), 77.

75. For discussions about everyday issues in city administration in this period, see *Vilniaus miesto vykdomojo komiteto posėdžių protokolai 1940-1941 m.* (Vilnius: Pergalė, 1975). These meetings took place from November 14, 1940 to June 17, 1941; the original documents are located at LCVA, R776, ap. 7, bb. 9, 14, 109, 163, 169, 179, 200, 296, 339.

76. This proposed name change is rather perplexing, though the desire to get rid of the famous religious leader of the late eighteenth century, the Gaon ("genius") is readily understandable. Samuel Strashun, who had died in 1872, was also a well-known local Talmudist (who left a rich library of religious works to the city) and for that reason was probably unpalatable to communists. Dr. Shabad had been a distinguished physician and community leader who had died recently, in 1935. Mark Antokol'skii was, of course, born in Vilna but made his career in St. Petersburg and Paris. As a russified (at least by language) and non-religious Jew, he was probably less offensive than Strashun to communist sensibilities.

77. Vilniaus Apskrities Archyvas (VAA), f. 761, ap. 9, b. 71.
78. VAA, f. 761, ap. 4, b. 135.
79. Truska, *Lietuva 1938-1953*, 89; see also Helena Pasierbska, *Wileńskie Łukiszki na tle wydarzeń lat wojny 1939-1944* (Gdańsk: Drukarnia Oruńska, 2003).
80. Journalist Rapolas Mackonis remarked on the "chekists" carrying out mass arrests and trains waiting to whisk these people away from Vilnius: R. Mackonis, *Amžiaus liudininko užrašai. Atsiminimai* (Vilnius: Lietuvos rašytojų sąjungos leidykla, 2001), 291-292. See also the personal memoir of an arrested student in VMID, 526.
81. Arūnas Bubnys, *Vokiečių okupuota Lietuva (1941-1944)* (Vilnius: Lietuvos gyventojų genocido ir rezistencijos tyrimo centras, 1998), 23-68.
82. For a personal memoir of this anti-Soviet uprising, see Vytautas Rimkus, *Lietuvių sukilimas Vilniuje 1941 m. Iš asmeniškų prisiminimų ir išgyvenimų* (London: Nida Press, 1969).
83. M. Römeris, *Dienoraštis* in *Kultūros barai*, no. 9 (September 1991), 77-78 [June 22-24, 1941] and no. 10 (October 1991), 78 [June 24-26, 1941].
84. Truska, *Lietuva*, 102-105.
85. Arūnas Bubnys, *Lietuvių tautos sukilimas 1941 m. birželio 22-28 d.* (Vilnius: Lietuvos gyventojų genocido ir rezistencijos tyrimo centras, 2011), 451-462. It is indicative of the uprising's minor important for Vilnius that Bubnys devotes to the city only ten pages of a huge (600+ pp.) tome.
86. Joanna Mackiewiczowa, *Polacy na Litwie w latach II wojny światowej* (Bydgoszcz: TMW i ZW, 1996), 84-93.
87. LCVA, f. 419, ap. 2, b. 168, ll. 1-3.
88. See, for example, the announcement "Jaunieji Lietuviai!," *Naujoji Lietuva*, no. 22 (178), January 27, 1942, 1.
89. "Vasario šešioliktąją dirbame," *Naujoi Lietuva*, no. 39 (195), February 15, 1941, 1.
90. Ibid., no. 42 (February 19, 1941), 57 (March 18, 1942), 94 (April 22, 1942), 97 (April 25, 1942).
91. *Naujoji Lietuva* announced the closing of the university in no. 66, March 18, 1943. For a Soviet account of the university closing, see *Tiesa*, no. 95 (156), October 28, 1944, 2.
92. Biržiška, *Vilniaus universiteto*, 58; and *Vilniaus universiteto istorija 1940 1979* (Vilnius: Mokslas, 1979), 27-44. The latter account calls Biržiška an "active collaborator" with the German authorities" (30).
93. On this difficult period, see Pšibilskis, *Mykolas Biržiška*, 338-360.
94. Donata Linčiuvienė, ed., *Kultūrinis Vilniaus gyvenimas 1939-1945* (Vilnius: Lietuvių literatūros ir tautosakos institutas, 1999).
95. The best overall treatment of Nazi policy in Lithuania is Christoph Dieckmann, *Deutsche Besatzungspolitik in Litauen 1941-1944* (Göttingen: Wallstein Verlag, 2011). Useful but on the whole one-sided are Juozas Bulavas, *Vokiškųjų fašistų okupacinis Lietuvos valdymas (1941-44 m.)* (Vilnius: LTSR MA Ekonomikos institutas, 1969); and Arūnas Bubnys, *Vokiečių okupuota Lietuva (1941-1944)* (Vilnius: Lietuvos gyventojų genocido ir rezistencijos tyrimo centras, 1998).
96. Maria Wardzyńska, *Sytuacja ludności polskiej w Generalnym Komisariacie Litwy czerwiec 1941-lipiec 1944* (Warsaw: Instytut pamięci narodowej, 1993), 45-47.
97. Ibid., 57-65.
98. Ibid., 88-96; Lewandowska, *Życie codzienne*, 65-67.
99. For a short biography of Reinys (mainly on the period before 1914), see Rapolas Mackonis, *Dvylika Vilniaus kunigų* (Vilnius: Unitas, 1994), 34-36. See also Irena Mikłaszewicz, "Postawa biskupów wobec próby przeciwstania interesów katolików Polaków i Litwinów w Wilnie w latach 1944-1953" in Feliksiak-2002, 1:241-262.
100. On the sufferings of Poles during the war and their strained relations with Lithuanians, see, e.g., Helena Pasierbska, *Wileńskie Ponary* (Gdańsk: Nakł. autora, 1996); Dariusz Ratajczak, *Polacy na Wilenszczyźnie 1939-1944* (Warsaw: Wydaw. O.N-a, 1990); Witold Staniewicz, *Wilno w latach Drugiej Wojny Światowej* (Poznań, 1946); Krzysztof Tarka, "Spór o Wilno. Ze stosunków polsko-litewskich w latach Drugiej Wojny Światowej," *Zeszyty Historyczne*, no. 114 (1995), 60-83.

101. See, for example, Joanna Mackiewiczowa, *Polacy na Litwie w latach II Wojny Światowej* (Bydgoszcz: Tow. Miłośników Wilna, 1998). On the sensitive issue of collaboration, see the careful and perceptive essays by V. Liulevičius, Chr. Dieckmann, S. Sužiedėlis, M. McQueen, and E. Aleksandravičius in Joachim Tauber, ed., *"Kollaboration" in Nordosteuropa. Erscheinungsform und Deutungen im 20. Jahrhundert* (Wiesbaden: Harrassowitz Verlag, 2006), 118-191.

102. See, for example, Helen Holzman, *"Dies Kind soll leben"* (Frankfurt/Main: List Taschenbuch, 2002), 12-15; N. N. Shneidman, *Jerusalem of Lithuania: The Rise and Fall of Jewish Vilnius, a Personal Perspective* (Oakville, Ontario: Mosaic Press, 1998), 43-48; Grigorii Shur (Šuras), *Evrei v Vil'no. Khronika 1941-1944 gg.* (Vilnius: Obrazovanie-Kul'tura, 2000), 33-37.

103. Kruk, *Last Days*, 49. See also the shocked reaction to the ease with which the Germans took Vilna in Yitskhok Rudashevski, *The Diary of the Vilna Ghetto* (Tel Aviv: Ghetto Fighters' House, 1973), 23-29.

104. Liudas Truska, *Lietuva 1938-1953 metais* (Kaunas: Šviesa, 1995), 98-105.

105. For two serious overviews of the issue, see Yitzhak Arad, "The Murder of the Jews in German-Occupied Lithuania (1941-1944)" and Arūnas Bubnys, "The Holocaust in Lithuania: An Outline of the Major Stages and Their Results" in *The Vanished World of Lithuanian Jews*, ed. Alvydas Nikžentaitis, Stefan Schreiner, and Darius Staliūnas (Amsterdam: Rodopi, 2004), 175-221.

106. "The Persecution and Mass Murder of Lithuanian Jews during Summer and Fall of 1941: Sources and Analysis" in Christoph Dieckmann and Saulius Sužiedėlis, *Lietuvos žydų persekiojimas ir masinės žudynės 1941 m. vasarą ir rudenį/The Persecution and Mass Murder of Lithuanian Jews during Summer and Fall of 1941* (Vilnius: Margi raštai, 2006), 99.

107. Saliamonas Vaintraubas, ed., *Garažas. Aukos—Budeliai—Stebėtojai* (Vilnius: Lietuvos žydų bendruomenė, 2002) compiles numerous eyewitness accounts as well as commentary.

108. Yitzhak Arad, "The Concentration of Refugees in Vilna on the Eve of the Holocaust," *Yad Vashem Studies* 9 (1973), 201-214.

109. Herman Kruk, *The Last Days of the Jerusalem of Lithuania: Chronicles from the Vilna Ghetto and the Camps, 1939-1944* (New Haven: Yale University Press, 2002), 46-60.

110. LCVA, R1421, ap. 1, b. 525 (USHMM microfilm 1999.A.0105, reel 24).

111. Failure to wear the yellow star (i.e., attempting to pass as non-Jewish) figures prominently in the arrest records of Jews, especially in the early period. LCVA, R689, ap. 3, bb. 68, 74, 241, 275, 284 (USHMM microfilm 1999.A.0108, reels 4, 8). At this point failure to wear the yellow star was punished by a fine of 1000 rubles or 30 days arrest. It should be noted that these are records of Vilnius city police, kept entirely in Lithuanian.

112. For a contemporary Nazi German overview of "Judenghettos im Baltikum," focusing mainly on "Wilna, Kauen, Kedanen" but with a broader historical overview, see LCVA, R1421, ap. 1, b. 233 (United States Holocaust Memorial Museum [USHMM] microfilm 1999.A.0105, reel 13).

113. A printed trilingual proclamation accusing two Jews of shooting at German soldiers and forbidding all Jews from leaving their dwellings between 3 p.m. and 10 a.m. was posted on the streets on September 1. LCVA, R614, ap. 1, b. 695 (USHMM microfilm 1999.A.0108, reel 17).

114. On the "Great Provocation," see Yitzak Arad, *Ghetto in Flames: The Struggle and Destruction of the Jews in Vilna in the Holocaust* (Jerusalem: Yad Vashem, 1980), 102-105; Mark Dvorzshetski (Dworzecki), *Yerushalayim delita in kampf un umkum* (Paris: L'union populaire juive en France, 1948), 51-57; Shur, *Evrei*, 44-46; Kruk, *Last Days*, 81-93. Kruk, unlike the others, mentions a German soldier being wounded in the arm.

115. Henri Minczeles, *Vilna, Wilno, Vilnius. La Jérusalem de Lituanie* (Paris: Editions la découverte, 1993), 383-386; Kruk, *Last Days*, 95-110.

116. For some documents on the duties of the Vilnius ghetto police, see LCVA, R1421, ap. 1, bb. 34, 36, 38 (USHMM 1999.A.0105, reel 2). The latter document (b. 38) is a list in Russian, dated 1948 and marked "translation from German," giving the names of ghetto policemen.

117. Arad, *Ghetto*, 133-142; N. N. Shneidman, *Jerusalem of Lithuania: The Rise and Fall of Jewish Vilnius, a Personal Perspective* (Oakville, Ontario: Mosaic Press, 1998), 59-61.

118. Kruk, *Last Days*, 133 (these words were written around December 21, 1941).

119. Dvorzshetski speaks of the "stabilizatsie epokhe fun geto," Dvorzshetski, *Yerushalayim delita*, 140-145.
120. More generally on the differences between the Kaunas and Vilnius Jewish ghetto administrations, see Dina Porat, "The Jewish Councils of the Main Ghettos of Lithuania: A Comparison," *Modern Judaism* 13, no. 2 (1993), 149-163; and Yitzhak Arad, "The Judenräte of the Lithuanian Ghettos of Kovno and Vilna" in *Patterns of Jewish Leadership in Nazi Europe 1933-1945* (Jerusalem: Yad Vashem, 1979), 93-112.
121. Minczeles, *Vilna*, 380-383; Arad, *Ghetto*, 95-98; Kruk, *Last Days*, 52-55, 67-70, 80.
122. The best overall discussion of this controversial figure is N. N. Shneidman, *The Three Tragic Heroes of the Vilnius Ghetto: Witenberg, Sheinbaum, Gens* (Oakville, Ontario: Mosaic Press, 2002), 103-131. See also Arad, *Ghetto*, 125-127, 284-291 and *passim*. Soviet historiography denigrated him as a "Lithuanian bourgeois nationalist" and "fascist," e.g., *Masinės žudynės Lietuvoje (1941-1944). Dokumentų rinkinys* (Vilnius: "Mintis," 1965), 1:172n.
123. Kruk, *Last Days*, 148 (entry for January 1, 1942).
124. On the Vilna myth, see Samuel Kassow, "The Uniqueness of Jewish Vilna" in Larisa Lempertienė, ed., *Vilniaus Žydų intelektualinis gyvenimas iki antrojo pasaulinio karo/Jewish Intellectual Life in Pre-War Vilna* (Vilnius: Lietuvos žydų bendruomenė, 2004), 147-161.
125. On the "paper brigade," as it was called, see David E. Fishman, *Dem Feuer entrissen. Die Rettung jüdischer Kulturschätze in Wilna* (Hannover: Laurentius, 1998).
126. Kruk, *Last Days*, 212.
127. *Vilniaus geto afišos/Vilna Ghetto Posters. Albumas—katalogas* (Vilnius: Baltos Lankos, 2006). For the original posters, see LCVA, R1421, ap. 2, bb. 1-221 (each file contains one poster). These files—unfortunately photographed in black and white only—are available on microfilm at USHMM, 1999.A.0105, reel 32.
128. Kruk, *Last Days*, 174 (entry for January 17, 1942).
129. Joshua Sobol, "The Passion of Life in the Ghetto" in *The Days of Memory/Atminties dienos* (Vilnius: Baltos Lankos, 1995), 247-250. For reports (in Yiddish) on the activities of the cultural section in the Vilnius ghetto, see LCVA, R1421, ap. 1, bb. 226, 246-270 (USHMM microfilm 1999.A.0105, reels 13-14).
130. The Germans were also interested in religious life in Jewish Vilnius, at least from the historical perspective, as reports on the "Stadtsynagoge" and "Klausen" (*kloyzn*) show: LCVA, R1421, ap. 1, b. 505 (USHMM microfilm 1999.A.0105, reel 23).
131. For details on the use of Jewish slave labor, see LCVA, R614, ap. 1, b. 249 (USHMM microfilm 1999.A.0108, reel 3).
132. LCVA, R614, ap. 1, b. 307 (USHMM microfilm 1999.A.0108, reel 3).
133. On confiscated Jewish property, Jewish property stolen by Lithuanians (and claimed by the Nazi authorities), and attempts to collect back taxes on confiscated Jewish real estate, see LCVA, R614, ap. 1, b. 408, 409, 409a (USHMM microfilm 1999.A.0108, reel 8); R643, ap. 1, bb. 434, 750, 759 (USHMM microfilm 1999.A.0108, reel 13); R643, ap. 3, bb. 44, 198-200 (USHMM microfilm 1999.A.0108, reel 2).
134. LCVA, R614, ap. 3, b. 435, parts ("tomai") I-IV (USHMM microfilm 1999.A.0108, reels 13-14).
135. The remarkable documentary film "Partisans of Vilna" (1986, directed by Joshua Waletzky), must also be noted here. Actual participants in the events of September 1943 appear in the film, including Abba Kovner.
136. Kovner, quoted in Arad, *Ghetto*, 231-232. Another memoir of the ghetto fights in Vilna, with a strong Betar-Zionist emphasis (though the author also participated in F.P.O.), is Chaim Lazar, *Destruction and Resistance: A History of the Partisan Movement in Vilna* (New York: Shengold Publishers, 1985).
137. Shneidman, *Jerusalem of Lithuania*, 72-91.
138. Shneidman, *Three Tragic Heroes*, 43-64.
139. On the F.P.O. and its members see, for example, Rachilė Margolis, "Pogrindinė antifašistinė organizacija FPO Vilniaus Gete (1942-1943)" in *Days of Memory*, 296-311.

140. Shneidman, *Jerusalem of Lithuania*, 92–108; Dvorzshetski, *Yerushalayim delita*, 466–474; Marija Rolnikaitė, "Paskutinės Vilniaus Geto dienos" in *Days of Memory*, 155–164; Arad, *Ghetto*, 420–440.

141. Reuben Ainsztein, *Jewish Resistance in Nazi-Occupied Eastern Europe* (New York: Barnes & Noble, 1974), 486–518: "Vilno: The Tragic Failure."

142. Ehrenburg and Grossman, *Complete Black Book*, 285–287; Mendel Balberyszski, *Likwidacja getta wileńskiego* (Warsaw: WINW, 1946).

143. It should be stressed that thousands of Poles and Lithuanians were murdered in Ponary, but the largest number of victims were Jews. For somewhat Polonocentric (but still valuable) accounts, see Helena Pasierbska, *Wileńskie Ponary* (Gdańsk: Nakł. Autora, 1996); and Monika Tomkiewicz, *Zbrodnia w Ponarach 1941–1944* (Warsaw: IPN, 2008).

144. On the very difficult issue of Lithuanians and the Holocaust, see Alfonsas Eidintas, *Žydai, lietuviai ir holokaustas* (Vilnius: Vaga, 2002); and Karen Ehrlich Friedman, "German/Lithuanian Collaboration in the Final Solution 1941–1944" (Ph.D. diss., University of Illinois at Chicago, 1994).

145. Kazimierz Sakowicz, *Ponary Diary 1941–1943. A Bystander's Account of a Mass Murder* (New Haven: Yale University Press, 2005); translation of *Dziennik pisany w Ponarach od 11 lipca 1941 r. do 6 listopada 1943 r.* (Bydgoszcz: Tow. Miłośników Wilna, 1999). The original handwritten diary was discovered in the Lithuanian Central State Archive (LCVA) in Vilnius by Rachel Margolis.

146. Bubnys, *Vokiečių okupuota Lietuva*, 374–383.

147. Zygmunt Mieczysław Grunt Mejer, *Partyzancka Brygada "Kmcica." Wileńszczyzna 1943* (Bydgoszcz: Tow. Miłośników Wilna, 1997).

148. Bernhard Chiari, "Kein Pakt mit Slawen. Deutsch-polnische Kontakte im Wilna-Gebiet 1944," *Osteuropa* 50, no. 4 (2000), 133–153; Stanisława Lewandowska, "Wileńskie rozmowy niemiecko-polskie w lutym 1944 r.," *Dzieje Najnowsze* 34, no. 1 (2002), 101–145.

149. "Dienoraštis," *Kultūros barai*, no. 2 (February 1992), 74 (entry for February 28, 1944).

150. Lewanska, *Życie codzienne*, 301–308; Tomaszewski, *Kronika*, 476–498. For documents (from the Lithuanian Soviet point of view) on the uprising, see Liudas Truska, "1944 m. liepa. Lenkų Armijos Krajovos operacija 'Ostra Brama' ir lietuvos TSR vadovų pozicija" in *Vilniaus istorijos metraštis* (2007), 249–252. See also the essays in Jarosław Wołkonowski, ed., *Sympozjum historyczne "Rok 1944 na Wileńszczyźnie"* (Warsaw: "Efekt," 1996).

151. Aleksander Srebrakowski, "Liczba Polaków na Litwie według danych spisu ludności z 27 maja 1942 roku," *Wrocławskie Studia wschodnie*, no. 1 (1997), 169–186; Nastazija Kairiūkštytė, "Vilniaus krašto gyventojų sudėties pokyčiai 1939–1946," *Lietuvos Rytai*, 281–298.

152. Stanisława Lewandowska, *Wilno 1944–1945. Oczekiwanie ii nastroje* (Warsaw: Neriton, 2007), 65.

153. "Podpisanie Układu," *Prawda Wileńska*, no. 57 (319), September 26, 1944, 1. It is remarkable that after this front-page announcement of the signing of this agreement, the planned evacuations are not mentioned again until the very end of the year. "Zawiadomienie do Polaków i byłych obywateli polskich narodowości żydowskiej, zamieszkałych w Litewskiej SRR," in no. 135 (397), December 27, 1944, 1.

154. LCVA, f. R841, ap. 10, b. 9.

155. *Gazeta Wileńska* 1, no. 1 (July 17, 1944).

156. *Gazeta Wileńska* 1, no. 65 (327) (October 5, 1944).

157. Lewandowska, *Wilno 1944–1945*, 55–57; Lewandowska, "Społeczność polska Wilna wobec nowej rzeczywistości. Postawy i nastroje 1944–1945," *Dzieje Najnowsze* 37, no. 4 (2005), 77–91.

158. LCVA, f. R754, ap. 13, b. 40, ll. 20–24, 88–91. The excerpts from letters, in Russian translation (with the remark "translated from Polish"), formed part of frequent NKVD *spetssoobshcheniia* (special reports).

159. Lewandowska, *Życie codzienne*, 330.

160. Theodore R. Weeks, "Population Politics in Vilnius 1944–1947: A Case Study of Socialist-Sponsored Ethnic Cleansing," *Post-Soviet Affairs* 23, no. 1 (2007), 76–95.

161. LCVA, f. R841, ap. 10, b. 27, l. 64.

162. For correspondence regarding individuals of "doubtful" nationality, see LCVA, f. R841, ap. 10, b. 37.
163. Aleksander Srebrakowski, *Polacy w Litewskiej SSR* (Toruń: Adam Marszałek, 2001), 98. Original source: AAN, Akta Gł. Pełnomocnika d/s Ewakuacji..., sygn. 167.
164. On the repatriation, from Polish and Lithuanian points of view, see Vitalija Stravinskienė, *Tarp gimtinės ir tėvynės. Lietuvos SSR gyventojų repatriacija į Lenkiją (1944-1947, 1955-1959 m.)* (Vilnius: LII, 2011); Jan Czerniakiewicz, *Repatriacja ludności polskiej z ZSRR 1944-1948* (Warsaw: PWN, 1987); Nastazija Kairiūkštytė, "Lenkų repatriacija iš Lietuvos 1944-1947 m." in *Rytų Lietuva* (Vilnius: Mokslas, 1992), 124-141.
165. The "repatriation" of Poles from Vilnius was just one part of a much larger wave of "unmixing of nationalities" after World War II. For a broader perspective, see Krystyna Kersten, *Repatriacja ludności polskiej po II wojnie światowej. Studium historyczne* (Wrocław: Ossolineum, 1974); and Philipp Ther, *Die dunkle Seite der Nationalstaaten. "Ethnische Säuberungen" im modernen Europa* (Göttingen: Vandenhoeck & Ruprecht, 2011).
166. VAA, f. 761, ap. 9, b. 71. The documents in this file are a remarkable mixture of Lithuanian and Russian texts, including one (ll. 72-73) pointing out that the Russian versions of street names should not simply be transliterations of the Lithuanian but should follow Russian grammar (e.g., not "Antokoľskio" in Russian but Antokoľskogo). This suggestion was not, however, consistently adopted in Soviet times.
167. Vladislovas Mikučianis, *Norėjau dirbti Lietuvoje* (Vilnius: Vilniaus dailės akademijos leidykla, 2001), 64.
168. VAA, f. 5, bb. 1014 and 598 contain dozens of pictures of the devastated city in late 1944 and early 1945.
169. For photographs of the destroyed Jewish part of Vilnius in1944, see Leyzer Ran, *Yerushalayim de Lita = Jerusalem of Lithuania* (New York: Laureate Press, 1974), 2:515-522.
170. Mikučianis, *Norėjau dirbti Lietuvoje*, 69.
171. For more on the training of architects in postwar Vilnius, see Algimantas Mačiulis, "Prieštaringas dešimtmetis," *Acta Academiiae Artium Vilnensis/Vilniaus Dailės Akademijos darbai* 2 (1993), 138-149.
172. Mikučianis, *Norėjau dirbti Lietuvoje*, 75-77. The temporary monument was in place already for the May 1, 1945 holiday: see *Tiesa*, no. 102 (632), May 4, 1945, 3.
173. Mikučianis, *Norėjau dirbti Lietuvoje*, 78-79. See also the details and photo of the "House of Scientists" in *Vilnius 1900-2005: A Guide to Modern Architecture* (Vilnius: Architektūros fondas, 2005), G1.
174. *Vilnius 1900-2005*, G2-G6.
175. V. B. Pšibilskis, "Byla dėl Vilniaus Arkikatedros. 1949-1956," *Kultūros barai*, no. 5 (May 1995), 66-72.
176. Mikučianis, *Norėjau dirbti Lietuvoje*, 86-88.
177. Kazys Misius, "Bažnyčių uždarinėjimas Vilniuje pokario metais," in Manelis and Samavičius, eds., VMIS, 812-815.
178. On the structure and personnel of the security apparatus in the first years of the LSSR, see Liudas Truska, Arvydas Anušauskas, Inga Petravičiūtė, *Sovietinis saugumas Lietuvoje 1940-1953 metais* (Vilnius: Lietuvos gyventojų genocido ir rezistencijos tyrimo centras, 1999).
179. For a final (Soviet) report on the evacuations of Poles, see LCVA, f. R841, ap. 10, b. 27, ll. 94-A somewhat different report covering the same events was published by Edward Kołodziej, "Sprawozdania Głównego Pełnomocnika Rządu RP do spraw Ewakuacji Ludności Polskiej z Litewskiej SRR w Wilnie z przebiegu zbiorowej repatriacji w latach 1945-1946," *Teki Archywalne*, no. 2 (24) (1997), 167-194.
180. L. Bagrowska, "Muzeum żydowskie w Vilnius" [sic], *Prawda Wileńska*, no. 52 (452), March 4, 1945, 2.
181. "Ponary—okrutna przeszłość," *Prawda Wileńska*, no. 30 (August 25, 1944).
182. "Do Narodu Litewskiego" (signed by the Lithuanian communists "J. Paleckis, M. Gedwilas, A. Snieczkus"), *Prawda Wileńska*, no. 33 (433) February 10, 1945, 1-2.

183. "Bystree vosstanovim stolitsu Sovetskoi Litvy," *Sovetskaia Litva*, no. 66 (1716), March 20, 1949, 1.
184. J. Milinis, "Dėmesio! Kalba Vilnius!" *Tiesa*, no. 6 (536), January 9, 1945, 2.
185. See especially the entire issue of *Tiesa*, no. 77 (607), April 4, 1945; and the interesting article by architect J. Kumpis on plans to rebuild the capital in no. 81 (611), April 8, 1945.
186. "Obóz śmierci w Oswięcimiu," *Prawda Wileńska*, no. 88 (350), November 1, 1944, 2.
187. "Kombinat śmierci w Oświęcimie," *Prawda Wileńska*, no. 46 (446), 2.
188. David Fishman, *Dem Feuer entrissen*, 23-31.
189. See the several dozen files in LCVA, f. R1390. These files are available in microfilm at the United States Holocaust Memorial Museum, General Directorate of Lithuania Archives collection, 1998.A.0073, reel 52. Unfortunately in many cases we do not have the artifacts or documents themselves, only lists of material that was later lost.
190. Abraham (Avraam) Sutzkever, *Fun vilner geto* (Moscow: "Der emes," 1946); Shmerke Kaczerginski, *Khurbn vilne* (New York: Bikher-farlag, 1947).
191. Fishman writes that the museum was closed in 1948 but both Ran and Atamukas agree that the museum was closed down in April 1949. YdL, 2:524 (which includes a picture of the trilingual sign outside the museum in Yiddish, Lithuanian, and Russian); Solomonas Atamukas, *Lietuvos žydų kelias. Nuo XIV amžiaus iki XX a. pabaigos* (Vilnius: Alma littera, 2001), 300-303.
192. See, for example, the photographs from 1944 (before page 49) in G. Agranovskii, I. Guzenberg, *Litovskii Ierusalim. Kratkii putevoditel' po pamiatnym mestam evreiskoi istorii i kul'tury v Vil'niuse* (Vilnius: Lituanus, 1992). This guidebook, for all its interesting facts, is not always very helpful to the historian as it concentrates on Jewish sites that have survived. See also Genrikh Agranovskii and Irina Guzenberg, *Vil'na. Po sledam Litovskogo Ierusalima* (Vil'nius: Gosudarstvennyi evreiskii muzei, 2011).
193. Mikučianis, *Norėjau dirbti Lietuvoje*, 90-91.
194. On the Great Synagogue, with a number of excellent photographs—including one of the still-standing shell of the synagogue in 1946—see Aliza Cohen-Mushlin et al., *Synagogues in Lithuania: A Catalogue* (Vilnius: Vilnius Academy of the Arts, 2012), 2:239-242, 284-293.
195. Agranovskii/Guzenberg, *Litovskii Ierusalim*, 69-70.
196. On the old Jewish cemetery in Vilnius, see J. Klauzner, *Korot beit ha'almin ha'yasan bev-ilnah* (Wilno: G. Kleckin, 1935).
197. See the photographs of the old Jewish cemetery, taken in 1944, in Ran, *Yerushalayim de Lita*, 2:532.
198. Mikučianis, *Norėjau dirbti Lietuvoje*, 108. For more on this new Jewish cemetery at Šeškinė, see Agranovskii/Guzenberg, *Litovskii Ierusalim*, 64-66.
199. Ran, *Yerushalayim de Lita*, 2:533-4 has photographs of both monuments.
200. Šadžius, *Socialistinio Vilniaus darbininkai*, 83-120.
201. VMI, 2:249.
202. *Tiesa*, no. 87 (148), October 19, 1944, 3.
203. *VMI*, 2:265-268; *Vilniaus universiteto istorija 1940-1979*, 45-54, 83-102.
204. VMI, 2:261-262.
205. *Vil'nius. Kratkii putvoditel'. Istoricheskie pamiatniki i kul'turno-prosvetitel'nye uchrezhdeniia* (Vil'nius: Gosudarstvennoe izdatel'stvo politicheskoi i nauchnoi literatury, 1950), 5-6.
206. Juozas Jurginis and Vladislavas Mikučianis, *Vilnius. Tarybų Lietuvos sostinė* (Vilnius: Valstybinė politinės ir mokslinės literatūros leidykla, 1956), 33-35.
207. *Vil'nius. Kratkii putvoditel'*, 18-22.
208. For an excellent photograph of the square, ca. 1955, see Jurginis and Mikučianis, *Vilnius*, 56-57. On the monument, see the entry in *Lietuvos TSR istorijos ir kultūros paminklų sąvadas* (Vilnius: Vyriausioji Enciklopedijų leidykla, 1988), 1:120-121.
209. See the view along the Neris with construction cranes in Jurginis and Mikučianis, *Vilnius*, 50-51; on industrial development, 69-79.
210. Officially the bridge was known as Černiachovskio tiltas until the late 1980s. See the

entry in *LTSR istorijos ... paminklų sąvadas*, 1:126-127.
211. Jurginis and Mikučianis, *Vilnius*, 110-111.
212. On street names and changes, see Jonas Jurkštas, *Vilniaus vietovardžiai* (Vilnius: Mokslas, 1985); and Antanas Čaplinskas, *Vilniaus gatvės. Istorija, vardynas, žemėlapiai* (Vilnius: Charibdė, 2000), 217-221 and *passim*.
213. Juozas Maniušis, *Tarybų Lietuvos statybose* (Vilnius: Valst. Polit. ir moksl. lit. leid., 1955), 8-28.
214. Jurginis and Mikučianis, *Vilnius*, 158-169.

## Notes to Chapter 7

1. VMID, 670.
2. For a brilliant examination of the complicated interplay of ideology and everyday life "performance," see Alexei Yurchak, *Everything Was Forever, Until It Was No More: The Last Soviet Generation* (Princeton: Princeton University Press, 2006). Most of Yurchak's examples are from the late 1970s and 1980s, but these processes, attitudes, and behaviors began to take shape, I believe, in the 1960s.
3. Geoffrey Hosking, *Rulers and Victims: The Russians in the Soviet Union* (Cambridge: Belknap Press of Harvard University Press, 2006), 275. Hosking gives the following figures (in millions of square meters): (1955) 640, (1964) 1182, (1980) 2202.
4. Mark B. Smith, *Property of Communists: The Urban Housing Program from Stalin to Khrushchev* (DeKalb: Northern Illinois University Press, 2010); Gregory D. Andrusz, *Housing and Urban Development in the USSR* (London: Macmillan, 1984).
5. While specific developments in Vilnius were unique, many general tendencies were echoed throughout the USSR. On this, see Blair A. Ruble, "From *khrushcheby* to *korobki*" in William C. Brumfeld and Blair A. Ruble, eds., *Russian Housing in the Modern Age: Design and Social History* (New York: Woodrow Wilson Center Press and Cambridge University Press, 1993), 232-270.
6. Leonid Brezhnev referred to the present period as one of "developed socialism" at the Twenty-Fourth Party Congress in 1971. In many ways, my term "socialist normalcy" coincides with this concept.
7. For an overview of the period 1939-1944 in Vilnius, see Theodore R. Weeks, "A Multiethnic City in Transition: Vilnius's Stormy Decade, 1939-1949," *Eurasian Geography and Economics* 47, no. 2 (2006), 153-175.
8. See, for example, the still very helpful—though not at all points!—two-volume history of the city published in this period, J. Jurginis, V. Merkys et al., *Vilniaus miesto istorija* (here VMI, vols. 1 and 2). Not surprisingly for a work published in 1968 and 1972, the Great October Socialist Revolution provides the break between volumes.
9. For a sophisticated examination of Lithuanian culture and memory in the postwar, see Violeta Davoliūtė, *The Making and Breaking of Soviet Lithuania: Memory and Modernity in the Wake of War* (London: Routledge, 2013).
10. *Vil'nius. Statisticheskii sbornik 1945-1964 gody* (Vil'nius: TsSU LSSR Statisticheskoe upravlenie goroda Vil'niusa, 1965), 8. See also Vida Kasparavičienė et al., eds., *Vilniečio portretas. Sociologiniai matmenys* (Vilnius: Filosofijos, sociologijos ir teisės institutas, 1995).
11. Antanas Papšys, *Vilnius. Mažasis vadovas* (Vilnius: Mintis, 1988), 33-40.
12. Inga Liutkevičienė, *Déjà vu Vilnius 1974-1990* (Vilnius: "Balto Print," 2012).
13. "Vilniaus miesto partinės organizacijos viekla socializmo įtvirtinimo ir socialistinės visuomenės sukūrimo laikotarpiu" in VMI, 2:254-259.
14. *Vilniaus miesto darbo žmonių deputatų Tarybos ir jos vykdomojo komiteto svarbesnių sprendimų rinkinys* (Vilnius: Valstybinė politinės ir mokslinės literatūros leidykla, 1959).
15. *Trumpa informacija apie Vilniaus miesto darbo žmonių deputatų Tarybos Vydomojo komiteto veiklą 1970 metais* (Vilnius: LKP CK leid. Ap., 1970).
16. *Vilniaus miesto darbo žmonių deputatų Tarybos ir jos vykdomojo komiteto svarbesnių spren-*

*dimų rinkinys* (Vilnius: Valstybinė politinės ir mokslinės literatūros leidykla, 1973).

17. Gediminas Valiuškis, *Vilniaus architektūra šiandien ir rtyoj* (Vilnius: "Mintis," 1965). This is a double-sided illustrated flyer without page numbering.

18. *LTSR paminklų sąvadas*, 1:338–342. This guide of architectural monuments is arranged by streets; hence, the articles on these buildings follow one another. On the post office reconstruction, see also Iu. Iaraov, "Pochtamt v Vil'niuse" in *Arkhitekturnoe tvorchestvo SSSR* (Moscow: Stroizdat, 1973), vol. 1.

19. *LTSR paminklų sąvadas*, 1:347–352.

20. Antanas Papšys, *Vilnius: A Guide* (Moscow: Progress Publishers, 1980), 135–137.

21. *LTSR paminklų sąvadas*, 1:336–337.

22. Ibid., 1:354–355.

23. The new Opera is pictured in the Lithuanian SSSR architects' monthly for November 1974 specifically connecting the opening of this building with the fifty-seventh anniversary of the Great October Revolution. *Statyba ir architektūra* (November 1974), 1.

24. Vytautas Jurkštas [V. Iurkshtas], *Novaia arkhitektura v tsentre starogo Vil'niusa* (Vil'nius: LitINTI, 1983), 10–12.

25. The issue of keeping the Old Town from decay while preserving it from unwanted changes concerned Vilnius architects vitally. On this topic, see, for example, Vytautas Jurkštas, *Senamiesčių regeneracija. Architektūros harmonizavivo problema* (Vilnius: Technika, 1994); Vytautas Kriščiūnas, Mykolas Prikšaitis, "Besaugant Vilniaus paveikslų galerijos pastatą," *Statyba ir architektūra* (April 1975), 23–24; Vytautas Jurkštas, "Senamiestis—mūsų pasididžiavimas ir rūpestis," *Statyba ir architektūra* (June 1976), 6–9; R. Kaminskas and J. [Ia.] Jaloveckas [Ialovetskas], "Regeneratsiia istoricheskogo iadra Vil'niusa," *Arkhitektura SSSR* (mart–aprel' 1984), 42–45.

26. Andrusz quotes the Central Party and Council of Ministers resolution of February 3, 1970 "O sereznykh narusheniiakh gosudarstvennoi distsipliny v gorodskom stroitel'stve i zhilishchnom khoziaistve," which complained that "in many cities, especially Republican capitals [i.e., capitals of Soviet republics] . . . administrative buildings, entertainment and sports complexes" were going up rather than schools, housing, and hospitals. Andrusz, *Housing*, 52.

27. "Televizijos ir radijo laidų perdavimo stoties bokšto statyboje," *Statyba ir architektūra* (April 1975), 6–9; Jurijus Ferdmanas, "Televizijos bokštai," *Statyba ir architektūra* (February 1980), 20–21.

28. On Soviet urban planning in the two largest Soviet cities, see Blair Ruble, *Leningrad: Shaping a Soviet City* (Berkeley: University of California Press, 1990); and Timothy Colton, *Moscow: Governing the Socialist Metropolis* (Cambridge: Belknap Press, 1995). On early urban planning in the USSR, see Anatole Kopp, *Town and Revolution: Soviet Architecture and City Planning, 1917–1935* (New York: G. Bazilier, 1970).

29. On this conflict in a slightly different context, see David Crowley, "Paris or Moscow? Warsaw Architects and the Image of the Modern City in the 1950s," *Kritika: Explorations in Russian and Eurasian History* 9, no. 4 (Fall 2008), 769–798.

30. Steven E. Harris, "'I Know All the Secrets of My Neighbors': The Quest for Privacy in the Era of the Separate Apartment" in Lewis Siegelbaum, ed., *Borders of Socialism: Private Spheres of Soviet Russia* (New York: Palgrave Macmillan, 2006), 171–189. Unfortunately, none of the very interesting essays in this collection deal with non-Russian regions of the USSR.

31. For a discussion of nineteenth-century plans for Vilnius' city development, see Jonas Jurkštas and Vytautas Jurkštas, "Trys pirmieji perspektyviiai planai," *Statyba ir architektūra* (March 1976), 29–32.

32. To be sure, in the 1950s development of the construction industry in general created the possibility of the rapid shift to prefab methods in the 1960s. Petras Savickas, "Penkmečių pakopomis," *Statyba ir architektūra* (April 1980), 20–21.

33. *Vil'nius. Statisticheskii sbornik 1945–1964* (Vil'nius: TsSU LSSR Statisticheskoe upravlenie goroda Vil'niusa, 1965), 86–87.

34. Juozas Maniušis, *Tarybų Lietuvos statybose* (Vilnius: Valst. polit. ir moksl. lit. l-kla, 1955),

8-28.
35. Juozas Maniušis, *Tarybų Lietuva pramonės kilimas* (Vilnius: Valst. polit. ir moksl. lit. 1-kla, 1958), 77-92.
36. Juozas Maniušis [Iu. Maniushis], *Promyshlennost' Sovetskoi Litvy na puti tekhnicheskogo progressa* (Vil'nius: Gos. Izdatel'stvo politicheskoi i nauchnoi literatury Litovskoi SSR, 1960), 44-71, 119.
37. A. Spelskis, "Perspektyvinis Lietuvos miestų gyvenamųjų rajonų, mikrorajonų planavimas ir statyba," *Statyba ir architektūra* (March 1960), 48-51; V. Kuplianskas, "Pasparintinti gyvenamųjų namų statyba," *Statyba ir architektūra* (October 1960), 225-228; S. Rokas, "Vilniaus perspektyvinio ugdymo problemos," *Statyba ir architektūra* (December 1964), 13-16.
38. *SLTSR paminklų sąvadas*, 1:71-73; Vaclovas Balčiūnas, "Svarbiausios Vilniaus užstatymo problemos," *Statyba ir architektūra* (December 1968), 2-4. A number of articles in this issue discuss Žirmūnai, which had recently been completed (and whose architects had received a major prize).
39. A. Cibas, "Sostinės genplanas suderintas," *Statyba ir architektūra* (September 1965), 19-20.
40. On the future downtown, including making Lenino into a pedestrian zone, see A. Cibas, "Kaip atrodys ateityje Vilniaus miesto centras," *Statyba ir architektūra* (November 1964), 18-25.
41. Jurgis Dragūnas, "Vilnius, dešinysis Neries krantas," *Statyba ir architektūra* (January 1970), 2-5; Vaclovas Balčiūnas, "Prie Vilniaus centro rekonstrukcijos projekto," *Statyba ir architektūra* (June 1973), 2-5; "Naujasis Miesto Centras" in *LTSR paminklų sąvadas*, 1:506-509. The April 1976 issue of *Statyba ir architektūra* features photos of the still under construction Hotel Lietuva in this new city center.
42. On the fascinating story of personal automobiles in the USSR, see Lewis H. Siegelbaum, *Cars for Comrades: The Life of the Soviet Automobile* (Ithaca: Cornell University Press, 2008). The ambitious plans for a five-story parking garage are included in A. Reventas and Z. Sušinskas, "Individualių automobilių garažų statybos klausimu," *Statyba ir architektūra* (November 1968), 10-12.
43. Vaclovas Balčiūnas, "Kur statysime butus vilniečiams," *Statyba ir architektūra* (June 1964), 20-24 contains a number of alternative sites for housing areas; S. Rokas, "Vilniaus perspektyvinio ugdymo problemos," *Statyba ir architektūra* (December 1964), 13-16; apparently even in the 1970s a housing estate (to be named "Žalgiris") was proposed for a location closer to the city center, but it was not built: Gediminas Girčys, "Minčys apie būsimąjį 'Žalgirio' rajoną," *Statyba ir architektūra* (February 1975), 4-7.
44. "Senojo Vilniaus atgimimas," *Statyba ir architektūra* (July 1964), 16-17.
45. "Kiekvienam naujam kompleksui—savitą veidą," *Statyba ir architektūra* (January 1975), 3-8.
46. The literature on Lazdynai is remarkably large and almost entirely laudatory. See, e.g., Vaclovas Balčiūnas, "Lazdynai inžineriniu požiūriu," *Statyba ir architektūra* (April 1974), 7-10; Balčiūnas, "Vilnius, Lazdynai," *Statyba ir architektūra* (February 1973), 1-4; and the illustrated brochures Liudas Verbliugevičius, *Lazdynai* (Vilnius: "Mintis," 1978), and Vytautas Balčiūnas, Jurgis Vanagas, *Lazdynai* (Vilnius: Mosklas, 1983). During construction, however, complaints about low quality work were also expressed: Vytautas Sūdžius, "Lazdynuose reikalai turi pagerėti," *Statyba ir architektūra* (March 1970), 18-19.
47. For the sanitized view, see, e.g., Papšys, *Vilnius: A Guide* (1980), 142-6. See also *LTSR Paminklų sąvadas*, 1:69-71.
48. Andrusz cites the astonishing statistic that 65.5% of the urban housing in the USSR had been constructed in the two decades from 1960 to 1980 (Andrusz, *Housing and Urban Development*, 177). It would appear that perhaps in Vilnius the percentage was even higher.
49. *Statyba ir architektūra*, 1960, January, February, March.
50. *Statyba ir architektūra*, 1961, January, April, June, April, December.
51. *Statyba ir architektūra*, 1965, February, April, July, September.
52. *Statyba ir architektūra*, 1970, January, February, May, June, August, October.
53. *Statyba ir architektūra*, 1975, January, February, April.
54. *Statyba ir architektūra*, 1980, January, June, August, October, December.
55. More generally on architecture in Soviet Lithuania, see Jonas Minkevičius, *Arkhitektura Sovetskoi Litvy* (Moscow: Stroiizdat, 1987); Eduardas Budreika, *Arkhitektura Sovetskoi Litvy* (Leningrad: Izdatelstvo literatury po stroitel'stvu, 1971); Budreika, *Architektas Vytautas Edmundas Čekanaus-*

*kas* (Vilnius: Vilniaus dailės akademijos leidykla, 1998).

56. *Vil'nius. Kratkaia adresno-spravochnaia kniga* (1957), 195-222.

57. On the rise of petty-bourgeois materialism earlier in Soviet history, see Vera Dunham, *In Stalin's Time: Middleclass Values in Soviet Fiction* (Cambridge: Cambridge University Press, 1976).

58. Gediminas Valiuškis, "Vilniečiams—šiuolaikinius patogumus," *Statyba ir architektūra* (June 1973), 12-13.

59. Robert Edelman, *Serious Fun: A History of Spectator Sports in the USSR* (New York: Oxford University Press, 1993), 120-121.

60. *LTSR Paminklų sąvadas*, 1:36-37.

61. Albertas Cibas, "Dideli architektų uždaviniai," *Statyba ir architektūra* (October 1970), 1-2.

62. In 1980, for example, nearly every issue of the Lithuanian Young Communists' (Komjaunimas) monthly magazine, *Jaunimo Gretos*, featured basketball teams (both male and female) as well as news about the Moscow Summer Olympics. Similarly, in one description of present-day Vilnius, the section on "physical culture and sport" spends much more time on spectator sports than on individual fitness: Algirdas Motulas, *Vilnius dabartis ir rytdiena* (Vilnius: Mintis, 1980), 103-108.

63. Vaclovas Balčiūnas, "Prie Vilniaus centro rekonstrukcijos projekto," *Statyba ir architektūra* (June 1973), 2-5; Juozas Vaškevičius, "Vilniaus centre, ties dešiuoju Neries krantu," *Statyba ir architektūra* (April 1976), 2-8.

64. *Trumpa informacija apie Vilniaus miesto darbo žmonių deputatų tarybos vykdomojo komiteto veiklą 1970 metais/Kratkaia informatsiia o rabote ispolkoma vil'niusskogo gorodskogo soveta deputatov trudiashchikhsia za 1970 god* (Vilnius: Vilniaus miesto darbo žmonių deputatų tarybos vykdomojo komitetas, 1970), 23-25.

65. Motulas, *Vilnius Dabartis ir rytdiena*, 63.

66. *LTSR Paminklų sąvadas*, 1:347; M. Urbelis and V. Brėdikis, "Naujoji kavinė 'Neringa' Vilniuje," *Statyba ir architektūra* (March 1960), 67-71; Algimantas Mačiulis, "Nuo 'Neringos' iki urbanistininių spredimų," *Kulturos barai*, no. 4 (1978), 7-14.

67. Another ambitious restaurant opened in this period was the "Bull's Horn" ("Tauro ragas"), the largest "beer restaurant" in the Baltic, opened in early 1974, *Statyba ir architektūra* (March 1974), 10. New movie theaters were opened in this period as well, for example the "Vilnius" on Lenino (now a Benetton store), opened in 1963 with 600 seats (*LTSR Paminklų sąvadas*, 1:337), and "Moscow" in the Old Town, opened in 1974 with 980 seats (Jurkštas, *Novaia arkhitektura v tsentre starogo Vil'niusa*, 10-12).

68. Vytautas Merkys, ed., *Vilniaus universiteto istorija (1579-1803, 1803-1940, 1940-1979)* (Vilnius: Mokslas, 1979).

69. Kamilla Mrozowska, ed., *Studia z dziejów uniwerystetu Wileńskiego* (Kraków: Zeszyty narukowe UJ no. 554, 1979).

70. Alvydas Jancevičius, *Vilniaus universitetui—400* (Vilnius: Mokslas, 1979), 78-98.

71. Ibid., 98-102, 174-186.

72. A. Bendžius et al., eds., *Academia et universitas vilnensis* (Vilnius: Mokslas, 1979).

73. A. Bendžius (Bendzhius) et al., eds., *Istoriia vil'niusskogo universiteta (1579-1979)* (Vilnius: Mokslas, 1979).

## Notes to Chapter 8

1. On the end of the USSR in a broader perspective, see Stephen Kotkin, *Armageddon Averted: The Soviet Collapse, 1970-2000* (Oxford: Oxford University Press, 2008).

2. For a detailed and sophisticated account of the Lithuanian course from Soviet republic to independence, see Česlovas Laurinavičius and Vladas Sirutavičius, eds., *Lietuvos Istorija, XII tomas, I dalis. Sąjūdis. Nuo "persitvarkymo" iki kovo 11-osios* (Vilnius: baltos lankos, 2008).

3. The juxtaposition of Old Town and new Soviet housing estates is nicely captured in a photo

of the cathedral (in Soviet times, a "picture gallery") with the concrete blocks of Žirmūnai behind it, in Romualdas Ratkauskas and Antanas Sutkus, *Vilniaus šiokiadieniai* (Vilnius: Mintis, 1967), 2.

    4. *Tarybų Lietuvai 45. Tarybų valdžios atkūrimo Lietuvoje 45-ųjų metinių šventė* (Vilnius: Mintis, 1985). This small book contains many excellent pictures of the celebration, all of them apparently from Vilnius or its surroundings, along with speeches and programs held during the festivities (including some in Russian).

    5. A. Motulas, *Vil'nius. Ekonomicheskii ocherk* (Vil'nius: "Mintis", 1984), 16–21.

    6. Ibid., 39–40. For photographs of these new buildings, see Jonas Minkevičius, *Naujoji Lietuvos architektūra* (Vilnius: Mintis, 1982). For an enthusiastic description (with illustrations) of the new ballet and opera house, written immediately after its completion, see Vaclovas Survila, "Iki atidarymo liko . . ." *Literatūra ir menas*, no. 35 (1448) (August 31, 1974), 8–9.

    7. *LTSR Paminklų sąvadas*, 120–121.

    8. Ibid., 321–323.

    9. Pictures of most of these statues (not the Green Bridge, however) and other "sights" of Soviet Vilnius appear in a useful guidebook that appeared in both Lithuanian and Russian: Algirdas Vileikis, *Vilnius. Tarybų Lietuvos Sostinė* (Vilnius: Mintis, 1986). For more detail, see *LTSR Paminklų sąvadas*, 126–127 ("Černiachiovkio tiltas"); 191–192 (Mickevičius-Kapsukas monument); 381–382 (Dzierżyński house and monument); 438 (Lenin and Kapsukas monument).

    10. Ibid., 348 (Žemaitė, 1970); 473 (L. Gira, 1977); 515 (K. Donalaitis, 1964).

    11. Ibid., 398 (Pushkin); and 181 (Moniuszko).

    12. Ibid., 241–242.

    13. Algirdas Motulas, *Vilniaus dabartis ir rytdiena* (Vilnius: Mintis, 1980).

    14. Vileikis, *Vilnius*.

    15. It is interesting that in the best Western account of this period in Lithuanian history, the "declaration of independence" of February 16, 1918 is mentioned once as "just an edited version of the earlier one" and not described in any detail. Alfred Senn, *The Emergence of Modern Lithuania* (New York: Columbia UP, 1959), 32. In Senn's account the Soviet date, December 29, 1918, appears similarly unimportant (69).

    16. Zenonas Petrauskas, "Šventė, kurios nebuvo," *Jaunimo gretos*, no. 1 (January 1988), 6–8.

    17. See, for example, Donald Raleigh, ed., *Soviet Historians and Perestroika: The First Phase* (Armonk, NY: M.E. Sharpe, 1989).

    18. While Lithuanian historians did take part in the larger debates on the October Revolution and Stalinism; still, the era of the incorporation of their country into the USSR captured the most attention. See, for example, Alfonsas Eidintas and Gediminas Rudis, eds., *Novyi vzgliad na istoriiu Litvy* (Kaunas: Šviesa, 1991).

    19. VMI, 2:123.

    20. See, for example, Vytautas Merkys, *Razvitie promyshlennosti i formirovaniia proletariata Litvy v XIX v.* (Vilnius: Mintis, 1969); Merkys, *Negalioji lietuvių spauda kapitalizmo laikotarpiu (ligi 1904)* (Vilnius: Mokslas, 1978). As late as 1988 Merkys co-authored a very traditional Soviet-style textbook on Lithuanian history: *Lietuvos istorija. Nuo seniausių laikų iki 1917 metų* (Vilnius: Mokslas, 1988).

    21. After the fall of the USSR, Merkys published a thick tome on the life and influence of an important Lithuanian bishop and writer: *Motiejus Valanačius. Tarp katalikiškojo universalizmo ir tautiškumo* (Vilnius: Mintis, 1999). It is clear that the amazingly detailed research for this book (over 800 pages long) was not all undertaken after the fall of the USSR.

    22. An excellent overview of this period and the founding of the first independent (not communist-controlled) organizations in Soviet Lithuania is Arvydas Anušauskas et al., eds., *Lietuva 1940–1990. Okupuotos Lietuvos istorija* (Vilnius: Lietuvos gyventojų genocido ir rezistencijos tyrimo centras, 2005), 598–611.

    23. An excellent overview of this period by an American specialist on Lithuanian history is Alfred Erich Senn, *Lithuania Awakening* (Vilnius: Mokslo ir enciklopedijų leidybos institutas, 2002; originally published by University of California Press in 1990).

    24. *Sovetskaia Litva*, no. 39 (13552), February 17, 1988, 2.

25. *Sovetskaia Litva*, no. 38 (13551), February 16, 1988, 3.

26. The Angarietis monument was located on a small square at the corner of Komunarų and Angariečio Streets (now Jakšto and Kaštonu). *LTSR Paminklų sąvadas*, 75-76, describes the monument (erected in 1972 on the 90th anniversary of Angarietis's birth) and shows a picture of it.

27. "Pochtili pamiat' zhertv kul'ta lichnosti," *Sovetskaia Litva*, no. 119 (13632), May 22, 1988, 1, 3. This entire article is a superb example of Soviet "wooden language" that does not entirely come through in translation. One paragraph exemplifies this bureaucratese nicely: "V khode pretvoreniia v zhizn' reshenii XVII s"ezda KPSS predaiutsia glasnosti oshibki proshlogo, fakty proizvola. Nadeemsia, chto i segodniashnimi vystupleniiami my budem sposobstvovat' utverzhdeniiu atmosfery perestroiki." A more interesting account of Stalinist denunciations is Rita Patamystė, "'Demaskuotojai,'" *Jaunimo gretos*, no. 6 (June 1988), 18-19. Patamystė takes all of her examples from the (Russian) Soviet press, not from local Lithuanian sources.

28. For a compilation and reprint of the *Sąjūdžio Žinios* issues from this crucial period, see *Sąjūdžio Žinios 1988-1989* (Vilnius: Lietuvos Respublikos Apsaugos Ministerija, 2005).

29. "Za chestnoe i otkrytoe izuchenie istorii," *Sovetskaia Litva*, no. 197 (13710), August 25, 1988, 3. Actually there are two articles: the first, by V. Ianov, is about the demonstration in Vingis Park, and the second, by G. Lopukhin, is about the "incidents" afterward.

30. Jurga Ivanauskaitė, "Netektis atgimimas 1939-1988," *Sąjūdžio Žinio*, no. 30 (ca. August 30, 1988—date illegible), 1.

31. Alfred Senn, *Gorbachev's Failure in Lithuania* (New York: St. Martin's Press, 1995), 37. See also, in connection with the Vingis Park gathering, "Šūvis į dešimtuką—ar greta?" *Jaunimo gretos*, no. 9 (September 1988), 15-16, 25.

32. *Sąjūdžio Žinios*, no. 41 (September 29, 1988), 3. An announcement on page 2 asked any eyewitnesses to the events of that night to send their accounts to *Sąjūdžio Žinios*.

33. The young communists not only condemned the use of force on September 28 ("Klausimai be atsakymų?" *Jaunimo gretos*, no. 11 [November 1988], 12-13) but published articles about the raising of the Lithuanian tricolor over Gediminas castle on October 7 ("Kas iškėlė tautinę vėliavą?" JG, nr 12 [December 1988], 3), along with a favorable discussion of Sąjūdis and its influence in Lithuania (Bronius Genzelis, "Po suviažiavimo," JG, no. 12 [December 1988], 6-7). It should not be forgotten that, as with Solidarność in Poland, many of Sąjūdis's members were communists who left the communist party.

34. *Sovetskaia Litva*, no. 225 (13738), 1.

35. On the events of September 28, 1988, see Senn, *Gorbachev's Failure*, 41.

36. See his memoirs on this period: Algirdas Brazauskas, *Lietuviškos skyrybos* (Vilnius: Politika, 1992) and *Self-Determination 1988-1991* (Vilnius: Vaga, 2004).

37. *Jaunimo gretos*, no. 10 (October 1989), 2-3. See also the articles on the Red Army's march into Vilnius on November 7, 1940 (November 1989, 2-3); on the newly formed Lithuanian police (*milicija*) (December 1989, 24-25); and on the Russo-Finnish War (Liudas Truska, "105 dienų karas," December 1989, 30-31). The events in Eastern Europe do not appear to have interested *Jaunimo Gretos* (or they may have been too hot to handle). No article on the fall of the Berlin wall or events in Prague that November appeared here.

38. See, e.g., no. 2 (February 2, 1989) and no. 4 (March 14, 1989).

39. The Lithuanian Historical Institute has copies of *Soglasie* up to 52 (74) December 31, 1990. It is unclear to me whether publication continued in 1991. See also the memoirs of one of *Soglasie*'s editors: Georgii Efremov, *My liudi drug drugu. Litva. Budni svobody 1988-1989* (Moscow: Progress, 1990).

40. On the Poles during this period, see the documents collected (in German translation) in Hans-Werner Rautenberg, ed., *Der "Ring um die Hauptstadt." Die polnische Minderheit in Litauen 1989-1993* (Marburg: J.G. Herder-Institut, 1994). This collection is very useful but contains nearly exclusively documents taken from the Polish press—some Lithuanian voices would have increased its value.

41. "Prebyvanie M. S. Gorbacheva v Litve," *Sovetskaia Litva*, no. 9 (14122), January 12, 1990, 1.

42. At this time political parties were also formally legalized in Lithuania, thereby ending the monopoly of the communists on legal politics. See the draft of this law in *Sovetskaia Litva*, no. 29

(14142), February 6, 1990, 1.
  43. Brazauskas, *Lietuviškos skyrybos*, 96–97. *Sovetskaia Litva*, no. 32 (14145), 3.
  44. "Informatsionnoe soobshchenie o pervoi sessii Verkhovnogo Soveta Litovskoi Respubliki pervogo sozyva," *Sovetskaia Litva*, no. 59 (14172), March 13, 1990, 1. The temporary constitution ("fundamental law") was published in *Sovetskaia Litva*, no. 62 (14175). For the Lithuanian text, see VMID, 589.
  45. *Ekho Litvy*, no. 63 (14176), March 16, 1990, 1.
  46. V. Šapalas, *Vilnius, kelias į savivaldą* (Vilnius: Šasta, 1994). See also VMIS, 863–867.
  47. *Soglasie*, no. 21 (43), May 21–27, 1990, 2; *Ekho Litvy*, no. 109 (14222), May 19, 1990, 2.
  48. On the March 11 declaration and Soviet blockade, see Senn, *Gorbachev's Failure*, 89f and Anatol Lieven, *The Baltic Revolutions* (New Haven: Yale UP, 1993), 230–241.
  49. In Kaunas, for example, the statue of Lenin was already removed in early August—though the counterpart in Vilnius would stand for several more months. "Paminklai griūva vidurdienį," *Lietuvos rytas*, no. 140 (11545), August 7, 1990, 1.
  50. *Lietuvos aidas*, no. 55 (5601), 1. The monument was finally completed and dedicated in September 1996, though not according to any of the three proposals depicted here.
  51. "Lietuvos valanda Vašingtone," *Lietuvos aidas*, no. 142 (5688), December 12, 1990, 1.
  52. *Lietuvos aidas*, no. 154 (5700), 4–5.
  53. *Ekho Litvy*, no. 1 (14380), January 3, 1991, 1.
  54. *Ekho Litvy*, no. 5 (14384), 1; *Lietuvos aidas*, no. 5 (5705), 1.
  55. Because of the occupation of the press center, *Ekho Litvy* could not be published from January 12 to 15. See the explanation in no. 8 (14387), January 16, 1991, 1.
  56. For a detailed chronology of the events of early January, see *Lietuva 1991.01.13. Dokumentai, liudijimai, atgarsiai* (Vilnius: Spaudos departamentas, 1991), 15–22. See also Lieven, *The Baltic Revolutions*, 245–255 and Senn, *Gorbachev's Failure*, 127–141.
  57. *Lietuvos aidas*, no. 8 (5708), 1.
  58. For their names and short biographies, see *Lietuva 1991.01.13*, 39–67. See also the documents from these crucial days in VMID, 598–601.
  59. "Mat' Litva proshchaetsia so svoimi det'mi," *Ekho Litvy*, no. 9 (14388), January 17, 1991, 1; *Lietuvos aidas*, no. 9 (5709), January 15, 1991, 3–4.
  60. "Nusprendė Gorbačiovas," *Lietuvos aidas*, no. 16 (5716), 1.
  61. "Demontirovany pamiatniki," *Ekho Litvy*, no. 166 (14545), August 27, 1991, 2.
  62. *Ekho Litvy*, no. 170 (14549), August 31, 1991, 2.
  63. Čaplinskas, *Vilniaus gatvės*, 221–222.
  64. The new street names figured in a contemporary newspaper article: "Prazdnik v Vil'niuse," *Ekho Litvy*, no. 189 (14568), 27 Sept. 1991, 1.
  65. Ibid., 223–224. For a quite detailed explanation of post-Soviet Vilnius street names (in particular with biographies of the eponymous individuals), see Antanas Čaplinskas, *Vilniaus atminimo knyga. Mieste įamžintos asmenybės* (Vilnius: Charibdė, 2011).
  66. *Ekho Litvy*, no. 188 (14567), 26 Sept. 1991, 7, describes the new police force's ranks.
  67. VMID, 673.
  68. *Ekho Litvy*, no. 186 (14565), 1.
  69. *Vilniaus miesto bendrasis planas* (Vilnius: Vilniaus miesto taryba, 1999).
  70. A. Kairienė, ed., *Vilniaus senamiesčio atgavinimo strategija* (Vilnius: R. Paknio leidykla, 1997), 13.
  71. *Vilnius ir vilniečiai. Gyvenimo kokybės vertinimas* (Vilnius: Filosofijos, sociologijos ir teisės institutas, 1995), 17.
  72. Ibid., 9–11.
  73. Ibid., 12.
  74. Jolita Lenkevičiūtė, *Vilnius im Wandel. Wohnsegregation in einer ostmitteleuropäischen Hauptstadt* (Berlin: Wissenschaftlicher Verlag, 2006), 187.
  75. Ibid., 202.

76. Ibid., 252.
77. Ibid., 261.
78. Ibid., passim. Lenkevičiūtė includes a number of very interesting case studies of individual families and interviewees but her desire to avoid "stigmatizing" specific housing estates at times makes it difficult to figure out just which area is being discussed. On the post-Soviet period, see also Terence M. Milstead, *Housing and Urban Development in a Post-Soviet City: A Case Study of Vilnius, Lithuania* (Ph.D. diss., Florida State University, 2008).
79. Zbigniew Kurcz, *Mniejszość polska na Wileńszczyźnie. Studium socjologiczne* (Wrocław: Wydawnictwo Uniwersytetu Wrocławskiego, 2005), 168–172.
80. Ibid., 174.
81. On the Vilnius Poles in historical context and especially in the early 1990s, see Rautenberg, *Ring um die Hauptstadt*.
82. On Poles in Vilnius after 1990, see the article by Severinas Vaitiekus in VMIS, 876–881.
83. Lenkevičiūtė, *Vilnius im Wandel*, 408 (table 25).
84. Solomonas Atamukas, *Lietuvos žydų kelias. Nuo XIV amžiaus iki XX a. pabaigos* (Vilnius: Alma Littera, 2001), 309. On the postwar Jewish community, see also Vladas Sirutavičius, Darius Staliūnas, Jurgita Šiaučiūnaitė-Verbickienė, eds., *Lietuvos Žydai. Istorinė studija* (Vilnius: Baltos Lankos, 2012), 485–529.
85. For remarkable images of the castle (upper as well as lower—both in ruins at this time) from the late eighteenth and early nineteenth centuries, see Vladas Drėma, *Dingęs Vilnius* (Vilnius: Vaga, 1991), 102–112.
86. John Czaplicka, "The Palace Ruins and Putting the Lithuanian Nation in Place: Historical Stagings in Vilnius" in Daniel J. Walkowitz and Lisa Maya Knauer, eds., *Memory and the Impact of Political Transformation in Public Space* (Durham: Duke University Press, 2004), 167–190. On the lower castle by one of the historians most involved in its reconstruction, see Napoleonas Kitkauskas, *Lietuvos Didžiosios Kunigaikštytės valdovų rūmai* (Vilnius: Kultūros leidykla, 2009).
87. Zigmas Zinkevičius, *Rytų Lietuva praeityje ir dabar* (Vilnius: Mokslo ir enciklopedijų leidykla, 1993), see in particular pp. 102–241.
88. Zigmas Zinkevičius, *Lietuvos sostinė. Visuomeninė ir kultūrinė veikla Vilniuje, paroda 1994.10.20 - 1995.02.12* (Vilnius: Lietuvos nacionalinis muziejus, 1994). For all its one-sidedness, this catalogue is a wonderful source of images, maps, and information about Lithuanian culture in Vilnius during these years.
89. Angelė Mičiūnienė, *Literatūrinis Vilnius. Individualioji programa* (Vilnius: Gimtasis žodis, 1996); Angelė Mičiūnienė, *Ką pasakoja Vilniaus gatvės. Kelionė po literatūrinį ir kultūrinį Vilnių* (Vilnius: Vilniaus knyga, 2001).
90. Eugenijus Manelis and Romualdas Samavičius, eds., *Vilniaus miesto istorijos skaitiniai* (Vilnius: Vilniaus knyga, 2001); Eugenijus Manelis and Romualdas Samavičius, eds., *Vilniaus miesto istorijos dokumentai. Vilniaus miesto istorijos skaitinių chrestomatija. Mokymo priemonė* (Vilnius: Vilniaus knyga, 2003).
91. Marija Skirmantienė and Jonas Varnauskas, eds., *Nukentėję paminklai* (Vilnius: Mokslo ir encikl. leidykla, 1994).
92. Antanas Čaplinskas, *Vilniaus gatvių istorija. Valdovų kelias* (Vilnius: Charybdė, 2001-2005), 3 vols. (Rūdninkų gatvė; Didžioji gatvė; Pilies gatvė); Antanas Čaplinskas, *Vilniaus istorija. Legendos ir tikrovė* (Vilnius: Charibdė, 2010).
93. Vladas Drėma, *Dingęs Vilnius/Lost Vilnius* (Vilnius: Vaga, 1991).
94. Genrikh Agranovskii, Irina Guzenberg, *Vil'nius. Po sledam litovskogo Ierusalima* (Vilnius: Gosudarstvennyi evreiskii muzei, 2011).
95. Herman Kruk, *Paskutinės Lietuvos Jeruzalės dienos. Vilniaus geto ir stovyklų kronikos, 1939-1944* (Vilnius: Lietuvos gyventojų genocido ir rezistencijos tyrimo centras, 2004); Lucy Dawidowicz, *Iš tos vietos ir laiko. Atsiminimai, 1938-1947* (Vilnius: Garnelis, 2003).
96. Anna Lipphardt, *Vilne. Die Juden aus Vilnius nach dem Holocaust. Eine transnationale Beziehungsgeschichte* (Paderborn: Friedrich Schöningh, 2010). See also Marina Dmitrieva and Heidemarie Petersen, eds., *Jüdische Kultur(en) im Neuen Europa. Wilna 1918-1939* (Wiesbaden: Harrasso-

witz, 2004).

97. For a collection of their letters and essays on Vilnius and Lithuania, see Czesław Miłosz and Tomas Venclova, *Grįžimai Lietuvon* (Vilnius: Vaga, 2014).

98. These letters are published in English translation in Tomas Venclova, *Forms of Hope* (Riverdale-on-Hudson: The Sheep Meadow Press, 1999), 5–31; and Czeslaw Milosz, *Beginning with My Streets* (New York: Farrar, Straus, Giroux, 1991), 23–57.

99. Tomas Venclova, *Vilnius. Vadovas po miestą* (Vilnius: R. Paknio leidykla, 2001).

100. Tomas Venclova, *Vilniaus vardai* (Vilnius: R. Paknio leidykla, 2006). See especially the entry "Muravjov Michail," 163–165.

101. For more on Venclova, see Leonidas Donskis, *Identity and Freedom: Mapping Nationalism and Social Criticism in Twentieth-Century Lithuania* (London: Routledge, 2002), 121–162 ("Tomas Venclova: Ethical Universalism and the Discovery of the Other"); and "Tomas Venclowa [sic]—głos wołającego na puszczy" in Aleksandr Srebrakowski, *Polacy w Litewskiej SRR, 1944–1989* (Toruń: Adam Marszałek, 1993), 301–303.

102. See, for example, Alvydas Nikžentaitis and Aivas Ragauskas, eds., *Santykis su istorine praeitimi XXI amžiaus Vilniuje* (Vilnius: Vilniaus miesto savivaldybė, 2004); Alfredas Bumblauskas, Šarūnas Liekis, Grigorijus Potašenko, eds., *Naujasis Vilniaus perskaitymas. Didieji Lietuvos istoriniai pasakojimai ir daugiakultūris miesto paveldas* (Vilnius: Vilniaus universiteto leidykla, 2009).

103. Laimonis Briedis, *Vilnius: City of Strangers* (Vilnius: Baltos Lankos, 2008).

## Notes to Conclusions

1. Theodore R. Weeks, "Vilna, Wilno, Vilnius 1863–1939. Une étude de cas sur les cultures parallèles et sur 'l'Autre' invisible," *Revue Germanique Internationale*, special thematic volume *Villes baltiques. Une mémoire partagée* 11 (2010), 79–102.

# Select Bibliography

See also the list of abbreviations for frequently used published works.

## Archives

Lietuvos Centrinis Valstybės Archyvas. Vilnius. (LCVA)
Lietuvos Valstybės Istorijos Archyvas. Vilnius. (LVIA)
Lietuvos Ypatingasis Archyvas. Vilnius. (LYA)
Vilniaus Apskrities Archyvas. Vilnius. (VAA)
Lietuvos Mokslo Akademijos Biblioteka, Rankraščių skyrius (Lithuanian Academy of Sciences Library, Manuscript Division, Vilnius). (LMAB)
Russian State Historical Archive. St. Petersburg. (RGIA)

## Published Works

Abramowicz, Hirsz. *Profiles of a Lost World: Memoirs of East European Jewish Life before World War II.* Detroit: Wayne State University Press, 1999.
Abramowicz, Ludwik. *Cztery wieki drukarstwa w Wilnie 1525–1925.* Wilno: Ludwik Chomiński, 1925.
Abramowicz, Ludwik, ed. *Litwa podczas wojny. Zbiór dokumentów.* Warsaw: Wydawnictwo Departamentu Spraw Politycznych, 1918.
Agranovskii, Genrikh. *Stanovlenie evreiskogo knigopechataniia v Litve.* Vilnius: "Academia," 1994.
Agranovskii, Genrikh, and Irina Guzenberg. *Vil'na. Po sledam Litovskogo Ierusalima.* Vil'nius: Gosudarstvennyi evreiskii muzei, 2011.
Andrusz, Gregory D. *Housing and Urban Development in the USSR.* London: Macmillan, 1984.
An-ski, Sh., ed. *Pinkas far der geshikhte fun vilne in di yorn fun milhome un okupatsie.* Vilne: n.p., 1922.
Arad, Yitzak. *Ghetto in Flames: The Struggle and Destruction of the Jews in Vilna in the Holocaust.* Jerusalem: Yad Vashem, 1980.
Balberyszski, Mendel. *Likwidacja getta wileńskiego.* Warsaw: WINW, 1946.
Balčiūnas, Vytautas, and Jurgis Vanagas. *Lazdynai.* Vilnius: Mosklas, 1983.
Baliński, Michał. *Historya miasta Wilna.* 2 vols. Wilno: A. Marcinkowski, 1836.
Baliński, Michał. *Opisanie statystyczne miasta Wilna.* Wilno: Józef Zawadzki, 1835.
Balkelis, Tomas. *The Making of Modern Lithuania.* New York: Routledge, 2009.
Bańkowski, Witold. *Wilno przyszłości. Rozważania na tematy urbanistyczne.* Wilno: Dru. A. Zwierzyńskiego, 1937.

# SELECT BIBLIOGRAPHY

Baranowski, Henryk. *Bibliografia Wilna. 1: Uniwersytet Wileński 1579-1939. 2: Miasto.* Toruń: Wydawnictwo Uniwersytetu Mikołaja Kopernika, 1996, 2000.
Beauvois, Daniel. *Lumières et société en Europe de l'Est. L'Université de Vilna et les écoles polonaises de l'Empire Russe 1803-1832.* Paris: H. Champion, 1977.
Berezowski, Henryk. *Towarzystwo Radiotechniczne Elektrit. Wilno 1925-1939.* Warsaw: Nakładem autora, 2011.
Bernatskii, N. *Sobytiia v Vil'ne vo vremia Otechestvennoi voiny.* Vil'na: n.p., 1912.
Berwaldt, Adam, ed. *10 lat rozgłośni wileńskiej. Radio dla miasta i wsi (Wilno 1928-1938).* Wilno: Referat Prasowo-Propagandowy rozgłośni wileńskiej, 1938.
Bieliński, Józef. *Szubrawcy w Wilnie (1817-1822).* Wilno: Nakładem Korwina, 1910.
Bieliński, Józef. *Uniwersytet Wileński (1579-1831).* Kraków: W. L. Anczyc, 1899-1900.
Biržiška, Mykolas. *Na posterunku wileńskim.* Wilno: "Głos Litwy," 1922.
Biržiška, Mykolas. *Vilniaus Golgota. Okupuotosios Lietuvos lietuvių ir kančių dienoraštis.* Kaunas: Vilniui vaduoti s-ga, 1930.
Brensztejn, Michał. *Adam-Honor Kirkor, wydawca, redaktor i właściciel drukarni w Wilnie od roku 1834 do 1867.* Wilno: Wydawnictwo Towarzystwa pomocy naukowej im. E. i E. Wróblewskich, 1930.
Briedis, Laimonas. *Vilnius: City of Strangers.* Vilnius: Baltos Lankos, 2008.
Bujnicki, Tadeusz. *Szkice Wileńskie. Rozprawy i eseje.* Kraków: Collegium Columbinum, 2002.
Bumblauskas, Alfredas, Šarūnas Liekis, and Grigorijus Potašenko, eds. *Naujasis Vilniaus perskaitymas. Didieji Lietuvos istoriniai pasakojimai ir daugiakultūris miesto paveldas.* Vilnius: Vilniaus universiteto leidykla, 2009.
Butėnas, Domas, et al., eds. *Academia et universitas Vilnensis. Vilniaus universiteto steigimo dokumentai.* Vilnius: Kultūra, 2004.
Butrimas, Adomas, ed. *Vilniaus architektūros mokykla XVIII-XX a.* Vilnius: Vilniaus darbės akademija, 1993.
Čaplinskas, Antanas Rimvydas. *Vilniaus istorija. Legendos ir tikrovė.* Vilnius: Charibdė, 2010.
Cicėnas, Jeronimas. *Vilnius tarp audrų.* Vilnius: Mokslo ir enciklop. leidykla, 1993.
*Conflit polono-lithuanien. Question de Vilna 1918-1924. Documents diplomatiques.* Kaunas: République de Lithuanie Ministère des affaires étrangères, 1924.
Cybulski, Radosław. *Józef Zawadzki. Księgarz, drukarz, wydawca.* Wrocław: Ossolineum, 1972.
Czarkowski, Ludwik. *Wilno w latach 1867-1875 (z wspomnień osobistych).* Wilno: "Pogoń," 1929.
Dąbrowski, Przemysław. *Rozpolitykowane miasto. Ustrój polityczny państwa w koncepcjach polskich ugrupowań działających w Wilnie w latach 1918-1939.* Gdańsk: Arche, 2012.
Daugudis, Vytautas. *Iš Vilniaus miesto praeitis.* Vilnius: Mokslo ir enciklopedijų leidykla, 1993.
Davoliūtė, Violeta. *The Making and Breaking of Soviet Lithuania: Memory and Modernity in the Wake of War.* London: Routledge, 2013.
Dieckmann, Christoph. *Deutsche Besatzungspolitik in Litauen 1941-1944.* Göttingen: Wallstein Verlag, 2011.
Dmitrieva, Marina, and Heidemarie Peterson, eds. *Jüdische Kultur(en) im Neuen Europa. Wilna 1918-1939.* Wiesbaden: Harrassowitz Verlag, 2004.
Dobaczewska, Wanda. *Wilno i Wileńszczyzna w latach 1914-1920.* Wilno: Dziennik Urzędowy Kuratorjum Okr. Szk. Wileńskiego, 1934.
Dobrianskii, Flavian Nikolaevich. *Staraia i novaia Vil'na.* 3rd ed. Vil'na: A. G. Syrkin, 1904.
Dobrianskii, Florian. *Putevoditel' po Vilenskoi publichnoi biblioteke.* Vil'na: I. Ia. Ialovtser, 1879.
Dohrn, Verena. "Das Rabbinerseminar in Wilna (1847-1873). Zur Geschichte der ersten staatlichen höheren Schule für Juden im Russischen Reich." *Jahrbücher für Geschichte Osteuropas* 45, no. 3 (1997), 379-401.
Drėma, Vladas. *Dingęs Vilnius.* Vilnius: Vaga, 1991.
Dunin-Horkawicz, Janusz. *Co było a nie jest—czyli kilka lat młodości mojej w Wilnie.* Łódź: "Poprzeczna Oficyna," 1992.
Eidintas, Alfonsas, and Gediminas Rudis, eds. *Novyi vzgliad na istoriiu Litvy.* Kaunas: Šviesa, 1991.

Fedorowicz, Irena. *W służbie ziemie ojczystej. Czesław Jankowski w życiu kulturalnym Wilna lat 1905–1929*. Kraków: Collegium Columbinum, 2005.
*Ferdynand Ruszczyc. Życie ir dzieło*. Wilno: "Grafyka," 1939.
Filipajtis, Eugeniusz. *Lewica akademicka w Wilnie 1930–pocz 1935*. Białystok: Białostockie Towarzystwo Naukowe. Komisja Historii Najnowszej, 1965.
Fishman, David E. *Dem Feuer entrissen. Die Rettung jüdischer Kulturschätze in Wilna*. Hannover: Laurentius, 1998.
Frank, Józef. *Pamiętniki*. 3 vols. Wilno: "Lux," 1923.
Frick, David. "The Bells of Vilnius: Keeping Time in a City of Many Calendars." In *Making Contact: Maps, Identity and Travel*. Edmonton: University of Alberta Press, 2003, 23–59.
Frick, David. *Kith, Kin, & Neighbors: Communities and Confessions in Seventeenth-Century Wilno*. Ithaca: Cornell University Press, 2013.
Frick, David, ed. *Wilniane. Żywoty siedemnastowieczne*. Warsaw: Studium Europy Wschodniej, 2008.
Gimžauskas, Edmundas, ed. *Lietuva vokiečių okupacijoje pirmojo pasaulinio karo metais 1915–1918. Lietuvos nepriklausomos valstybės genezė*. Vilnius: LII, 2006.
Gizbert-Studnicki, Wacław. *Wilno. Przewodnik ilustrowany po mieście i okolicy*. Wilno: A. Żukowski i W. Borkowicz, 1910.
Glaser, Stefan. *Okupacja niemiecka na Litwie w latach 1915–1918. Stosunki prawne*. Lwów: Wydawnictwo Wschód, 1929.
Greble, Emily. *Sarajevo, 1941–1945: Muslims, Christians, and Jews in Hitler's Europe*. Ithaca: Cornell University Press, 2011.
Griškaitė, Reda. *Mykolas Balinskis. Kova dėl istorijos?* Vilnius: Eugrimas, 2005.
Grossmann, Moritz. *Yidishe vilne in wort un bild*. Vilne: Farlag drikeray "Hirsh Mats," 1925.
Gulczyński, Eugenjusz. *Rok 1830–1831 w Wilnie*. Wilno: Druk "Lux," 1933.
Hernik-Spalińska, Jagoda. *Wileńskie Środy Literackie (1927–1939)*. Warsaw: Instytut Badań Literackich, 1998.
Jałowiecki, Mieczysław. *Dawne Wilno i ludzie zapomniani*. London: Wydawnictwo Klubu Londyńskiego Społeczności Akademickiej Uniwersytetu Stefana Batorego, 1955.
Jankevičienė, Algė, ed., *Vilniaus architektūra*. Vilnius: Mokslas, 1985.
Jankevičienė, Algė. *Vilniaus Didžiojo Sinagoga—Great Synagogue of Vilnius*. Vilnius: Savastis, 1996.
Janowski, Ludwik. *W promieniach Wilna i Krzemieńca*. Wilno: Józef Zawadzki, 1923.
Jogėla, Vytautas, Elmantas Meilus, and Virgilijus Pugačiauskas. *Lukiškės. Nuo priemiesčio iki centro (XV a.–XX a. pradžia). Kolektyvinė monografija*. Vilnius: Diemedžio leidykla, 2008.
Jurginis, Juozas. *1905 metų revoliucijos įvykiai Vilniuje*. Vilnius: Politinės ir Mokslinės Literatūros Leidykla, 1958.
Jurginis, Juozas, and Vladislovas Mikučianis. *Vilnius. Tarybų Lietuvos sostinė*. Vilnius: Valstybinė politinės ir mokslinės literatūros leidykla, 1956.
Jurkštas, Jonas. *Vilniaus vietovardžiai*. Vilnius: Mokslas, 1985.
Jurkštas, Vytautas. *Novaia arkhitektura v tsentre starogo Vil'niusa*. Vil'nius: LitINTI, 1983.
Kahan, Arcadius. *Essays in Jewish Social and Economic History*. Chicago: University of Chicago Press, 1986.
Kairienė, A., ed. *Vilniaus senamiesčio atgavinimo strategija*. Vilnius: R. Paknio leidykla, 1997.
Kairiūkštytė, Nastazija. *Vilniaus vadavimo sąjunga 1925 04 26–1938 11 25*. Vilnius: LII, 2001.
Karosas, Jonas. *Mówią kamienie Wilna*. Warsaw: Książka ir Wiedza, 1968.
Kazlauskaitė, Jadvyga. *Vilniaus periodiniai leidiniai 1760–1918*. Vilnius: "Mintis," 1988.
Kiezuń, Anna, ed. *Kultura międzywojennego Wilna*. Białystok: Towarzystwo Literackie im. Adama Mickiewicza, 1994.
Kirkor, Adam H. *Przewodnik historyczny po Wilnie i jego okolicach*. Wilno: J. Zawadzki, 1880.
Klausner, Israel. *Vilnah, Yerushalayim de-lita. Dorot rishonim 1495–1881*. Tel Aviv: Bet lohame hagetaʾot, 1988.
Klimas, Petras. *Mūsų kova dėl Vilniaus 1322/23–1922/23*. Kaunas: A. ir P. Klimų leidinys, 1923.

Kłos, Juljusz. *Wilno. Przewodnik krajoznawczy (szkic monografii historyczno-archytektonicznej)*. Wilno: Wydaw. Oddz. Wileńskiego Pol. Tow. Krajozawczego Touring-Klubu, 1929.
Kon, Pinchas. *Dawny Uniwersytet Wileński a Żydzi*. Wilno: Lux 1926.
Kosman, Marceli. *Uniwersytet Wileński 1579–1979*. Wrocław: Ossolineum, 1981.
Kozłowska, Mirosława, ed. *Wilno teatralne*. Warsaw: Ogólnopolski klub miłośników Litwy, 1998.
Kraszewski, Józef Ignacy. *Wilno od początków do roku 1750*. Wilno: Józef Zawadzki, 1840–1842. 4 vols.
Kruk, Herman. *The Last Days of the Jerusalem of Lithuania: Chronicles from the Vilna Ghetto and the Camps, 1939–1944*. New Haven: Yale University Press, 2002.
Kryczyński, Leon. *Historia meczetu w Wilnie (Próba monografii)*. Warsaw: "Przegląd Islamski," 1937.
Krzyżanowski, Bronisław. *Wileński matecznik 1939–1944 (z dziejów "Wachlarza" ir armii krajowej)*. Paris: Instytut literacki, 1979.
*Księga pamiątkowa ku uczczeniu 350 rocznicy założenia Uniw. Wileńskiego*. Wilno: Uniwersytet Stefana Batorego, 1929.
Kudrinskii, F. A. *Vil'na v 1812 godu*. Vil'na: Izdanie Vilenskago Uchenago Okruga, 1912.
Kuznitz, Cecile Esther. *YIVO and the Making of Modern Jewish Culture: Scholarship for the Yiddish Nation*. Cambridge: Cambridge University Press, 2014.
Laučkaitė, Laima. *Vilniaus dailė XX amžiaus pradžioje*. Vilnius: Baltos Lankos, 2002.
Lazar, Chaim. *Destruction and Resistance: A History of the Partisan Movement in Vilna*. New York: Shengold Publishers, 1985.
Lempert, Israel. "Der goral fun YIVO in historishn iberbroch (1939–1941)." *YIVO-Bleter*, new ser., vol. 3 (1997), 9–42.
Lenkevičiūtė, Jolita. *Vilnius im Wandel. Wohnsegregation in einer ostmitteleuropäischen Hauptstadt*. Berlin: Wissenschaftlicher Verlag, 2006.
Levin, Dov. "The Jews of Vilna under Soviet Rule, September 19–October 28, 1939." *Polin* 9 (1996), 107–137.
Lewandowska, Stanisława. *Wilno 1921–1944. Czasy i ludzie*. Warsaw: Neriton, 2009.
Liekis, Šarūnas. "The Transfer of the Vilna District into Lithuania, 1939." *Polin* 14 (2001), 212–222.
Linčiuvienė, Donata, ed. *Kultūrinis Vilniaus gyvenimas 1939–1945*. Vilnius: Lietuvių literatūros ir tautosakos institutas, 1999.
Linčiuvienė, Donata, ed. *Vilniaus kultūrinis gyvenimas ir Petras Vileišis*. Vilnius: Lietuvių literatūros ir tautsakos institutas, 2001.
Lipphardt, Anna. *Vilne. Die Juden aus Vilnius nach dem Holocaust. Eine transnationale Beziehungsgeschichte*. Paderborn: Friedrich Schöningh, 2010.
Lisek, Joanna. *Jung Wilne. Żydowska grupa artystyczna*. Wrocław: Wydawnictwo Uniwersytetu Wrocławskiego, 2005.
*Das Litauen-Buch. Eine Auslese aus der Zeitung der 10. Armee*. N.p. [Wilna]: Druck und Verlag Zeitung der 10. Armee, 1918.
Liulevicius, Vejas. *War Land on the Eastern Front*. Cambridge: Cambridge University Press, 2000.
Liutkevičienė, Inga. *Déjà vu Vilnius 1974–1990*. Vilnius: "Balto Print," 2012.
Lorentz, Stanisław. *Album wileńskie*. Warsaw: PIW, 1986.
Łossowski, Stanisław. *Stosunki polsko-litewskie, 1921–1939*. Warsaw: Instytut Historii PAN, 1997.
Łowicki, Maciej. *Duch Akademji Wileńskiej. Z czasów Szymona Konarskiego pamiętnika ucznia wileńskiej akademji medyczno-chirurgicznej*. Edited by Wacław Gizbert-Studnicki. Wilno: Książnica Atlas, 1925.
Łowmiańska, Maria. *Wilno przed najazdem moskiewskim 1655 roku*. Wilno: Magistratu m. Wilna, 1929.
Łukomski, Grzegorz, and Rafał E. Stolarski. *Walka o Wilno. Z dziejów samoobrony Litwy i Białorusi 1918–1919*. Warsaw: "Adiutor," 1994.
Lukšionytė-Tolvaišienė, Nijolė. *Istorizmas ir modernas Vilniaus architektūroje*. Vilnius: Vilniaus Dailės Akademija, 2000.
Lunsky, Haikl. *Me-hageto havilnai. Tipusim ve-tslalim*. Vilna: Agudat ha-sofrim veha-zhurnalistim ha'ivriyim veVilna, 1921.

SELECT BIBLIOGRAPHY 299

Łysakowski, Adam, ed. *Bibljoteki wileńskie*. Wilno: "Znicz," 1932.
Mackonis, Rapolas. *Amžiaus liudininko užrašai. Atsiminimai*. Vilnius: Lietuvos rašytojų sąjungos leidykla, 2001.
Maliukevičius, Rokas. *Vil'niusskoe podpol'e*. Vilnius: Vaga, 1966.
Maniušis, Juozas. *Tarybų Lietuva pramonės kilimas*. Vilnius: Valst. polit. ir moksl. lit. 1-kla, 1958.
Marten-Finnis, Susanne. *Vilna as a Centre of the Modern Jewish Press, 1840–1926*. Oxford: Peter Lang, 2004.
Merkys, Vytautas, ed. *Vilniaus universiteto istorija (1579–1803, 1803–1940, 1940–1979)*. Vilnius: Mokslas, 1979.
Mianowski, Stanisław. *Świat, który odszedł. Wspomnienia Wilnianina 1945–1895*. Warsaw: Oficyna wydawnicza Rytm, 1995.
Mienicki, Ryszard. *Wileńska Komisja Archeograficzna (1864–1915)*. Wilno: Nakładem Towarzystwa Przyjaciół Nauk w Wilnie, 1925.
Milosz, Czeslaw. *Beginning with My Streets*. New York: Farrar Straus Giroux, 1991.
Miłosz, Czesław, and Tomas Venclova. *Grįžimai Lietuvon*. Vilnius: Vaga, 2014.
Milovidov, A. I. *K 50-letiiu russkoi Vil'ny*. Vil'na: "Russkii pochin," 1914.
Minczeles, Henri. *Vilna, Wilno, Vilnius. La Jérusalem de Lituanie*. Paris: Editions la découverte, 1993.
Minkevičius, Jonas. *Arkhitektura Sovetskoi Litvy*. Moscow: Stroiizdat, 1987.
Monty, Paul. *Wanderstunden in Wilna*. 3rd ed. Wilna: Verlag der Wilnaer Zeitung, 1918.
Morelowski, Marian. *Co będzie z placem katedralnym, co ze starym Wilnem? Niebezpieczeństwa modernistycznej urbanistyki w głównych centrach wielkiej przeszłości*. Wilno: Znicz, 1937.
Mościcki, Henryk. *Ze stosunków wileńskich w okresie 1816–1823. Z Filareckiego świata*. Warsaw: "Bibljoteka polska," 1924.
Motieka, Egidijus. *Didysis Vilniaus seimas*. Vilnius: Saulabolis, 1996.
Motulas, Algirdas. *Vil'nius. Ekonomicheskii ocherk*. Vil'nius: "Mintis," 1984.
Naruniec, Romuald. *Michał Baliński jako mecenas polsko-litewskich więzi kulturowych*. Warsaw: Semper, 1995.
Nikžentaitis, Alvydas, and Aivas Ragauskas, eds. *Santykis su istorine praeitimi XXI amžiaus Vilniuje*. Vilnius: Vilniaus miesto savivaldybė, 2004.
Niwiński, Piotr. *Garnizon konspiracyjny miasta Wilna*. Toruń: Wydaw. Adama Marszałka, 1999.
O'Connor, Mark Francis. "Cultures in Conflict: A Case Study in Russian-Polish Relations—The University at Wilno." Ph.D. diss., Boston College, 1977.
Osica, Janusz. *Politycy anachronizmu. Konserwatyści wileńskiej grupy "Słowa" 1922–1928*. Warsaw: PWN, 1982.
Osteika, Darius, and Jūratė Tytlytė, eds. *Vilnius 1900–2005. Naujosios architektūros gidas*. Vilnius: Architektūros fondas, 2005.
Papšys, Antanas. *Vilnius. Mažasis vadovas*. Vilnius: Mintis, 1988.
Pasierbska, Helena. *Wileńskie Łukiszki na tle wydarzeń lat wojny 1939–1944*. Gdańsk: Drukarnia Oruńska, 2003.
Piechnik, Ludwik. *Początki Akademii Wileńskiej 1570–1599*. Rome: apud Institutum Historicum Societatis Jesu, 1990.
Pigoń, Stanisław. *Z dawnego Wilna. Szkice obyczajowe i literackie*. Wilno: Wydawnictwo Magistratu, 1929.
*Poland and Lithania: The Question of Wilno*. Warsaw: Straż Kresowa, 1921.
Pugačiauskas, Virgilijus. *Napoleonas ir Vilnius. Karinio gyvenimo kasdienybės bruožai*. Vilnius: Arlila, 2004.
Pukszto, Andrzej. *Między stołecznością a partykularizmem. Wielunarodowościowe społeczeństwo Wilna w latach 1915–1920*. Toruń: Adam Marszalek, 2006.
Puzynina, Gabriela z Güntherów. *W Wilnie i w dworach litewskich. Pamiętniki z lat 1815–1843*. Wilno: Józef Zawadzki, 1928; reprint Kraków, 1990.
Rabinowiczówna, Sara. *Wilno w powstaniu roku 1830/31*. Wilno: Wydawnictwo Magistratu, 1932.
Ran, Leyzer. *Jerusalem of Lithuania*. New York: Laureate Press, 1976. 3 vols.

Ratkauskas, Romualdas, and Antanas Sutkus. *Vilniaus šiokiadieniai*. Vilnius: Mintis, 1967.
Rautenberg, Hans-Werner, ed. *Der "Ring um die Hauptstadt." Die polnische Minderheit in Litauen 1989-1993*. Marburg: J. G. Herder-Institut, 1994.
Remer, Jerzy. *Wilno*. Poznań: Wydawnictwo Polskie, 1934.
*Rocznik statystyczny Wilna 1937*. Wilno: Zarząd miejski, 1939.
Romanowski, Andrzej. *Młoda Polska Wileńska*. Kraków: "Universitas," 1999.
Romanowski, Andrzej. *Pozytywizm na Litwie. Polskie życie kulturalne na ziemiach litewsko-białorusko-inflanckich w latach 1864-1914*. Kraków: "Universitas," 2003.
Römeris, Mykolas. *Lietuvos Sovietizacija 1940-1941. Istorinė Lietuvos sovietizacijos apžvalga ir konstitucinis jos įvertinimas*. Vilnius: Lituanus, 1989.
Romer-Ocheńkowska, Helena. *Dwudziestopięciolecie wskrzeszonego Teatru Polskiego w Wilnie*. Wilno: Nakładem Komitetu Obchodu, 1932.
Rosiak, Stefan. *Księgarnia 'E. Orzeszkowa i S-ka' w Wilnie 1879-1882*. Wilno: Wydawnictwo magistratu m. Wilna, 1938.
Rudashevski, Yitskhok. *The Diary of the Vilna Ghetto*. Tel Aviv: Ghetto Fighters' House, 1973.
Rudnitski, Yisrael, ed. *Vilner zamlbukh / Me'asef vilnah*. Tel Aviv: Igud olami shel yotsei Vilnah veh-asvivah be'Israel, 1974.
Rülf, Jichak (Isaac). *Drei Tage in Jüdisch-Russland. Ein Cultur- und Sittenbild*. Frankfurt a/M: Verlag von J. Kauffmann, 1882.
*Russkaia Vil'na. Prilozhenie k puteshestviiu po sv. mestam russkim*. Vil'na: A. Syrkin, 1865.
Rygiel, Stefan. *Polskie czasopiśmiennictwo wileńskie w r. 1928*. Wilno: "Lux," 1928.
Šadžius, Henrikas. *Socialistinio Vilniaus darbininkai (Pereinamuoju iš kapitalizmo į socializmą laikotarpiu)*. Vilnius: "Mokslas," 1980.
Sakowicz, Kazimierz. *Ponary Diary 1941-1943. A Bystander's Account of a Mass Murder*. New Haven: Yale University Press, 2005.
Šapoka, Adolfas. *Vilnius in the Life of Lithuania*. Toronto: Lithuanian Association of the Vilnius Region, 1962.
Senn, Alfred Erich. *The Great Powers, Lithuania, and the Vilna Question 1920-1928*. Leiden: E. J. Brill, 1966.
Senn, Alfred Erich. "Lithuania's Fight for Independence. The Polish Evacuation of Vilnius, July 1920." *Baltic Review* 23 (1961), 32-39.
Shcherbitskii, O. V. *Vilenskii prechistenskii sobor. Istoricheskii ocherk v sviazi s tserk.-rel. zhizn'iu g. Vil'ny*. Vil'na: Russkii pochin, 1908.
Shneidman, N. N. *Jerusalem of Lithuania: The Rise and Fall of Jewish Vilnius, a Personal Perspective*. Oakville, Ontario: Mosaic Press, 1998.
Siedlaczek, Aleksandra. *Wileńskie Towarzystwo Opieki nad Dziećmi w latach 1901-1940*. Częstochowa: Wydawnictwo WSP, 1998.
Sierpowski, Stanisław. *Piłsudski w Genewie. Dyplomatyczny spór o Wilno w roku 1927*. Poznań: Instytut Zachodni, 1990.
Skirmantienė, Marija, and Jonas Varnauskas, eds. *Nukentėję paminklai*. Vilnius: Mokslo ir encikl. leidykla, 1994.
Smith, Mark B. *Property of Communists: The Urban Housing Program from Stalin to Khrushchev*. DeKalb: Northern Illinois University Press, 2010.
Solak, Zbigniew. *Między Polską i Litwą. Życie i działalność Michała Römera*. Kraków: Arcana, 2004.
Srebrakowski, Aleksander. *Sejm wileński 1922 roku. Idea i jej realizacja*. Wrocław: Wydawnictwo Uniwersytetu Wrocławskiego, 1993.
Steponaitis, Vytautas. *Vilniaus lietuvių spauda 1919-1928*. Kaunas: Vilniui vaduoti sąjunga, 1931.
Stern, Eliyahu. *The Genius: Elijah of Vilnius and the Making of Modern Judaism*. New Haven: Yale University Press, 2013.
Stolzman, Małgorzata. *"Nigdy od ciebie miasto . . ." Dzieje kultury wileńskiej lat międzypowstaniowych (1832-1863)*. Olsztyn: Wydawnictwo Pojezierze, 1987.

## SELECT BIBLIOGRAPHY 301

Stravinskienė, Vitalija. *Tarp gimtinės ir tėvynės. Lietuvos SSR gyventojų repatriacija į Lenkiją (1944–1947, 1955–1959 m.)*. Vilnius: LII, 2011.
Studnicki, Władysław. *Ziemia wileńska, jej stan gospodarczy i pożądany statut*. Wilno: Ludwik Chomiński, 1922.
Sukiennicki, Wiktor. *Legenda i rzeczywistość. Wspomnienia i uwagi o dwudziestu latach Uniwersytetu Stefana Batorego w Wilnie*. Paris: Instytut Literacki, 1967.
Syrokomla, Władysław. *Wycieczki po Litwie w promieniach od Wilna*. Wilno: A. Ass, 1857–1860.
Tamulevičienė, Eglė. *Rusijos geografų draugijos Šiaurės Vakarų krašto skyrius (1867–1915)* in *Moskslo draugijos Lietuvoje*. Vilnius: "Mokslas," 1979.
*Tarybų Lietuvai 45. Tarybų valdžios atkūrimo Lietuvoje 45-ųjų metinių šventė*. Vilnius: Mintis, 1985.
Tauber, Joachim, and Talph Tuchtenhagen. *Vilnius. Kleine Geschichte der Stadt*. Cologne: Böhlau, 2008.
Tomaszewski, Longin. *Wileńszyzna lat wojny i okupacji 1939–1945*. Warsaw: Rytm, 2001.
Vasil'evskii, V. G. *Ocherk istorii goroda Vil'ny*. In *Pamiatniki russkoi stariny zapadnych gubernii*. Edited by P. N. Batiushkov, vyp. 5–6. St. Petersburg: Tip. A. Transhelia, 1872.
Veilentienė, Audronė, ed. *Vilniaus klausimas Lietuvos respublikos diplomatijoje (1918–1940)*. Kaunas: "Jumena," 2003.
Venclova, Tomas. *Vilniaus vardai*. Vilnius: R. Paknio leidykla, 2006.
Vileikis, Algirdas. *Vilniius. Tarybų Lietuvos Sostinė*. Vilnius: Mintis, 1986.
*Vil'na v karmane*. Vil'na: Izd. M. Tassel'krauta, 1912.
*Vilniaus autobusai*. Vilnius: Transporto pasaulis, 2003.
*Vilniaus geto afišos/Vilna Ghetto Posters. Albumas—katalogas*. Vilnius: Baltos Lankos, 2006.
*Vilnius ir vilniečiai gyvenimo kokybės vertinimas*. Vilnius: Filosofijos, sociologijos ir teisės institutas, 1995.
Vinogradov, A. A., ed. *Kak sozdalsia v Vil'ne pamiatnik grafu M.N. Murav'evu*. Vil'na: Komitet po sooruzheniiu pamiatnika, 1898.
Vinogradov, A. A. *Pravoslavnye sviatyni g. Vil'ny*. Vil'na: Gubernskaia tipografiia, 1906.
Walasek, Stefania. *Polska oświata w gubernii wileńskiej w latach 1864–1915*. Kraków: "Impuls," 2003.
Waligóra, Bolesław. *Walka o Wilno. Okupacja Litwy i Bialorusi w 1918–1919 roku przez Rosję Sowiecką*. Wilno: Wydawnictwo Zarządu Miejskiego, 1938.
Weeks, Theodore R. *From Assimilation to Antisemitism: The "Jewish Question" in Poland, 1850–1914*. DeKalb: Northern Illinois University Press, 2006.
Weeks, Theodore R. *Nation and State in Late Imperial Russia: Nationalism and Russification on the Western Frontier, 1863–1914*. DeKalb: Northern Illinois University Press, 1996.
*Wileńszczyzna w latach 1926–1930*. Warsaw: Wydaw. Bezpartyjnego Bloku Współpracy z Rządem, 1930.
*Wilno i ziemia wileńska. Zarys monograficzny*. Wilno: Wydawnictwo wojewódzkiego komitetu regjonalnego, 1930.
Wołkonowski, Jarosław. *Okręg Wileński Związku Walki Zbrojnej Armii krajowej w latach 1939–1945*. Warsaw: Adiutor, 1996.
Wolkonowski, Jarosław. *Stosunki polsko-żydowskie w Wilnie i na Wileńszczyźnie 1919–1939*. Białystok: Wydawnictwo Uniwersytetu w Białymstoku, 2004.
Worobiejczyk, Mojżesz. *Ein Ghetto im Osten (Vilna)*. Zürich/Leipzig: O. Füssli, 1931.
*Wybory do Sejmu w Wilnie, 8 stycznia 1922. Oświetlenie akcji wyborczej i jej wyników na podstawie źródeł urzędowych*. Wilno: Generalny Komisarjat Wyborczy, 1922.
Wrzosek, Adam. *Wskrzeszenie Uniwersytetu Wileńskiego w r. 1919*. Wilno: Zawadzki, 1919.
Yeshurin, Yefin. *Vilne. A zamelbukh gevidmet der shtot Vilne*. Vilna: Vilner brentsh 367 Arbeyter Ring, 1935.
Zahorski, Władysław. *Podania i legendy wileńskie*. Wilno: Zawadzki, 1925.
Żak, Andrzej. *Wilno 1919–1920*. Warsaw: Bellona, 1993.
Zalkin, Mordekhai. "Beit hamidrash lerabanim bevilnah—bein dimui lematsiut." *Gal-Ed* 14 (1995), 59–71 (Hebrew numeration).

Žepkaitė, Regina. *Vilniaus istorijos atkarpa, 1939 m. spalio 27 d.–1940 m. birželio 15 d.* Vilnius: Mosklas, 1990.
Zinov'ev, N. *Vil'na, po perepisi aprelia 1875 goda.* Vil'na: Tipografiia A. G. Syrkina, 1881.
Znamierowska-Prüfferowa, Maria. *Wilno. Miasto serce najbliższe.* Edited by Krystyna Jakowska. Białystok: Towarzystwo Literackie im. Adama Mickiewicza, 1997.
Žukas, Vladas. *Marijos ir Jurgio Šlapelių lietuvių knygynas Vilniuje.* Vilnius: Mokslo ir enciklopedijų leidybos institutas, 2000.
Żytkowicz, Leonid. *Rządy Repnina na Litwie w latach 1794–1797.* Wilno: Nakładem Towarzystwa Przyjaciół Nauk w Wilnie, 1938.

# Index

## A

Abramowicz, Hirsz, 76, 99, 100, 102, 112
Alexander Jagiellończyk (king), 141
Alexander I (Tsar), 28, 33, 39, 40, 71
Alexander II (Tsar), 22, 60, 74
Angarietis, Zigmas, 218, 290n26
Antakalnis, 62, 156, 195, 198, 199, 202, 227, 229, 246n23
antisemitism, 95, 120, 122, 129, 137, 138–139, 146, 150, 161–162
Antokol'skii, Mark, 70–71, 72, 277n76
Arad, Yitzhak, 162
Armia Krajowa, 176
artisans, 12, 19, 25, 46, 76, 78, 147, 148
Auschwitz, 183
Auszra, 88
Aušros Vartai. See Ostra Brama
automobiles, 107, 127, 199, 287n42

## B

Baliński, Michał, 17–20, 23–25
Balkelis, Tomas, 108
Barbara Radziwiłłówna, 141
Basanavičius, Jonas, 90, 102, 110, 143, 151, 160, 187, 215
Basilian (monastery), 47, 65, 182
basketball, 205, 288n62
Batiushkov, P. N., 67, 68, 71, 254n37
Belarusians, 9, 12, 36, 43, 61, 67, 94, 100, 103, 122, 124, 129, 131, 132, 151, 156, 158, 175, 182, 185, 239, 253n27
Belgium, 34, 134
Berezina (river), 33
Berlin Wall, 223
Białystok, 113, 147
Bielinskis, Kipras, 86

Biržiška, Mykolas, 119, 130, 151–153, 162, 164, 168, 279n92
Biržiška, Vaclovas, 151
Biržiška, Viktoras, 151
Black Sea, 12
Bolsheviks, 110, 112, 131, 143, 152, 157, 175
Borodino (battle), 32
Brazauskas, Algirdas, 211, 217, 222, 223, 227
Brezhnev, Leonid, 189, 201, 210, 285n6
Briedis, Laimonis, 80, 235–236
Bujnicki, Teodor, 135
Bułhak, Jan, 143
bund (party), 79, 93, 111, 122, 146, 237, 256n75
bus (service in Vilnius), 127, 187, 195, 213, 269n13

## C

Calvinism, 13, 14, 17
Čaplinskas, Antanas, 226, 233
Castle Hill, 25, 29, 31, 54, 62, 66, 69, 143, 181
"Cat." See Mackiewicz, Stanisław
Catherine II (Empress), 39, 69, (monument) 70–72, 81, 98, 157
Catholicism, 5, 12, 14, 17, 24, 36, 47, 59, 61, 66, 76, 81, 82, 89, 93, 107, 117, 134, 142, 181, 209, 239, 253n27, 277n37
cathedral, 25–26, 30, 44, 49, 62, 65, 66, 69, 72, 134, 166, 196, 220, 230
census, (1875) 77, 252n7; (1897) 62, 89; (1923) 124–125; (1931) 145, 243n2; (1944) 176; (1951) 185; (1950, 1959, 1988) 192; (1970) 212
Cherniakhovskii, Ivan, 180, 186, 196, 199, 211, 213, 214
Chernikover, Elias, 149

Chodkiewicz (family), 13, 15
cholera, 81
Choral Synagogue, 63, 80, 107, 213
Church Slavonic (language), 15
Čiurlionis, Mikolajus, 143
Cook, Thomas, 142
cinema, 73, 94, 127–128, 181, 187, 191, 195, 197, 202, 288n67
Cossacks, 86, 97
Counter Reformation, 14
Cracow, 17, 82, 119, 126, 132, 136, 147
Curzon line, 125
Cyrillic (alphabet), 13, 60, 89, 133
Cywiński, Stanisław, 97, 110
Czarkowski, Ludwik, 74
Czartoryski, Adam, 32, 45
Czechoslovakia, 154
Czechot, Jan, 39

## D

Daukantas, Simonas, 21
Dawidowicz, Lucy, 154, 233
Decembrists, 38
Dekanozov, Vladimir, 163
Diebitsch, Hans, 34
Dimanshtein, Semen, 112
Długski, Michał, 30
Dobaczewska, Wanda, 97
Dobrianskii, F. N., 80–81
Domeyko, Ignacy, 38
Dorpat, 41, 140
Dostoevsky, Fyodor, 80
Drėma, Vladas, 233
Dubnov, Simon, 149
Duchy of Warsaw, 32
Duma, (Russian State) 85, 93, 238; (Vilnius city) 92–93, 260n169
Dunin-Horkawicz, Janusz, 139
*Dziennik Wileński*, 40
Dzierżyński, Feliks, 192, 214, 226

## E

East Prussia, 89
*Edinstvo*, 223, 224, 225
Ehrenkreutz, Stefan, 162
*Einsatzstab Rosenberg*, 172–173, 183
electricity, 126, 187
Eliahu ben Shlomo Zalman, 1, 21, 44, 133, 143, 165, 184, 237, 277n76
Elkes, Elkhanan, 172
Elizavetgrad, 77
Esperanto, 150, 270n34

Estonia, 22, 175, 216, 222, 240
ethnic cleansing, 3
European Union (EU), 7, 211, 227

## F

F.P.O. (partisan organization), 174, 175, 281n139
Filareci, 38, 39
Filomaci, 38, 39
Frank, Józef, 38, 42

## G

Galicia, 142
Gaon. *See Eliahu ben Shlomo Zalman*
Gediminas, 11, 133–134, 160, 166, 179, 187, 213, 217, 227, 244n4
genocide, 3, 155, 168–169, 185, 188
Gens, Jacob, 172–175
Gestapo, 167, 172
ghetto (World War II), 171, 173–175, 188
Gira, Liūdas, 105, 214
Gorbachev, Mikhail S., 9, 190, 208, 210–211, 215, 221, 222, 223, 224, 225, 226, 240
Gordon, A., 78
Goskind, Shaul and Yitzak, 145
Grand Duchy of Lithuania, 1, 11, 93, 118
Green Bridge, 4, 28, 48, 62, 81, 99, 156, 166, 186, 214
Gregorian Calendar, 10
Grodno, 27, 71, 77, 90, 107, 117, 136, 185
Grunwald. *See Žalgiris*

## H

Haskalah, 45
Haman, 32
Hebrew, 10, 45, 46, 76, 130, 131, 149, 150, 164
Heder, 76, 77
Helsinki, 64, 198, 205
Hogendorp, Dirk, 30
Hoskins, Geoffrey, 190
Hulewicz, Witold, 141
Hymans, Paul, 117

## I

Iceland, 226
imperialism, 157
Iron Wolf, 11, 227
Ivan IV (Tsar), 68

## J

Jabłkowski (merchants), 125–126, 127, 141, 158
Jankowski, Czesław, 98, 99–100, 101, 136

# INDEX 305

Jankowski, Jan, 39
January Insurrection (1863–1864), 8, 22, 24, 26, 59–60, 68, 134
*Jaunimo Gretos*, 205, 215–216, 218, 221, 222
Jesuits, 14
Jogaila (Jagiełło), 11
*Judenrat*, 170, 172
Jurginis, Juozas, 179, 187

## K

Kaczerginski, Shmerke, 182, 183, 184fx
Kahan, Arcadius, 147, 150
Karaites, 9, 95, 124, 140, 153
Kassow, Samuel, 146
Kaunas, 77, 89, 96, 98, 109, 120, 153, 154, 158, 162, 166, 167, 170, 172
Kazan, 140
Kazimierz (town), 75
KGB, 169, 184, 220, 226
Kiev, 41, 64, 196
Kirkor, Adam Honory, 43, 81
Klaczko, Juljan, 145
Klaipėda, 78, 154, 160, 185
Klimas, Petras, 72, 97, 109
Kłos, Juljusz, 136, 144–145
Knyva, A., 179
Konarski, Szymon, 42
Kornilov, I. P., 67
Korwin-Milewski, Hipolit, 254n48
Korwin-Milewski, Ignacy, 63
Kościuszko Uprising, 21, 26, 118
Kossakowski, J. N., 30
Kovner, Abba, 174, 281n135
Kovno. See Kaunas
*Krajowcy*, 92, 95, 261n188
Kraszewski, Józef Ignacy, 17–20
Krewo, Union of (1385), 11, 67
Kridl, Manfred, 150
Kruk, Herman, 157, 170, 172, 173, 233
Krzyżanowski, Bronisław, 158
Kapsukas. See Mickevičius-Kapsukas
Kudirka, Vincas, 136, 213
Kuna, Henryk, 137
Kurier Litewski, 40, 43, 87
Kuznitz, Cecile 148

## L

Landsbergis, Vytautas, 216, 219, 224, 225, 227
Latvia, 175, 216, 240
Laurinavičius, Česlovas, 113
Lavrinovich, M., 31
Lazdynai, 201, 203, 212, 229

Le Corbusier (architect), 203
League of Nations, 115
Lekert, Hirsh, 79, 179
Lelewel, Joachim, 34, 179
Lenin, Vladimir Ilyich, 4, 164, 165, 181, 186, 192, 193, 194, 196, 203, 213, 218, 226
Leningrad, 201, 212
Lestschinski, Jacob, 148, 149
Lietūkis garage, 170
libraries, 41, 43, 66, 105, 107, 114, 130, 132, 149, 158, 172, 173, 183, 186, 188
Listowsky, Paul, 107–108
*Litas (currency)*, 21, 161, 227, 277n45
Lithuania, 7, 12, 17, 109, 115–116, 119, 120, 124, 151, 152, 154, 155, 156, 159–162, 238, 239, 276n31
Łódź, 87
*Łopalewski, Tadeusz*, 141
*Lorentz, Stanisław*, 126
*Lublin (Union of)*, 118
*Ludendorff, Erich von*, 100–101
Lukiškės prison, 47, 62, 126, 171
Lukiškės Square, 4, 26, 64, 82, 181, 204, 226, 227, 246n5
Lunski, Khaykel, 105
Lutherans, 5, 13, 24
Lwów, 113, 120, 125, 126, 136, 147
Lysenko, Trofim, 216

## M

Mackiewicz, Stanisław, 129, 135
Magdeburg Law, 12, 13
Makabi (football team), 150
Manelis, Eugenijus, 232–233
Maniušis, Juozas, 187
masons, 40
Matulewicz, Jerzy, 135
Mazovia, 142
McDonald's (restaurant), 227
Memel. See Klaipėda
Mendelsohn, Moses, 45
Mensheviks, 112
Merkys, Vytautas, 207, 217
Meysztowicz, Aleksander, 121, 123
Mianowski, Stanisław and Krzysztof, 139–141
Michnik, Adam, 210
Mickevičius-Kapsukas, Vincas, 186, 214, 215
Mickiewicz, Adam, 1, 38, 39, 41, 42, 71, 94, 110, 130, 133, 136–137, 140, 141, 144, 160, 214, 246n21, 249n98, 271n60
"Middle Lithuania," 114–115, 119–123, 125, 131, 146

*Mikrorajonas,* 195, 197, 203, 212
*Mikučianis, Vladislovas,* 180, 181, 184, 187
*Miłosz, Czesław,* 127, 128, 135, 143, 146, 222
*Milovidov, A. I.,* 67, 68–69
*Minsk,* 78, 108, 138, 185
*Mitnagdim,* 45
*Młoda Polska,* 138
*Molotov, V. M.,* 179, 217
*Molotov-Ribbentrop Pact,* 154, 157, 217, 219, 221
*Moniuszko, Stanisław,* 214
*Montwiłł, Józef,* 64
*Monty, Paul,* 106–107
*Morelowski, Marian,* 126
Moscow, 32–33, 64, 85, 87–88, 143, 151, 158, 162, 197, 212, 226, 239
Motulas, Algirdas, 206, 214
Multiculturalism, 6
Muraviev, M. N., 35–36, 60, 67, (monument) 69–70, 72, 77, 81, 98, 139, 144, 157, 252n4
Muscovy, 12, 68
Muslims, 5, 122

## N

Napoleon, 26, 28, 29–34, 46, 63, 81, 96
National Democrats (ND), 115, 129, 146, 150
nationality, 4, 237–238
NATO, 211
Nazis, 3, 138, 151, 154, 155, 159, 165, 166, 173, 183, 188
Neringa (café), 202, 207
Neris (river), 11, 62, 64, 99, 140, 156, 180, 184, 186, 196, 199, 200, 204, 214
Nicholas I (Tsar), 33–34, 39, 40
Nicholas II (Tsar), 70, 85
NKVD, 155, 156–157, 164, 167, 176, 178
Northern War, 17
November Uprising (1830–1831), 8, 30, 34–36, 37, 47, 130, 181, 238, 248n77

## O

*Ober Ost,* 104
Obiezierska, Helena, 138–139
October Manifesto (1905), 85, 87
Odessa, 64, 147
Olympics, 205
Orthodox (religion), 5, 13, 15, 24, 31, 47, 61, 65–66, 69, 75, 81, 142, 253n27
Orzeszkowa, Eliza, 74, 136, 180
Ostra Brama, 28, 44, 65, 72, 114, 130, 143, 226, 237, 246n14
Ostrovsky, Aleksandr, 80

## P

Paleckis, Justas, 163
Paneriai. *See Ponary*
Pasternak, Leonid, 216
Paul I (Tsar), 27, 71
Pease, Neil, 135
Pelikan, Wacław, 34–35
*Pfeil, Graf (count),* 100, 102
Piłsudski, Józef, 112, 113, 123, 129, 130, 131, 134, 140, 141, 143, 160
plebiscite (1921) 97, 118, 122, 134, 146
Poalei Tsiyon (party), 79
pogroms, (1881) 77; (April 1919) 113, 120, 146, 152
Poland, 7, 11, 34, 217
Polish underground (World War II), 169
Ponary, 169, 171, 175, 176, 182, 183, 185
Poznań, 131, 136
prefab concrete housing, 195, 198–201, 212–213
printers and publishing, 40, 45, 66, 73, 85–86, 91, 105, 135–136, 149, 151
Pronaszka, Zbigniew, 136–137, 140
prostitution, 76, 253n15, 255n72
Pushkin, 69, 81, 214
Putrament, Jerzy, 129
Puzyna, Nikodem, 30
Puzynina, Gabriela, 35, 39, 42

## R

Rabbinical School, 46, 76
Radziwiłł (family), 12, 13, 15, 29
radio, 128, 141, 156, 158, 162, 167, 170, 182, 238, 269n20
railroads, 22, 59, 72, 80, 85, 166, 181, 238
Rasų. *See Rossa*
Red Army, 7, 111, 112, 114, 126, 131, 140, 145, 156–158, 163, 176, 177, 180, 188, 190, 192, 198, 202, 209, 225, 226, 290n37
reformation, 13
Reinys, Mečislovas, 169
"Repatriation," 155, 177–178, 183
*Rejzen, Zalman,* 149
Remer, Jerzy 143–144
Repnin, N. V., 27
Revolutions: (1905) 74, 82, 83–92, 238; (1917) 110, 164
Ribbentrop, Joachim, 154, 275n135
Riga, 197
Rimskii-Korsakov, Aleksandr, 34
Roma, 153
Romanov (dynasty), 68

INDEX 307

Römer, Michał, 34, 95
Römeris, Mykolas, 159, 161, 165, 167, 175, 278n62
Romm (publishers), 45
Ropp, Edward, 71, 93
Roosevelt, Theodore, 7
Rossa (cemetery), 140, 144, 152
Rozenbaum, M., 117
Rubinsztejn, Isaac, 121, 131
Rülf, Isaac, 78–79, 80
Russian Empire, 6, 17, 92, 96, 134, 145, 237, 238, 249n98
Russian Geographical Society, 66–67
Russification, 5, 8, 21, 43, 59–61, 64–72, 73, 232, 252n1
Russo-Japanese War, 82
Ruszczyc, Ferdynand, 137–138
Ruthenian, 11, 13

S

St. Petersburg, 10, 22, 64, 78, 80, 87, 141, 238
Sąjūdis, 217, 219, 220–221, 222, 224, 290n33
Sakowicz, Kazimierz, 175
Samavičius, Romualdas, 232–233
Sapieha (family), 12, 13, 15, 29
Sarajevo, 6
*Saugumas,* 164, 167
Sawicz, Franciszek, 41–42
*Scandinavia,* 12
Seimas: ("Great," 1905) 90
Senn, Erich Alfred, 110, 220
*Shtif, Nochem,* 149
*Šiauliai,* 172
*Siedlecki, M., 131–132*
Sierakowski, Józef, 30
*Sigismund I (Grand Duke),* 13
*Singer, Isaac Bashevich,* 157
Skarga, Piotr, 14
*Šlapelis, Marija and Jurgis,* 92
*Slendziński, Ludomir, 138*
*Słowacki, Juliusz, 1,* 145
Smetona, Antanas, 72, 163
Śniadecki, Jan, 37
Šnipiškės, 47, 48, 63, 64
Socialism, 84, 87, 88, 189, 221, 239, 258n139
*Solidarność (Solidarity Trade Union),* 210, 217, 290n33
Solzhenitsyn, Aleksandr, 216
Soslovie, 61
Soviets, 111–112, 133, 151, 155, 189, 218, 239
sports, 150, 189, 195, 203, 204, 205, 208, 213, 286n126

Stalin, Joseph, 153, 165, 166, 177, 179, 186, 194, 216, 218
Stefan Batory (King), 13, 113, 130
Stockholm, 198, 202
Straszun Library, 107, 165, 173, 278n76
Strong, Anna Louise, 163–164
Studnicki, Władysław, 125
Subbotin, A. P., 78–79
Sukiennicki, Wiktor, 128–129, 151
Supreme Soviet (LSSR), 163, 165, 203, 204, 213, 217, 223
Sutzkever, Abraham, 183, 184
Suzin, Adam, 39
Sviatopolk-Mirskii, Petr, 71–72
Švenčionys, 28
Synagogue (Great), 78, 148, 171, 184, 281n130, 284n194
Syrokomla, Władysław, 43
Szabad, Cemach, 147, 165, 277n76
Szlachta, 71, 75
Szubrawcy, 40
Szumski, Stanisław, 35, 42

T

Tallinn, 197, 211
Talmud, 45
*Talonas,* 227
Tambov, 34
Tarnowski, Stanisław, 74–75
*Taryba,* 109
Tatars, 9, 13, 62, 95, 124, 140, 153, 226
Tashkent, 64, 196, 203
Television, 187–188, 193, 196, 203, 225
Teutonic Knights, 12
Thirty Years War, 15
Three Crosses (monument), 181
Tilsit (Treaty, 1807), 28
Totleben, E. I., 77, 78, 256n84
Torah, 45
Trakai, 11
Trotskii, V. N., 70
Trotsky, Lev, 216
Truska, Liudas, 166
*Tugendbund,* 38
*Tygodnik Wileński,* 40
Tyszkiewicz, Eustachy, 42
Tyszkiewicz, Klementyna, 63

U

Ukraine, 77
Uniate Church, 15, 24, 27, 36, 43, 47, 65
university (in Vilnius), 14, 34–35, 37–38, 39,

41, 43, 46, 103, 113–114, 125, 129–133, 134, 138–139, 142–143, 150–151, 153, 156, 162, 164–165, 168, 186, 191, 207–208, 230, 238–239, 244n14, 270n34, 277n53
Urbšys, Juozas, 163
USSR, 6, 7, 97, 119, 124, 128, 134, 154, 158, 159, 163, 166, 178, 182, 186, 192, 204, 210, 218, 225, 226, 229, 239

## V

Valiuškis, Gediminas, 205
*Varpas*, 89
Venclova, Tomas, 222, 234–235
Viekšniai, 151
Vileišis, Petras, 63, 72, 91
Vileikis, Algirdas, 192, 215, 218
Vilnia (river), 11
*Vilniaus Žinios*, 83, 85
Vilnius Archaeological Commission, 42
"Vilnius passports," 153
Voldemaras, Augustinas, 72, 116–117, 130
Volga (river), 140
*Volksdeutsche*, 5

## W

Wahl, Victor von, 79
Warsaw, 6, 17, 22, 46, 59, 64, 77, 80, 96, 97, 125, 136, 138, 140, 147, 157
Wat, Aleksander, 157
Weber, Paul, 108
Wehrmacht, 167, 190
Weinrich, Max, 149
Wilhelm von Urach of Württemburg (Duke), 111
Wilson, Woodrow, 104

Witenberg, Yitzhak, 174
Witte, Sergei, 85
Wołkonowski, Jarosław, 146
World War I, 7, 92, 96–123, 140, 145, 151, 218, 238
World War II, 7, 9, 97, 126, 137, 151, 155–183, 204, 221, 239
Wrzosek, A., 130
Wygodzki, Jakob, 120, 121, 172, 267n125

## Y

Yeltsin, Boris, 211
Yiddish, 45, 59, 74, 75, 76, 94, 100, 106, 121, 124, 130, 131, 132, 146, 148, 150, 185, 230, 237, 238, 256n75
YIVO (Jewish Scientific Institution), 126, 149, 164, 183
Yom Kippur, 96

## Z

Žalgiris (battle, 1410), 12–13, 244n7
Žagary, 135
Zahorski, Władysław, 142
Zan, Tomasz, 38
Zawadzki (printers), 40, 43, 73
Zawadzki, Władysław, 109–110
Zawisza, Szymon, 40
Żeligowski, Lucjan, 97, 114–115, 119, 121, 123, 131, 133, 136, 143, 160, 232
Žemaitė, 214
Zhitomir, 46
Zinkevičius, Zigmas, 231–232
Zionism, 79–80, 93, 122, 131, 172
Žirmūnai, 199–200, 201, 206, 227, 229, 289n3
Žvėrynas, 62, 63, 66, 198, 206, 229

www.ingramcontent.com/pod-product-compliance
Lightning Source LLC
Chambersburg PA
CBHW021847300426
44115CB00005B/40